Plant-Based Diet Cookbook 2020

The Ultimate Guide for Beginners with 800 Delicious Whole Food Recipes and 21-Day Plant-Based Meal Plan

By Annie Oliver

Table of Content

Introduction

Have you been struggling to lose weight unsuccessfully?
Do you wish to eat food that is nutritious and with no health issues?

Are you trying to find a diet that prevents health conditions such as low blood pressure, cancer, obesity, diabetes and others?

Do you want a meal that will improve the health of your organs such as kidney, heart and liver?

If you answered yes, I am going to show you a great solution in which you can do improve yourself through the food you eat. The health of our body systems is so dependent on the food we eat and so is our health and wellbeing too.

Not very long ago, my mum's health was not good. Before I tell you about her, I need to mention that she loved eating meat products and more so junk foods. Cheese burgers, pizzas, chicken breasts, BBQs and other "nice" animal food products were her favorite. She had gained weight over the years and had been trying different ways to lose it but it didn't work.

Her health had not only become a concern for her alone but also the immediate family members which included my dad, my siblings and I. Dad enrolled her on a gym nearby so that she could exercise and lose her weight. My sister and I also joined her as a way of encouraging her to do the workouts. We went to the gym for a month but then there was only a small change on her weight. We were a bit discouraged.

We thought that this may be more than meets the eye. During the next visit to the doctor she was diagnosed with diabetes and her blood pressure

was high. This was very worrying piece of news for us all. The doctor advised her to change her lifestyle in terms of the food she ate. He recommended her switching to a plant-based diet. He said that it would help her reverse her conditions and generally improve her health. Mum was not ready to stop eating her favorite recipes and make the switch. We tried talking with her to make her change her mind. She only agreed after we promised that we will also join her in the journey of plant-based diet. She is our mum and we'd do anything for her. Wouldn't you do the same for your loved one? I believe you would.

I must say it was really tough for us at the beginning. However, right now, our family only eats plant-based meals and we got used to it. Would you believe it if I told you that mum lost almost half her weight? Yes, she did. The diabetes was no more and her blood pressure had gone back to normal. All this thanks to the plant-based lifestyle that she chose to follow. We are now all happy as a family because of the healthy eating we practice.

Plant-based died is known to have many benefits to us; from weight loss to reversing some health conditions and many more as you will find in this book. If you are thinking of living a happy healthy life, consider switching to a plant-based lifestyle and you will always be happy for that decision.

This book contains information about the plant-based diet that will help you in this journey. It has 800 plant-based recipes that are carefully selected with ingredients that are easily available in the stores.
Enjoy reading and all the best I your plant-based diet journey!

Chapter 1: Plant-Based Diet Primer

What is a Plant-Based Diet?

A plant-based diet is a diet that comprises lots of products from plants, and very little or no amounts of animal products and processed foods.

Why Plant-Based Diet?

Research suggests that those eating a plant-based diet tend to have a lower Body Mass Index (BMI) and therefore are slimmer, healthier and more energetic. Additionally, this means they tend to have lower rates of diabetes, heart disease and stroke than those who eat diets based around meat, especially processed meats.

This may be because plant-based foods such as fresh vegetables, fruits and nuts tend to be higher in complex carbs and fiber so keep you feeling fuller for longer. When you're full, you're far less likely to reach for unhealthy foods that won't nourish your body or mind.

They're also high in antioxidant, vitamins and minerals which are in a natural state and so more readily absorbed by the body.

Additionally, a plant-based diet has been shown to help reduce cholesterol, reduce high blood pressure and even certain types of cancer.

Difference Between Plant-Based Diet and Vegan, Vegetarian Diet

A plant-based diet is all about easy healthy plant food option that includes fruits, vegetables, lentils, beans, and more. Other than the hardcore plant diet options, it allows the intake of low-fat dairy products that includes low-fat milk, low-fat cottage, mozzarella and cheddar cheese as well. Having a plant-based diet doesn't require that you avoid all the animal-based products.

A vegan diet states that one should eat all the vegetables and avoid any meat products. It is simply that a person prefers eating vegetables and fruits instead of meat and other fats. Vegan culture

Types of Plant-Based Diet

Vegan: Diet includes vegetables, seeds, nuts, legumes, grains, and fruit and excludes all animal products (i.e. no animal flesh, dairy, or eggs). There are variations within the vegan diet as well such as the fruitarian diet made up mainly of fruits and sometimes nuts and seeds and the raw vegan diet where food is not cooked.

Vegetarian: Diet includes vegetables, fruit, nuts, legumes, grains, and seeds and excludes meat but may include eggs or dairy. The Ovo-lacto vegetarian diet incorporates dairy and eggs while the Ovo-vegetarian diet incorporates eggs and excludes dairy and the lacto vegetarian diet incorporates dairy but excludes eggs.

Semi-Vegetarianism: Diet is mostly vegetarian but also incorporates some meat and animal products. The macrobiotic diet is a type of semi-vegetarian diet that emphasizes vegetables, beans, whole grains, naturally processed foods, and may include some seafood, meat, or poultry. The pescatarian diet includes plant foods, eggs, dairy, and seafood but no other types of animal flesh. People who subscribe to a semi-vegetarian diet sometimes describe themselves as flexitarians as well.

involves not using any other animal products not in food nor any daily use.

A vegetarian diet is about focusing on plant foods but also eating animal products such as honey and milk. The main difference with veganism is that vegans avoid any form of animal products while vegetarians do not eat meat but they eat animal products like honey and milk.

Benefits of a Plant-Based Diet

- *Environmentally Friendly:* Plant-based diet is all environmentally friendly. When masses are following the plant-based diet that means there will be more plants and no more packing food. No processed or packaged food means there won't be any disposal or trash out there. On the other hand, more plants will provide more oxygen for people and give them nutrients through food. It is an overall a good package for the ultimate healthy and happy society.

- *Better Organ Health:* Plant-based diet is good for not only a specific organ like liver, heart or kidneys, but it helps your overall body to have a perfect mechanism. It gives proper attention to all the organs and make it possible for a person to have the best of health in any manner. Other than organs, the diet helps to increase muscular strength, make bones stronger, hair longer and many more. It is all about how you are managing the diet and you will be able to get the best results within a few days of starting with it.

- *Benefits Beyond Health:* The benefits of plant-based diet are not limited to the health and fitness only. It is a complete package of ultimate benefits that prolong in society and help each aspect of the society to grow better. Since the diet is all about plants, it means one needs to have fresh vegetables and fruits available in surroundings. Moreover, it

-

enhances the consumption and utilization of all the products and bi-products. Here are some of the value-added benefits of the plant-based diet that is commendable:

- *Lowers Blood Pressure:* One of the reasons why plant-based foods contribute to low blood pressure is that they tend to have high amount of potassium, which in turn helps you manage your blood pressure (Physicians Committee for Responsible Medicine, n.d.). Additionally, potassium has also been known to reduce anxiety and stress. Now, guess what meat has little of? That's right. Potassium. Some foods that have a high amount of potassium are fruits, whole grains, nuts, and legumes.

- *Prevents Chronic Diseases:* Obesity? Cancer? Diabetes? These are illnesses that you can avoid or minimize the risk of with a plant-based diet. People who are already suffering from chronic diseases are asked to live on plant-based food because they help improve lifespans (Nordqvist, 2012).

- *Lowers Blood Sugar Levels:* One thing that plant-based diets are rich in is fiber. When you consume fiber, your body reduces the amount of sugar it absorbs into the bloodstream. Additionally, fiber does not make you feel hungry really fast. When you do not feel full, you end up consuming more food than necessary. Plant-based foods help prevent such a situation from arising.

- *Ideal for Weight Loss:* When you are consuming a plant-based diet, you are cutting down on excess fats and maintaining a healthy level of weight. You don't even have to worry about calorie restrictions! Weight loss is possible with a plant-based diet simply because of the fiber we mentioned previously. It helps you manage your hunger, and you also receive the necessary amount of minerals, proteins, and vitamins from your green meal.

- *Saves Time and Money:* Plant-based foods are not as difficult to prepare as meat-based foods. In fact, you will take less time to prepare an organic meal. When you really need, you can easily put together some healthy ingredients and make a quick salad. Furthermore, you spend less money by preparing food using plant-based ingredients. When you source local and organic products, you end up shelling out less cash for the items that you would like to buy.

- *Lowers Cholesterol Level:* This might sound like a myth, but plants contain no cholesterol. Even if you pick out coconut and cocoa plants, they do not contain any cholesterol. Hence, when you are at risk of having a high level of cholesterol, a plant-based diet will help you bring it back down to a much healthier level.

Chapter 2: Plant -Based Diet Blue Print

Foods to Eat

Vegetables: tomatoes, cauliflower, spinach, carrots, kale, asparagus, peppers, and broccoli.

Whole Grains: rolled oats, quinoa, pastas made with brown rice, barley, faro, and brown rice, wild rice, amaranth, buckwheat, spelt, kamut, and couscous.

Legumes: chickpeas, peanuts, black beans, peas, and lentils.

Fruits: citrus fruits, bananas, apples, pineapples, berries, and pears.

Starchy Vegetables: sweet potatoes, squash, regular potatoes.

Healthy Fats: avocados, unsweetened coconut, olive oils, and coconut oils.

Seeds: Nut Butters, and Nuts: Macadamia nuts, sunflower seeds, pumpkin seeds, almond butter, cashews, almonds, and tahini.

Plant-Based Milks: almond milk, coconut milk, cashew milk. For this category, it might be tempting to get the sweetened varieties to help you get accustomed to the taste. Initially, that is okay, however, for the long-term, the sweeteners in these milks are not great for your overall health. Perhaps eventually, you can experiment with making some great nut-milk at home, where you can control how much it's sweetened.

Spices and Seasonings: rosemary, turmeric (this spice in particular is great for reducing internal inflammation), curry, sea salt, basil, black pepper.

Drinks: unsweetened coffees and teas, fresh fruit and vegetable juices or smoothies, plain water, sparkling water. There are some great new brands of flavored and sparkling waters available that are sugar-free and help abstain from pop and sweetened juice. No matter what diet you choose, drinking loads of water is great for your body. Additionally, if you really want to boost your immunity and also help your body detox naturally, try adding some berries, sliced orange/lemon/cucumber, mint or lavender to your water. They each make for a tasty flavored water combination either altogether or individually as well.

Condiments: mustard, vegan mayonnaise, soy sauce, tamari, vinegar (apple cider vinegar is wonderful), lemon juice, salsa, and nutritional yeasts.

Plant-based Proteins: tempeh and tofu. A little later, we will provide fabulous recipes for these meatless, yet protein packed, plant-based options.

Foods to Avoid

Animal Foods

Yes, no duh! Being plant-based means that you should avoid animal foods as much as possible. Whether you are doing this for health purposes or for the love of animals, just be sure you try to avoid animal products as much as possible. Some of the more popular options include

Meat: Organs, Veal, Pork, Lamb, and Beef, etc.

Poultry: Duck, Goose, Turkey, Chicken, etc.

Eggs: Any Type of Egg

Dairy: Ice Cream, Butter, Cheese, Yogurt, etc.

Seafood and Fish: All Fish, Lobster, Crab, Mussels, Shrimp, etc.

Bee Products: Honey, Royal Jelly, etc.

Animal Derived Ingredients & Additives: This is where it can get a bit tricky when it comes to living a plant-based diet. One moment you are enjoying one of your favorite snacks, the next you are reading the label and realizing it has an ingredient that has been derived from an animal. Of course, we all make mistakes, but by being educated, you can avoid this mistake in the first place!

Tips to Get Started

As a newbie to plant-based diets, you should understand that this is not something you can just jump into. Your body needs time to adapt to the new style of eating. As you take this important step in your life, here are a few pointers to help you get started.

Find Your Motivation

Before making any changes to your diet, it is essential to take a step back and determine the reasons why you need to make this step. Why do you want to try a plant-based diet? Maybe you are suffering from a disease and this is the best strategy for you to reduce the effects of the disease. Alternatively, it could be that you are looking for a way of improving your health as a means to your overall happiness. Good health means a good heart. It doesn't matter what reasons you have for taking this path. What you need to do is write down your motivation and remind yourself of it every time you wake up.

Start Slow

This is the second most important consideration you should bear in mind. You need to initiate your transition slowly. Select a few foods that are plant-based and begin rotating them for about a week. A good tip here is to select foods that you often enjoy. They can range from lentil stew, oatmeal, jacket potatoes, beans, or veggie stir-fry. Human beings are creatures of habit. Therefore, make a list of the most common plant-based foods that interest you. This should be your starting point as you help your body make a smooth transition.

Cut Down on Processed Foods and Meat

A slow transition guarantees that your body adapts well to the change in diet. In line with this, you shouldn't just avoid processed foods and meat from the get-go. This should be done gradually. Begin by cutting down on your meat intake. Increase the portions of veggies on your plate while reducing the meat portions. After some time, get rid of them entirely as you will have gained the perception that you can do without them. Later on, work on your recipes. If you were a huge fan of beef chili, you can swap the meat with portobello mushrooms. The idea is to continue eating your favorite meals, but as a plant-based version of what you used to have.

Try a Plant-Based Breakfast

After making a few attempts here and there, your next step should be to grab a plant-based meal every day. It would be a good idea for you to start your morning with a vegetarian breakfast. Maybe you are worried that you don't know where to start. There are several plant-based recipes for breakfast, lunch, and dinner that will be provided in this guide. They should help you get started on adopting a plant-based lifestyle.

Surround Yourself with Wholesome Foods

If you are going to adopt a healthy lifestyle, then it is important that you surround yourself with healthy foods. In this case, no other forms of food will be okay; you should only have plant-based foods. Walk around your kitchen as you try and evaluate whether the foods around you are helpful to your goal. If not, don't hesitate to throw them away or donate them. Just because you bought them doesn't imply that you will be wasting food if you choose not to eat them.

Watch Your Protein Portions

The Dietary Reference Intake recommends that the average amount of protein that the body needs is about 0.8 grams per kilogram of body weight. This implies that the typical, sedentary man will require about 56 grams of daily protein intake, whereas a woman will require about 46 grams (Gunnars, 2018). This shows that we only need a fraction of our protein intake to supplement the body with what it needs. Unfortunately, most dieters over-consume proteins with the idea that the body requires the nutrients. What we forget is that too much of something can be toxic and dangerous.

Whether the body needs it or not, watching our portions is vital. While striving to live on a plant-based diet, you should be careful of the amounts of protein you consume. Excessive intake will undeniably lead to negative health effects. What you need to do is make sure that your plant foods have enough calories to provide your body with the energy it needs for metabolism and other purposes.

Educate Yourself

In addition to focusing on food, you should also invest your time and money in educating yourself, just like you are doing by reading this book. It is unfortunate that digital media and advertising has polluted our minds. We are blinded from realizing that plant-based foods are the best foods for our bodies and the planet we live on. Educating yourself is the surest way to get the answers to lifestyle-related questions. You should recognize that, by taking the time to learn, you will be motivated to focus on your goal since you know what you are after.

Find Like-Minded People

Relating to like-minded individuals will be helpful in good and bad times. These are people who are also looking to benefit from eating plant-based foods. Therefore, by relating to them, you can share success stories as well as help each other out in times of need. With the advent of the Internet, it should not be difficult for you to find other people who are vegetarians. Browse through social media pages and join their groups. Here, you will find significant information about your new diet plan. For instance, some people will be eager to share tasty, plant-based recipes with you.

Chapter 3: 21-Day Meal Plan

Day 1
Breakfast: Cinnamon Rolls with Cashew Frosting
Lunch: California Quinoa Bowl
Dinner: Stuffed Bell Peppers
Dessert: Banana Green Smoothie

Day 2
Breakfast: Sundried Tomato & Asparagus Quiche
Lunch: Grilled Veggie Burrito Bowl
Dinner: Summer garlic scape and zucchini pasta
Dessert: Peppermint Monster Smoothie

Day 3
Breakfast: Gingerbread Waffles
Lunch: Italian Lunch Bowls
Dinner: Veggie pasta
Dessert: Raspberry Lime Smoothie

Day 4
Breakfast: Almond Butter Banana Overnight Oats
Lunch: Thai Tempeh Buddha Bowl
Dinner: Roasted Sweet Potatoes and Rice with Spicy Thai Peanut Sauce
Dessert: Blueberry Protein Shake

Day 5
Breakfast: Tasty Oatmeal and Carrot Cake
Lunch: Roasted Vegetable Buddha Bowls with Almond Butter Dressing
Dinner: Spanish Vegetable Paella
Dessert: Hidden Kale Smoothie

Day 6
Breakfast: Quiche with Cauliflower & Chickpea
Lunch: Black Bean-Quinoa Buddha Bowl
Dinner: Sweet Potato & Black Bean Veggie Burgers
Dessert: Creamy Chocolate Shake

Day 7
Breakfast: Tempeh Bacon Smoked to Perfection
Lunch: Thai Sweet Potato Noodle Bowls
Dinner: Sugar Snap Pea and Carrot Soba Noodles
Dessert: Go-Green Smoothie

Day 8
Breakfast: Perfect Polenta with a Dose of Cranberries & Pears
Lunch: Vegetarian Grain Bowl
Dinner: Vegan Mac and Cheese
Dessert: Amazing Blueberry Smoothie

Day 9
Breakfast: Amazing Almond & Banana Granola
Lunch: Delicious Sloppy Joes with No Meat
Dinner: Quinoa Lentil Burger
Dessert: Plant-Power Chopped Salad

Day 10
Breakfast: Fruit and Nut Oatmeal
Lunch: Cauliflower Sushi
Dinner: Ground Beef with Marinara Tomato Sauce
Dessert: Banana Mango Ice Cream

Day 11
Breakfast: Cashew Cheese Spread
Lunch: Raw Zoodles with Avocado 'N Nuts
Dinner: Slow Cooker Chili
Dessert: Banana Creamy Pie

Day 12
Breakfast: Cardamom & Blueberry Oatmeal
Lunch: Sushi Rice Bowls
Dinner: Maple Glazed Tempeh with Quinoa and Kale
Dessert: Avocado-based Chocolate Mousse

Day 13
Breakfast: Hot Sausage and Pepper Breakfast
Casserole
Lunch: Avocado and Cauliflower Hummus
Dinner: Lentil Vegetable Loaf
Dessert: Banana Muffins

Day 14
Breakfast: Breakfast: No-Bake Chewy Granola
Bars
Lunch: Mango and Red Cabbage Slaw
Dinner: Broccoli and Mushroom Stir-Fry
Dessert: Raspberry Chia Pudding Shots

Day 15
Breakfast: Oatmeal Fruit Shake
Lunch: Chickpea 'N Spinach Tomato Salad
Dinner: Baked Enchilada Bowls
Dessert: Date Porcupines

Day 16
Breakfast: Easy Hummus Toast
Lunch: Apple Mint Salad with Pine Nut Crunch
Dinner: Cuban Tempeh Buddha Bowl
Dessert: Raw Energy Squares

Day 17
Breakfast: Fluffy Garbanzo Bean Omelete
Lunch: Zucchini Sandwich with Balsamic
Dressing
Dinner: Green Thai Curry
Dessert: Plant-based Taco Salad

Day 18
Breakfast: Smoky Sweet Potato Tempeh Scramble
Lunch: Sweet Potato Sandwich Spread
Dinner: Tahini Falafels
Dessert: Brown Rice Pudding

Day 19
Breakfast: Greek Garbanzo Beans on Toast
Lunch: Sun-dried Tomato Spread
Dinner: Coconut Tofu Curry
Dessert: Cinnamon Coffee Shake

Day 20
Breakfast: Vegan Mango Almond Milkshake
Lunch: Spicy Hummus and Apple Wrap
Dinner: Red Beans & Rice
Dessert: Sautéed Bosc Pears with Walnuts

Day 21
Breakfast: Blueberry French Toast Breakfast Muffins
Lunch: Sloppy Joes Made with Lentils and Bulgur
Dinner: Sweet Potato Sushi
Dessert: Mango & Papaya After-Chop

Chapter 4: Breakfast Recipes

Oatmeal & Peanut Butter Breakfast Bar

Prep time 10 minutes / Cook time 0 minutes / Serves 8

Ingredients

- 1½ cups date, pit removed
- ½ cup peanut butter
- ½ cup old-fashioned rolled oats

Instructions:

1. Grease and line an 8" x 8" baking tin with parchment and pop to one side.
2. Grab your food processor, add the dates and whizz until chopped.
3. Add the peanut butter and the oats and pulse.
4. Scoop into the baking tin then pop into the fridge or freezer until set.
5. Serve and enjoy.

Nutrition Facts Per Serving:

Calories 459, Total Fat 8.9g, Saturated Fat 1.8g, Cholesterol 0mg, Sodium 77mg, Total Carbohydrate 98.5g, Dietary Fiber 11.3g, Total Sugars 79.1g, Protein 7.7g, Calcium 51mg, Potassium 926mg

Chocolate Chip Banana Pancake

Prep time 15 minutes / Cook time 3 minutes / Serves 6

Ingredients

- 1 large ripe banana, mashed
- 2 tablespoons coconut sugar
- 3 tablespoons coconut oil, melted
- 1 cup coconut milk
- 1 ½ cups whole wheat flour
- 1 teaspoon baking soda
- ½ cup vegan chocolate chips
- Olive oil, for frying

Instructions:

1. Grab a large bowl and add the banana, sugar, oil and milk. Stir well.
2. Add the flour and baking soda and stir again until combined.
3. Add the chocolate chips and fold through then pop to one side.
4. Place a skillet over a medium heat and add a drop of oil.
5. Pour ¼ of the batter into the pan and move the pan to cover.
6. Cook for 3 minutes then flip and cook on the other side.
7. Repeat with the remaining pancakes then serve and enjoy.

Nutrition Facts Per Serving:

Calories 315, Total Fat 18.2g, Saturated Fat 15.1g, Cholesterol 0mg, Sodium 221mg, Total Carbohydrate 35.2g, Dietary Fiber 2.6g, Total Sugars 8.2g, Protein 4.7g, Potassium 209mg

Black Bean Breakfast Burritos

Prep time 30 minutes / Cook time 10 minutes / Serves 4

Ingredients

- ¾ cup white rice
- 1 ½ cups water
- ¼ teaspoon sea salt
- ½ lime, juiced
- ¼ cup fresh cilantro, chopped
- 4 small red potatoes, cut into bite-sized pieces
- ½ red onion, sliced into rings
- 1-2 tablespoons olive oil
- Salt & pepper, to taste
- 1 cup cooked black beans
- ¼ teaspoon each ground cumin garlic powder, and chili powder
- Salt & pepper, to taste
- ¼ ripe avocado
- 1 lime, juiced
- 1 cup purple cabbage, thinly sliced
- 1 jalapeno, seeds removed, thinly sliced
- Pinch salt and black pepper
- 2 large vegan flour tortillas white or wheat
- ½ ripe avocado sliced

- ¼ cup salsa
- Hot sauce

Instructions:
1. Place the rice, water and salt in a pan and bring to the boil.
2. Cover and cook on low until fluffy then remove from the heat and pop to one side.
3. Place a skillet over a medium heat, add 1-2 tablespoons olive oil and add the potatoes and onion.
4. Season well then leave to cook for 10 minutes, stirring often.
5. Remove from the heat and pop to one side.
6. Take a small pan then add the beans, cumin, garlic and chili. Stir well.
7. Pop over a medium heat and bring to simmer. Reduce the heat to keep warm.
8. Take a small bowl and add the avocado and lime. Mash together.
9. Add the cabbage and jalapeno and stir well. Season then pop to one side.
10. Grab the cooked rice and add the lime juice and cilantro then toss with a fork.
11. Gently warm the tortillas in a microwave for 10-20 seconds then add the fillings.
12. Roll up, serve and enjoy.

Nutrition Facts Per Serving:
Calories 588, Total Fat 17.1g, Saturated Fat 3.4g, Sodium 272mg, Total Carbohydrate 94.8g, Dietary Fiber 16.2g, Total Sugars 5g, Protein 18.1g, Calcium 115mg, Iron 6mg, Potassium 1964mg

Avocado and 'Sausage' Breakfast Sandwich

Prep time 15 minutes / Cook time 2 minutes / Serves 1

Ingredients
- 1 vegan sausage patty
- 1 cup kale, chopped
- 2 teaspoons extra virgin olive oil
- 1 tablespoon pepitas
- Salt and pepper, to taste
- 1 tablespoon vegan mayo
- 1/8 teaspoon chipotle powder
- 1 teaspoon jalapeno chopped
- 1 English muffin, toasted
- ¼ avocado, sliced

Instructions:
1. Place a sauté pan over a high heat and add a drop of oil.
2. Add the vegan patty and cook for 2 minutes.
3. Flip the patty then add the kale and pepitas.
4. Season well then cook for another few minutes until the patty is cooked.
5. Find a small bowl and add the mayo, chipotle powder and the jalapeno. Stir well to combine.
6. Place the muffin onto a flat surface, spread with the spicy may then top with the patty.
7. Add the sliced avocado then serve and enjoy.

Nutrition Facts Per Serving:
Calories 571, Total Fat 42.3g, Saturated Fat 10.1g, Cholesterol 36mg, Sodium 1334mg, Total Carbohydrate 38.6g, Dietary Fiber 6.6g, Total Sugars 3.7g, Protein 14.4g, Calcium 193mg

Cinnamon Rolls with Cashew Frosting

Prep time 30 minutes / Cook time 25 minutes / Serves 12

Ingredients
- 3 tablespoons vegan butter
- ¾ cup unsweetened almond milk
- ½ teaspoon salt
- 3 tablespoons caster sugar
- 1 teaspoon vanilla extract
- ½ cup pumpkin puree
- 3 cups all-purpose flour
- 2 ¼ teaspoons dried active yeast
- 3 tablespoons softened vegan butter
- 3 tablespoons brown sugar
- ½ teaspoon cinnamon
- ½ cup cashews, soaked 1 hour in boiling water
- ½ cup icing sugar
- 1 teaspoon vanilla extract
- 2/3 cup almond milk

Instructions:
1. Grease a baking sheet and pop to one side.
2. Find a small bowl, add the butter and pop into the microwave to melt.

3. Add the sugar and stir well then set aside to cool.
4. Grab a large bowl and add the flour, salt and yeast. Stir well to mix together.
5. Place the cooled butter into a jug, add the pumpkin puree, vanilla and almond milk. Stir well together.
6. Pour the wet ingredients into the dry and stir well to combine.
7. Tip onto a flat surface and knead for 5 minutes, adding extra flour as needed to avoid sticking.
8. Pop back into the bowl, cover with plastic wrap and pop into the fridge overnight.
9. Next morning, remove the dough from the fridge and punch down with your fingers.
10. Using a rolling pin, roll to form an 18" rectangle then spread with butter.
11. Find a small bowl and add the sugar and cinnamon. Mix well then sprinkle with the butter.
12. Roll the dough into a large sausage then slice into sections.
13. Place onto the greased baking sheet and leave in a dark place to rise for one hour.
14. Preheat the oven to 350°F.
15. Meanwhile, drain the cashews and add them to your blender. Whizz until smooth.
16. Add the sugar and the vanilla then whizz again.
17. Add the almond milk until it reaches your desired consistency.
18. Pop into the oven and bake for 20 minutes until golden.
19. Pour the glaze over the top then serve and enjoy.

Nutrition Facts Per Serving:
Calories 226, Total Fat 6.5g, Saturated Fat 3.4g, Cholesterol 0mg, Sodium 113mg, Total Carbohydrate 38g, Dietary Fiber 1.9g, Total Sugars 11.3g, Protein 4.9g, Calcium 34mg, Iron 2mg, Potassium 153mg

Blueberry French Toast Breakfast Muffins

Prep time 55 minutes / Cook time 25 minutes / Serves 12

Ingredients
- 1 cup unsweetened plant milk
- 1 tablespoon ground flaxseed
- 1 tablespoon almond meal
- 1 tablespoon maple syrup
- 1 teaspoon vanilla extract
- 1 teaspoon cinnamon
- 2 teaspoons nutritional yeast
- ¾ cup frozen blueberries
- 9 slices soft bread
- ¼ cup oats
- 1/3 cup raw pecans
- ¼ cup coconut sugar
- 3 tablespoons coconut butter, at room temperature
- 1/8 teaspoon sea salt
- 9 slices bread, each cut into 4

Instructions:
1. Preheat your oven to 375°F and grease a muffin tin. Pop to one side.
2. Find a medium bowl and add the flax, almond meal, nutritional yeast, maple syrup, milk, vanilla and cinnamon.
3. Mix well using a fork then pop into the fridge.
4. Grab your food processor and add the topping ingredients (except the coconut butter.) Whizz to combine.
5. Add the butter then whizz again.
6. Grab your muffin tin and add a teaspoon of the flax and cinnamon batter to the bottom of each space.
7. Add a square of the bread then top with 5-6 blueberries.
8. Sprinkle with 2 teaspoons of the crumble then top with another piece of bread.
9. Place 5-6 more blueberries over the bread, sprinkle with more of the topping then add the other piece of bread.
10. Add a tablespoon of the flax and cinnamon mixture over the top and add a couple of blueberries on the top.
11. Pop into the oven and cook for 25-25 minutes until the top begins to brown.
12. Serve and enjoy.

Nutrition Facts Per Serving:
Calories 228, Total Fat 14.4g, Saturated Fat 5.1g, Cholesterol 0mg, Sodium 186mg, Total Carbohydrate 22.9g, Dietary Fiber 4g, Total Sugars 7.8g, Protein 4.3g, Calcium 87mg, Iron 2mg, Potassium

Sundried Tomato & Asparagus Quiche

Prep time 1 hour 20 minutes / Cook time 40 minutes / Serves 8

Ingredients

- 1 ½ cup all-purpose flour
- ½ teaspoon salt
- ½ cup vegan butter
- 2-3 tablespoons ice cold water
- 1 tablespoon coconut or vegetable oil
- ¼ cup white onion, minced
- 1 cup fresh asparagus, chopped
- 3 tablespoons dried tomatoes, chopped
- 1 x 14 oz. block medium/firm tofu, drained
- 3 tablespoons nutritional yeast
- 1 tablespoon non-dairy milk
- 1 tablespoon all-purpose flour
- 1 teaspoon dehydrated minced onion
- 2 teaspoons fresh lemon juice
- 1 teaspoon spicy mustard
- ½ teaspoon sea salt
- ½ teaspoon turmeric
- ½ teaspoon liquid smoke
- 3 tablespoons fresh basil, chopped
- 1/3 cup vegan mozzarella cheese
- Salt and pepper, to taste

Instructions:

1. Preheat your oven to 350°F and grease 4 x 5" quiche pans and pop to one side.
2. Grab a medium bowl and add the flour and salt. Stir well.
3. Then cut the butter into chunks and add to the flour, rubbing into the flour with your fingers until it resembles breadcrumbs.
4. Add the water and roll together.
5. Roll out and place into the quiche pans.
6. Bake for 10 minutes then remove from the oven and pop to one side.
7. Place a skillet over a medium heat, add the oil and then add the onions.
8. Cook for five minutes until soft.
9. Throw in the asparagus and tomatoes and cook for 5 more minutes. Remove from the heat and pop to one side.
10. Grab your food processor and add the tofu, nutritional yeast, milk, flour, onions, turmeric, liquid smoke, lemon juice and salt.
11. Whizz until smooth and pour into a bowl.
12. Add the asparagus mixture, the basil and the cheese and stir well.
13. Season with salt and pepper.
14. Spoon into the pie crusts and pop back into the oven for 15-20 minutes until set and cooked through.
15. Remove from the oven, leave to cool for 20 minutes then serve and enjoy.

Nutrition Facts Per Serving:

Calories 175, Total Fat 5.1g, Saturated Fat 2.3g, Cholesterol 1mg, Sodium 286mg, Total Carbohydrate 24.2g, Dietary Fiber 2.7g, Total Sugars 1.2g, Protein 9.4g, Calcium 118mg, Iron 3mg, Potassium 252mg

Fluffy Garbanzo Bean Omelet

Prep time 20 minutes / Cook time 7 minutes / Serves 2

Ingredients

- ¼ cup besan flour
- 1 tablespoon nutritional yeast
- ½ teaspoon baking powder
- ¼ teaspoon turmeric
- ½ teaspoon chopped chives
- ¼ teaspoon garlic powder
- 1/8 teaspoon black pepper
- ½ teaspoon Ener-G egg replacer
- ¼ cup water
- ½ cup Romaine Leafy Green Fresh Express
- ½ cup Veggies
- 1 tablespoon Salsa
- 1 tablespoon Ketchup
- 1 tablespoon Hot sauce
- 1 tablespoon Parsley

Instructions:

1. Grab a medium bowl and combine all the ingredients except the greens and veggies. Leave to stand for five minutes.
2. Place a skillet over a medium heat and add the oil.
3. Pour the batter into the pan, spread and cook for 3-5 minutes until the edges pull away from the pan.

4. Add the greens and the veggies of your choice then fold the omelet over.
5. Cook for 2 more minutes then pop onto a plate.
6. Serve with the topping of your choice.
7. Serve and enjoy.

Nutrition Facts Per Serving:
Calories 104, Total Fat 1.3g, Saturated Fat 0.2g, Cholesterol 0mg, Sodium 419mg, Total Carbohydrate 17.9g, Dietary Fiber 4.6g, Total Sugars 4.7g, Protein 6.6g, Calcium 69mg, Iron 3mg, Potassium 423mg

Gingerbread Waffles

Prep time 30minutes / Cook time 20 minutes / Serves 6
Ingredients
- 1 slightly heaping cup spelt flour
- 1 tablespoon ground flax seeds
- 2 teaspoons baking powder
- ¼ teaspoon baking soda
- ¼ teaspoon salt
- 1 ½ teaspoons ground cinnamon
- 2 teaspoons ground ginger
- 4 tablespoons coconut sugar
- 1 cup non-dairy milk
- 1 tablespoon apple cider vinegar
- 2 tablespoons black strap molasses
- 1½ tablespoons olive oil

Instructions:
1. Find your waffle iron, oil generously and preheat.
2. Find a large bowl and add the dry ingredients. Stir well together.
3. Put the wet ingredients into another bowl and stir until combined.
4. Add the wet to dry then stir until combined.
5. Pour the mixture into the waffle iron and cook on a medium temperature for 20 minutes
6. Open carefully and remove.
7. Serve and enjoy.

Nutrition Facts Per Serving:
Calories 256, Total Fat 14.2g, Saturated Fat 2g, Cholesterol 0mg, Sodium 175mg, Total Carbohydrate 31.2g, Dietary Fiber 3.4g, Total Sugars 13.2g, Protein 4.2g, Calcium 150mg, Iron 2mg, Potassium 369mg

Greek Garbanzo Beans on Toast

Prep time 30 minutes / Cook time 5 minutes / Serves 2
Ingredients
- 2 tablespoons olive oil
- 3 small shallots, finely diced
- 2 large garlic cloves, finely diced
- ¼ teaspoon smoked paprika
- ½ teaspoon sweet paprika
- ½ teaspoon cinnamon
- ½ teaspoon salt
- ½-1 teaspoon sugar, to taste
- Black pepper, to taste
- 1 x 6 oz. can peel plum tomatoes
- 2 cups cooked garbanzo beans
- 4 slices of crusty bread, toasted
- Fresh parsley and dill
- Pitted Kalamata olives

Instructions:
1. Pop a skillet over a medium heat and add the oil.
2. Add the shallots to the pan and cook for five minutes until soft.
3. Add the garlic and cook for another minute then add the other spices to the pan.
4. Stir well then add the tomatoes.
5. Turn down the heat and simmer on low until the sauce thickens.
6. Add the garbanzo beans and warm through.
7. Season with the sugar, salt and pepper then serve and enjoy.

Nutrition Facts Per Serving:
Calories 1296, Total Fat 47.4g, Saturated Fat 8.7g, Cholesterol 11mg, Sodium 1335mg, Total Carbohydrate 175.7g, Dietary Fiber 36.3g, Total Sugars 25.4g, Protein 49.8g, Calcium 313mg, Iron 17mg, Potassium 1972mg

Smoky Sweet Potato Tempeh Scramble

Prep time 17 minutes / Cook time 13 minutes / Serves 8

Ingredients

- 2 tablespoons olive oil
- 1 small sweet potato, finely diced
- 1 small onion, diced
- 2 garlic cloves, minced
- 8 oz. package tempeh, crumbled
- 1 small red bell pepper, diced
- 1 tablespoon soy sauce
- 1 tablespoon ground cumin
- 1 tablespoon smoked paprika
- 1 tablespoon maple syrup
- Juice of ½ lemon
- 1 avocado, sliced
- 2 scallions, chopped
- 4 tortillas
- 2 tbsp. Hot sauce

Instructions:

1. Place a skillet over a medium heat and add the oil.
2. Add the sweet potato and cook for five minutes until getting soft.
3. Add the onion and cook for another five minutes until soft.
4. Stir through the garlic and cook for a minute.
5. Add the tempeh, pepper, soy, cumin, paprika, maple and lemon juice and cook for two more minutes.
6. Serve with the optional extras then enjoy.

Nutrition Facts Per Serving:
Calories 200, Total Fat 12.3g, Saturated Fat 2.2g, Cholesterol 0mg, Sodium 224mg, Total Carbohydrate 19g, Dietary Fiber 3.7g, Total Sugars 6.5g, Protein 7.5g, Calcium 64mg, Iron 2mg, Potassium 430mg

Easy Hummus Toast

Prep time 10 minutes / Cook time 0 minutes / Serves 1

Ingredients

- 2 slices sprouted wheat bread
- ¼ cup hummus
- 1 tablespoon hemp seeds
- 1 tablespoon roasted unsalted sunflower seeds

Instructions:

1. Start by toasting your bread.
2. Top with the hummus and seeds then eat!

Nutrition Facts Per Serving:
Calories 445, Total Fat 16.3g, Saturated Fat 2.2g, Cholesterol 0mg, Sodium 597mg, Total Carbohydrate 54.5g, Dietary Fiber 10.5g, Total Sugars 6.1g, Protein 22.6g, Calcium 116mg, Iron 6mg, Potassium 471mg

No-Bake Chewy Granola Bars

Prep time 10 minutes / Cook time 10 minutes / Serves 8

Ingredients

- ¼ cup coconut oil
- ¼ cup honey or maple syrup
- ¼ teaspoon salt
- 1 teaspoon vanilla extract
- ½ teaspoon cardamom
- ¼ teaspoon cinnamon
- Pinch of nutmeg
- 1 cup old-fashioned oats
- ½ cup sliced raw almonds
- ¼ cup sunflower seeds
- ¼ cup pumpkin seeds
- 1 tablespoon chia seeds
- 1 cup chopped dried figs

Instructions:

1. Line a 6" x 8" baking dish with parchment paper and pop to one side.
2. Grab a saucepan and add the oil, honey, salt and spices.
3. Pop over a medium heat and stir until it melts together.
4. Reduce the heat, add the oats and stir to coat.
5. Add the seeds, nuts and dried fruit and stir through again.
6. Cook for 10 minutes.
7. Remove from the heat and transfer the oat mixture to the pan.
8. Press down until it's packed firm.
9. Leave to cool completely then cut into 8 bars.

14

10. Serve and enjoy.
Nutrition Facts Per Serving:
Calories 243, Total Fat 13.3g, Saturated Fat 6.7g, Cholesterol 0mg, Sodium 78mg, Total Carbohydrate 30.8g, Dietary Fiber 4.3g, Total Sugars 21.1g, Protein 4.2g, Calcium 67mg, Iron 2mg, Potassium 285mg

Hot Sausage and Pepper Breakfast Casserole

Prep time 57 minutes / Cook time 50 minutes / Serves 8
Ingredients
- 10 cup white bread, cubed
- 2¾ cups ice water
- 1 ¼ cup plant-based unsweetened creamer
- 2 tablespoons extra-virgin olive oil
- 3 vegan sausage, sliced
- 1 bell pepper, seeded and chopped
- 1 medium onion, chopped
- 2 garlic cloves, minced
- 5 cups spinach leaves
- 1 cup vegan parmesan, grated
- 1 teaspoon ground sea salt, or to taste
- ½ teaspoon ground nutmeg
- ½ teaspoon ground black pepper
- 1 tablespoon fresh parsley, chopped
- 1 teaspoon fresh rosemary, chopped
- 1 teaspoon fresh thyme, chopped
- 1 teaspoon fresh oregano, chopped
- 1 tablespoon vegan butter

Instructions:
1. Preheat your oven to 375°F and grease a 13" x 8" baking dish.
2. Grab a medium bowl and add the water, milk and nutmeg. Whisk well until combined.
3. Pop a skillet over a medium heat and add the oil.
4. Add the sausage to the pan and cook for 8-10 minutes until browned. Remove from the pan and pop to one side.
5. Add the onions and cook for 3 minutes.
6. Add the peppers and cook for 5 minutes.
7. Add the garlic, salt and pepper and cook for 2 minutes then remove from the pan and pop to one side.
8. Add the spinach to the pan and cook until wilted.
9. Remove the spinach from the pan then chop. Squeeze out the water.
10. Grab the greased baking dish and add half the cubed bread to the bottom.
11. Add half the spinach to the top followed by half the spinach and half of the onion and pepper mixture.
12. Sprinkle with half the parmesan then repeat.
13. Whisk the egg mixture again then pour over the casserole.
14. Pop into the oven and bake for 30 minutes until browned.
15. Serve and enjoy.
Nutrition Facts Per Serving:
Calories 263, Total Fat 8.2g, Saturated Fat 1g, Cholesterol 0mg, Sodium 673mg, Total Carbohydrate 31.8g, Dietary Fiber 3.4g, Total Sugars 3.6g, Protein 12.9g, Calcium 239mg, Iron 3mg, Potassium 377mg

Cardamom & Blueberry Oatmeal

Prep time 10 minutes / Cook time 3 minutes / Serves 1
Ingredients
- ¾ cup quick oats
- 1¼ cup water
- ½ cup unsweetened almond milk, divided
- 2 tablespoons pure maple syrup
- ¼ heaping teaspoon cinnamon
- 1/8 teaspoon cardamom
- Handful walnuts
- Handful dried currants

Instructions:
1. Place the water into a small saucepan and bring to the boil.
2. Add the oats, stir through, reduce the heat to medium and cook for 3 minutes.
3. Add half of the milk, stir again and cook for another few seconds.

4. Remove from the heat and leave to stand for 3 minutes.
5. Transfer to a bowl and to with the remaining ingredients.
6. Drizzle with the milk then serve and enjoy.

Nutrition Facts Per Serving:
Calories 568, Total Fat 24.4g, Saturated Fat 1.9g, Cholesterol 0mg, Sodium 118mg, Total Carbohydrate 77g, Dietary Fiber 10.4g, Total Sugars 26.8g, Protein 16.5g, Vitamin D 1mcg, Calcium 263mg, Iron 5mg, Potassium 651mg

Cashew Cheese Spread

Prep Time: 5 minutes / Cook Time: 0 minutes / Serves: 5

Ingredients:
- 1 cup water
- 1 cup raw cashews
- 1 tsp. nutritional yeast
- ½ tsp. salt
- Optional: 1 tsp. garlic powder

Instructions:
1. Soak the cashews for 6 hours in water.
2. Drain and transfer the soaked cashews to a food processor.
3. Add 1 cup of water and all the other ingredients and blend.
4. For the best flavor, serve chilled.
5. Enjoy immediately, or store for later.

Nutrition Facts Per Serving:
Calories 162, Total Fat 12.7g, Saturated Fat 2.5g, Cholesterol 0mg, Sodium 239mg, Total Carbohydrate 9.7g, Dietary Fiber 1.1g, Total Sugars 1.5g, Protein 4.6g, Calcium 15mg, Iron 2mg, Potassium 178mg

Fruit and Nut Oatmeal

Prep Time: 5 minutes / Cook Time: 10 minutes / Serves: 2

Ingredients
- ¾ cup rolled oats
- ¼ cup berries, fresh
- ½ ripe banana, sliced
- 2 tablespoons nuts, chopped
- ½ teaspoon cinnamon
- ¼ teaspoon salt
- 2 tablespoons Maple syrup

Instructions:
1. Put the oats in a small saucepan and add 1½ cups of water. Stir and over high heat, boil. Reduce to low heat and cook for about 5 minutes, or until the water has been absorbed.
2. Stir in the cinnamon and add the pinch of salt. Serve in 2 bowls and top each with the chopped fruit and nuts. You can also add a little bit of maple syrup if you want.

Nutrition Facts Per Serving:
Calories 257, Total Fat 6.6g, Saturated Fat 1g, Cholesterol 0mg, Sodium 352mg, Total Carbohydrate 45.7g, Dietary Fiber 5.6g, Total Sugars 17.5g, Protein 6g, Vitamin D 0mcg, Calcium 45mg, Iron 2mg, Potassium 334mg

Amazing Almond & Banana Granola

Prep Time: 5 minutes / Cook Time: 70 minutes / Serves: 8

Ingredients:
- 2 peeled and chopped ripe bananas
- 4 cups of rolled oats
- 1 teaspoon of salt
- 2 cups of freshly chopped and pitted dates
- 1 cup of slivered and toasted almonds
- 1 teaspoon of almond extract

Instructions:
1. Heat the oven to 275°F.
2. With parchment paper, line two 13 x 18-inch baking sheets.
3. In an average saucepan, add water, 1 cup and the dates, and boil. On medium heat, cook them for about 10 minutes. The dates will be soft and pulpy. Keep on adding water to the saucepan so that the dates do not stick to the pot.
4. After removing the dates from the high temperature, allow them to cool before you blend them with salt, bananas, almond extract.
5. You will have a creamy and smooth puree.

16

6. To the oats, add this mixture, and give it a thorough mix.
7. Divide the mixture into equal halves and spread over the baking sheets.
8. Bake for about 30-40 minutes, and stir every 10 minutes or so.
9. You will know that the granola is ready when it becomes crunchy.
10. After removing the baking sheets from the cooker, allow them to cool. Then, add the almonds.
11. You can store your granola in a container and enjoy it whenever you are hungry.

Nutrition Facts Per Serving:
Calories 603, Total Fat 14.2g, Saturated Fat 1.5g, Cholesterol 0mg, Sodium 471mg, Total Carbohydrate 112.7g, Dietary Fiber 15.9g, Total Sugars 52.4g, Protein 14.9g, Calcium 116mg, Iron 4mg, Potassium 1014mg

Perfect Polenta with a Dose of Cranberries & Pears

Prep Time: 5 minutes / Cook Time: 10 minutes / Serves: 4

Ingredients:
- 2 pears freshly cored, peeled, and diced
- 1 cup warm basic polenta
- ¼ cup of brown rice syrup
- 1 teaspoon of ground cinnamon
- 1 cup of dried or fresh cranberries

Instructions:
1. Warm the polenta in a medium-sized saucepan. Then, add the cranberries, pears, and cinnamon powder.
2. Cook everything, stirring occasionally. You will know that the dish is ready when the pears are soft.
3. The entire dish will be done within 10 minutes.
4. Divide the polenta equally among 4 bowls. Add some pear compote as the last finishing touch.
5. Now you can dig into this hassle-free breakfast bowl full of goodness.

Nutrition Facts Per Serving:
Calories 178, Total Fat 0.3g, Saturated Fat 0g, Cholesterol 0mg, Sodium 17mg, Total Carbohydrate 44.4g, Dietary Fiber 4.9g, Total Sugars 23.8g, Protein 1.9g, Calcium 20mg, Iron 0mg, Potassium 170mg

Tempeh Bacon Smoked to Perfection

Prep Time: 5 minutes / Cook Time: 10 minutes / Serves: 4

Ingredients:
- 3 tablespoons of maple syrup
- 8 ounce package of tempeh
- ¼ cup of soy sauce
- 2 teaspoons of liquid smoke

Instructions:
1. In a steamer basket, steam the block of tempeh.
2. Mix the tamari, maple syrup, and liquid smoke in a medium-sized bowl.
3. Once the tempeh cools down, slice into stripes and add to the prepared marinade. Remember: the longer the tempeh marinates, the better the flavor will be. If possible, refrigerate overnight. If not, marinate for at least half an hour.
4. In a sauté pan, cook the tempeh on medium-high heat with a bit of the marinade.
5. Once the strips get crispy on one side, turn them over so that both sides are evenly cooked.
6. You can add some more marinade to cook the tempeh, but they should be properly caramelized. It will take about 5 minutes for each side to cook.
7. Enjoy the crispy caramelized tempeh with your favorite dip.

Nutrition Facts Per Serving:
Calories 157, Total Fat 6.2g, Saturated Fat 1.3g, Cholesterol 0mg, Sodium 905mg, Total Carbohydrate 16.6g, Dietary Fiber 0.1g, Total Sugars 9.2g, Protein 11.5g, Calcium 76mg, Iron 2mg, Potassium 299mg

Quiche with Cauliflower & Chickpea

Prep Time: 10 minutes / Cook Time: 30 minutes / Serves: 3

Ingredients:

- ½ teaspoon of salt
- 1 cup of grated cauliflower
- 1 cup of chickpea flour
- ½ teaspoon of baking powder
- ½ zucchini, thinly sliced into half moons
- 1 tablespoon of flax meal
- 1 cup of water
- 4 tbsp fresh rosemary
- ½ teaspoon of Italian seasoning
- ½ freshly sliced red onion

Instructions:

1. In a bowl, combine all the dry ingredients.
2. Chop the onion and zucchini.
3. Grate the cauliflower so that it has a rice-like consistency, and add it to the dry ingredients. Now, add the water and mix well.
4. Add the zucchini, onion, and rosemary last. You will have a clumpy and thick mixture, but you should be able to spoon it into a tin.
5. You can use either a silicone or a metal cake tin with a removable bottom. Now put the mixture in the tin and press it down gently.
6. The top should be left messy to resemble a rough texture.
7. Bake at 350o F for about half an hour. You will know your quiche is ready when the top is golden.
8. You can serve the quiche warm or cold, as per your preference.

Nutrition Facts Per Serving:

Calories 280, Total Fat 5.3g, Saturated Fat 0.5g, Cholesterol 1mg, Sodium 422mg, Total Carbohydrate 46.6g, Dietary Fiber 14.2g, Total Sugars 9.4g, Protein 14.7g, Calcium 136mg, Iron 5mg, Potassium 916mg

Vegan Mango Almond Milkshake

Prep Time: 4 minutes / Cook Time: 5 minutes / Serves: 1

Ingredients

- 1 ripe mango, pulp
- ¾ cup almond milk, unsweetened
- ½ cup Ice

Instructions:

1. Grab your blender, add the ingredients and whizz until smooth.
2. Serve and enjoy.

Nutrition Facts Per Serving:

Calories 232, Total Fat 3.9g, Saturated Fat 0.5g, Cholesterol 0mg, Sodium 142mg, Total Carbohydrate 51.8g, Dietary Fiber 6.1g, Total Sugars 45.9g, Protein 3.5g, Vitamin D 1mcg, Calcium 266mg, Iron 1mg, Potassium 708mg

Tasty Oatmeal and Carrot Cake

Prep Time: 5 minutes / Cook Time: 10 minutes / Serves: 2

Ingredients:

- 1 cup of water
- ½ teaspoon of cinnamon
- 1 cup of rolled oats
- Salt
- ¼ cup of raisins
- ½ cup of shredded carrots
- 1 cup of soy milk
- ¼ teaspoon of allspice
- ½ teaspoon of vanilla extract

Toppings:

- ¼ cup of chopped walnuts
- 2 tablespoons of maple syrup
- 2 tablespoons of shredded coconut

Instructions:

1. Put a small pot on low heat and bring the non-dairy milk, oats, and water to a simmer.
2. Now, add the carrots, vanilla extract, raisins, salt, cinnamon and allspice. You need to simmer all of the ingredients, but do not forget to stir them. You will know that they are ready when the liquid is fully absorbed into all of the ingredients (in about 7-10 minutes).

3. Transfer the thickened dish to bowls. You can drizzle some maple syrup on top or top them with coconut or walnuts.
4. This nutritious bowl will allow you to kickstart your day.

Nutrition Facts Per Serving:
Calories 442, Total Fat 15.5g, Saturated Fat 2.7g, Cholesterol 0mg, Sodium 384mg, Total Carbohydrate 66.3g, Dietary Fiber 7.9g, Total Sugars 29g, Protein 13.6g, Vitamin D 1mcg, Calcium 224mg, Iron 5mg, Potassium 520mg

Almond Butter Banana Overnight Oats

Prep Time: 5 minutes / Cook Time: 10 minutes / Serves: 2
Ingredients
- ½ cup rolled oats
- 1 cup almond milk
- ½ oz chia seeds
- ¼ teaspoon vanilla extract
- ½ teaspoon ground cinnamon
- 1 tablespoon honey
- 1 banana, sliced
- ½ oz almond butter

Instructions:
1. Take a large bowl and add the oats, milk, chia seeds, vanilla, cinnamon and honey.
2. Stir to combine then divide half of the mixture between two bowls.
3. Top with the banana and peanut butter then add the remaining mixture.
4. Cover then pop into the fridge overnight.
5. Serve and enjoy.

Nutrition Facts Per Serving:
Calories 789, Total Fat 60.1g, Saturated Fat 28.1g, Cholesterol 0mg, Sodium 121mg, Total Carbohydrate 49.4g, Dietary Fiber 14.9g, Total Sugars 22.1g, Protein 20g, Vitamin D 0mcg, Calcium 234mg, Iron 4mg, Potassium 638mg

Peach & Chia Seed Breakfast Parfait

Prep Time: 5 minutes / Cook Time: 10 minutes / Serves: 4
Ingredients
- ½ oz chia seeds
- 1 tablespoon pure maple syrup
- 1 cup coconut milk
- 1 teaspoon ground cinnamon
- 3 medium peaches, diced small
- 2/3 cup granola

Instructions:
1. Find a small bowl and add the chia seeds, maple syrup and coconut milk.
2. Stir well then cover and pop into the fridge for at least one hour.
3. Find another bowl, add the peaches and sprinkle with the cinnamon. Pop to one side.
4. When it's time to serve, take two glasses and pour the chia mixture between the two.
5. Sprinkle the granola over the top, keeping a tiny amount to one side to use to decorate later.
6. Top with the peaches and top with the reserve granola and serve.

Nutrition Facts Per Serving:
Calories 261, Total Fat 25.5g, Saturated Fat 14.5g, Cholesterol 0mg, Sodium 20mg, Total Carbohydrate 40.8g, Dietary Fiber 8.2g, Total Sugars 23.6g, Protein 9.1g, Vitamin D 0mcg, Calcium 73mg, Iron 3mg, Potassium 618mg

Avocado Toast with White Beans

Prep Time: 4 minutes / Cook Time: 6 minutes / Serves: 4
Ingredients
- ½ cup canned white beans, drained and rinsed
- 2 teaspoons tahini paste
- 2 teaspoons lemon juice
- ½ teaspoon salt
- ½ avocado, peeled and pit removed
- 4 slices whole grain bread, toasted
- ½ cup grape tomatoes, cut in half

Instructions:
1. Grab a small bowl and add the beans, tahini, ½ the lemon juice and ½ the salt. Mash with a fork.

2. Take another bowl and add the avocado and the remaining lemon juice and salt. Mash together.
3. Place your toast onto a flat surface and add the mashed beans, spreading well.
4. Top with the avocado and the sliced tomatoes then serve and enjoy.

Nutrition Facts Per Serving:
Calories 245, Total Fat 8g, Saturated Fat 1.3g, Cholesterol 0mg, Sodium 431mg, Total Carbohydrate 33.8g, Dietary Fiber 10g, Total Sugars 3.3g, Protein 11g, Vitamin D 0mcg, Calcium 77mg, Iron 4mg, Potassium 642mg

Homemade Granola

Prep time: 5 minutes / Cook time: 1 hour 15 minutes / Serves: 7
Ingredients:
- 5 cups rolled oats
- 1 cup almonds, slivered
- ¾ cup coconut, shredded
- ¾ tsp salt
- ¼ cup coconut oil
- ½ cup maple syrup

Instructions:
1. Preheat oven to 250°F.
2. Mix all ingredients in a large bowl.
3. Spread granola evenly on two rimmed sheet pans.
4. Bake at 250°F for 1 hour 15 minutes, stirring every 20-25 min.
5. Let cool in pans, and serve.

Nutrition Facts Per Serving:
Calories 456, Total Fat 21.3g, Saturated Fat 10.5g, Cholesterol 0mg, Sodium 255mg, Total Carbohydrate 58.9g, Dietary Fiber 8.4g, Total Sugars 15.1g, Protein 10.8g, Vitamin D 0mcg, Calcium 82mg, Iron 4mg, Potassium 387mg

Country Breakfast Cereal

Prep time: 5 minutes / Cook time: 40 minutes / Serves: 6
Ingredients:
- 1 cup brown rice, uncooked
- ½ cup raisins, seedless
- 1 tsp cinnamon, ground
- ¼ Tbsp butter
- 2 ¼ cups water
- 1 tablespoon Honey, to taste
- ½ cup Nuts, toasted

Instructions:
1. Combine rice, butter, raisins, and cinnamon in a saucepan. Add 2 ¼ cups water. Bring to boil.
2. Simmer covered for 40 minutes until rice is tender.
3. Fluff with fork. Add honey and nuts to taste.

Nutrition Facts Per Serving:
Calories 234, Total Fat 7.3g, Saturated Fat 1.3g, Cholesterol 1mg, Sodium 85mg, Total Carbohydrate 39.8g, Dietary Fiber 2.8g, Total Sugars 10.6g, Protein 4.8g, Vitamin D 0mcg, Calcium 31mg, Iron 1mg, Potassium 248mg

Oatmeal Fruit Shake

Prep time: 10 minutes / Cook time: 0 minutes / Serves: 2
Ingredients:
- 1 cup oatmeal, already prepared, cooled
- 1 apple, cored, roughly chopped
- 1 banana, halved
- 1 cup baby spinach
- 2 cups coconut water
- 2 cups ice, cubed
- ½ tsp ground cinnamon
- 1 tsp pure vanilla extract

Instructions:
1. Add all ingredients to blender.
2. Blend from low to high for several minutes until smooth.

Nutrition Facts Per Serving:
Calories 322, Total Fat 3.6g, Saturated Fat 1g, Cholesterol 0mg, Sodium 275mg, Total Carbohydrate 66.8g, Dietary Fiber 11.6g, Total Sugars 25.8g, Protein 8.5g, Vitamin D 0mcg, Calcium 110mg, Iron 4mg, Potassium 1170mg

Amaranth Banana Breakfast Porridge

Prep time: 10 minutes / Cook time: 25 minutes / Serves: 8

Ingredients:

- 2 cup amaranth
- 2 cinnamon sticks
- 4 bananas, diced
- 10 pieces pecans
- 4 cups water

Instructions:

1. Combine the amaranth, water, and cinnamon sticks, and banana in a pot. Cover and let simmer around 25 minutes.

2. Remove from heat and discard the cinnamon. Places into bowls, and top with pecans.

Nutrition Facts Per Serving:

Calories 390, Total Fat 8g, Saturated Fat 1.6g, Cholesterol 0mg, Sodium 114mg, Total Carbohydrate 72g, Dietary Fiber 6.9g, Total Sugars 15.5g, Protein 10.7g, Vitamin D 0mcg, Calcium 86mg, Iron 5mg, Potassium 391mg

Breakfast Quinoa with Figs and Honey

Prep time: 5 minutes / Cook time: 15 minutes / Serves: 4

Ingredients:

- 2 cups water
- 1 cup white quinoa
- 1 cup dried figs, sliced
- 1 cup walnuts, chopped
- 1 cup almond milk
- ½ tsp cinnamon, ground
- ¼ tsp cloves, ground
- 1 tablespoon Honey, to taste

Instructions:

1. Rinse quinoa under cool water.

2. Combine it with water, cinnamon, and cloves. Bring to boil.
3. Simmer covered for 10-15 minutes.
4. Add dried figs, nuts, milk. Garnish with honey. Serve.

Nutrition Facts Per Serving:

Calories 512, Total Fat 33.9g, Saturated Fat 13.8g, Cholesterol 0mg, Sodium 19mg, Total Carbohydrate 50.3g, Dietary Fiber 9.3g, Total Sugars 31.3g, Protein 12.1g, Vitamin D 0mcg, Calcium 122mg, Iron 3mg, Potassium 666mg

Maple Walnut Teff Porridge

Prep time: 5 minutes / Cook time: 20 minutes / Serves: 2

Ingredients:

- 1 ½ cups water
- 1 cup teff, whole grain
- ½ cup coconut milk
- ½ tsp cardamom, ground
- ¼ cup walnuts, chopped
- 1 tsp sea salt
- 1 Tbsp maple syrup

Instructions:

1. Combine the water and coconut oil in a medium pot. Bring to boil, then stir in the teff.

2. Add the cardamom, and simmer uncovered for 15-20 minutes.
3. Mix in the maple syrup and walnuts. Serve.

Nutrition Facts Per Serving:

Calories 352, Total Fat 24.1g, Saturated Fat 13.2g, Cholesterol 0mg, Sodium 954mg, Total Carbohydrate 30.4g, Dietary Fiber 4.5g, Total Sugars 8.1g, Protein 8.7g, Vitamin D 0mcg, Calcium 83mg, Iron 3mg, Potassium 267mg

PB & J Overnight Oatmeal

Prep time: 25 minutes / Cook time: 8 hours 20 minutes / Serves: 4

Ingredients:

- 1½ cups blueberries, frozen
- 1 oz chia seeds, divided
- 2 cups rolled oats

- 3 cups almond milk
- 4 pitted dates
- 2 Tbsp peanut butter

Instructions:

1. Microwave blueberries in 1 Tbsp water for 2-3 minutes.
2. Stir in 2 Tbsp chia seed to the blueberries. Refrigerate for 20 minutes.
3. Put ½ cup oats and ½ Tbsp chia seeds into 4 jars.
4. Blend milk, dates, and peanut butter. Pour it into the jars.
5. Add blueberry chia jam to the jars. Refrigerate for 6-8 hours.

Nutrition Facts Per Serving:
Calories 788, Total Fat 52.5g, Saturated Fat 39.6g, Cholesterol 0mg, Sodium 69mg, Total Carbohydrate 77.3g, Dietary Fiber 16.5g, Total Sugars 32.2g , Protein 14.4g, Vitamin D 0mcg, Calcium 100mg, Iron 9mg, Potassium 910mg

Southwest Tofu Scramble

Prep time: 10 minutes / Cook time: 15 minutes / Serves: 4

Ingredients:

- 8 oz package firm tofu, crumbled
- 1-2 tsp ground cumin
- ½ cup nutritional yeast
- 2 tsp tamari
- 2 tsp extra-virgin olive oil
- 1 zucchini, diced
- 1 bell pepper, diced
- 1 onion, diced

Instructions:

1. Mix first four ingredients with a fork.
2. In a heavy skillet, combine the zucchini, pepper, shallot, and olive oil. Sauté for 5 minutes.
3. Stir in tofu and cook for another 10 minutes. Serve.

Nutrition Facts Per Serving:
Calories 263, Total Fat 10.8g, Saturated Fat 1.5g, Cholesterol 0mg, Sodium 247mg, Total Carbohydrate 20g, Dietary Fiber 8.7g, Total Sugars 3.6g, Protein 26.8g, Vitamin D 0mcg, Calcium 337mg, Iron 8mg, Potassium 720mg

Amaranth Polenta with Wild Mushrooms

Prep time: 10 minutes / Cook time: 30 minutes / Serves: 3

Ingredients:

- ½ ounce dried porcini
- 1 Tbsp olive oil
- ¼ cup shallots, chopped
- 1 cup amaranth
- ¼ tsp salt
- 1 tsp fresh thyme, chopped
- ¼ tsp Ground pepper, to taste

Instructions:

1. Combine 1 ¾ cups boiling water and mushrooms. Leave for 10 minutes to soften.
2. In a saucepan, cook shallots in olive oil for 1 minutes. Add amaranth, mushrooms, and soaking liquid. Simmer for 15 minutes.
3. Add pepper, thyme, and salt. Simmer for another 15 minutes.
4. Serve in small bowls.

Nutrition Facts Per Serving:
Calories 306, Total Fat 9.1g, Saturated Fat 1.8g, Cholesterol 0mg, Sodium 209mg, Total Carbohydrate 46.9g, Dietary Fiber 7.3g, Total Sugars 1.4g, Protein 11.1g, Vitamin D 0mcg, Calcium 112mg, Iron 6mg, Potassium 287mg

Berry Breakfast Bars

Prep time: 8 minutes / Cook time: 27 minutes / Serves: 9

Ingredients:

- 1 ½ cup Rolled oats
- ½ cup Applesauce
- 1 tablespoon Flaxseed meal
- 2 cups Almond flour
- ¼ Salt
- ¼ cup Blackstrap molasses
- ½ teaspoon Baking powder
- 1 teaspoon Vanilla extract
- ¼ cup Almond butter
- 1 teaspoon Apple cider vinegar

- ½ cup Oat milk
- ¼ cup Maple syrup
- 1 tablespoon Agar agar
- 3 cups Mixed frozen berries
- 1 teaspoon Lemon juice

Instructions:

1. You'll need an oven-safe dish, preferably a baking dish. Square is better to get nine full-portioned squares from it, but any shape will do. Your oven should be heated to 350°F and your baking dish should be lined with baking paper.
2. Mix together the oat milk, applesauce, molasses, vanilla, and almond butter. Add the almond flour and flaxseed meal and mix. If it looks too thick at this point, add a little water (maybe a tablespoon or two) to ensure it is runny enough to accept the oats. Stir in the oats and baking powder then add the salt and mix really well to get a nice thick batter.
3. Spoon all but about one cup of mixture into the bottom of your dish and press it down with your fingers to get an even base and bake for 15 minutes.
4. While this is in the oven, get a saucepan and over medium-high heat, cook down the frozen berries and agar-agar with half a cup of cold water. Keep an eye on it and once it comes to a boil, you should turn down the heat to medium-low and let it simmer for around five minutes while stirring as it thickens. Then take it off the heat and add the lemon juice and maple syrup, stir again and then leave to thicken.
5. Pour this over the oat base and with your fingers, roughly crumble the cup of oat mixture you put aside over the top of the berry filling.
6. Put the baking dish back in the oven for another 12 minutes then take out. The oat mixture on top should be beautifully browned. Allow it to cool before you put it in the fridge to set for an hour or so.
7. Cut into squares or bars or whatever makes you happy. Then wrap individually in baking paper or cling film and keep in the fridge or freezer!

Nutrition Facts Per Serving:
Calories 188, Total Fat 5g, Saturated Fat 0.4g, Cholesterol 0mg, Sodium 19mg, Total Carbohydrate 33.1g, Dietary Fiber 5g, Total Sugars 16.8g, Protein 3.9g, Vitamin D 6mcg, Calcium 86mg, Iron 2mg, Potassium 252mg

Tasty Oatmeal Muffins

Prep time 10 minutes / Cook time 20 minutes / Serves 12

Ingredients:

- ½ cup of hot water
- ½ cup of raisins
- ¼ cup of ground flaxseed
- 2 cups of rolled oats
- ¼ teaspoon of sea salt
- ½ cup of walnuts
- ¼ teaspoon of baking soda
- 1 banana
- 2 tablespoons of cinnamon
- ¼ cup of maple syrup

Instructions:

1. Whisk the flaxseed with water and allow the mixture to sit for about 5 minutes.
2. In a food processor, blend all the ingredients along with the flaxseed mix. Blend everything for 30 seconds, but do not create a smooth substance. To create rough-textured cookies, you need to have a semi-coarse batter.
3. Put the batter in cupcake liners and place them in a muffin tin. As this is an oil-free recipe, you will need cupcake liners. Bake everything for about 20 minutes at 350 degrees.
4. Enjoy the freshly-made cookies with a glass of warm milk.

Nutrition Facts Per Serving:
Calories 143, Total Fat 4.8g, Saturated Fat 0.4g, Cholesterol 0mg, Sodium 70mg, Total Carbohydrate 22.8g, Dietary Fiber 3.4g, Total Sugars 8.9g, Protein 3.8g, Vitamin D 0mcg, Calcium 30mg, Iron 2mg, Potassium 194mg

Omelet with Chickpea Flour

Prep time 10 minutes / Cook time 20 minutes / Serves 1

Ingredients:

- ½ teaspoon, onion powder
- ¼ teaspoon, black pepper
- 1 cup, chickpea flour
- ½ teaspoon, garlic powder
- ½ teaspoon, baking soda
- 1/3 cup, nutritional yeast
- 3 finely chopped green onions
- 4 ounces, sautéed mushrooms

Instructions:

1. In a small bowl, mix the onion powder, white pepper, chickpea flour, garlic powder, black and white pepper, baking soda, and nutritional yeast.
2. Add 1 cup of water and create a smooth batter.
3. On medium heat, put a frying pan and add the batter just like the way you would cook pancakes.
4. On the batter, sprinkle some green onion and mushrooms. Flip the omelet and cook evenly on both sides.
5. Once both sides are cooked, serve the omelet with spinach, tomatoes, hot sauce, and salsa.
6. Enjoy a guilt-free meal.

Nutrition Facts Per Serving:

Calories 1006, Total Fat 15.4g, Saturated Fat 1.7g, Cholesterol 0mg, Sodium 722mg, Total Carbohydrate 168.1g, Dietary Fiber 52g, Total Sugars 28g, Protein 66.1g, Vitamin D 0mcg, Calcium 293mg, Iron 24mg, Potassium 3315mg

White Sandwich Bread

Prep time 10 minutes / Cook time 20 minutes / Serves 16

Ingredients:

- 1 cup warm water
- 2 tablespoons active dry yeast
- 4 tablespoons oil
- 2 ½ teaspoons salt
- 2 tablespoons raw sugar
- 1 cup warm almond milk
- 6 cups all-purpose flour

Instructions:

1. Add warm water, yeast and sugar into a bowl and stir. Set aside for 5 minutes or until lots of tiny bubbles are formed, sort of frothy.
2. Add flour and salt into a mixing bowl and stir. Pour the oil, yeast mix and milk and mix into dough. If the dough is too hard, add a little water, a tablespoon at a time and mix well each time. If the dough is too sticky, add more flour, a tablespoon at a time. Knead the dough for 8 minutes until soft and supple. You can use your hands or use the dough hook attachment of the stand mixer.
3. Now spray some water on top of the dough. Keep the bowl covered with a towel. Let it rest until it doubles in size.
4. Remove the dough from the bowl and place on your countertop. Punch the dough.
5. Line a loaf pan with parchment paper. You can also grease with some oil if you prefer. You can use 2 smaller loaf pans if you want to make smaller loaves, like I did.
6. Place the dough in the loaf pan. Now spray some more water on top of the dough. Keep the loaf pan covered with a towel. Let it rest until the dough doubles in size.
7. Bake in a preheated oven at 370° F for about 40 – 50 minutes or a toothpick when inserted in the center of the bread comes out without any particles stuck on it.
8. Let it cool to room temperature.
9. Cut into 16 equal slices and use as required. Store in a breadbox at room temperature.

Nutrition Facts Per Serving:

Calories 245, Total Fat 7.5g, Saturated Fat 3.7g, Cholesterol 0mg, Sodium 369mg, Total Carbohydrate 38.7g, Dietary Fiber 1.9g, Total Sugars 2.1g, Protein 5.8g, Vitamin D 0mcg, Calcium 11mg, Iron 3mg, Potassium 120mg

A Toast to Remember

Prep time 10 minutes / Cook time 15 minutes / Serves 4

Ingredients:

- 8 oz black beans
- ¼ teaspoon sea salt
- 2 pieces whole-wheat toast
- ¼ teaspoon chipotle spice
- ¼ teaspoon black pepper
- 1 teaspoon garlic powder
- 1 freshly juiced lime
- 1 freshly diced avocado
- ¼ cup corn
- 3 tablespoons, finely diced onion
- ½ freshly diced tomato
- ¼ cup Fresh cilantro

Instructions:

1. Mix the chipotle spice with the beans, salt, garlic powder, and pepper. Stir in the lime juice.
2. Boil all of these until you have a thick and starchy mix.
3. In a bowl, mix the corn, tomato, avocado, red onion, cilantro, and juice from the rest of the lime. Add some pepper and salt.
4. Toast the bread and first spread the black bean mixture followed by the avocado mix.
5. Take a bite of wholesome goodness!

Nutrition Facts Per Serving:

Calories 355, Total Fat 12g, Saturated Fat 2.4g, Cholesterol 0mg, Sodium 215mg, Total Carbohydrate 50.7g, Dietary Fiber 13.1g, Total Sugars 3g, Protein 14.6g, Vitamin D 0mcg, Calcium 82mg, Iron 4mg, Potassium 1167mg

Tasty Panini

Prep time 5 minutes / Cook time 0 minutes / Serves 1

Ingredients:

- ¼ cup hot water
- 1 teaspoon cinnamon
- ¼ cup raisins
- 2 teaspoons cacao powder
- 1 ripe banana
- 2 slices whole-grain bread
- ¼ cup natural peanut butter

Instructions:

1. In a bowl, mix the cinnamon, hot water, raisins, and cacao powder.
2. Spread the peanut butter on the bread.
3. Cut the bananas and put them on the toast.
4. Mix the raisin mixture in a blender and spread it on the sandwich.

Nutrition Facts Per Serving:

Calories 807, Total Fat 34.2g, Saturated Fat 6.6g, Cholesterol 0mg, Sodium 269mg, Total Carbohydrate 103.2g, Dietary Fiber 20.6g, Total Sugars 45.9g , Protein 31.2g, Vitamin D 0mcg, Calcium 252mg, Iron 12mg, Potassium 704mg

Tasty Oatmeal and Carrot Cake

Prep time 10 minutes / Cook time 10 minutes / Serves 1

Ingredients:

- 1 cup water
- ½ teaspoon cinnamon
- 1 cup rolled oats
- ¼ teaspoon salt
- ¼ cup raisins
- ½ cup shredded carrots
- 1 cup almond milk
- ¼ teaspoon allspice
- ½ teaspoon vanilla extract

Toppings:

- ¼ cup chopped walnuts
- 2 tablespoons maple syrup
- 2 tablespoons shredded coconut

Instructions:

1. Put a small pot on low heat and bring the non-dairy milk, oats, and water to a simmer.
2. Now, add the carrots, vanilla extract, raisins, salt, cinnamon and allspice. You need to simmer all of the ingredients, but do not forget to stir them. You will know that they are ready when the liquid is fully absorbed

into all of the ingredients (in about 7-10 minutes).
3. Transfer the thickened dish to bowls. You can drizzle some maple syrup on top or top them with coconut or walnuts.

Nutrition Facts Per Serving:
Calories 1336, Total Fat 84.6g, Saturated Fat 55.7g, Cholesterol 0mg, Sodium 678mg, Total Carbohydrate 135.8g, Dietary Fiber 20g, Total Sugars 58.1g , Protein 25.8g, Vitamin D 0mcg, Calcium 186mg, Iron 11mg, Potassium 1671mg

Onion & Mushroom Tart with a Nice Brown Rice Crust

Prep time 10 minutes / Cook time 55 minutes / Serves 1

Ingredients:
- 1 ½ pounds mushrooms
- 1 cup short-grain brown rice
- 2 ¼ cups water
- ½ teaspoon ground black pepper
- 1 large onion
- 7 ounces extra-firm tofu
- 1 cup almond milk
- 2 teaspoons onion powder
- 1 tablespoon low-sodium soy
- 1 teaspoon molasses
- ¼ teaspoon ground turmeric
- ¼ cup white wine
- ¼ cup tapioca

Instructions:
1. Cook the brown rice and put it aside for later use.
2. Slice the onions into thin strips and sauté them in water until they are soft. Then, add the molasses, and cook them for a few minutes.
3. Next, sauté the mushrooms in water. Once the mushrooms are cooked and they are soft, add the white wine or sherry. Cook everything for a few more minutes.
4. In a blender, combine milk, tofu, arrowroot, turmeric, and onion powder till you have a smooth mixture

5. On a pie plate, create a layer of rice, spreading evenly to form a crust. The rice should be warm and not cold. It will be easy to work with warm rice. You can also use a pastry roller to get an even crust. With your fingers, gently press the sides.
6. Take half of the tofu mixture and the mushrooms and spoon them over the tart dish. Smooth the level with your spoon.
7. Now, top the layer with onions followed by the tofu mixture. You can smooth the surface again with your spoon.
8. Sprinkle some black pepper on top.
9. Bake the pie at 350°F for about 45 minutes. Toward the end, you can cover it loosely with tin foil. This will help the crust to remain moist.
10. Allow the pie crust to cool down, so that you can slice it. If you are in love with vegetarian dishes, there is no way that you will not love this pie.

Nutrition Facts Per Serving:
Calories 1375, Total Fat 72.7g, Saturated Fat 51.9g, Cholesterol 0mg, Sodium 647mg, Total Carbohydrate 140.8g, Dietary Fiber 20.1g, Total Sugars 36.2g, Protein 54.9g, Vitamin D 2449mcg, Calcium 485mg, Iron 29mg, Potassium 3514mg

Perfect Breakfast Shake

Prep time 5 minutes / Cook time 0 minutes / Serves 2

Ingredients:
- 3 tablespoons raw cacao powder
- 1 cup almond milk
- 2 bananas
- 3 tablespoons natural peanut butter

Instructions:
1. Use a powerful blender to combine all the ingredients.

2. Process everything until you have a smooth shake.
3. Enjoy a hearty shake to kickstart your day.

Nutrition Facts Per Serving:
Calories 546, Total Fat 41.3g, Saturated Fat 27.9g, Cholesterol 0mg, Sodium 27mg, Total Carbohydrate 40.4g, Dietary Fiber 8.6g, Total Sugars 19.9g , Protein 12.2g, Vitamin D 0mcg, Calcium 25mg, Iron 5mg, Potassium 738mg

Beet Gazpacho

Prep time 10 minutes / Cook time 2 minutes / Serves 4

Ingredients:

- ½ large bunch young beets with stems, roots and leaves
- 2 small cloves garlic, peeled,
- ¼ teaspoon Salt
- ¼ teaspoon Pepper
- ½ teaspoon liquid stevia
- ½ cup coconut milk kefir
- 1 teaspoon chopped dill
- ½ tablespoon canola oil
- 1 small red onion, chopped
- 1 tablespoon apple cider vinegar
- 2 cups vegetable broth or water
- 1 tablespoon chopped chives
- 1 scallion, sliced
- 1 cup Roasted baby potatoes

Instructions:

1. Cut the roots and stems of the beets into small pieces. Thinly slice the beet greens.
2. Place a saucepan over medium heat. Add oil. When the oil is heated, add onion and garlic and cook until onion turns translucent.
3. Stir in the beets, roots and stem and cook for a minute.
4. Add broth, salt and water and cover with a lid. Simmer until tender.
5. Add stevia and vinegar and mix well. Taste and adjust the stevia and vinegar if required.
6. Turn off the heat. Blend with an immersion blender until smooth.
7. Place the saucepan back over it. When it begins to boil, add beet greens and cook for a minute. Turn off the heat.
8. Cool completely. Chill if desired.
9. Add rest of the ingredients and stir.
10. Serve in bowls with roasted potatoes if desired.

Nutrition Facts Per Serving:

Calories 97, Total Fat 3.8g, Saturated Fat 1.2g, Cholesterol 1mg, Sodium 580mg, Total Carbohydrate 12.4g, Dietary Fiber 2g, Total Sugars 2.6g, Protein 4g, Vitamin D 0mcg, Calcium 97mg, Iron 1mg, Potassium 198mg

Vegetable Rice

Prep time 7 minutes / Cook time 15 minutes / Serves 4

Ingredients:

- ½ cup brown rice, rinsed
- 1 cup water
- ½ teaspoon dried basil
- 1 small onion, chopped
- 2 tablespoons raisins
- 5 ounces frozen peas, thawed
- 10 pieces pecans, halves and toasted
- 1 medium carrot, cut into matchsticks
- 4 green onions, cut into 1-inch pieces
- 1 tablespoon olive oil
- ½ teaspoon salt or to taste
- ¼ teaspoon Ground pepper or to taste

Instructions:

1. Place a small saucepan with water over medium heat.
2. When it begins to boil, add rice and basil. Stir.
3. When it again begins to boil, lower the heat and cover with a lid. Cook for 15 minutes until all the water is absorbed and rice is cooked. Add more water if you think the rice is not cooked well.
4. Meanwhile, place a skillet over medium high heat. Add carrots, raisins and onions and sauté until the vegetables are crisp as well as tender.
5. Stir in the peas, salt, and pepper.
6. Add pecans and rice and stir.
7. Serve.

Nutrition Facts Per Serving:

Calories 419, Total Fat 29.3g, Saturated Fat 3.2g, Cholesterol 0mg, Sodium 333mg, Total Carbohydrate 36g, Dietary Fiber 7.9g, Total Sugars 7.4g, Protein 8.1g, Vitamin D 0mcg, Calcium 66mg, Iron 2mg, Potassium 400mg

Courgette Risotto

Prep time 10 minutes / Cook time 5 minutes / Serves 8

Ingredients:

- 2 tablespoons olive oil
- 4 cloves garlic, finely chopped
- 1.5 pounds Arborio rice
- 6 tomatoes, chopped
- 2 teaspoons chopped rosemary
- 6 courgettes, finely diced
- 1 ¼ cups peas, fresh or frozen
- 12 cups hot vegetable stock
- ¼ teaspoon Salt to taste
- ¼ teaspoon Freshly ground pepper

Instructions:

1. Place a large heavy bottomed pan over medium heat. Add oil. When the oil is heated, add onion and sauté until translucent.
2. Stir in the tomatoes and cook until soft.
3. Next stir in the rice and rosemary. Mix well.
4. Add half the stock and cook until dry. Stir frequently.
5. Add remaining stock and cook for 3-4 minutes.
6. Add courgette and peas and cook until rice is tender. Add salt and pepper to taste.
7. Stir in the basil. Let it sit for 5 minutes.
8. Serve hot.

Nutrition Facts Per Serving:

Calories 422, Total Fat 7.6g, Saturated Fat 3.7g, Cholesterol 0mg, Sodium 1180mg, Total Carbohydrate 85g, Dietary Fiber 6.5g, Total Sugars 9.3g, Protein 9.7g, Vitamin D 0mcg, Calcium 53mg, Iron 3mg, Potassium 734mg

Nutty Breakfast Cookies

Prep time 5 minutes / Cook time 10 minutes / Serves 12

Ingredients:

- 1 tsp Vanilla
- 1 tsp Cinnamon
- ½ cup filtered water
- 1 tsp Sunflower Seeds
- ¼ cup Maple syrup
- ½ cup Nut Butter
- 2 cups Rolled or Old Fashion Oats
- ¼ cup Raisins

Ingredients:

1. Heat oven to 350 degrees.
2. Use parchment paper on a cookie sheet.
3. Mix your warm water, and raisins. Let sit for five minutes.
4. Lightly blend one cup of oats. In large bowl, add the other cup of oats with this mixture.
5. Add nut butter to dry mixture. Make sure to create an even mix.
6. Mix in chia/raisin and water mixture. Using a wooden spoon, blend well.
7. Add sunflower seeds, maple syrup, cinnamon, and vanilla. Mix well.
8. Use a scooper to scoop even amounts onto cookie sheet. Or with wet hands, form into small balls and flatten with a spoon.
9. Let bake for 10 minutes. Once cool, keep in airtight container. Enjoy!

Nutrition Facts Per Serving:

Calories 117, Total Fat 6.3g, Saturated Fat 1.3g, Cholesterol 0mg, Sodium 51mg, Total Carbohydrate 11.6g, Dietary Fiber 2.1g, Total Sugars 1.2g, Protein 4.5g, Vitamin D 0mcg, Calcium 10mg, Iron 2mg, Potassium 121mg

Cinnamon Peanut Butter Banana Overnight Oats

Prep time 15 minutes / Cook time 0 minutes / Serves 5

Ingredients:

- ½ cup Sliced Ripe Bananas
- 1 cup almond Milk
- ½ tsp Cinnamon
- 1 cup Oats
- 1 tbsp Peanut Butter

Instructions:

1. Use any glass container or jar.
2. Add milk, oats, and cinnamon to the container.

3. Mix well. You can add more liquid or more oats depending on how thin or thick you may want it.
4. Cover with lid or plastic wrap.
5. Place in refrigerator for at least 3 hours.
6. Add sliced bananas and peanut butter on top. Enjoy!

Nutrition Facts Per Serving:
Calories 205, Total Fat 14.2g, Saturated Fat 10.7g, Cholesterol 0mg, Sodium 23mg, Total Carbohydrate 18g, Dietary Fiber 3.4g, Total Sugars 3.9g, Protein 4.2g, Vitamin D 0mcg, Calcium 19mg, Iron 2mg, Potassium 261mg

Savory Sweet Potato Hash with Black Beans

Prep time 5 minutes / Cook time 15 minutes / Serves 3

Ingredients:
- 1 cup Black Beans, cooked
- ¼ cup Chopped green onions
- 2 cups Diced Sweet Potatoes
- 1 cup Chopped Onion
- 2 cloves Minced Garlic
- 2 tsp Chili Powder
- 1/3 cup Vegetable Broth
- 4 tbsp Cilantro

Instructions:
1. Sauté onions and garlic in non-stick skillet.
2. Add one to two teaspoons of broth, and then add sweet potatoes and chili powder, Coat everything well.
3. Cook until potatoes are soft and cooked through. Mix to keep from sticking by adding broth as needed.
4. Add green onions and black beans. Cook for 15 minutes until beans are heated through.
5. Adjust seasoning to personal preferences.
6. Serve with cilantro on top. Enjoy!

Nutrition Facts Per Serving:
Calories 370, Total Fat 1.6g, Saturated Fat 0.4g, Cholesterol 0mg, Sodium 118mg, Total Carbohydrate 74.2g, Dietary Fiber 15.6g, Total Sugars 3.9g, Protein 17g, Vitamin D 0mcg, Calcium 122mg, Iron 4mg, Potassium 1925mg

Super Protein Chia Pudding

Prep time 5 minutes / Cook time 0 minutes / Serves 4

Ingredients:
- ¼ tsp Vanilla
- 1/5 tsp Cinnamon
- ¼ cup Cooked Quinoa
- ¼ oz Chia Seeds
- ¾ cup almond Milk
- 2 tsps. Maple syrup
- ½ cup Hemp Seeds for topping
- ½ cup Chopped peanuts
- 1 mango

Instructions:
1. Mix together, chia seeds, cooked quinoa, almond milk, cinnamon, and maple syrup.
2. Put in a glass container, small mason jar or bowl
3. Place in refrigerator and leave for about 2 hours.
4. Once already set, add the mango toppings that you like. Enjoy!

Nutrition Facts Per Serving:
Calories 442, Total Fat 28.1g, Saturated Fat 11.4g, Cholesterol 0mg, Sodium 14mg, Total Carbohydrate 40.2g, Dietary Fiber 5.8g, Total Sugars 13.7g, Protein 13.2g, Vitamin D 0mcg, Calcium 61mg, Iron 4mg, Potassium 596mg

Cinnamon Apple Muffins

Prep time 10 minutes / Cook time 25 minutes / Serves 12

Ingredients:
- ½ cup Apples, peeled and chopped
- ½ cup Raisins
- 1 tsp Apple Cider Vinegar
- ½ cup almond Milk
- 1 tsp Vanilla
- 1 tsp Cinnamon
- 1.5 cups Apple Sauce
- ½ cup Brown Sugar

- ¼ tsp All Spice
- ¼ tsp Salt
- 1 tsp Baking Powder
- 1 tsp Baking Soda
- 2 cups Whole Wheat Flour

Instructions:
1. Heat oven to 350°F
2. Mix together all dry ingredients into a big bowl. Set aside flour, sugar, salt, baking powder and soda, allspice, cinnamon.
3. Mix together all wet ingredients in a smaller bowl using a whisk. Set aside apple sauce, milk, vanilla, and vinegar.
4. Mix together both mixtures until smooth.
5. Add apples and raisins; coat well.
6. Scoop batter into silicone or non-stick muffin pan.
7. Let bake for 25 minutes. Let cool. Enjoy!

Nutrition Facts Per Serving:
Calories 153, Total Fat 2.6g, Saturated Fat 2.1g, Cholesterol 0mg, Sodium 165mg, Total Carbohydrate 30.3g, Dietary Fiber 1.5g, Total Sugars 12.2g, Protein 2.6g, Vitamin D 0mcg, Calcium 33mg, Iron 1mg, Potassium 165mg

Quick Chickpea Omelet

Prep time 30 minutes / Cook time 5 minutes / Serves 5

Ingredients:
- ¾ cup sautéed mushrooms
- ½ cup green Onions
- ½ tsp Baking Soda
- 1/3 cup Nutritional Yeast
- ¾ tsp Black Pepper
- ½ tsp Garlic Powder
- ½ tsp Onion Powder
- 1 cup Chickpea Flour

Instructions:
1. In a small bowl mix together: Baking soda, yeast, both types of pepper, garlic powder, onion powder, and chickpea flour.
2. Add one cup of water to the mixture and mix well. Make a smooth batter.
3. Heat up a non-stick skillet. Add plant-based oil if desired.
4. Using the same method as making pancakes, do add batter into the pan.
5. Add green onions and mushrooms in the middle of the omelet.
6. Flip twice once each side is a golden brown color.
7. Let it cool. Enjoy!

Nutrition Facts Per Serving:
Calories 196, Total Fat 3.2g, Saturated Fat 0.3g, Cholesterol 0mg, Sodium 199mg, Total Carbohydrate 31.7g, Dietary Fiber 10.5g, Total Sugars 5.1g, Protein 13.4g, Vitamin D 5mcg, Calcium 61mg, Iron 5mg, Potassium 726mg

Carrot Cake-Like Overnight Oats

Prep time 15 minutes / Cook time 0 minutes / Serves 5

Ingredients:
- ½ cup Shredded carrots
- 1 cup almond Milk
- ¼ tsp Cinnamon
- 1 cup Oats
- 1 tsp Pitted dates
- ¼ tsp Nutmeg
- 1/3 tsp Grated or dried Ginger
- ¼ tsp Vanilla
- ¼ tbsp Hemp Seeds

Instructions:
1. Use any glass container or jar.
2. Add all ingredients together in a container.
3. Mix well. You can add more liquid or more oats depending on how thin or thick you may want it.
4. Cover with lid or plastic wrap.
5. Place in refrigerator for at least 3 hours.
6. Once set, mix together. Enjoy!

Nutrition Facts Per Serving:
Calories 185, Total Fat 12.9g, Saturated Fat 10.4g, Cholesterol 0mg, Sodium 16mg, Total Carbohydrate 15.7g, Dietary Fiber 3.2g, Total Sugars 2.8g, Protein 3.6g, Vitamin D 0mcg, Calcium 22mg, Iron 2mg, Potassium 235mg

Fruity Muesli

Prep time 5 minutes / Cook time 0 minutes / Serves 3

Ingredients:

- ½ cup Plant-Based Milk
- 2 tsp Maple Syrup
- ¼ cup Chopped Nuts
- ½ cup mango
- 1 cup sliced bananas
- 1 cup Rolled Oats

Instructions:

1. In a bowl mix together milk, maple syrup, oats, fruit, and nuts.

2. Add milk to eat immediately like cereal.
3. Add milk and refrigerate for an overnight version.
4. Enjoy!

Nutrition Facts Per Serving:
Calories 336, Total Fat 17.5g, Saturated Fat 9.6g, Cholesterol 0mg, Sodium 85mg, Total Carbohydrate 42.1g, Dietary Fiber 6.4g, Total Sugars 14.7g, Protein 7.3g, Vitamin D 0mcg, Calcium 37mg, Iron 2mg, Potassium 506mg

Easy Oat and Waffles

Prep time 30 minutes / Cook time 0 minutes / Serves 10

Instructions:

- 1/3 cup Ripe Mashed Bananas
- ½ tsp Cinnamon
- ¼ cup ground flax Seeds
- ½ cup unsweetened Almond Milk
- 2 cups Rolled Oats
- ¼ cup Lemon Zest
- 1 cup Sliced Bananas
- 1 cup Strawberries

Instructions:

1. Using a food processor, mix oats, flax seeds, cinnamon, and lemon zest. Form a powder.

2. Add milk and mashed bananas to make a thick batter.
3. Using a preheated waffle iron add some of the batter and close lid.
4. Repeat until finish batter. Top with fresh sliced fruit. Enjoy!

Nutrition Facts Per Serving:
Calories 115, Total Fat 2.3g, Saturated Fat 0.4g, Cholesterol 0mg, Sodium 11mg, Total Carbohydrate 21.1g, Dietary Fiber 3.6g, Total Sugars 5.6g, Protein 3.2g Vitamin D 0mcg,Iron 2mg, Potassium 221mg

Ayurvedic oatmeal

Prep time 5 minutes / Cook time 10 minutes / Serves 4

Ingredients

- ½ tsp turmeric powder
- ¼ tsp cardamom
- ¼ tsp ground cloves
- 4 Cinnamon sticks
- 11 ounces soy milk
- 3 ounces Oatmeal flakes
- ½ tablespoons raisins
- ½ tablespoons pumpkin seeds
- 1 oz Sliced fresh pumpkin
- 7 ounces tap water

Instructions:

1. Boil the shredded pumpkin in water in low heat till soft and well done.

2. Put in the soy milk then bring the mixture to boil once again.
3. Include the turmeric, cardamom powder, cinnamon sticks, and the oatmeal in the mixture.
4. Let the food cook for 10minutes.
5. Include the pumpkin seeds by sprinkling them in the dish.
6. It is now ready to serve.

Nutrition Facts Per Serving:
Calories 133, Total Fat 2.7g, Saturated Fat 0.3g, Cholesterol 0mg, Sodium 177mg, Total Carbohydrate 23.2g, Dietary Fiber 3g, Total Sugars 9g, Protein 5.1g, Vitamin D 0mcg, Calcium 26mg, Iron 8mg, Potassium 134mg

Cantaloupe with dates oatmeal and mint-melon relish

Prep time 5 minutes / Cook time 109 minutes / Serves 5

Ingredients

- ¼ tsp Salt
- ¼ cup quick cook steel cut oats
- ¼ cup coconut milk
- ¼ tsp coconut oil
- 2 dates pitted and chopped
- 1 cup cantaloupe
- 1 tsp minced mint leaves
- 2 blackberries, fresh

Instructions:

1. Puree the coconut oil, dates and cantaloupe in a food processor.
2. Pour the puree in a pan and add the coconut milk, and simmer the mixture for 10 minutes.
3. Include salt and oats and simmer.
4. As the moisture simmers, start on the mint-melon relish.
5. Slice the blackberries and cantaloupe into a quarter inch sized piece.
6. With fresh mint, toss the blackberries and cantaloupe mixture.
7. Put the cooked oatmeal in a bowl once it is cooked to your satisfaction.
8. Add the mint-melon relish on top of the oatmeal and splash some coconut milk over the dish.

Nutrition Facts Per Serving:

Calories 82, Total Fat 3.6g, Saturated Fat 2.8g, Cholesterol 0mg, Sodium 124mg, Total Carbohydrate 12.6g, Dietary Fiber 4.1g, Total Sugars 7.9g, Protein 1.7g, Vitamin D 0mcg, Calcium 24mg, Iron 1mg, Potassium 233mg

Granola bars

Prep time 6 minutes / Cook time 30 minutes / Serves 5

Ingredients

- 1 stick dark chocolate, melted
- 1 tsp almond extract
- 1/3 organic coconut oil
- ½ glass pure maple syrup
- ½ glass pure natural almond butter
- ¾ tsp sea salt
- 2 tbsps. cinnamon
- ¼ cup natural desiccated coconut
- ½ cup raw pumpkin seeds
- ¼ cup raw sunflower seeds
- ¼ hemp seeds
- ½ cup raw walnuts, chopped
- 1 cup dried cherries
- 1 cup raw almonds, chopped
- 2 ½ cups rolled gluten free oats

Instructions:

1. Line your oven with a standard parchment cookie sheet and preheat to 325F.
2. Mix the salt, cinnamon, hemp seeds, coconut, pumpkin seeds, sunflower seeds, walnuts, the presoaked cherries, almonds, and oats, in a bowl and put aside.
3. In low heat and in a small pot, put the coconut oil, almond butter, and the maple syrup. Keep stirring as it melts. Remove from the heat and mix in the almond extract.
4. To the dry ingredients, you had set aside, add the wet mixture, and keep mixing until satisfied with the outcome.
5. Firmly on the baking sheet, press the granola in a layer and make it spread evenly.
6. In the preheated oven, let it cook for a maximum of 30 minutes then remove it and let it cool down.
7. Once cold, cut into pieces of your liking.
8. Drizzle the pieces with the melted chocolate.

Nutrition Facts Per Serving:

Calories 611, Total Fat 46.5g, Saturated Fat 9.4g, Cholesterol 0mg, Sodium 341mg, Total Carbohydrate 38.4g, Dietary Fiber 11g, Total Sugars 10.8g , Protein 19.9g, Vitamin D 0mcg, Calcium 167mg, Iron 6mg, Potassium 419mg

Chapter 5: Lunch Recipes

Vegan Mushroom Pho

Prep time 10 minutes / Cook time 30 minutes / Serves 3

Ingredients:
- 14-oz. block firm tofu, drained
- 6 cups vegetable broth
- 3 green onions, thinly sliced
- 1 tsp. minced ginger
- 1 tbsp. olive oil
- 3 cups mushrooms, sliced
- 2 tbsp. hoisin sauce
- 1 tbsp. sesame oil
- 2 cups gluten-free rice noodles
- 1 cup raw bean sprouts
- 1 cup matchstick carrots
- 1 cup bok choy, chopped
- 1 cup cabbage, chopped
- ¼ tsp Salt
- ¼ tsp pepper

Instructions:
1. Cut the tofu into ¼-inch cubes and set it aside.
2. Take a deep saucepan and heat the vegetable broth, green onions, and ginger over medium high heat.
3. Boil for 1 minute before reducing the heat to low; then cover the saucepan with a lid and let it simmer for 20 minutes.
4. Take another frying pan and heat the olive oil in it over medium-high heat.
5. Add the sliced mushrooms to the frying pan and cook until they are tender, for about 5 minutes.
6. Add the tofu, hoisin sauce, and sesame oil to the mushrooms.
7. Heat until the sauce thickens (around 5 minutes), and remove the frying pan from the heat.
8. Prepare the gluten-free rice noodles according to the package instructions.
9. Top the rice noodles with a scoop of the tofu mushroom mixture, a generous amount of broth, and the bean sprouts.
10. Add the carrots, and optional cabbage and/or bok choy (if desired), right before serving.
11. Top with salt and pepper to taste and enjoy, or, store ingredients separately!

Nutritional facts per serving:
Calories 610, Total Fat 18.9g, Saturated Fat 3.5g, Cholesterol 0mg, Sodium 2098mg, Total Carbohydrate 83g, Dietary Fiber 5.4g, Total Sugars 9.4g, Protein 29.6g, Vitamin D 252mcg, Calcium 366mg, Iron 7mg, Potassium 1132mg

Ruby Red Root Beet Burger

Prep time 20 minutes / Cook time 21 minutes / Serves 6

Ingredients:
- 1 cup dry chickpeas
- ½ cup dry quinoa
- 2 large beets
- 2 tbsp. olive oil
- 2 tbsp. garlic powder
- 1 tbsp. balsamic vinegar
- 2 tsp. onion powder
- 1 tsp. fresh parsley, chopped
- ¼ tsp Salt
- ¼ tsp pepper
- 2 cups spinach, fresh or frozen, washed and dried
- 6 buns or wraps of choice

Instructions:
1. Preheat the oven to 400°F.
2. Peel and dice the beets into ¼-inch or smaller cubes, put them in a bowl, and coat the cubes with 1 tablespoon of olive oil and the onion powder.
3. Spread the beet cubes out across a baking pan and put the pan in the oven.
4. Roast the beets until they have softened, approximately 10-15 minutes. Take them out and set aside so the beets can cool down.
5. After the beets have cooled down, transfer them into a food processor and add the cooked chickpeas and quinoa, vinegar, garlic, parsley, and a pinch of pepper and salt.

6. Pulse the ingredients until everything is crumbly, around 30 seconds.
7. Use your palms to form the mixture into 6 equal-sized patties and place them in a small pan.
8. Put them in a freezer, up to 1 hour, until the patties feel firm to the touch.
9. Heat up the remaining 1 tablespoon of olive oil in a skillet over medium-high heat and add the patties.
10. Cook them until they're browned on each side, about 4-6 minutes per side.
11. Store or serve the burgers with a handful of spinach, and if desired, on the bottom of the optional bun.
12. Top the burger with your sauce of choice.

Nutritional value per serving
Calories 353, Total Fat 9.2g, Saturated Fat 1.5g, Cholesterol 0mg, Sodium 351mg, Total Carbohydrate 57.8g, Dietary Fiber 9g, Total Sugars 9.2g, Protein 13.9g, Vitamin D 0mcg, Calcium 103mg

Teriyaki Tofu Wraps

Prep time 30 minutes / Cook time 15 minutes / Serves 3
Ingredients:
- 1 14-oz. drained, package extra firm tofu
- 1 small white onion, diced
- 1 cup chopped pineapple
- ¼ cup soy sauce
- 2 tbsp. sesame oil
- 1 garlic clove, minced
- 1 tsp. coconut sugar
- 4 large lettuce leaves
- 1 tbsp. roasted sesame seeds
- ¼ tsp Salt
- ¼ tsp pepper

Instructions:
1. Take a medium-sized bowl and mix the soy sauce, sesame oil, coconut sugar, and garlic.
2. Cut the tofu into ½-inch cubes, place them in the bowl, and transfer the bowl to the refrigerator to marinate, up to 3 hours.
3. Meanwhile, cut the pineapple into rings or cubes.
4. After the tofu is adequately marinated, place a large skillet over medium heat, and pour in the tofu with the remaining marinade, pineapple cubes, and diced onions; stir.
5. Add salt and pepper to taste, making sure to stir the ingredients frequently, and cook until the onions are soft and translucent—about 15 minutes.
6. Divide the mixture between the lettuce leaves and top with a sprinkle of roasted sesame seeds.
7. Serve right away, or, store the mixture and lettuce leaves separately.

Nutritional facts per serving:
Calories 247, Total Fat 16.2g, Saturated Fat 2.6g, Cholesterol 0mg, Sodium 1410mg, Total Carbohydrate 16.1g, Dietary Fiber 3.1g, Total Sugars 9g, Protein 13.4g, Vitamin D 0mcg, Calcium 315mg, Iron 4mg, Potassium 371mg

Creamy Squash Pizza

Prep time 25 minutes / Cook time 21 minutes / Serves 4
Ingredients:
- 3 cups butternut squash, fresh or frozen, cubed
- 2 tbsp. minced garlic
- 1 tbsp. olive oil
- 1 tsp. red pepper flakes
- 1 tsp. cumin
- 1 tsp. paprika
- 1 tsp. oregano

Crust:
- 2 cups dry French green lentils
- 2 cups water

- 2 tbsp. minced garlic
- 1 tbsp. Italian seasoning
- 1 tsp. onion powder

Toppings:
- 1 tbsp. olive oil
- 1 medium green bell pepper, pitted, diced
- 1 cup chopped broccoli
- 1 small purple onion, diced

Instructions:
1. Preheat the oven to 350°F.

2. Prepare the French green lentils according to the method.
3. Add all the sauce ingredients to a food processor or blender, and blend on low until everything has mixed and the sauce looks creamy. Set the sauce aside in a small bowl.
4. Clean the food processor or blender; then add all the ingredients for the crust and pulse on high speed until a dough-like batter has formed.
5. Heat a large deep-dish pan over medium-low heat and lightly grease it with 1 tablespoon of olive oil.
6. Press the crust dough into the skillet until it resembles a round pizza crust and cook until the crust is golden brown—about 5-6 minutes on each side.
7. Put the crust on a baking tray covered with parchment paper.
8. Coat the topside of the crust with the sauce using a spoon, and evenly distribute the toppings across the pizza.
9. Bake the pizza in the oven until the vegetables are tender and browned, for about 15 minutes.
10. Slice into 4 equal pieces and serve, or store.

Nutritional facts per serving:
Calories 258, Total Fat 9.2g, Saturated Fat 1.2g, Cholesterol 2mg, Sodium 21mg, Total Carbohydrate 38.3g, Dietary Fiber 9.7g, Total Sugars 6.2g, Protein 9g, Vitamin D 0mcg, Calcium 111mg, Iron 4mg, Potassium 838mg

Lasagna Fungo

Prep time 20 minutes / Cook time 40 minutes / Serves 8

Ingredients:
- 10 lasagna sheets
- 2 cups matchstick carrots
- 1 cup mushrooms, sliced
- 2 cups raw kale
- 1 14-oz. package extra firm tofu, drained
- 1 cup hummus
- ½ cup nutritional yeast
- 2 tbsp. Italian seasoning
- 1 tbsp. garlic powder
- 1 tbsp. olive oil
- 4 cups marinara sauce
- 1 tsp. salt

Instructions:
1. Preheat the oven to 400°F.
2. Cook the lasagna noodles or sheets according to method.
3. Take a large frying pan, put it over medium heat, and add the olive oil.
4. Throw in the carrots, mushrooms, and half a teaspoon of salt; cook for 5 minutes.
5. Add the kale, sauté for another 3 minutes, and remove the pan from the heat.
6. Take a large bowl, crumble in the tofu, and set the bowl aside for now.
7. Take another bowl and add the hummus, nutritional yeast, Italian seasoning, garlic, and ½ teaspoon salt; mix everything together.
8. Coat the bottom of an 8x8 baking dish with 1 cup of the marinara sauce.
9. Cover the sauce with a couple of the noodles or sheets, and top these with the tofu crumbles.
10. Add a layer of the vegetables on top of the tofu.
11. Continue to build up the lasagna by stacking layers of marinara sauce, noodles or sheets, tofu, and vegetables, and top it off with a cup of marinara sauce.
12. Cover the lasagna with aluminum foil, and bake in the oven for 20-25 minutes.
13. Remove the foil and put back in the oven for an additional 5 minutes.
14. Allow the lasagna to sit for 10 minutes before serving, or store for another day!

Nutritional facts per serving:
Calories 491, Total Fat 13.1g, Saturated Fat 2.2g, Cholesterol 30mg, Sodium 959mg, Total Carbohydrate 73.5g, Dietary Fiber 9g, Total Sugars 13.3g, Protein 23.3g, Vitamin D 32mcg, Calcium 176mg, Iron 5mg, Potassium 903mg

Sweet and Sour Tofu

Prep time 40 minutes / Cook time 21 minutes / Serves 4

Ingredients:

- 14-oz. package extra firm tofu, drained
- 2 tbsp. olive oil
- 1 large red bell pepper, pitted, chopped
- 1 medium white onion, diced
- 2 tbsp. minced garlic
- ½-inch minced ginger
- 1 cup pineapple chunks
- 1 tbsp. tomato paste
- 2 tbsp. rice vinegar
- 2 tbsp. low sodium soy sauce
- 1 tsp. cornstarch
- 1 tbsp. cane sugar
- ¼ tsp Salt
- ¼ tsp pepper

Instructions:

1. In a small bowl, whisk together the tomato paste, vinegar, soy sauce, cornstarch, and sugar.
2. Cut the tofu into ¼-inch cubes, place in a medium bowl, and marinate in the soy sauce mixture until the tofu has absorbed the flavors (up to 3 hours).
3. Heat 1 tablespoon of the olive oil in a frying pan over medium-high heat.
4. Add the tofu chunks and half of the remaining marinade to the pan, leaving the rest for later.
5. Stir frequently until the tofu is cooked golden brown, approximately 10-12 minutes. Remove the tofu from the heat and set aside in a medium-sized bowl.
6. Add the other tablespoon of olive oil to the same pan, then the garlic and ginger; heat for about 1 minute.
7. Add in the peppers and onions. Stir until the vegetables have softened, about 5 minutes.
8. Pour the leftover marinade into the pan with the vegetables and heat until the sauce thickens while continuously stirring, around 4 minutes.
9. Add the pineapple chunks and tofu cubes to the pan while stirring and continue to cook for 3 minutes.
10. Serve and enjoy right away, or, let the sweet and sour tofu cool down and store for later!

Nutritional facts per serving:

Calories 290, Total Fat 16.9g, Saturated Fat 2.6g, Cholesterol 0mg, Sodium 512mg, Total Carbohydrate 19.5g, Dietary Fiber 3.3g, Total Sugars 9.1g, Protein 15.9g, Vitamin D 0mcg, Calcium 138mg, Iron 1mg, Potassium 434mg

Stuffed Sweet Potatoes

Prep time 30 minutes / Cook time 1 hour 16 minutes / Serves 3

Ingredients:

- ½ cup dry black beans
- 3 small or medium sweet potatoes
- 2 tbsp. olive oil
- 1 large red bell pepper, pitted, chopped
- 1 small sweet yellow onion, chopped
- 2 tbsp. garlic, minced or powdered
- 1 8-oz. package tempeh, diced into ¼" cubes
- ½ cup marinara sauce
- ½ cup water
- 1 tbsp. chili powder
- 1 tsp. parsley
- ½ tsp. cayenne
- ¼ tsp Salt
- ¼ tsp pepper

Instructions:

1. Preheat the oven to 400°F.
2. Using a fork, poke several holes in the skins of the sweet potatoes.
3. Wrap the sweet potatoes tightly with aluminum foil and place them in the oven until soft and tender, or for approximately 45 minutes.
4. While sweet potatoes are cooking, heat the olive oil in a deep pan over medium-high heat. Add the onions, bell peppers, and garlic; cook until the onions are tender, for about 10 minutes.
5. Add the water, together with the cooked beans, marinara sauce, chili powder, parsley, and cayenne. Bring the mixture to a boil and then lower the heat to medium or low. Allow

the mixture to simmer until the liquid has thickened, for about 15 minutes.

6. Add the diced tempeh cubes and heat until warmed, around 1 minute.
7. Blend in salt and pepper to taste.
8. When the potatoes are done baking, remove them from the oven. Cut a slit across the top of each one, but do not split the potatoes all the way in half.
9. Top each potato with a scoop of the beans, vegetables, and tempeh mixture. Place the filled potatoes back in the hot oven for about 5 minutes.
10. Serve after cooling for a few minutes, or, store for another day!

Nutritional facts per serving:
Calories 548, Total Fat 19.7g, Cholesterol 1mg, Sodium 448mg, Total Carbohydrate 76g, Dietary Fiber 12.4g, Total Sugars 15.2g, Protein 25.3g, Vitamin D 0mcg, Calcium 185mg, Iron 5mg, Potassium 1132mg

Sweet Potato Quesadillas

Prep time 30 minutes / Cook time 1 hour 9 minutes / Serves 3

Ingredients:
- 1 cup dry black beans
- ½ cup dry rice of choice
- 1 large sweet potato, peeled and diced
- ½ cup salsa
- 4 tortilla wraps
- 1 tbsp. olive oil
- ½ tsp. garlic powder
- ½ tsp. onion powder
- ½ tsp. paprika

Instructions:
1. Preheat the oven to 350°F.
2. Line a baking pan with parchment paper.
3. Cut the sweet potato into ½-inch cubes and drizzle these with olive oil. Transfer the cubes to the baking pan.
4. Place the pan in the oven and bake the potatoes until tender, for around 1 hour.
5. Allow the potatoes to cool for 5 minutes and then add them to a large mixing bowl with the salsa and cooked rice. Use a fork to mash the ingredients together into a thoroughly combined mixture.
6. Heat a saucepan over medium-high heat and add the potato/rice mixture, cooked black beans, and spices to the pan.
7. Cook everything for about 5 minutes or until it is heated through.
8. Take another frying pan and put it over medium-low heat. Place a tortilla in the pan and fill half of it with a heaping scoop of the potato, bean, and rice mixture.
9. Fold the tortilla in half to cover the filling, and cook the tortilla until both sides are browned—about 4 minutes per side.
10. Serve the tortillas with some additional salsa on the side.

Nutritional facts per serving:
Calories 683, Total Fat 12.7g, Saturated Fat 2.3g, Cholesterol 0mg, Sodium 980mg, Total Carbohydrate 121g, Dietary Fiber 18.5g, Total Sugars 8.3g, Protein 24.9g, Vitamin D 0mcg, Calcium 184mg, Iron 9mg, Potassium 1425mg

Satay Tempeh with Cauliflower Rice

Prep time 60 minutes / Cook time 15 minutes / Serves 4

Ingredients:
- ¼ cup water
- 4 tbsp. peanut butter
- 3 tbsp. low sodium soy sauce
- 2 tbsp. coconut sugar
- 1 garlic clove, minced
- 1 tbsp ginger, minced
- 2 tsp. rice vinegar
- 1 tsp. red pepper flakes
- 4 tbsp. olive oil
- 2 8-oz. packages tempeh, drained
- 2 cups cauliflower rice
- 1 cup purple cabbage, diced
- 1 tbsp. sesame oil
- 1 tsp. agave nectar

Instructions:

1. Take a large bowl, combine all the ingredients for the sauce, and then whisk until the mixture is smooth and any lumps have dissolved.
2. Cut the tempeh into ½-inch cubes and put them into the sauce, stirring to make sure the cubes get coated thoroughly.
3. Place the bowl in the refrigerator to marinate the tempeh for up to 3 hours.
4. Before the tempeh is done marinating, preheat the oven to 400°F.
5. Spread the tempeh out in a single layer on a baking sheet lined with parchment paper or lightly greased with olive oil.
6. Bake the marinated cubes until browned and crisp—about 15 minutes.
7. Heat the cauliflower rice in a saucepan with 2 tablespoons of olive oil over medium heat until it is warm.
8. Rinse the large bowl with water, and then mix the cabbage, sesame oil, and agave together.
9. Serve a scoop of the cauliflower rice topped with the marinated cabbage and cooked tempeh on a plate or in a bowl and enjoy. Or, store for later.

Nutritional facts per serving:
Calories 554, Total Fat 38.8g, Saturated Fat 7.1g, Cholesterol 0mg, Sodium 614mg, Total Carbohydrate 32.3g, Dietary Fiber 2.1g, Total Sugars 13.9g, Protein 28.1g, Vitamin D 0mcg, Calcium 140mg, Iron 5mg, Potassium 655mg

Tex-Mex Tofu & Beans

Prep time 25 minutes / Cook time 12 minutes / Serves 2

Ingredients:
- 1 cup dry black beans
- 1 cup dry brown rice
- 1 14-oz. package firm tofu, drained
- 2 tbsp. olive oil
- 1 small purple onion, diced
- 1 medium avocado, pitted, peeled
- 1 garlic clove, minced
- 1 tbsp. lime juice
- 2 tsp. cumin
- 2 tsp. paprika
- 1 tsp. chili powder
- ¼ tsp Salt
- ¼ tsp pepper

Instructions:
1. Cut the tofu into ½-inch cubes.
2. Heat the olive oil in a large skillet over high heat. Add the diced onions and cook until soft, for about 5 minutes.
3. Add the tofu and cook an additional 2 minutes, flipping the cubes frequently.
4. Meanwhile, cut the avocado into thin slices and set aside.
5. Lower the heat to medium and mix in the garlic, cumin, and cooked black beans.
6. Stir until everything is incorporated thoroughly, and then cook for an additional 5 minutes.
7. Add the remaining spices and lime juice to the mixture in the skillet. Mix thoroughly and remove the skillet from the heat.
8. Serve the Tex-Mex tofu and beans with a scoop of rice and garnish with the fresh avocado.
9. Enjoy immediately, or, store the rice, avocado, and tofu mixture separately.

Nutritional facts per serving:
Calories 1175, Total Fat 46.8g, Saturated Fat 8.8g, Cholesterol 0mg, Sodium 348mg, Total Carbohydrate 152.1g, Dietary Fiber 28.8g, Total Sugars 5.7g, Protein 47.6g, Vitamin D 0mcg, Calcium 601mg, Iron 13mg, Potassium 2653mg

Vegan Friendly Fajitas

Prep time 30 minutes / Cook time 19 minutes / Serves 6

Ingredients:
- 1 cup dry black beans
- 1 large green bell pepper, seeded, diced
- 1 poblano pepper, seeded, thinly sliced
- 1 large avocado, peeled, pitted, mashed
- 1 medium sweet onion, chopped
- 3 large portobello mushrooms
- 2 tbsp. olive oil
- 6 tortilla wraps

- 1 tsp. lime juice
- 1 tsp. chili powder
- 1 tsp. garlic powder
- ¼ tsp. cayenne pepper
- ¼ tsp Salt

Instructions:

1. Prepare the black beans according to the method.
2. Heat 1 tablespoon of olive oil in a large frying pan over high heat.
3. Add the bell peppers, poblano peppers, and half of the onions.
4. Mix in the chili powder, garlic powder, and cayenne pepper; add salt to taste.
5. Cook the vegetables until tender and browned, around 10 minutes.
6. Add the black beans and continue cooking for an additional 2 minutes; then remove the frying pan from the stove.
7. Add the portobello mushrooms to the skillet and turn heat down to low. Sprinkle the mushrooms with salt.
8. Stir/flip the ingredients often, and cook until the mushrooms have shrank down to half their size, around 7 minutes. Remove the frying pan from the heat.
9. Mix the avocado, remaining 1 tablespoon of olive oil, and the remaining onions together in a small bowl to make a simple guacamole. Mix in the lime juice and add salt and pepper to taste.
10. Spread the guacamole on a tortilla with a spoon and then top with a generous scoop of the mushroom mixture.
11. Serve and enjoy right away, or, allow the prepared tortillas to cool down and wrap them in paper towels to store!

Nutritional facts per serving:
Calories 429, Total Fat 16.8g, Saturated Fat 3.2g, Cholesterol 0mg, Sodium 627mg, Total Carbohydrate 59.2g, Dietary Fiber 12.7g, Total Sugars 4.2g, Protein 14.8g, Vitamin D 0mcg, Calcium 113mg, Iron 4mg, Potassium 899mg

Tofu Cacciatore

Prep time 45 minutes / Cook time 35 minutes / Serves 3

Ingredients:

- 1 14-oz. package extra firm tofu, drained
- 1 tbsp. olive oil
- 1 cup matchstick carrots
- 1 medium sweet onion, diced
- 1 medium green bell pepper, seeded, diced
- 1 28-oz. can diced tomatoes
- 1 4-oz. can tomato paste
- ½ tbsp. balsamic vinegar
- 1 tbsp. soy sauce
- 1 tbsp. maple syrup
- 1 tbsp. garlic powder
- 1 tbsp. Italian seasoning
- ¼ tsp Salt
- ¼ tsp pepper

Instructions:

1. Chop the tofu into ¼- to ½-inch cubes.
2. Heat the olive oil in a large skillet over medium-high heat.
3. Add the onions, garlic, bell peppers, and carrots; sauté until the onions turn translucent, around 10 minutes. Make sure to stir frequently to prevent burning.
4. Now add the balsamic vinegar, soy sauce, maple syrup, garlic powder and Italian seasoning.
5. Stir well while pouring in the diced tomatoes and tomato paste; mix until all ingredients are thoroughly combined.
6. Add the cubed tofu and stir one more time.
7. Cover the pot, turn the heat to medium-low, and allow the mixture to simmer until the sauce has thickened, for around 20-25 minutes.
8. Serve the tofu cacciatore in bowls and top with salt and pepper to taste, or, store for another meal!

Nutritional facts per serving:
Calories 319, Total Fat 12g, Saturated Fat 2.1g, Cholesterol 3mg, Sodium 1156mg, Total Carbohydrate 43.1g, Dietary Fiber 10.4g, Total Sugars 27.1g , Protein 17.6g, Vitamin D 0mcg, Calcium 359mg, Iron 5mg, Potassium 961mg

Portobello Burritos

Prep time 50 minutes / Cook time 40 minutes / Serves 4

Ingredients:
- 3 large portobello mushrooms
- 2 medium potatoes
- 4 tortilla wraps
- 1 medium avocado, pitted, peeled, diced
- ¾ cup salsa
- 1 tbsp. cilantro
- ½ tsp salt
- 1/3 cup water
- 1 tbsp. lime juice
- 1 tbsp. minced garlic
- ¼ cup teriyaki sauce

Instructions:
1. Preheat the oven to 400°F.
2. Lightly grease a sheet pan with olive oil (or alternatively, line with parchment paper) and set it aside.
3. Combine the water, lime juice, teriyaki, and garlic in a small bowl.
4. Slice the portobello mushrooms into thin slices and add these to the bowl. Allow the mushrooms to marinate thoroughly, for up to three hours.
5. Cut the potatoes into large matchsticks, like French fries. Sprinkle the fries with salt and then transfer them to the sheet pan. Place the fries in the oven and bake them until crisped and golden, around 30 minutes. Flip once halfway through for even cooking.
6. Heat a large frying pan over medium heat. Add the marinated mushroom slices with the remaining marinade to the pan. Cook until the liquid has absorbed, around 10 minutes. Remove from heat.
7. Fill the tortillas with a heaping scoop of the mushrooms and a handful of the potato sticks. Top with salsa, sliced avocados, and cilantro before serving.
8. Serve right away and enjoy, or, store the tortillas, avocado, and mushrooms separately for later!

Nutritional facts per serving:
Calories 391, Total Fat 14.9g, Saturated Fat 3.1g, Cholesterol 0mg, Sodium 1511mg, Total Carbohydrate 57g, Dietary Fiber 10.8g, Total Sugars 5.1g, Protein 11.2g, Vitamin D 0mcg, Calcium 85mg, Iron 3mg, Potassium 956mg

Barbecued Greens & Grits

Prep time 60 minutes / Cook time 35 minutes / Serves 4

Ingredients:
- 1 14-oz. package tempeh
- 3 cups vegetable broth
- 3 cups collard greens, chopped
- ½ cup BBQ sauce
- 1 cup gluten-free grits
- ¼ cup white onion, diced
- 2 tbsp. olive oil
- 2 garlic cloves, minced
- 1 tsp. salt

Instructions:
1. Preheat the oven to 400°F.
2. Cut the tempeh into thin slices and mix it with the BBQ sauce in a shallow baking dish. Set aside and let marinate for up to 3 hours.
3. Heat 1 tablespoon of olive oil in a frying pan over medium heat, then add the garlic and sauté until fragrant.
4. Add the collard greens and ½ teaspoon of salt and cook until the collards are wilted and dark. Remove the pan from the heat and set aside.
5. Cover the tempeh and BBQ sauce mixture with aluminum foil. Place the baking dish into the oven and bake the ingredients for 15 minutes. Uncover and continue to bake for another 10 minutes, until the tempeh is browned and crispy.
6. While the tempeh cooks, heat the remaining tablespoon of olive oil in the previously used frying pan over medium heat.
7. Cook the onions until brown and fragrant, around 10 minutes.
8. Pour in the vegetable broth and bring it to a boil; then turn the heat down to low.

9. Slowly whisk the grits into the simmering broth. Add the remaining ½ teaspoon of salt before covering the pan with a lid.
10. Let the ingredients simmer for about 8 minutes, until the grits are soft and creamy.
11. Serve the tempeh and collard greens on top of a bowl of grits and enjoy, or store for later!

Nutritional facts per serving:
Calories 374, Total Fat 19.1g, Saturated Fat 3.5g, Cholesterol 0mg, Sodium 1519mg, Total Carbohydrate 31.1g, Dietary Fiber 2g, Total Sugars 9g, Protein 23.7g, Vitamin D 0mcg, Calcium 163mg, Iron 4mg, Potassium 645mg

Brown Basmati Rice Pilaf

Prep time 10 minutes / Cook time 3 minutes / Serves 2
Ingredients:
- ½ tablespoon vegan butter
- ½ cup mushrooms, chopped
- ½ cup brown basmati rice
- 3 tablespoons water
- 1/8 teaspoon dried thyme
- Ground pepper to taste
- ½ tablespoon olive oil
- ¼ cup green onion, chopped
- 1 cup vegetable broth
- ¼ teaspoon salt
- ¼ cup chopped, toasted pecans

Instructions:
1. Place a saucepan over medium-low heat. Add butter and oil.
2. When it melts, add mushrooms and cook until slightly tender.
3. Stir in the green onion and brown rice. Cook for 3 minutes. Stir constantly.
4. Stir in the broth, water, salt and thyme.
5. When it begins to boil, lower heat and cover with a lid. Simmer until rice is cooked. Add more water or broth if required.
6. Stir in the pecans and pepper.
7. Serve.

Nutritional facts per serving:
Calories 256, Total Fat 8.8g, Saturated Fat 1.3g, Cholesterol 0mg, Sodium 318mg, Total Carbohydrate 39.8g, Dietary Fiber 1.6g, Total Sugars 1g, Protein 4.5g, Vitamin D 63mcg, Calcium 26mg, Iron 1mg, Potassium 144mg

Stuffed Indian Eggplant

Prep time 90 minutes / Cook time 1 hour 10 minutes / Serves 5
Ingredients:
- ½ cup dry black beans
- 6 medium eggplants, peeled
- 3 large roma tomatoes, diced
- 1 large purple onion, chopped
- 1 large yellow bell pepper, chopped
- 2 cups raw spinach
- 2 tbsp. olive oil
- 2 cloves garlic, minced
- 1 tbsp. tomato paste
- 1 tsp. coconut sugar
- 1 tsp. cumin
- 1 tsp. turmeric
- Salt and pepper to taste
- 2 tbsp. thyme, chopped

Instructions:
1. Preheat the oven to 400°F.
2. Line a large baking sheet or pan with parchment paper and set it aside.
3. Cut the peeled eggplants open across the top from one side to the other, being careful not to slice all the way through.
4. Sprinkle the inside of the cut eggplants with salt and wrap them in a paper towel to drain the excess water. This could take up to 30 minutes.
5. Place the eggplants on the baking sheet, and bake in the oven for 15 minutes. Remove the baking sheet from the oven and set it aside.
6. Heat 1 tablespoon of olive oil in a large skillet over medium-high heat. Add the chopped onions and sauté until soft, around 5 minutes.
7. Stir frequently, adding in the bell peppers and garlic. Cook the ingredients until the onions are translucent and peppers are tender, for about 15 minutes.

8. Season the spinach with sugar, cumin, turmeric, salt, and pepper.
9. Stir everything well to coat the ingredients evenly; then mix in the tomatoes, black beans, spinach, and tomato paste.
10. Heat everything for about 5 minutes, and then remove the skillet from the heat and set aside.
11. Stuff the eggplants with heaping scoops of the vegetable mixture. Sprinkle more salt and pepper to taste on top.
12. Drizzle the remaining 1 tablespoon of olive oil across the eggplants, return them to the oven, and bake until they shrivel and flatten—for 20-30 minutes.
13. Serve the eggplants, and if desired, garnish with the optional fresh thyme.
14. Enjoy right away, or, store to enjoy later!

Nutritional facts per serving:
Calories 308, Total Fat 7.5g, Saturated Fat 1g, Cholesterol 0mg, Sodium 152mg, Total Carbohydrate 57g, Dietary Fiber 25.6g, Total Sugars 23.5g, Protein 11.9g, Vitamin D 0mcg, Calcium 134mg, Iron 5mg, Potassium 2027mg

Moroccan Eggplant Stew

Prep time 45 minutes / Cook time 32 minutes / Serves 4

Ingredients:
- 1 cup dry green lentils
- 1 cup dry chickpeas
- 1 tsp. olive oil
- 1 large sweet onion, chopped
- 1 medium green bell pepper, seeded, diced
- 1 large eggplant
- 1 cup vegetable broth
- ¾ cup tomato sauce
- ½ cup golden raisins
- 2 tbsp. turmeric
- 1 garlic clove, minced
- 1 tsp. cumin
- ½ tsp. allspice
- ¼ tsp. chili powder
- ¼ tsp Salt
- ¼ tsp pepper

Instructions:
1. Heat the olive oil in a medium-sized skillet over medium high heat.
2. Add the onions and cook until they begin to caramelize and soften, in 5-8 minutes.
3. Cut the eggplant into ½-inch eggplant cubes and add it to the skillet along with the bell pepper, cumin, allspice, garlic, and turmeric.
4. Stir the ingredients to combine everything evenly and heat for about 4 minutes; then add the vegetable broth and tomato sauce.
5. Cover the skillet, turn the heat down to low, and simmer the ingredients until the eggplant feels tender, or for about 20 minutes. You should be able to easily insert a fork into the cubes.
6. Uncover and mix in the cooked chickpeas and green lentils, as well as the raisins and chili powder. Simmer the ingredients until all the flavors have melded together, or for about 3 minutes.
7. Store the stew for later, or, serve in a bowl, top with salt and pepper to taste, and enjoy!

Nutritional facts per serving:
Calories 506, Total Fat 6g, Saturated Fat 0.8g, Cholesterol 0mg, Sodium 604mg, Total Carbohydrate 91.7g, Dietary Fiber 30.9g, Total Sugars 25.8g, Protein 26.7g, Vitamin D 0mcg, Calcium 133mg, Iron 10mg, Potassium 1714mg

Mushroom Madness Stroganoff

Prep time 30 minutes / Cook time 25 minutes / Serves 4

Ingredients:
- 2 cups gluten-free noodles
- 1 small onion, chopped
- 2 cups vegetable broth
- 2 tbsp. almond flour
- 1 tbsp. tamari
- 1 tsp. tomato paste
- 1 tsp. lemon juice
- 3 cups mushrooms, chopped
- 1 tsp. thyme
- 3 cups raw spinach
- 1 tbsp. apple cider vinegar
- 1 tbsp. olive oil

- ¼ tsp Salt
- ¼ tsp pepper
- 2 tbsp. fresh parsley

Instructions:
1. Prepare the noodles according to the package instructions.
2. Heat the olive oil in a large skillet over medium heat.
3. Add the chopped onion and sauté until soft—for about 5 minutes.
4. Stir in the flour, vegetable broth, tamari, tomato paste, and lemon juice; cook for an additional 3 minutes.
5. Blend in the mushrooms, thyme, and salt to taste, then cover the skillet.
6. Cook until the mushrooms are tender, for about 7 minutes, and turn the heat down to low.
7. Add the cooked noodles, spinach, and vinegar to the pan and top the ingredients with salt and pepper to taste.
8. Cover the skillet again and let the flavors combine for another 8-10 minutes.
9. Serve immediately, topped with the optional parsley if desired, or, store and enjoy the stroganoff another day of the week!

Nutritional facts per serving:
Calories 240, Total Fat 11.9g, Saturated Fat 1.3g, Cholesterol 0mg, Sodium 935mg, Total Carbohydrate 26.1g, Dietary Fiber 4.3g, Total Sugars 4.9g, Protein 9.9g, Vitamin D 189mcg, Calcium 71mg, Iron 4mg, Potassium 463mg

Refined Ratatouille

Prep time 90 minutes / Cook time 1 hour / Serves 2

Ingredients:
- 1 14-oz. block extra firm tofu, drained
- 2 large heirloom tomatoes
- 1 large eggplant
- 1 large zucchini
- 1 large sweet yellow onion, diced
- 1 cup chopped kale
- 1 cup tomato sauce
- 2 tbsp. olive oil
- 1 tbsp. minced garlic
- ¼ tsp. chili powder
- ¼ tsp. apple cider vinegar
- 1/8 tsp. fennel seeds
- ¼ tsp Salt
- ¼ tsp pepper
- 5 large basil leaves, finely chopped

Instructions:
1. Preheat the oven to 350°F.
2. Lightly grease an 8x8" square dish with 1 tablespoon of olive oil and set it aside.
3. Combine the tomato sauce, vinegar, remaining 1 tablespoon of olive oil, garlic, fennel seeds, and chili powder in a large mixing bowl.
4. Add salt and pepper to taste and stir until all ingredients are evenly coated.
5. Pour the mixture into the baking dish and use a spoon to smear the ingredients out evenly across the bottom of the dish.
6. Lay out the kale in one even layer on top of the mixture.
7. Vertically slice the tomatoes, eggplant, zucchini, and onion into thick, round discs; they should look like miniature plates or saucers.
8. Cut the tofu into thin slices, each similar in size to the vegetable discs for even cooking.
9. Layer the vegetable discs and tofu slices on top of the kale in the baking dish with an alternating pattern. For instance: tomato, eggplant, tofu, zucchini, squash, onion, repeat.
10. Fill up every inch of the pan with all the slices and stack them against the edge.
11. Place the baking dish into the oven and bake until the tomato sauce has thickened and the vegetable slices have softened, around 50 minutes to an hour.
12. Scoop the ratatouille into a bowl and garnish it with the chopped basil.
13. Serve and enjoy, or, store for another day!

Nutritional facts per serving:
Calories 493, Total Fat 27g, Saturated Fat 3.2g, Cholesterol 0mg, Sodium 999mg, Total Carbohydrate 47g, Dietary Fiber 16.7g, Total Sugars 23g, Protein 29.1g, Vitamin D 0mcg, Calcium 498mg, Iron 7mg, Potassium 2324mg

Sweet Potato Sushi

Prep Time: 90 minutes / Cook Time: 35 minutes / Serves: 3

Ingredients:

- 1 14-oz. package silken tofu, drained
- 3 nori sheets
- 1 large sweet potato, peeled
- 1 medium avocado, pitted, peeled, sliced
- 1 cup water
- ¾ cup dry sushi rice
- 1 tbsp. rice vinegar
- 1 tbsp. agave nectar
- 1 tbsp. amino acids

Instructions:

1. Preheat the oven to 400°F / 200°C.
2. Stir the amino acids (or tamari) and agave nectar together in a small bowl until it is well combined, and then set aside.
3. Cut the sweet potato into large sticks, around ½-inch thick. Place them on a baking sheet lined with parchment and coat them with the tamari/agave mixture.
4. Bake the sweet potatoes in the oven until softened—for about 25 minutes—and make sure to flip them halfway so the sides cook evenly.
5. Meanwhile, bring the sushi rice, water, and vinegar to a boil in a medium-sized pot over medium heat, and cook until liquid has evaporated, for about 10 minutes.
6. While cooking the rice, cut the block of tofu into long sticks. The sticks should look like long, thin fries. Set aside.
7. Remove the pot from heat and let the rice sit for 10-15 minutes.
8. Cover your work area with a piece of parchment paper, clean your hands, wet your fingers, and lay out a sheet of nori on the parchment paper.
9. Cover the nori sheet with a thin layer of sushi rice, while wetting the hands frequently. Leave sufficient space for rolling up the sheet.
10. Place the roasted sweet potato strips in a straight line across the width of the sheet, about an inch away from the edge closest to you.
11. Lay out the tofu and avocado slices right beside the potato sticks and use the parchment paper as an aid to roll up the nori sheet into a tight cylinder.
12. Slice the cylinder into 8 equal pieces and refrigerate. Repeat the process for the remaining nori sheets and fillings.
13. Serve chilled, or, store to enjoy this delicious sushi later!

Nutritional facts per serving:

Calories 467, Total Fat 17.1g, Saturated Fat 3.4g, Cholesterol 0mg, Sodium 81mg, Total Carbohydrate 64g, Dietary Fiber 7.6g, Total Sugars 11g, Protein 15.4g, Vitamin D 0mcg, Calcium 78mg, Iron 6mg, Potassium 921mg

Mexican Rice

Prep time 10 minutes / Cook time 15 minutes / Serves 4

Ingredients:

- ½ can diced tomatoes with its liquid
- 2 ounces corn
- ½ can tomatoes with green chilies with its liquid
- 1 small onion, chopped
- ½ can black beans, drained, rinsed
- 1 small green bell pepper, chopped
- 1 tablespoon olive oil
- ½ cup white rice
- ¾ cup water
- 2 tablespoons picante style salsa
- 2 tablespoons black olives, pitted, sliced
- 1 jalapeno pepper, sliced

Instructions:

1. Place a pan over medium heat. Add oil. When the oil is heated, add bell pepper and onions and sauté until tender.
2. Add rest of the ingredients except vegan sour cream and cheese. Stir and bring to the boil.
3. Lower the heat. Cover and cook for 15 minutes until rice is tender and serve.

Nutrition Facts Per Serving:

Calories 298, Total Fat 5.5g, Saturated Fat 0.9g, Cholesterol 0mg, Sodium 163mg Total Carbohydrate 55.3g, Dietary Fiber 8g, Total Sugars 7.2g, Protein 10.6g, Vitamin D 0mcg, Calcium 57mg, Iron 5mg, Potassium 761mg

Artichoke & Eggplant Rice

Prep time 5 minutes / Cook time 10 minutes / Serves 3

Ingredients:

- 2 tablespoons olive oil
- 1 medium onion, finely chopped
- 1 cup parsley, chopped
- 1 teaspoon turmeric powder
- 3 cups vegetable stock
- 2 tablespoons lemon juice
- 1 eggplant, chopped into chunks
- 1 clove garlic, crushed
- 1 teaspoon smoked paprika
- 7 ounces paella rice
- 1 package chargrilled artichoke
- 3 Lemon wedges to serve

Instructions:

1. Place a nonstick pan or paella pan over medium heat. Add 1 tablespoon oil. When the oil is heated, add eggplant and cook until brown all over.
2. Remove with a slotted spoon and place on a plate lined with paper towels.
3. Add 1 tablespoon oil. When the oil is heated, add onion and sauté until translucent.
4. Stir in garlic and parsley stalks. Cook for 10 minutes. Add all the spices and rice and stir-fry for a few minutes until rice is well coated with the oil.
5. Add salt and mix well. Pour half the broth and cook until dry. Stir occasionally.
6. Add eggplant and artichokes and stir. Pour remaining stock and cook until rice is tender. Add parsley leaves and lemon juice and stir.
7. Serve hot with lemon wedges.

Nutrition Facts Per Serving:
Calories 381, Total Fat 24.4g, Saturated Fat 3.5g, Cholesterol 0mg, Sodium 1289mg, Total Carbohydrate 36.6g, Dietary Fiber 12.5g, Total Sugars 8.5g, Protein 6.7g, Vitamin D 0mcg, Calcium 67mg, Iron 3mg, Potassium 575mg

Coconut Veggie Wraps

Prep time 8 minutes / Cook time 0 minutes / Serves 3

Ingredients:

- 1½ cups shredded carrots
- 1 red bell pepper, seeded and thinly sliced
- 2½ cups kale
- 1 ripe avocado, thinly sliced
- 1 cup fresh cilantro, chopped
- 5 coconut wraps
- 2/3 cups hummus
- 6½ cups green curry paste

Instructions:

1. Slice, chop and shred all the vegetables.
2. Lay a coconut wrap on a clean flat surface and spread two tablespoons of the hummus and one tablespoon of the green curry paste on top of the end closest to you.
3. Place some carrots, bell pepper, kale and cilantro on the wrap and start rolling it up, starting from the edge closest to you. Roll tightly and fold in the ends.
4. Place the wrap, seam down, on a plate to serve.

Nutrition Facts Per Serving:
Calories 1501, Total Fat 86.7g, Saturated Fat 3.6g, Cholesterol 0mg, Sodium 13658mg, Total Carbohydrate 170.6g, Dietary Fiber 18.6g, Total Sugars 12.3g, Protein 14.8g, Vitamin D 0mcg, Calcium 484mg, Iron 8mg, Potassium 2350mg

Black Beans and Rice

Prep time 6 minutes / Cook time 15 minutes / Serves 3

Ingredients:

- 1 tablespoon vegetable oil
- 8 oz can black beans
- 1 ½ teaspoons dried oregano
- ½ cup uncooked rice
- 1 large onion, chopped
- ¼ teaspoon creole seasoning
- ¼ teaspoon ground cumin
- ¾ teaspoon garlic powder

- ½ teaspoon salt or to taste
- 1 cup water
- 2 tablespoon Cilantro to garnish

Instructions:
1. Place a saucepan over medium heat. Add oil. When the oil is heated, add onions and sauté until tender. Add rest of the ingredients except rice and beans and mix well.
2. When it begins to boil, add rice and mix well.
3. Lower the heat and cover with a lid. Simmer for 15 minutes until rice is tender.
4. Turn off the heat. Let it sit covered for 5 minutes.
5. Fluff with a fork. Add beans and stir. Cover and let it sit for 5 minutes.
6. Garnish with cilantro if desired and serve.

Nutrition Facts Per Serving:
Calories 436, Total Fat 6g 8%, Saturated Fat 1.3g, Cholesterol 0mg, Sodium 488mg, Total Carbohydrate 77.6g, Dietary Fiber 13.4g, Total Sugars 4g, Protein 19.3g, Vitamin D 0mcg, Calcium 130mg, Iron 6mg, Potassium 1257mg

Artichoke White Bean Sandwich Spread

Prep time 10 minutes / Cook time 0 minutes / Serves 4

Ingredients:
- ½ cup raw cashews, chopped
- 3 cups Water
- 1 clove garlic, cut into half
- 1 tablespoon lemon zest
- 1 teaspoon fresh rosemary, chopped
- ¼ teaspoon salt
- ¼ teaspoon pepper
- 6 tablespoons almond
- 1 15.5-ounce can cannellini beans, rinsed and drained well
- 3 canned artichoke hearts, chopped
- ¼ cup hulled sunflower seeds
- 2 Green onions, chopped, for garnish

Instructions:
1. Soak the raw cashews for 15 minutes in enough water to cover them. Drain and dab with a paper towel to make them as dry as possible.
2. Transfer the cashews to a blender and add the garlic, lemon zest, rosemary, salt and pepper. Pulse to break everything up and then add the milk, one tablespoon at a time, until the mixture is smooth and creamy.
3. Mash the beans in a bowl with a fork. Add the artichoke hearts and sunflower seeds. Toss to mix.
4. Pour the cashew mixture on top and season with more salt and pepper if desired. Mix the ingredients well and spread on whole-wheat bread, crackers, or a wrap.

Nutrition Facts Per Serving:
Calories 612, Total Fat 15.4g, Saturated Fat 2.3g, Cholesterol 0mg, Sodium 324mg, Total Carbohydrate 90.9g, Dietary Fiber 37.8g, Total Sugars 5.5g, Protein 36.3g, Vitamin D 0mcg, Calcium 274mg, Iron 13mg, Potassium 2292mg

Cucumber Avocado Sandwich

Prep time 5 minutes / Cook time 10 minutes / Serves 2

Ingredients:
- ½ of a large cucumber, peeled, sliced
- ¼ teaspoon salt
- 4 slices whole-wheat bread
- 4 ounces goat cheese with or without herbs
- 2 Romaine lettuce leaves
- 1 large avocado, peeled, pitted, sliced
- 2 pinches lemon pepper
- 1 squeeze of lemon juice
- ½ cup alfalfa sprouts

Instructions:
1. Peel and slice the cucumber thinly. Lay the slices on a plate and sprinkle them with a quarter to a half teaspoon of salt. Let this set for 10 minutes or until water appears on the plate.
2. Place the cucumber slices in a colander and rinse with cold water. Let this drain, then place on a dry plate and pat dry with a paper towel.
3. Spread all slices with goat cheese and place lettuce leaves on the two bottom pieces of bread.

4. Layer the cucumber slices and avocado atop the bread.
5. Sprinkle one pinch of lemon pepper over each sandwich and drizzle a little lemon juice over the top.
6. Top with the alfalfa sprouts and place another piece of bread, goat cheese down, on top.

Nutrition Facts Per Serving:
Calories 511, Total Fat 33.6g, Saturated Fat 12.9g, Cholesterol 26mg, Sodium 773mg, Total Carbohydrate 35.6g, Dietary Fiber 11.2g, Total Sugars 5.6g, Protein 20.6g, Vitamin D 0mcg, Calcium 168mg, Iron 4mg, Potassium 778mg

Lentil Sandwich Spread

Prep time 10 minutes / Cook time 18 minutes / Serves 3
Ingredients:
- 1 tablespoon water or oil
- 1 small onion, chopped
- 2 cloves garlic, minced
- 1 cup dry lentils
- 2 cups vegetable stock
- 1 tablespoon apple cider vinegar
- 2 tablespoons tomato paste
- 3 sun-dried tomatoes
- 2 tablespoons maple or agave syrup
- 1 teaspoon dried oregano
- ½ teaspoon ground cumin
- 1 teaspoon coriander
- 1 teaspoon turmeric
- ½ lemon, juiced
- 1 tablespoon fresh parsley, chopped

Instructions:
1. Warm a Dutch oven over medium heat and add the water or oil.
2. Immediately add the onions and sauté for two to three minutes or until softened. Add more water if this starts to stick to the pan.
3. Add the garlic and sauté for one minute.
4. Add the lentils, vegetable stock and vinegar; bring to a boil. Turn down to a simmer and cook for 15 minutes or until the lentils are soft and the liquid is almost completely absorbed.
5. Ladle the lentils into a food processor and add the tomato paste, sun-dried tomatoes and syrup; process until smooth.
6. Add the oregano, cumin, coriander, turmeric and lemon; processes until thoroughly mixed.
7. Remove the spread to a bowl and apply it to bread, toast, a wrap, or pita. Sprinkle With toppings as desired.

Nutrition Facts Per Serving:
Calories 318, Total Fat 1.4g, Saturated Fat 0.2g, Cholesterol 0mg, Sodium 58mg, Total Carbohydrate 59.6g, Dietary Fiber 23g, Total Sugars 15.6g, Protein 19g, Vitamin D 0mcg, Calcium 87mg, Iron 7mg, Potassium 1138mg

Pita Pizza

Prep time 3 minutes / Cook time 10 minutes / Serves 2
Ingredients:
- 1 pita
- 1 cup Hummus
- 3 tbsp Marinara sauce
- 2 cups various chopped vegetables, onions, cauliflower, broccoli, mushrooms etc.
- ½ cup Shredded cheese, vegan

Instructions:
1. Preheat the oven to 350 degrees, Fahrenheit.
2. Place the pita bread on a baking pan coated with nonstick spray.
3. Spread the pita with hummus and then spoon on a light layer of marinara sauce.
4. Lay down your vegetables on top and sprinkle with cheese.
5. Bake for five to 10 minutes until everything is hot and bubbly.

Nutrition Facts Per Serving:
Calories 317, Total Fat 14.2g, Saturated Fat 2.1g, Cholesterol 0mg, Sodium 729mg, Total Carbohydrate 36.6g, Dietary Fiber 8.9g, Total Sugars 2.3g, Protein 14.7g, Vitamin D 0mcg, Calcium 102mg, Iron 5mg, Potassium 732mg

Mediterranean Tortilla Pinwheels

Prep time 3 minutes / Cook time 0 minutes / Serves 2

Ingredients:
- ½ cup water
- 4 tablespoons white vinegar
- 3 tablespoons lemon juice
- 3 tablespoons tahini paste
- 1 clove garlic, minced
- ¼ teaspoon Salt
- ¼ teaspoon pepper
- 8 oz Canned artichokes, drained, thinly sliced
- 3 Cherry tomatoes, thinly sliced
- ½ cup Olives, thinly sliced
- 1 cup Lettuce or baby spinach
- 2 wheat Tortillas

Instructions:
1. In a bowl, combine the water, vinegar, lemon juice and Tahini paste; whisk together until smooth.
2. Add the garlic, salt and pepper to taste; whisk to combine. Set the bowl aside.
3. Lay a tortilla on a flat surface and spread with one tablespoon of the sauce.
4. Lay some lettuce or spinach slices on top, then scatter some artichoke, tomato and olive slices on top.
5. Tightly roll the tortilla and fold in the sides. Cut the ends off and then slice into four or five pinwheels.

Nutrition Facts Per Serving:
Calories 357, Total Fat 18.5g, Saturated Fat 2.4g, Cholesterol 0mg, Sodium 975mg, Total Carbohydrate 40.2g, Dietary Fiber 19.9g, Total Sugars 7g, Protein 12.9g, Vitamin D 0mcg, Calcium 204mg, Iron 6mg, Potassium 1052mg

Rice and Bean Burritos

Prep time 5 minutes / Cook time 15 minutes / Serves 4

Ingredients:
- 2 16-ounce cans fat-free refried beans
- 6 tortillas
- 2 cups cooked rice
- ½ cup salsa
- 1 tablespoon olive oil
- 8 green onions, chopped
- 2 bell peppers, finely chopped
- 7 oz Guacamole

Instructions:
1. Preheat the oven to 375 degrees, Fahrenheit.
2. Dump the refried beans into a saucepan and place over medium heat to warm.
3. Heat the tortillas and lay them out on a flat surface.
4. Spoon the beans in a long mound that runs across the tortilla, just a little off from center.
5. Spoon some rice and salsa over the beans; add the green pepper and onions to taste, along with any other finely chopped vegetables you like.
6. Fold over the shortest edge of plain tortilla and roll it up, folding in the sides as you go.
7. Place each burrito, seam side down, on a nonstick-sprayed baking sheet.
8. Brush with olive oil and bake for 15 minutes.
9. Serve with guacamole.

Nutrition Facts Per Serving:
Calories 770, Total Fat 15.4g, Saturated Fat 2.8g, Cholesterol 18mg, Sodium 1052mg, Total Carbohydrate 137.5g, Dietary Fiber 19.4g, Total Sugars 6.5g, Protein 23.6g, Vitamin D 0mcg, Calcium 170mg, Iron 9mg, Potassium 1070mg

Ricotta Basil Pinwheels

Prep time 5 minutes / Cook time 0 minutes / Serves 4

Ingredients:
- ½ cup unsalted cashews
- 3 cups Water
- 7 ounces firm tofu, cut into pieces
- ¼ cup almond milk
- 1 teaspoon white wine vinegar
- 1 clove garlic, smashed
- 20 fresh basil leaves
- ¼ teaspoon Salt
- ¼ teaspoon pepper
- 8 wheat tortillas

- 7 ounces fresh spinach
- ½ cup black olives, sliced
- 2 tomatoes, cut into small pieces

Instructions:
1. Soak the cashews for 30 minutes in enough water to cover them. Drain them well and pat them dry with paper towels.
2. Place the cashews in a blender along with the tofu, almond milk, vinegar, garlic, basil leaves, salt and pepper to taste. Blend until smooth and creamy.
3. Spread the resulting mixture on the eight tortillas, dividing it equally.
4. Top with spinach leaves, olives and tomatoes.
5. Tightly roll each loaded tortilla.
6. Cut off the ends with a sharp knife and slice into four or five pinwheels.

Nutrition Facts Per Serving:
Calories 546, Total Fat 25.7g, Saturated Fat 5.5g, Cholesterol 0mg, Sodium 1011mg, Total Carbohydrate 66.9g, Dietary Fiber 10.6g, Total Sugars 4.7g, Protein 19.3g, Vitamin D 0mcg, Calcium 192mg, Iron 4mg, Potassium 890mg

Sloppy Joes Made with Lentils and Bulgur

Prep time 5 minutes / Cook time 35 minutes / Serves 6

Ingredients:
- 5 tablespoons vegetable stock
- 2 stalks celery, diced
- 1 small onion, diced
- 1 small red bell pepper, diced
- 1 teaspoon garlic powder
- 1 teaspoon chili powder
- 1 teaspoon ground cumin
- 1 teaspoon salt
- 1 cup cooked bulgur wheat
- 1 cup red lentils
- 1 15-ounce can tomato sauce
- 4 tablespoons tomato paste
- 3½ cups water
- 2 teaspoons balsamic vinegar
- 1 tablespoon Hoisin sauce

Instructions:
1. In a Dutch oven, heat up the vegetable stock and add the celery, onion and bell pepper. Sauté until vegetables are soft, about five minutes.
2. Add the garlic powder, chili powder, cumin and salt and mix in.
3. Add the bulgur wheat, lentils, tomato sauce, tomato paste, water, vinegar and Hoisin sauce. Stir and bring to a boil.
4. Turn the heat down to a simmer and cook uncovered for 30 minutes. Stir occasionally to prevent sticking and scorching.
5. Taste to see if the lentils are tender.
6. When the lentils are done, serve on buns.

Nutrition Facts Per Serving:
Calories 246, Total Fat 1.2g, Saturated Fat 0.2g, Cholesterol 0mg, Sodium 889mg, Total Carbohydrate 48.2g, Dietary Fiber 16.9g, Total Sugars 8.1g, Protein 13.5g, Vitamin D 0mcg, Calcium 70mg, Iron 4mg, Potassium 843mg

Zucchini Sandwich with Balsamic Dressing

Prep time 5 minutes / Cook time 3 minutes / Serves 4

Ingredients:
- 2 small zucchinis
- 1 tablespoon olive oil
- 4 cloves garlic, thinly sliced
- 1 tablespoon balsamic vinegar
- 1 large roasted red pepper, chopped
- 1 cup cannellini beans, rinsed, drained
- 2 whole-wheat sandwich rolls
- 6 basil leaves
- ½ teaspoon pepper

Instructions:
1. Add the oil to a hot skillet and sauté the garlic for one or two minutes or until it just starts to brown.
2. Add the zucchini strips and sauté in batches and lay out on a plate until they are all finished.
3. Reduce heat to medium and place all the zucchini strips back in the pan.
4. Add the vinegar and sauté for about a minute.
5. In the blender, process the red pepper and beans until smooth.

6. Toast the buns and spoon onto the bottom halves the bean and pepper mixture.
7. Lay basil leaves on top and then the zucchini.
8. Grind some pepper on top and close the sandwich with the top of the bun.
9. The next chapter will give you some salads that can also make a great lunch.

Nutrition Facts Per Serving:
Calories 269, Total Fat 5.1g, Saturated Fat 0.8g, Cholesterol 0mg, Sodium 156mg, Total Carbohydrate 43.9g, Dietary Fiber 14.5g, Total Sugars 3.9g, Protein 15g, Vitamin D 0mcg, Calcium 84mg, Iron 5mg, Potassium 852mg

Spicy Hummus and Apple Wrap

Prep time 7 minutes / Cook time 0 minutes / Serves 3

Ingredients:
- 4 tablespoons hummus
- 2 tablespoons mild salsa
- ½ cup broccoli slaw
- ½ teaspoon fresh lemon juice
- 2 teaspoons plain yogurt
- ¼ teaspoon salt
- ¼ teaspoon pepper
- 1 tortilla
- Lettuce leaves
- 2 oz Granny Smith, cored and thinly sliced

Instructions:
1. In a small bowl, mix the hummus with the salsa. Set the bowl aside.
2. In a large bowl, mix the broccoli slaw, lemon juice and yogurt. Season with the salt and pepper.
3. Lay the tortilla on a flat surface and spread on the hummus mixture.
4. Lay down some lettuce leaves on top of the hummus.
5. On the upper half of the tortilla, place a pile of the broccoli slaw mixture and cover with the apples.
6. Fold and wrap.

Nutrition Facts Per Serving:
Calories 146, Total Fat 2.2g, Saturated Fat 0.4g, Cholesterol 0mg, Sodium 335mg, Total Carbohydrate 30.8g, Dietary Fiber 5.4g, Total Sugars 17.6g, Protein 3.4g, Vitamin D 0mcg, Calcium 43mg, Iron 1mg, Potassium 119mg

Sun-dried Tomato Spread

Prep time 10 minutes / Cook time 0 minutes / Serves 4

Ingredients:
- 1 cup sun-dried tomatoes
- 1 cup raw cashews
- ½ cup water
- 1 clove garlic, minced
- 1 green onion, chopped
- 5 large basil leaves
- ½ teaspoon lemon juice
- ¼ teaspoon salt
- 1 dash pepper
- ¼ cup Hulled sunflower seeds, salted or unsalted

Instructions:
1. Soak tomatoes and cashews for 30 minutes in separate bowls, with enough water to cover them. Drain and pat dry.
2. Put the tomatoes and cashews in a food processor and puree them, drizzling the water in as it purees to make a smooth, creamy paste.
3. Add the garlic, onion, basil leaves, lemon juice, salt and pepper and mix thoroughly.
4. Scrape into a bowl, cover and refrigerate overnight.
5. Spread on bread or toast and sprinkle with sunflower seeds for a little added crunch.

Nutrition Facts Per Serving:
Calories 225, Total Fat 17.5g, Saturated Fat 3.3g, Cholesterol 0mg, Sodium 157mg, Total Carbohydrate 14.2g, Dietary Fiber 2g, Total Sugars 3.1g, Protein 6.5g, Vitamin D 0mcg, Calcium 33mg, Iron 3mg, Potassium 343mg

Sweet Potato Sandwich Spread

Prep time 10 minutes / Cook time 0 minutes / Serves 5

Ingredients:
- 1 large sweet potato baked and peeled
- 1 teaspoon cumin
- 1 teaspoon chili powder
- 1 teaspoon garlic powder
- ¼ teaspoon Salt
- ¼ teaspoon pepper
- 2 slices whole-wheat bread
- 8 oz pinto beans, drained
- 3 Lettuce leaves

Instructions:
1. Bake and peel the sweet potato and mash it in a bowl. If it is too thick, add a little almond or coconut milk.
2. Mix in the cumin, chili powder, garlic powder, salt and pepper.
3. Spread the mixture on a slice of bread and spoon some beans on top.
4. Top with lettuce leaves and the other slice of bread.

Nutrition Facts Per Serving:
Calories 222, Total Fat 1.1g, Saturated Fat 0.2g, Cholesterol 0mg, Sodium 184mg, Total Carbohydrate 41.4g, Dietary Fiber 8.1g, Total Sugars 1.8g, Protein 12g, Vitamin D 0mcg, Calcium 70mg, Iron 3mg, Potassium 689mg

Apple Mint Salad with Pine Nut Crunch

Prep time 10 minutes / Cook time 0 minutes / Serves 2

Ingredients:
- 1 medium apple, diced
- 1 tablespoon lemon juice
- 1 teaspoon maple syrup
- ½ teaspoon dried mint
- 1 tablespoon fresh pomegranate seeds
- 1 teaspoon pine nuts or sliced almonds

Instructions:
1. Toast the nuts in a pan on the stove. Stir constantly so they don't burn and let them turn a golden brown. Set the pan aside until cooled to room temperature.
2. Place the diced apple in a small bowl with the lemon juice and stir around so all the apple is coated.
3. Add the maple syrup and dried mint and stir it in.
4. Sprinkle the top of the salad with pomegranate seeds and toasted nuts.

Nutrition Facts Per Serving:
Calories 128, Total Fat 1.3g, Saturated Fat 0.1g, Cholesterol 0mg, Sodium 3mg, Total Carbohydrate 30g, Dietary Fiber 3.3g, Total Sugars 19.8g, Protein 1.1g, Vitamin D 0mcg, Calcium 4mg, Iron 1mg, Potassium 146mg

Chickpea 'N Spinach Tomato Salad

Prep time 7 minutes / Cook time 0 minutes / Serves 2

Ingredients:
- 2 cups canned or cooked chickpeas
- 4 medium tomatoes, chopped
- 5 green onions, chopped
- 1 red bell pepper, seeded,chopped
- 1/3 cup fresh parsley, chopped
- 1 cup baby spinach leaves
- 2 tablespoons olive oil
- ½ lemon, juiced
- 1 tablespoon balsamic vinegar
- 2 tablespoons flaxseed
- 2 tablespoons sesame seeds

Instructions:
1. Combine the chickpeas, tomatoes, onion, bell pepper, parsley and baby spinach in a large salad bowl.
2. In a jar with a lid, combine the oil, lemon juice and balsamic vinegar; shake until well mixed.
3. Pour the dressing over the salad and sprinkle with the flaxseed and sesame seeds.

Nutrition Facts Per Serving:
Calories 1025, Total Fat 33.6g, Saturated Fat 4.3g, Cholesterol 0mg, Sodium 89mg, Total Carbohydrate 144.8g, Dietary Fiber 43.6g, Total Sugars 32.4g, Protein 45.8g, Vitamin D 0mcg, Calcium 389mg, Iron 18mg, Potassium 2812mg

Mango and Red Cabbage Slaw

Prep time 15 minutes / Cook time 0 minutes / Serves 5

Ingredients:

- 2 ripe mangos, sliced
- ¼ cup fresh cilantro, chopped
- 4 carrots, peeled and grated
- 4 cups red cabbage, shredded
- 1 splash of balsamic vinegar
- 1 lime, juiced
- 1 pinch kosher salt

Instructions:

1. Place the mango, cilantro, carrot and red cabbage in a large salad bowl.

2. Whisk together in another bowl the vinegar, lime juice and salt.
3. Pour the dressing over the salad and toss to coat.
4. For the most refreshing flavor, refrigerate for 20 minutes before serving.

Nutrition Facts Per Serving:

Calories 119, Total Fat 0.6g, Saturated Fat 0.1g, Cholesterol 0mg, Sodium 162mg, Total Carbohydrate 29.7g, Dietary Fiber 5.2g, Total Sugars 22.8g, Protein 2.3g, Vitamin D 0mcg, Calcium 58mg, Iron 1mg, Potassium 497mg

Avocado and Cauliflower Hummus

Prep time 5 minutes / Cook time 25 minutes / Serves 2

Ingredients:

- 1 medium cauliflower, stem removed and chopped
- 1 large Hass avocado, peeled, pitted, and chopped
- ¼ cup extra virgin olive oil
- 2 garlic cloves
- ½ tbsp. lemon juice
- ½ tsp. onion powder
- ¼ teaspoon Sea salt
- ¼ teaspoon ground black pepper
- 2 large carrots
- ¼ cup fresh cilantro, chopped

Instructions:

1. Preheat the oven to 450°F, and line a baking tray with aluminum foil.
2. Put the chopped cauliflower on the baking tray and drizzle with 2 tablespoons of olive oil.
3. Roast the chopped cauliflower in the oven for 20-25 minutes, until lightly brown.

4. Remove the tray from the oven and allow the cauliflower to cool down.
5. Add all the ingredients—except the carrots and optional fresh cilantro—to a food processor or blender, and blend the ingredients into a smooth hummus.
6. Transfer the hummus to a medium-sized bowl, cover, and put it in the fridge for at least 30 minutes.
7. Take the hummus out of the fridge and, if desired, top it with the optional chopped cilantro and more salt and pepper to taste; serve with the carrot fries, and enjoy!

Nutritional facts per serving:

Calories 312, Total Fat 27.7g, Saturated Fat 3.7g, Cholesterol 0mg, Sodium 326mg, Total Carbohydrate 17.4g, Dietary Fiber 5.8g, Total Sugars 7.1g, Protein 4.1g, Vitamin D 0mcg, Calcium 63mg, Iron 1mg, Potassium 668mg

Raw Zoodles with Avocado 'N Nuts

Prep time 10 minutes / Serves 2

Ingredients:

- 1 medium zucchini
- 1½ cups basil
- 1/3 cup water
- 5 tbsp. pine nuts
- 2 tbsp. lemon juice

- 1 medium avocado, peeled, pitted, sliced
- Optional: 2 tbsp. olive oil
- 6 yellow cherry tomatoes, halved
- Optional: 6 red cherry tomatoes, halved
- ¼ teaspoon Sea salt

- ¼ teaspoon black pepper

Instructions:
1. Add the basil, water, nuts, lemon juice, avocado slices, optional olive oil, salt, and pepper to a blender.
2. Blend the ingredients into a smooth mixture. Add more salt and pepper to taste and blend again.
3. Divide the sauce and the zucchini noodles between two medium-sized bowls for serving, and combine in each.

4. Top the mixtures with the halved yellow cherry tomatoes, and the optional red cherry tomatoes. Serve and enjoy!

Nutritional facts per serving:
Calories 571, Total Fat 49.8g, Saturated Fat 7.5g, Cholesterol 0mg, Sodium 275mg, Total Carbohydrate 31.3g, Dietary Fiber 14.2g, Total Sugars 13.2g, Protein 11.5g, Vitamin D 0mcg, Calcium 187mg, Iron 5mg, Potassium 1964mg

Cauliflower Sushi

Prep time 30 minutes / Serves 4

Ingredients:

Sushi Base:
- 6 cups cauliflower florets
- ½ cup vegan cheese
- 1 medium spring onion, diced
- 4 nori sheets
- ¼ teaspoon Sea salt
- ¼ teaspoon pepper to taste
- 1 tbsp. rice vinegar or sushi vinegar
- 1 medium garlic clove, minced

Filling:
- 1 medium Hass avocado, peeled, sliced
- ½ medium cucumber, skinned, sliced
- 4 asparagus spears
- ½ cup enoki mushrooms

Instructions:
1. Put the cauliflower florets in a food processor or blender. Pulse the florets into a rice-like substance. When using readymade cauliflower rice, add this to the blender.
2. Add the vegan cheese, spring onions, and vinegar to the food processor or blender. Top these ingredients with salt and pepper to taste, and pulse everything into a chunky mixture. Make sure not to turn the ingredients into a puree by pulsing too long.

3. Taste and add more vinegar, salt, or pepper to taste. Add the optional minced garlic clove to the blender and pulse again for a few seconds.
4. Lay out the nori sheets and spread the cauliflower rice mixture out evenly between the sheets. Make sure to leave at least 2 inches of the top and bottom edges empty.
5. Place one or more combinations of multiple filling ingredients along the center of the spread out rice mixture. Experiment with different ingredients per nori sheet for the best flavor.
6. Roll up each nori sheet tightly. (Using a sushi mat will make this easier.)
7. Either serve the sushi as a nori roll, or, slice each roll up into sushi pieces.
8. Serve right away with a small amount of wasabi, pickled ginger, and soy sauce!

Nutritional facts per serving:
Calories 82, Total Fat 2g, Saturated Fat 0.1g, Cholesterol 0mg, Sodium 183mg, Total Carbohydrate 13.5g, Dietary Fiber 5.3g, Total Sugars 4.8g, Protein 5.2g, Vitamin D 0mcg, Calcium 67mg, Iron 2mg, Potassium 609mg

Delicious Sloppy Joes with No Meat

Prep time 6 minutes / Cook time 5 minutes / Serves 4

Ingredients:
- 5 tablespoons vegetable stock
- 2 stalks celery, diced
- 1 small onion, diced
- 1 small red bell pepper, diced

- 1 teaspoon garlic powder
- 1 teaspoon chili powder
- 1 teaspoon ground cumin
- 1 teaspoon salt

- 1 cup cooked bulgur wheat
- 1 cup red lentils
- 1 15-ounce can tomato sauce
- 4 tablespoons tomato paste
- 3½ cups water
- 2 teaspoons balsamic vinegar
- 1 tablespoon Hoisin sauce

Instructions:
1. In a Dutch oven, heat up the vegetable stock and add the celery, onion and bell pepper. Sauté until vegetables are soft, about five minutes.
2. Add the garlic powder, chili powder, cumin and salt and mix in.
3. Add the bulgur wheat, lentils, tomato sauce, tomato paste, water, vinegar and Hoisin sauce. Stir and bring to a boil.
4. Turn the heat down to a simmer and cook uncovered for 30 minutes. Stir occasionally to prevent sticking and scorching.
5. Taste to see if the lentils are tender.
6. When the lentils are done, serve on buns.

Nutritional Facts Per Serving:
Calories 369, Total Fat 1.9g, Saturated Fat 0.3g, Cholesterol 0mg, Sodium 1334mg, Total Carbohydrate 72.3g, Dietary Fiber 25.3g, Total Sugars 12.1g , Protein 20.2g, Vitamin D 0mcg, Calcium 105mg, Iron 7mg, Potassium 1265mg

Vegetarian Grain Bowl

Prep time 6 minutes / Cook time 0 minutes / Serves 2

Ingredients:

For dressing:
- 1 tablespoon rice vinegar
- 1 tablespoon avocado oil
- 1 teaspoon fresh ginger, grated
- 1 tablespoon tamari
- 1 teaspoon toasted dark sesame oil

For bowl:
- ½ cup shredded carrot
- 1 cup cooked brown rice
- ½ cup chopped cucumber
- ½ cup shelled frozen edamame, thawed
- Sesame seeds to garnish
- ½ avocado, peeled, pitted, chopped
- ½ cup toasted nori, chopped

Instructions:

To make dressing:
1. Add rice vinegar, tamari, sesame oil, avocado oil and ginger into a bowl. Whisk well.
2. Take 2 bowls and add ½ cup brown rice in each bowl. Divide the vegetables, avocado and nori equally among the bowls.
3. Divide the dressing on it. Garnish with sesame seeds and serve.

Nutritional Facts Per Serving:
Calories 570, Total Fat 17.4g, Saturated Fat 2.3g, Cholesterol 0mg, Sodium 545mg, Total Carbohydrate 87g, Dietary Fiber 9.1g, Total Sugars 2.6g, Protein 16.4g, Vitamin D 0mcg, Calcium 243mg, Iron 6mg, Potassium 541mg

Thai Sweet Potato Noodle Bowls

Prep time 5 minutes / Cook time 4 minutes / Serves 2

Ingredients:
- 4 teaspoons toasted sesame oil, divided
- ½ cup red bell pepper, thinly sliced
- 1 large sweet potato, peeled
- Salt to taste
- 1 ½ cups baby spinach
- ¼ cup canned light coconut milk
- 1 tablespoon fresh curry paste
- Lime wedges to serve
- ½ cup red bell pepper, thinly sliced
- ¼ cup water, divided
- 4 ounces extra firm tofu, cut into ½ inch cubes
- 1 ½ tablespoons almond butter
- A handful cashews, unsalted

Instructions:
1. Make noodles of the sweet potato with a spiralizer or a julienne peeler. You should get 4 cups of sweet potato noodles.
2. Place a nonstick skillet over medium high heat. Add 2 teaspoons oil and heat. Add sweet potatoes noodles, bell pepper and salt. Sauté for 3-4 minutes.
3. Add 2 tablespoons water and stir. Cover the pan with a lid and cook for a couple of minutes. Toss well.

4. Remove the lid and cook for a couple of minutes. Transfer into a bowl and set aside.
5. Place the pan back on heat. Add remaining oil and heat. Add tofu and cook until light brown.
6. Mix together 2 tablespoons water, salt, coconut milk, curry paste and almond butter in a bowl.
7. Add half this sauce to the sweet potato noodles. Toss well and divide into 2 serving bowls.

8. Divide the tofu among the bowls. Drizzle the remaining sauce over the tofu. Sprinkle cashews and serve with lime wedges.

Nutritional Facts Per Serving:
Calories 489, Total Fat 34.9g, Saturated Fat 9.6g, Cholesterol 0mg, Sodium 357mg, Total Carbohydrate 38.5g, Dietary Fiber 8.4g, Total Sugars 10.9g, Protein 13.2g, Vitamin D 0mcg, Calcium 179mg, Iron 9mg, Potassium 931mg

Black Bean-Quinoa Buddha Bowl

Prep time 6 minutes / Cook time 0 minutes / Serves 2

Ingredients:
- 1 ½ cups cooked or canned black beans, rinsed, drained
- ½ cup hummus
- ½ medium avocado, peeled, pitted, cubed
- ¼ cup chopped fresh cilantro
- 1 1/3 cups cooked quinoa
- 2 tablespoons lime juice
- 6 tablespoons Pico de Gallo

Instructions:
1. Add hummus and lime juice into a bowl and mix well. Add a little water if you want a thinner dressing.

2. Add beans and quinoa into a bowl and stir. Divide into 2 serving bowls.
3. Divide and drizzle hummus mixture over the bean mixture.
4. Place avocado and Pico de Gallo on top. Garnish with cilantro and serve.

Nutritional Facts Per Serving:
Calories 1133, Total Fat 24.8g, Saturated Fat 4.3g, Cholesterol 0mg, Sodium 444mg, Total Carbohydrate 178.7g, Dietary Fiber 37.3g, Total Sugars 4.5g, Protein 53.4g, Vitamin D 0mcg, Calcium 265mg, Iron 14mg, Potassium 3205mg

Roasted Vegetable Buddha Bowls with Almond Butter Dressing

Prep time 10 minutes / Cook time 1 hour / Serves 2

Ingredients:
For roasted vegetables:
- 2 small heads broccoli, cut into bite size florets
- 1 clove garlic, minced
- Salt to taste
- Pepper to taste
- 1 large sweet potato, peeled, chopped into small cubes
- ½ tablespoon toasted sesame oil or olive oil

For coconut mango rice:
- 1 teaspoon unrefined coconut oil
- ½ cup water
- 1 medium ripe mango, peeled, pitted, diced
- ½ cup coconut milk or almond coconut milk, unsweetened
- ½ cup uncooked brown rice, rinsed

For almond butter dressing:
- 2 tablespoons natural creamy almond butter

- 1 teaspoon pure maple syrup
- ½ teaspoon toasted sesame oil
- 2 tablespoons fresh orange juice
- ¼ teaspoon apple cider vinegar

To garnish:
- 1 green onion, thinly sliced
- 2 teaspoons toasted sesame seeds
- Cilantro, chopped

Instructions:
To make mango coconut rice:
1. Place a pot over medium high heat.
2. Add coconut oil and let it melt. Add rice and stir- fry for 3-4 minutes until toasted.
3. Add water and coconut milk. When it begins to boil, lower the heat and cover with a lid.
4. Cook until dry. It should take 25-30 minutes. Turn off the heat and fluff the rice with a fork. Set aside for 10 minutes. Add mango and salt

and stir lightly until mango pieces are evenly distributed in the rice.

5. Meanwhile make the roasted vegetables as follow: Place a sheet of parchment paper on a baking sheet.
6. Place sweet potatoes in a microwave safe bowl. Microwave on High for 3 minutes.
7. Transfer on to the prepared baking sheet. Spread it evenly.
8. Spread the broccoli florets on the baking sheet. Sprinkle garlic over the vegetables.
9. Bake in a preheated oven at 375° F for about 20-25 minutes or until tender. Turn the vegetables half way through roasting.

To make dressing:
1. Add all the ingredients for dressing into a bowl and whisk well.
2. Divide the rice into 2 bowls. Scatter the roasted vegetables over the rice.
3. Drizzle the dressing on top.
4. Garnish with optional ingredients if using and serve.

Nutritional Facts Per Serving:
Calories 732, Total Fat 35.4g, Saturated Fat 17g, Cholesterol 0mg, Sodium 370mg, Total Carbohydrate 98.6g, Dietary Fiber 13.7g, Total Sugars 36.8g, Protein 14.1g, Vitamin D 0mcg, Calcium 173mg, Iron 7mg, Potassium 1368mg

Grilled Veggie Burrito Bowl

Prep time 5 minutes / Cook time 15 minutes / Serves 2

Ingredients:

For cilantro lime dressing:
- ¼ cup raw cashews, soaked in hot water for 20-30 minutes
- A large handful fresh cilantro
- ½ teaspoon salt
- ¼ cup water
- ½ lime Juice

For burrito bowl:
- 1 tablespoon olive oil, divided
- 1 clove garlic, peeled, minced
- ¾ cup water or vegetable stock
- ¼ teaspoon ground cumin
- ½ teaspoon dried oregano
- Pepper to taste
- ¼ teaspoon chili powder
- 1 small onion, diced
- ½ red bell pepper, sliced
- ½ cup rice, rinsed
- ½ teaspoon salt or to taste
- ½ can corn kernels, drained
- 1 cup canned or cooked beans, rinsed, drained
- ½ cup, fresh cilantro, chopped
- 1 cup, cherry tomatoes, halved, quartered
- ½ Lime, wedged to garnish
- ½ avocado, sliced to garnish

Instructions:

To make cilantro lime dressing:
1. Add all the ingredients for cilantro lime dressing into a blender and blend until smooth. Pour into a bowl and refrigerate for at least an hour.

To make burrito bowls:
1. Place a pot over medium-high heat. Add ½ tablespoon oil and heat. Add onion and garlic and sauté until onion turns pink. Stir in the rice. While you can use any variety of rice, personally I prefer short grain rice. Sauté for 15 minutes until it turns opaque. Add vegetable stock, tomato, spices, oregano and salt and mix well.
2. When it begins to boil, lower the heat and cook until rice is tender. If you think the rice is not cooked properly, add some more stock or water. Fluff the rice with a fork.
3. Add beans and toss well.
4. Meanwhile, place a grill pan over medium-high heat. Add corn and bell pepper. Drizzle remaining oil and season with salt. Grill to the desired doneness.
5. Remove the peppers and place on your cutting board. Chop into smaller pieces.

To assemble:
1. Divide the rice mixture among 2 bowls. Layer with grilled pepper and corn followed by tomatoes and avocado.
2. Sprinkle cilantro on top. Spoon cilantro lime dressing on top and serve.

Nutritional Facts Per Serving:
Calories 534, Total Fat 26.1g, Saturated Fat 4.9g, Cholesterol 0mg, Sodium 616mg, Total Carbohydrate 71.2g, Dietary Fiber 10.7g, Total Sugars 9.1g, Protein 11.1g, Vitamin D 0mcg, Calcium 94mg, Iron 6mg, Potassium 1017mg

Thai Tempeh Buddha Bowl

Prep time 10 minutes / Cook time 5 minutes / Serves 4

Ingredients:

For tempeh:
- 4 tablespoons coconut aminos
- 2 tablespoons rice vinegar
- 2 teaspoons sesame oil
- 2 packages (8 ounces each) tempeh

For freekeh:
- 1 cup uncooked freekeh
- 3 cups water

To assemble:
- 8 cups mixed greens
- 1 cup shredded purple cabbage
- 1 large avocado, peeled, pitted, chopped
- 1 red bell pepper, thinly sliced
- 2 small sweet potatoes, cubed, roasted

For cashew curry sauce:
- 3 tablespoons cashew butter
- 2 tablespoons coconut aminos
- 1 teaspoon red curry paste
- 3 tablespoons coconut milk
- 2 teaspoons rice vinegar

Instructions:

To make tempeh:

1. Add all the ingredients for tempeh into a bowl and stir. Set aside for 10 minutes.
2. Place a pan over medium heat. Add tempeh and cook for 5 minutes until golden brown and crisp.

To make freekeh:

1. Meanwhile, add freekeh and water into a saucepan. Place saucepan over medium-high heat. When it begins to boil, cover and cook until dry.

To make curry sauce:

1. Add all the ingredients for curry sauce into a bowl and whisk well.
2. Divide the mixed greens among 4 bowls. Layer with equal quantities of – tempeh, freekeh, cabbage, avocado, bell pepper and sweet potatoes.
3. Drizzle curry sauce on top and serve.

Nutritional Facts Per Serving:

Calories 800, Total Fat 34.4g, Saturated Fat 8.8g, Cholesterol 0mg, Sodium 247mg, Total Carbohydrate 90.8g, Dietary Fiber 23.3g, Total Sugars 14.5g, Protein 37.6g, Vitamin D 0mcg, Calcium 251mg, Iron 11mg, Potassium 1848mg

Italian Lunch Bowls

Prep time 5 minutes / Cook time 10 minutes / Serves 3

Ingredients:

For bowls:
- 1 cup dry quinoa, soaked in water for 15 minutes, rinsed
- 2 cups water
- 1 medium cucumber, chopped
- ½ pint cherry tomatoes, halved
- 1 green onion, thinly sliced, to garnish
- ½ pound leafy greens like spinach, lettuce etc.
- 1 bell pepper of any color, deseeded, chopped
- 1-2 radishes, trimmed, thinly sliced
- 1 ½ cups cooked beans

For creamy Italian dressing:
- ¼ cup raw tahini
- ½ teaspoon apple cider vinegar
- 1 clove garlic, peeled
- ¼ teaspoon dried oregano
- ¼ cup water
- ¼ teaspoon salt
- 2 tablespoons fresh lemon juice
- ¼ teaspoon onion powder

Instructions:

1. Add quinoa and water into a saucepan. Place the saucepan over high heat. When it begins to boil, reduce the heat and cover with a lid. Cook for 10 minutes until dry. Turn off the heat. Using a fork, fluff the quinoa.
2. Meanwhile, make the dressing by add all the ingredients of the dressing into a blender and blend until smooth.
3. Divide quinoa among 3 bowls. Divide the leafy greens and other vegetables and place over the quinoa. Spoon the dressing on top and serve.

Nutritional Facts Per Serving:

Calories 408, Total Fat 15g, Saturated Fat 2.1g, Cholesterol 0mg, Sodium 298mg, Total Carbohydrate 57.5g, Dietary Fiber 11.4g, Total Sugars 6.9g, Protein 16.4g, Vitamin D 0mcg, Calcium 248mg, Iron 8mg, Potassium 1347mg

Prep time 5 minutes / Cook time 25 minutes / Serves 3

Ingredients:

For roasted vegetables:
- 1 red bell pepper, cut into strips
- ½ red onion, thinly sliced
- 2 cloves garlic, thinly sliced
- ½ zucchini, julienned
- 2 tablespoons chopped walnuts
- 1 tablespoon extra-virgin olive oil
- ½ teaspoon fine sea salt
- A pinch crushed red pepper flakes
- ¼ teaspoon freshly ground pepper or to taste

For bean puree:
- ¾ cup cooked or canned cannellini beans, drained, rinsed
- 1 tablespoon lemon juice
- 3 tablespoons water
- Salt to taste
- ½ avocado, peeled, pitted, chopped
- 1 large clove garlic, peeled, sliced
- A handful fresh cilantro or parsley
- Freshly ground pepper to taste

For bowl:
- ½ cup sprouts
- 2 cups cooked, warmed quinoa

Instructions:

1. Place a sheet of parchment paper on a baking sheet.
2. Add vegetables, garlic, walnuts, spices and salt into a bowl and toss well.
3. Transfer on to a baking sheet. Spread it evenly.
4. Roast in a preheated oven at 425° F for about 20-25 minutes or until tender. Turn the vegetables half way through roasting.
5. Meanwhile, make the bean puree. To make that, add all the ingredients for bean puree into a blender and blend until smooth. Add more water if you prefer the puree of thinner consistency.
6. Divide the quinoa into 3 bowls. Divide the roasted vegetables and place over the quinoa. Drizzle bean puree over the vegetables. Scatter sprouts on top and serve.

Nutritional Facts Per Serving:
Calories 483, Total Fat 17.7g, Saturated Fat 2.4g, Cholesterol 0mg, Sodium 541mg, Total Carbohydrate 66.1g, Dietary Fiber 19.6g, Total Sugars 5.2g, Protein 20.1g, Vitamin D 0mcg, Calcium 124mg, Iron 7mg, Potassium 1143mg

Prep time 5 minutes / Cook time 20 minutes / Serves 6

Ingredients:

For rice:
- 2 cups short grain brown rice
- 2 tablespoons minced ginger
- 2 tablespoons vegetable oil
- 4 cups water

For topping:
- 2 teaspoons vegetable oil
- Salt to taste
- 2 avocadoes, peeled, pitted, chopped
- 10 slender asparagus stalks, cut into 1 inch pieces
- 2 bunches radish, do not remove the tops, rinsed, dried
- 1 sheet toasted nori, cut into strips
- 2 tablespoons sesame seeds, toasted
- ¼ teaspoon salt

For dressing:
- ¼ cup rice vinegar
- ¼ cup red miso paste
- 3 tablespoons dark brown sugar
- ¼ cup vegetable oil
- 2 tablespoons soy sauce
- 3 teaspoons toasted sesame oil

Instructions:

To make dressing:
1. Add rice vinegar, miso, oil, soy sauce and sesame oil and sugar into a bowl and whisk well. Set aside for a while for the flavors to blend in.

To make rice:

1. Place a saucepan over medium heat. Add oil. When the oil is heated, add ginger and rice and sauté for 10 minutes until aromatic. Add water and stir.
2. When it begins to boil, lower the heat and cook for 5 minutes until rice is tender and all the water has evaporated. If you think that the rice is still uncooked and there is no water left in the saucepan, then add some more water and cook until done.

To make toppings:
1. Place a nonstick pan over medium-high heat. Add oil. When the oil is heated, add asparagus and salt and cook for 5 minutes until crisp as well as tender. Turn off the heat.
2. Chop the tops of the radishes coarsely and add into a bowl. Slice the radishes thinly. Add into the bowl of chopped radishes. Drizzle 3-4 tablespoons dressing and toss well.

To assemble:
1. Divide the rice among 6 bowls. Sprinkle a tablespoon of dressing over the rice. Divide equally the radish tops and slices and place over the rice. Place asparagus and avocado slices. Drizzle remaining dressing on top.

Nutritional Facts Per Serving:
Calories 577, Total Fat 28g, Saturated Fat 5.1g, Cholesterol 0mg, Sodium 872mg, Total Carbohydrate 74.1g, Dietary Fiber 12.6g, Total Sugars 11.5g, Protein 9.8g, Vitamin D 0mcg, Calcium 86mg, Iron 2mg, Potassium 397mg

Chapter 6: Dinner Recipes

Black Bean & Quinoa Burgers

Prep time 40 minutes / Cook time 8 minutes / Serves 3

Ingredients:

- 1 cup dry black beans
- ½ cup dry quinoa
- ½ purple onion, chopped
- ¼ cup bell pepper
- 2 tablespoons garlic, minced
- ½ cup whole wheat flour
- 2 tbsp. olive oil
- ½ tsp. red pepper flakes
- ½ tsp. paprika
- 1 tsp. salt
- 1 tsp. pepper
- 2 cups lettuce leaves
- ½ cup Roasted sesame seeds

Instructions:

1. Heat 1 tablespoon of the olive oil in a frying pan over medium-high heat, and then add the onions, bell peppers, garlic, salt, and pepper.
2. Sauté until the ingredients begin to soften, for about 5 minutes. Remove the pan from the heat and let it cool down for about 10 minutes.
3. Once the veggies have cooled down, put them in a food processor along with the cooked beans, quinoa, flour, and remaining spices; pulse until it's a chunky mixture.
4. Lay out a pan covered with parchment paper and form the blended mixture into 6 evenly-sized patties.
5. Place the patties on the pan and place them in the freezer for about 5 minutes to prevent crumbling.
6. Heat the remaining oil in a frying pan over high heat and add the burgers.
7. Cook the patties until they have browned, for about 2-3 minutes per side.
8. Serve each burger wrapped in a lettuce leaf (or burger bun) and, if desired, top with the optional roasted sesame seeds. Alternatively, store to enjoy later.

Nutritional facts per serving:

Calories 651, Total Fat 24.3g, Saturated Fat 3.5g, Cholesterol 0mg, Sodium 785mg, Total Carbohydrate 86.5g, Dietary Fiber 16.9g, Total Sugars 2.9g, Protein 25.9g, Vitamin D 0mcg, Calcium 363mg, Iron 10mg, Potassium 1344mg

Stuffed Bell Peppers

Prep time 30 minutes / Cook time 27 minutes / Serves 6

Ingredients:

- 1 cup dry black beans
- ½ cup dry chickpeas
- ½ cup dry quinoa
- 3 bell peppers, red or yellow, seeded
- 2 tbsp. olive oil
- 1 sweet onion, chopped
- 2 tbsp. garlic, minced
- 2 tbsp. water
- 1 tbsp. parsley
- ½ cup kale, chopped, fresh or frozen
- ½ tbsp. dried basil
- ¼ teaspoon Salt
- ¼ teaspoon pepper

Instructions:

1. Preheat the oven to 400°F.
2. Slice the bell peppers in half and remove and discard the seeds, stem, and placenta. Place the peppers skin down on a large baking sheet and drizzle with 1 tablespoon of the olive oil, making sure the bell peppers are fully covered.
3. Bake the bell pepper halves for 10 minutes, or until the skins begin to soften.
4. While the peppers are baking, heat up 1 tablespoon of olive oil in a frying pan over medium heat.
5. Add the onion, cook until translucent (around 5 minutes), and stir in the garlic, parsley, basil, kale, and water.

6. Sauté for about 2 minutes and mix in the cooked quinoa, chickpeas, and black beans until warmed through.
7. Season the mixture to taste, stir for few minutes, and remove from heat.
8. Spoon the filling equally into the pepper halves, and place them back into the oven for about 10 minutes.
9. Remove the filled bell peppers from the oven when the peppers are soft and fragrant.
10. Store for later, or, serve right away and enjoy!

Nutritional facts per serving:
Calories 297, Total Fat 7.2g, Saturated Fat 1g, Cholesterol 0mg, Sodium 109mg, Total Carbohydrate 47.2g, Dietary Fiber 10.2g, Total Sugars 6.3g, Protein 13.4g, Vitamin D 0mcg, Calcium 88mg, Iron 4mg, Potassium 888mg

Coconut Tofu Curry

Prep time 30 minutes / Cook time 15 minutes / Serves 2

Ingredients:
- 1 14-oz. block firm tofu
- 2 tsp. coconut oil
- 1 medium sweet onion, diced
- 1 13-oz. can reduced-fat coconut milk
- 1 cup fresh tomatoes, diced
- 1 cup snap peas
- 1½ inch ginger, finely minced
- 1 tsp. curry powder
- 1 tsp. turmeric
- 1 tsp. cumin
- ½ tsp. red pepper flakes
- 1 tsp. agave nectar
- ¼ teaspoon Salt
- ¼ teaspoon pepper to taste

Instructions:
1. Cut the tofu into ½-inch cubes.
2. Heat the coconut oil in a large skillet over medium-high heat.
3. Add the tofu and cook for about 5 minutes.
4. Stir in the garlic and diced onions, and sauté until the onions are transparent (for about 5 to 10 minutes); add the ginger while stirring.
5. Add in the coconut milk, tomatoes, agave nectar, snap peas, and remaining spices.
6. Combine thoroughly, cover, and cook on low heat; remove after 10 minutes of cooking.
7. For serving, scoop the curry into a bowl or over rice.
8. Enjoy right away, or, store the curry in an airtight container to enjoy later!

Nutritional facts per serving:
Calories 751, Total Fat 58g, Saturated Fat 44.8g, Cholesterol 0mg, Sodium 356mg, Total Carbohydrate 44.8g, Dietary Fiber 13.5g, Total Sugars 23.9g, Protein 26.5g, Vitamin D 0mcg, Calcium 490mg, Iron 10mg, Potassium 1359mg

Sweet Potato Sushi

Prep time 90 minutes / Cook time 35 minutes / Serves 3

Ingredients:
- 1 14-oz. package silken tofu, drained
- 3 nori sheets
- 1 large sweet potato, peeled
- 1 medium avocado, pitted, peeled, sliced
- 1 cup water
- ¾ cup dry sushi rice
- 1 tbsp. rice vinegar
- 1 tbsp. agave nectar
- 1 tbsp. amino acids

Instructions:
1. Preheat the oven to 400°F
2. Stir the amino acids (or tamari) and agave nectar together in a small bowl until it is well combined, and then set aside.
3. Cut the sweet potato into large sticks, around ½-inch thick. Place them on a baking sheet lined with parchment and coat them with the tamari/agave mixture.
4. Bake the sweet potatoes in the oven until softened—for about 25 minutes—and make sure to flip them halfway so the sides cook evenly.
5. Meanwhile, bring the sushi rice, water, and vinegar to a boil in a medium-sized pot over

medium heat, and cook until liquid has evaporated, for about 10 minutes.

6. While cooking the rice, cut the block of tofu into long sticks. The sticks should look like long, thin fries. Set aside.
7. Remove the pot from heat and let the rice sit for 10-15 minutes.
8. Cover your work area with a piece of parchment paper, clean your hands, wet your fingers, and lay out a sheet of nori on the parchment paper.
9. Cover the nori sheet with a thin layer of sushi rice, while wetting the hands frequently. Leave sufficient space for rolling up the sheet.
10. Place the roasted sweet potato strips in a straight line across the width of the sheet,

about an inch away from the edge closest to you.

11. Lay out the tofu and avocado slices right beside the potato sticks and use the parchment paper as an aid to roll up the nori sheet into a tight cylinder.
12. Slice the cylinder into 8 equal pieces and refrigerate. Repeat the process for the remaining nori sheets and fillings.
13. Serve chilled, or, store to enjoy this delicious sushi later!

Nutritional facts per serving:
Calories 467, Total Fat 17.1g, Saturated Fat 3.4g, Cholesterol 0mg, Sodium 81mg, Total Carbohydrate 64g, Dietary Fiber 7.6g, Total Sugars 11g, Protein 15.4g, Vitamin D 0mcg, Calcium 78mg, Iron 6mg, Potassium 921mg

Baked Enchilada Bowls

Prep time 60 minutes / Cook time 45 minutes / Serves 4

Ingredients:
- 1 cup dry black beans
- 1 large sweet potato
- 4 tbsp. olive oil
- 2 cups enchilada sauce
- 1 green bell pepper, fresh or a frozen red/green mix
- ½ purple onion, diced
- 1 14-oz. package firm tofu
- ½ cup cashews, chopped
- 1 tsp. cumin
- 1 tsp. paprika
- 1 tsp. garlic powder
- 1 tsp. salt
- ½ cup vegan cheese
- 1 tbsp. chopped jalapeños

Instructions:
1. Preheat oven to 400°F
2. Cut the sweet potatoes into ¼-inch cubes and place them in a bowl with 2 tablespoons of the olive oil, the garlic powder, and ½ teaspoon of salt; toss well and make sure the sweet potatoes get coated evenly.
3. Arrange the sweet potatoes in a single layer on a baking pan. Place the pan in the oven and bake until the potato cubes begin to soften, for 15-20 minutes.

4. Meanwhile, dice up the bell pepper, onion, and tofu into ¼-inch cubes and place all in the previously used bowl with the remaining olive oil, cashews, and ½ teaspoon of salt.
5. Stir the ingredients thoroughly to make sure everything again is coated evenly.
6. After removing the potatoes from the oven, add the tofu, peppers, and onions to the baking pan and stir until combined.
7. Put the baking pan back into the oven for an additional 10 minutes, until the onions are browned and peppers are soft.
8. Remove the pan from the oven and place the contents into a casserole dish.
9. Add the cooked black beans, enchilada sauce, and spices to the casserole dish, mixing everything until it's evenly distributed.
10. Top with a layer of vegan cheese and return to oven until it is melted, around 15 minutes.
11. Serve in a bowl topped with the optional jalapeños if desired, or store for later!

Nutritional facts per serving:
Calories 573, Total Fat 28.4g, Saturated Fat 4.9g, Cholesterol 0mg, Sodium 641mg, Total Carbohydrate 64.4g, Dietary Fiber 16.7g, Total Sugars 7.9g, Protein 25.3g, Vitamin D 0mcg, Calcium 370mg, Iron 13mg, Potassium 1527mg

Red Beans & Rice

Prep time 25 minutes / Cook time 10 minutes / Serves 4

Ingredients:

- 1 cup dry brown rice
- 1½ cups dry red beans
- 2 tbsp. olive oil
- ½ cup sweet onion, chopped
- ½ cup celery ribs, diced
- ½ cup green bell pepper, fresh or frozen, chopped
- 1 large head of cauliflower
- 1 tbsp. garlic, minced
- 2 cups of water
- 2 tsp. cumin
- 1 tsp. paprika
- 1 tsp. chili powder
- ½ tsp. basil
- ½ tsp. parsley flakes
- ½ tsp. black pepper
- ¼ cup parsley
- ¼ cup basil

Instructions:

1. Heat up the olive oil in a large frying pan over medium-high heat.
2. Add the onion, celery, and green pepper and sauté until everything has softened, in about 7 minutes.
3. Place the cauliflower into a food processor. Pulse until it resembles rice, in about a 15 seconds. (Skip this step altogether when using frozen cauliflower rice.)
4. Add the cups of water, rice, beans, and remaining ingredients to the pan.
5. Mix all the ingredients until completely distributed and cook until the cauliflower rice is soft, about 10 minutes.
6. Serve into bowls and, if desired, garnish with the optional parsley and/or basil, or, store to enjoy later!

Nutritional value per serving

Calories 1144, Total Fat 11.6g, Saturated Fat 1.7g, Cholesterol 0mg, Sodium 99mg, Total Carbohydrate 203.7g, Dietary Fiber 45g, Total Sugars 10.4g, Protein 64.3g, Vitamin D 0mcg, Calcium 288mg, Iron 20mg, Potassium 4141mg

Tahini Falafels

Prep time 30 minutes / Cook time 25 minutes / Serves 4

Ingredients:

- 2 cups dry chickpeas
- ½ cup dry black beans
- 2 cups broccoli florets
- 1 garlic clove, minced
- 2 tsp. cumin
- 1 tsp. olive oil
- ½ tsp. lemon juice
- ½ tsp. paprika
- ¼ tsp. turmeric
- ¼ teaspoon salt
- 2 tbsp. tahini

Instructions:

1. Preheat the oven to 400°F
2. Meanwhile, place the broccoli florets in a large skillet and drizzle them with the olive oil and salt.
3. Roast the broccoli over medium-high heat until the florets are tender and brown, for 5 to 10 minutes; set aside and allow to cool a little.
4. Place the cooled broccoli with all the remaining ingredients—except the tahini—into a food processor. Blend on low for 2-3 minutes, until most large lumps are gone.
5. Line a baking pan with parchment paper. Press the falafel dough into 8 equal-sized patties, and place them evenly-spaced apart on the parchment.
6. Bake the falafels until they are brown and crisp on the outside, for roughly 10 to 15 minutes. Make sure to flip them halfway through to ensure even cooking.
7. Serve with tahini as topping, or, let the falafel cool down and store for later.

Nutritional facts per serving:

Calories 523, Total Fat 12g, Saturated Fat 1.5g, Cholesterol 0mg, Sodium 198mg, Total Carbohydrate 81.3g, Dietary Fiber 23.2g, Total Sugars 12.1g, Protein 27.4g, Vitamin D 0mcg, Calcium 200mg, Iron 9mg, Potassium 1442mg

Green Thai Curry

Prep time 30 minutes / Cook time 18 minutes / Serves 4

Ingredients:

- 1 cup white rice
- ½ cup dry chickpeas
- 2 tbsp. olive oil
- 1 14-oz. package firm tofu, drained
- 1 medium green bell pepper
- ½ white onion, diced
- 2 tbsp. green curry paste
- 1 cup reduced-fat coconut milk
- 1 cup water
- 1 cup peas, fresh or frozen
- 1/3 cup chopped fresh Thai basil
- 2 tbsp. maple syrup
- ½ tsp. lime juice
- ¼ teaspoon salt

Instructions:

1. Cut the tofu into ½-inch pieces.
2. Over medium-high heat, heat up the olive oil in a large skillet and fry the tofu about 3 minutes per side.
3. Remove the skillet from the stove and set the tofu aside in a medium-sized bowl with the cooked chickpeas.
4. Using the same skillet over medium-high heat, add the bell pepper and onions and sauté until they are softened, for about 5 minutes.
5. Remove the skillet from the heat, add the green curry paste, water (or vegetable broth), and coconut milk to the skillet.
6. Stir until the curry paste is well incorporated; then add the tofu, chickpeas, and peas to the mixture and cook for 10 more minutes.
7. Drop in the Thai basil, maple syrup, and salt, and bring the mixture back up to a low cooking bubble, stirring constantly for about 3 minutes. Remove from heat.
8. Serve with rice, topped with additional chopped Thai basil, or store for later!

Nutritional facts per serving:

Calories 621, Total Fat 29g, Saturated Fat 14.8g, Cholesterol 0mg, Sodium 482mg, Total Carbohydrate 75.2g, Dietary Fiber 9.7g, Total Sugars 15.5g, Protein 20.1g, Vitamin D 0mcg, Calcium 275mg, Iron 7mg, Potassium 771mg

Cuban Tempeh Buddha Bowl

Prep time 15 minutes / Cook time 15 minutes / Serves 5

Ingredients:

- 1 cup basmati rice
- 1 cup dry black beans
- 1 14-oz. package tempeh, thinly sliced
- 1 cup water
- 2 tsp. chili powder
- 1 tsp. lime juice
- 1¼ tsp. cumin
- 1 pinch of salt
- 1 tsp. turmeric
- 2 tbsp. coconut oil
- 1 medium avocado, pitted, peeled, diced

Instructions:

1. Mix the vegetable broth, chili powder, cumin, turmeric, salt, and lime juice in a large bowl.
2. Add the tempeh and let it marinate in the fridge for up to 3 hours.
3. Heat up a frying pan with the coconut oil on medium-high heat and add the tempeh with the marinating juices.
4. Bring everything to a boil, turn down the heat, and cook over low heat until the broth is gone—10 to 15 minutes.
5. Serve the tempeh in a bowl with a scoop of rice, and top with the cooked black beans and diced avocado.

Nutritional facts per serving:

Calories 559, Total Fat 23.1g, Saturated Fat 8.4g, Cholesterol 0mg, Sodium 35mg, Total Carbohydrate 66.2g, Dietary Fiber 9.7g, Total Sugars 1.2g, Protein 26.9g, Vitamin D 0mcg, Calcium 167mg, Iron 6mg, Potassium 1195mg

Broccoli and Mushroom Stir-Fry

Prep time 30 minutes / Cook time 2 minutes / Serves 4

Ingredients

- 2 cups broccoli, cut into small florets
- ¼ cup red onion, chopped small
- 3 cloves garlic, minced
- 2 cups sliced mushrooms
- ¼ teaspoon red pepper, crushed
- 2 teaspoons grated fresh ginger
- 1 tablespoon olive oil
- ¼ cup water or broth
- ½ cup shredded carrot
- ¼ cup cashews
- 2 tablespoons rice wine vinegar
- 2 tablespoons soy sauce
- 1 tablespoon coconut sugar
- 1 tablespoon sesame seeds

Instructions:

1. Pop a large skillet over a medium heat and add the olive oil.
2. Add the broccoli, onion, garlic, mushrooms, red pepper, ginger and water.
3. Cook until the veggies are soft.
4. Add the carrots, cashews, vinegar, soya and coconut sugar. Stir well and cook for 2 minutes.
5. Sprinkle with sesame seeds then serve and enjoy.

Nutritional facts per serving:
Calories 156, Total Fat 8.9g, Saturated Fat 1.5g, Cholesterol 0mg, Sodium 489mg, Total Carbohydrate 15.8g, Dietary Fiber 2.9g, Total Sugars 6.2g, Protein 5.1g, Vitamin D 126mcg, Calcium 61mg, Iron 3mg, Potassium 421mg

Lentil Vegetable Loaf

Prep time 45 minutes / Cook time 50 minutes / Serves 2

Ingredients

- 2 cups cooked lentils, drained well
- 1 tablespoon olive oil
- 1 small onion, diced
- 1 carrot, finely diced
- 1 stalk celery, diced
- 1 x 8 oz. package white or button mushrooms, cleaned and diced
- 3 tablespoons tomato paste
- 2 tablespoons soy sauce
- 1 tablespoon balsamic vinegar
- 1 cup old-fashioned oats, uncooked
- ½ cup almond meal
- 1 ½ teaspoons dried oregano
- 1/3 cup ketchup
- 1 teaspoon balsamic vinegar
- 1 teaspoon Dijon mustard

Instructions:

1. Preheat your oven to 400°F and grease a 5" x 7" loaf tin then pop to one side.
2. Add the olive oil to a skillet and pop over a medium heat.
3. Add the onion and cook for five minutes until soft.
4. Add the carrots, celery and mushrooms and cook until soft.
5. Grab your food processor and add the lentils, tomato paste, soy sauce, vinegar, oats almond and oregano. Whizz well until combined then transfer to a medium bowl.
6. Pop the vegies into the food processor and pulse until combined. Transfer to the bowl.
7. Stir everything together.
8. Transfer the lentil mixture into the loaf pan, press down and pop into the oven.
9. Cook for 35 minutes, add the topping then bake again for 15 minutes.
10. Remove from the oven, leave to cool for 10 minutes.
11. Serve and enjoy.

Nutritional facts per serving:
Calories 1078, Total Fat 23.3g, Saturated Fat 2.5g, Cholesterol 0mg, Sodium 1448mg, Total Carbohydrate 161g, Dietary Fiber 68.1g, Total Sugars 22.9g, Protein 64.3g, Vitamin D 408mcg, Calcium 242mg, Iron 21mg, Potassium 3003mg

Maple Glazed Tempeh with Quinoa and Kale

Prep time 40 minutes / Cook time 30 minutes / Serves 4

Ingredients

- 1 cup quinoa
- 1 ½ cups vegetable stock
- 8 oz. tempeh, cubed
- 2 tablespoons pure maple syrup
- 3 tablespoons dried cranberries
- 1 tablespoon fresh chopped thyme
- 1 tablespoon fresh chopped rosemary
- 1 tablespoon olive oil
- 1 orange, Juice
- 1 clove garlic, minced
- 4 oz. baby kale, chopped

Instructions:

1. Preheat the oven to 400°F and line a baking sheet with parchment paper.
2. Add the stock to a saucepan and pop over a medium heat. Bring to the boil and add the quinoa.
3. Reduce the heat, cover and simmer for 15 minutes until cooked.
4. Take a medium bowl, add the tempeh and pour the maple syrup and stir well until combined.
5. Place the tempeh onto the baking sheet and pop into the oven for 15 minutes until brown.
6. Meanwhile, grab a large bowl and add the rest of the ingredients. Stir well to combine.
7. Add the quinoa and cooked tempeh, season well with salt and pepper.
8. Serve and enjoy.

Nutritional facts per serving:

Calories 370, Total Fat 12.7g, Saturated Fat 2.2g, Cholesterol 0mg, Sodium 46mg, Total Carbohydrate 49.8g, Dietary Fiber 5.8g, Total Sugars 10.8g, Protein 18.3g, Vitamin D 0mcg, Calcium 167mg, Iron 5mg, Potassium 602mg

Slow Cooker Chili

Prep time 30 minutes / Cook time 9 hours / Serves 6

Ingredients

- 3 cups dry pinto beans
- 1 large onion, chopped
- 3 bell peppers, chopped
- 8 large green jalapeño peppers
- 2 x 14.5 oz. cans of diced tomatoes
- 1 tablespoon chili powder
- 2 tablespoons oregano flakes
- 1 tablespoon cumin powder
- 1 tablespoon garlic powder
- 3 bay leaves, freshly ground
- 1 teaspoon ground black pepper
- 1 tablespoon sea salt

Instructions:

1. Place the beans into a large pan, cover with water and leave to soak overnight.
2. The next morning, drain and transfer to a 6-quart slow cooker.
3. Cover with the salt and two inches of water. Cook on high for 6 hours until soft.
4. Drain the beans and add the other ingredients. Stir well to combine.
5. Cover and cook for another 3 hours on high.
6. Serve and enjoy.

Nutritional facts per serving:

Calories 210, Total Fat 1.2g, Saturated Fat 0.2g, Cholesterol 0mg, Sodium 679mg, Total Carbohydrate 38.7g, Dietary Fiber 10.4g, Total Sugars 5.8g, Protein 11.8g, Vitamin D 0mcg, Calcium 87mg, Iron 4mg, Potassium 953mg

Ground Beef with Marinara Tomato Sauce

Prep time 40 minutes / Cook time 30 minutes / Serves 10

Ingredients

- 1 cup quinoa, rinsed
- 2 cups vegetable broth
- ½ teaspoon black pepper
- ½ teaspoon salt,
- 1 cup finely diced raw walnuts
- 3 tablespoons tomato paste
- 1 tablespoon nutritional yeast
- ½ cup salsa

- ¼ teaspoon garlic powder
- 2 teaspoons chili powder
- 2 teaspoons cumin
- ½ cup vegan marinara sauce
- ¼ teaspoon garlic powder
- 2 teaspoons dried oregano

Instructions:

1. Take a medium pan and add the quinoa, broth, salt and pepper.
2. Cover and bring to the boil.
3. Reduce the heat and cook for 15 minutes until fluffy.
4. Cover with the lid and leave to rest for 5 minutes.
5. Preheat the oven to 400°F and line a baking sheet with parchment paper.
6. Take the lid off the quinoa then add the remaining ingredients. Stir to combine.
7. Spread the quinoa onto a baking sheet and bake for 15 minutes.
8. Remove from the oven then serve and enjoy.

Nutritional facts per serving:
Calories 166, Total Fat 9.1g, Saturated Fat 0.7g, Cholesterol 0mg, Sodium 370mg, Total Carbohydrate 15.7g, Dietary Fiber 3.1g, Total Sugars 1.6g, Protein 7.5g, Vitamin D 0mcg, Calcium 35mg, Iron 2mg, Potassium 339mg

Spicy Grilled Tofu with Szechuan Vegetables

Prep time 15 minutes / Cook time 3 minutes / Serves 4

Ingredients:

- 1 lb. firm tofu, frozen and thawed
- 3 tablespoons soy sauce
- 2 tablespoons toasted sesame oil
- 2 tablespoons apple cider vinegar
- 1 clove garlic, minced
- 1 teaspoon freshly grated ginger
- ¼ teaspoon red pepper flakes
- 1 tablespoon toasted sesame oil
- 1 lb. fresh green beans, trimmed
- 1 red bell pepper, sliced
- 1 small red onion, sliced
- 1 teaspoon soy sauce
- 1 teaspoon corn starch

Instructions:

1. Start by cutting the tofu into ½" slices then place into a shallow baking dish.
2. Take as small bowl and add the marinade ingredients. Stir well then pour over the tofu.
3. Pop into the fridge for at least 30 minutes (or overnight if you can).
4. Preheat the broiler to medium then grill the tofu until firm.
5. Fill a pot with water and pop over a medium heat.
6. Bring to the boil then add the beans.
7. Blanche for 2 minutes then drain and rinse.
8. Take a small bowl and add the corn starch and a teaspoon of cold water.
9. Place a skillet over a medium heat, add the oil then add the beans, red peppers and onions. Stir well.
10. Add the soy sauce and cook for another minute.
11. Add the cornstarch mixture and stir again.
12. Serve the vegies and the tofu together.
13. Enjoy!

Nutritional value per serving
Calories 236, Total Fat 15.2g, Saturated Fat 2.5g, Cholesterol 0mg, Sodium 812mg, Total Carbohydrate 16.4g, Dietary Fiber 5.9g, Total Sugars 4.8g, Protein 12.8g, Vitamin D 0mcg, Calcium 282mg, Iron 4mg, Potassium 534mg

Quinoa Lentil Burger

Prep time 30 minutes / Cook time 15 minutes / Serves 4

Ingredients

- 1½ tablespoon olive oil
- ¼ cup diced red onion
- 1 cup cooked quinoa
- 1 cup cooked brown lentils, drained
- 1 x 4 oz. can dice green chilies
- 1/3 cup rolled oats
- ¼ cup all-purpose flour
- 2 teaspoons cornstarch
- ¼ cup whole wheat panko breadcrumbs
- ¼ teaspoon garlic powder

- ½ teaspoon cumin
- 1 teaspoon paprika
- ¼ tsp Salt
- ¼ tsp pepper
- 2 tablespoons Dijon mustard
- 3 teaspoons honey

Instructions:
1. Place a skillet over a medium heat and add 2 teaspoons olive oil.
2. Add the onion and cook for five minutes until soft.
3. Grab a small bowl and add the honey and Dijon mustard.
4. Grab a large bowl and add the burger ingredients. Stir well.
5. Form into 4 patties with your hands.
6. Place a large skillet over a medium heat and add a tablespoon of oil.
7. Add the patties and cook for 10 minutes on each side.
8. Serve with the honey mustard and enjoy!

Nutritional facts per serving:
Calories 580, Total Fat 24.7g, Saturated Fat 3.4g, Cholesterol 0mg, Sodium 267mg, Total Carbohydrate 78g, Dietary Fiber 15.1g, Total Sugars 16.5g, Protein 17g, Vitamin D 0mcg, Calcium 48mg, Iron 5mg, Potassium 847mg

Vegan Mac and Cheese

Prep time 40 minutes / Cook time 14 minutes / Serves 4

Ingredients
- 2 cups whole-grain macaroni elbows, cooked
- 1 ½ to 2 cups broccoli, lightly cooked
- 1 ½ tablespoons extra-virgin olive oil
- 1 small yellow onion, chopped
- 1 medium potato, peeled and grated
- 3 cloves garlic, pressed or minced
- ½ teaspoon garlic powder
- ½ teaspoon onion powder
- ½ teaspoon dry mustard powder
- ½ teaspoon fine sea salt
- Pinch red pepper flakes
- 2/3 cup raw cashews
- 1 cup water, or as needed
- ¼ cup nutritional yeast
- 2 teaspoons apple cider vinegar

Instructions:
1. Place the cooked pasta and broccoli into a large bowl.
2. Pop a large saucepan over a medium heat and add the oil.
3. Add the onion and cook for 5 minutes until soft.
4. Add a pinch of salt, the potato, garlic, garlic powder, onion, onion powder, mustard powder and red pepper flakes. Stir well then leave to cook for another minute.
5. Add the cashews and water and stir. Simmer for 5-8 minutes until the potatoes have cooked.
6. Pour into a blender, add the nutritional yeast and vinegar and whizz until smooth.
7. Add the water slowly until the sauce reaches your desired consistency.
8. Pour over the pasta and broccoli, stir well then enjoy.

Nutritional facts per serving:
Calories 363, Total Fat 17.3g, Saturated Fat 2.9g, Cholesterol 0mg, Sodium 265mg, Total Carbohydrate 44g, Dietary Fiber 7.1g, Total Sugars 4.4g, Protein 14g, Vitamin D 0mcg, Calcium 59mg, Iron 5mg, Potassium 786mg

Sugar Snap Pea and Carrot Soba Noodles

Prep time 30 minutes / Cook time 5 minutes / Serves 6

Ingredients
- 6 oz. soba noodles
- 2 cups frozen edamame, roughly chopped
- 10 oz. sugar snap peas or snow peas
- 6 medium-sized carrots, peeled and sliced lengthways
- ½ cup chopped fresh cilantro
- ¼ cup sesame seeds
- ¼ cup soy sauce
- 2 tablespoons quality peanut oil
- 1 small lime, juiced
- 1 tablespoon toasted sesame oil
- 1 tablespoon honey or agave nectar

- 1 tablespoon white miso
- 2 teaspoons freshly grated ginger
- 1 oz chili garlic sauce or sriracha

Instructions:
1. Take a medium bowl and add the sauce ingredients. Stir well together.
2. Bring two pans of water to boil.
3. Pop a small pan over a medium heat and add the sesame seeds. Toast for 5 minutes then remove from the heat.
4. Place the noodles into one of the pots of boiling water and the edamame into the other.
5. Cook through then drain.
6. Pop the noodles, edamame, snap peas and carrots into a large bowl.
7. Cover with the dressing and toss.
8. Add the cilantro and sesame seeds.
9. Serve and enjoy.

Nutritional facts per serving:
Calories 305, Total Fat 11.9g, Saturated Fat 1.8g, Cholesterol 0mg, Sodium 1041mg, Total Carbohydrate 42.2g, Dietary Fiber 5.5g, Total Sugars 9.5g, Protein 12.4g, Vitamin D 0mcg, Calcium 152mg, Iron 4mg, Potassium 578mg

Sweet Potato & Black Bean Veggie Burgers

Prep time 1 hour 20 minutes / Cook time 45 minutes / Serves 8

Ingredients
- 1 ½ lb. sweet potatoes, sliced lengthways
- 1 cup cooked quinoa
- 1 cup old fashioned oats
- 1 x 15 oz. can black beans, rinsed and drained
- ½ small red onion, diced
- ½ cup fresh cilantro leaves, chopped
- 2 teaspoons cumin powder
- 1 teaspoon chili powder
- 1 teaspoon chipotle powder
- ½ teaspoon cayenne powder
- ½ teaspoon salt
- 1 tablespoon olive oil
- 2 tablespoons Olive oil, to cook burgers
- 8 whole wheat hamburger buns

Toppings
- avocado, tomato, Pico de Gallo, lettuce, sprouts, ketchup, mustard, pickles, cheese, etc.

Instructions:
1. Preheat the oven to 400°F and grease a baking sheet.
2. Place the sweet potatoes on top then cook for 30-40 minutes until soft.
3. Leave to cool then remove the skin and chop the insides.
4. Take a food processor and grind the oats.
5. Grab a large bowl and add the sweet potatoes, quinoa, black beans, onion, cilantro, cumin, chili, chipotle, cayenne and salt.
6. Mash well together then add the oats. Stir through.
7. Form into burgers with your hands.
8. Place the olive oil into a skillet and place over a medium heat.
9. Cook the burgers for about 5 minutes on each side until browned.
10. Toast the buns then add the burgers.
11. Serve and enjoy.

Nutritional facts per serving:
Calories 486, Total Fat 13.8g, Saturated Fat 2.1g, Cholesterol 3mg, Sodium 551mg, Total Carbohydrate 79.6g, Dietary Fiber 12.4g, Total Sugars 4.8g, Protein 13g, Vitamin D 0mcg, Calcium 106mg, Iron 5mg, Potassium 1224mg

Spanish Vegetable Paella

Prep time 1 hour 15 minutes / Cook time 1 hour / Serves 6

Ingredients
- 3 tablespoons divided extra-virgin olive oil
- 1 medium chopped fine yellow onion
- 1 ½ teaspoons fine sea salt, divided
- 6 garlic cloves, pressed or minced
- 2 teaspoons smoked paprika
- 1 x 15 oz. can dice tomatoes, drained
- 2 cups short-grain brown rice
- 1 x 15 oz. can garbanzo beans, rinsed and drained
- 3 cups vegetable broth
- 1/3 cup vegetable broth
- ½ teaspoon saffron threads, crumbled

- 1 x 14 oz. can quartered artichokes
- 2 red bell peppers, sliced into long, ½"-wide strips
- ½ cup Kalamata olives, pitted and halved
- Freshly ground black pepper
- ¼ cup chopped fresh parsley
- 2 tablespoons lemon juice
- ½ cup frozen peas

Instructions:

1. Preheat the oven to 350°F.
2. Place 2 tablespoons oil into a skillet and pop over a medium heat
3. Add the onion and cook for five minutes until soft.
4. Add a pinch of salt, the garlic and the paprika. Cook for 30 seconds.
5. Add the tomatoes, stir through and cook for 2 minutes.
6. Add the rice, stir through and cook again for a minute.
7. Add the garbanzo beans, broth, wine or stock, saffron and salt.
8. Increase the heat to high and bring to a boil.
9. Cover and pop into the oven for 50 minutes until the rice has been absorbed.
10. Line a baking sheet with parchment paper.
11. Grab a large bowl and add the artichoke, peppers, olives, 1 tablespoon olive oil, ½ teaspoon of salt and black pepper, to taste. Toss to combine then spread over the prepared baking sheet.
12. Pop into the oven and cook for 40 minutes.
13. Remove from the oven and leave to cook slightly.
14. Add the parsley, lemon juice and seasoning as required. Toss.
15. Pop the rice onto a stove, turn up the heat and bake the rice for five minutes.
16. Garnish and serve with the veggies.
17. Enjoy!

Nutritional facts per serving:
Calories 501, Total Fat 14.2g, Saturated Fat 1.9g, Cholesterol 0mg, Sodium 1236mg, Total Carbohydrate 76.5g, Dietary Fiber 20.6g, Total Sugars 14.7g, Protein 22.3g, Vitamin D 0mcg, Calcium 152mg, Iron 7mg, Potassium 1147mg

Veggie Pasta

Prep time 15 minutes / Cook time 15 minutes / Serves 8

Ingredients:

- 5 oz pasta
- 2 tablespoons olive oil
- 3 cubed tomatoes
- ½ cup chopped basil
- 6 oz drained and chopped broccoli
- 1 tablespoon vinegar
- 2 tablespoons chopped chives
- 1 tablespoons baby capers

Instructions:

1. Cook the pasta according to the given instructions on the package.
2. In a bowl add olive oil, vinegar, tomatoes, and capers and mix all the ingredients well.
3. Add the cooked pasta in it and toss it and leave it for around 5 minutes.
4. Now put all the remaining ingredients in it and whisk them well. It is ready to serve.

Nutritional facts per serving:
Calories 96, Total Fat 4.1g, Saturated Fat 0.6g, Cholesterol 13mg, Sodium 49mg, Total Carbohydrate 12.5g, Dietary Fiber 1g, Total Sugars 0.4g, Protein 3.2g, Vitamin D 0mcg, Calcium 18mg, Iron 1mg, Potassium 195mg

Roasted Sweet Potatoes and Rice with Spicy Thai Peanut Sauce

Prep time 50 minutes / Cook time 1 hour 25 minutes / Serves 4

Ingredients

- ½ cup creamy peanut butter
- ¼ cup reduced-sodium tamari or soy sauce
- 3 tablespoons apple cider vinegar
- 2 tablespoons honey or maple syrup
- 1 teaspoon grated fresh ginger
- 2 cloves garlic, pressed
- ¼ teaspoon red pepper flakes
- 2 tablespoons water

For the roasted vegetables…

- 2 sweet potatoes, peeled and sliced into ½" chunks
- 1 red bell pepper, sliced

- 2 tablespoons olive oil
- ¼ teaspoon cumin powder
- ¼ tsp Sea salt

For the rice and garnishes…
- 1 ¼ cup jasmine brown rice
- 2 green onions/chives
- ½ cup cilantro, torn
- ½ cup peanuts, crushed
- 2 tbsp Chili sauce

Instructions:
1. Place a large pot of water over a medium heat and bring to the boil
2. Preheat the oven to 425°F.
3. Find a large bowl and add the sweet potato with a tablespoon of the oil, the cumin and salt. Stir well.
4. Transfer to a baking sheet then pop into the oven for 35 mins.
5. Find a smaller bowl and add the bell pepper and the remaining coconut oil and salt.
6. Place onto a smaller baking sheet then place into the oven for 20 minutes.
7. Meanwhile, add the rice to the boiling water, cover with the lid then cook for 30 minutes until tender.
8. Drain the rice then return to the pot and cover with the lid. Leave to sit for 10 minutes.
9. Remove the lid and fluff with a fork.
10. Take a small bowl and add the sauce ingredients. Whisk well.
11. Grab your bowls and add the rice and roasted veggies.
12. Drizzle with the sauce and top with the onion, cilantro and peanuts.
13. Enjoy.

Nutritional facts per serving:
Calories 663, Total Fat 34.1g, Saturated Fat 6g, Cholesterol 0mg, Sodium 1483mg, Total Carbohydrate 76.5g, Dietary Fiber 7.5g, Total Sugars 16.3g, Protein 20.3g, Vitamin D 0mcg, Calcium 62mg, Iron 6mg, Potassium 663mg

Summer Garlic Scape And Zucchini Pasta

Prep time 10 minutes / Cook time 10 minutes / Serves 4

Ingredients:
- 4 zucchinis
- 1 8oz. small pack cooked pasta
- ½ thin sliced purple cabbage
- 1 tablespoon olive oil
- 10 minced garlic cloves
- 1 tablespoon lemon juice
- 1 cup lemon thyme
- 2 tablespoons chopped almonds
- ½ teaspoon salt
- ¼ tsp ground black pepper

Instructions:

1. Preheat the oven at 450F temperature and bake zucchini for around 8 minutes.
2. Take a large bowl, add baked zucchini, cabbage, and pasta in it, and whisk well.
3. Now add all the remaining items in it and mix it and it is ready to serve.

Nutritional facts per serving:
Calories 320, Total Fat 10.3g, Saturated Fat 1.3g, Cholesterol 41mg, Sodium 405mg, Total Carbohydrate 49g, Dietary Fiber 6.3g, Total Sugars 8.1g, Protein 11.9g, Vitamin D 0mcg, Calcium 106mg, Iron 4mg, Potassium 866mg

Chickpea Mushroom Pita Burgers

Prep time 10 minutes / Cook time 30 minutes / Serves 6

Ingredients:

Burgers:
- 6 pita breads
- 1 ½ cups cooked basmati rice
- 1 14-ounce can chickpeas
- 1 onion, chopped
- 4 cloves garlic, chopped
- 8 ounces mushrooms, chopped
- 2 tbsp soy sauce
- 1 ¼ cup chickpea flour

Spices:
- 1 tbsp coconut sugar
- ¼ cup nutritional yeast
- ½ tsp smoked paprika powder
- ½ tsp black pepper powder
- ½ tsp cumin powder
- ½ tsp coriander powder
- ¼ tsp allspice powder

Sauce:
- 2 tbsp vegan mayonnaise

- 1 tsp mustard
- 1 tsp gochujang
- Pinch of coconut sugar

Instructions:
1. Cook the rice and sauté onion and garlic. Add mushrooms and salt until tender.
2. Drain chickpeas and add everything apart from chickpea flour to a food processor. Pulse until combined but not mushy.
3. Add this mixture to a bowl and add chickpea flour until everything is combined.
4. Form into patties.
5. Pan-fry the patties or bake them in an oven. Once done, assemble into the pita.
6. For the sauce, whisk everything together. Serve with the patties.

Nutrition Facts Per Serving:
Calories 685, Total Fat 7.4g, Saturated Fat 0.8g, Cholesterol 6mg, Sodium 982mg, Total Carbohydrate 128.1g, Dietary Fiber 15.4g, Total Sugars 11.2g, Protein 27.9g, Vitamin D 136mcg, Calcium 166mg, Iron 9mg, Potassium 945mg

Sun-Dried Tomato Pesto Pasta

Prep time 15 minutes / Cook time 15 minutes / Serves 5

Ingredients:
- 1 cup fresh basil leaves
- 6 ounce sun-dried tomatoes
- 1 tablespoon lemon juice
- ½ teaspoon salt
- ¼ cup olive oil
- ¼ cup almonds
- 3 minced garlic cloves
- ½ teaspoon chopped red pepper flakes
- 8 ounces pasta

Instructions:
1. Cook the pasta according to the given instructions. For making, the pesto toasts the almonds over medium flame in a small skillet for around 4 minutes.
2. In a blender put sun-dried tomatoes, basil, garlic, lemon juice, salt, red pepper flakes, and toasted almonds and blend it. While blending adds olive oil in it and blend, it until it converts in the form of a pesto.
3. Now coat the pasta with the pesto and serve it.

Nutritional facts per serving:
Calories 256, Total Fat 13.7g, Saturated Fat 1.8g, Cholesterol 33mg, Sodium 247mg, Total Carbohydrate 28.1g, Dietary Fiber 1.2g, Total Sugars 1.2g, Protein 6.7g, Vitamin D 0mcg, Calcium 35mg, Iron 2mg, Potassium 225mg

Indian Mashed Potatoes

Prep time 10 minutes / Cook time 30 minutes / Serves 2

Ingredients:
- 2 pounds red potatoes
- 1 13-ounce can coconut milk
- 1/3 cup tomato sauce
- 2 tbsp olive oil
- 1 slice onion, chopped
- 1 tsp cumin seeds
- 1 tsp mustard seeds
- 1 tbsp coriander powder
- 1 tsp fenugreek powder
- 1 tsp turmeric powder
- ¼ tsp Salt
- ½ cup Frozen peas for garnish

Instructions:
1. Peel, chop, boil, and drain potatoes.
2. Sauté onion with salt.
3. Add cumin, mustard seeds, coriander powder, and turmeric. Mix well and take off from the heat.
4. Mash potatoes and add the spiced oil to them. Add salt to taste.
5. In a small pot, add a can of coconut milk and 1/3 cup tomato sauce. Mix 1 tsp each of turmeric, fenugreek, and coriander powder. Add salt and pepper to taste.
6. Pour curry gravy on potatoes and serve topped with green peas.

Nutrition Facts Per Serving:
Calories 643, Total Fat 26.4g, Saturated Fat 11.5g, Cholesterol 0mg, Sodium 578mg, Total Carbohydrate 89.3g, Dietary Fiber 11.2g, Total Sugars 11.6g , Protein 17g, Vitamin D 0mcg, Calcium 82mg, Iron 8mg, Potassium 2310mg

Chickpeas and Spinach Andalusian Style

Prep time 10 minutes / Cook time 15 minutes / Serves 4

Ingredients:

- 1 ¾ cup fresh spinach
- 14-ounce can chickpeas
- 1 tbsp cumin seeds
- 1 tbsp smoked paprika
- Pinch fresh cayenne pepper
- 2 slices bread
- 3 cloves garlic, thinly sliced
- 1 tbsp Sherry vinegar
- 1 tbsp salt
- 1 tbsp ground black pepper
- 6 tbsp extra virgin olive oil

Instructions:

1. Wash spinach and cook in boiling water for 3 minutes. Drain and set aside.
2. In a hot pan, heat olive oil and fry garlic until brown and crunchy. Set aside.
3. Using a mortar and pestle, grind together cumin seeds, salt, pepper, cayenne, bread, and garlic.
4. Add Sherry vinegar to the paste and a bit of water from the canned chickpeas.
5. Using the same saucepan, sauté spinach before adding the rest of previous ingredients.
6. Stir until cooked.

Nutrition Facts Per Serving:
Calories 576, Total Fat 27.8g, Saturated Fat 3.7g, Cholesterol 0mg, Sodium 1813mg, Total Carbohydrate 66.4g, Dietary Fiber 19g, Total Sugars 11.1g, Protein 20.7g, Vitamin D 0mcg, Calcium 153mg, Iron 9mg, Potassium 1045mg

Vegan Lasagna

Prep time 10 minutes / Cook time 60 minutes / Serves 4

Ingredients:

For sauce:

- 1 tablespoon vegetable oil
- 1 ½ tablespoons minced garlic
- ¾ cup chopped onions
- 2 cans (14.5 ounces each) stewed tomatoes
- ¼ cup fresh basil
- ¼ cup fresh parsley
- ¼ tsp Pepper
- ¼ tsp Salt
- 3 tablespoons tomato paste

For lasagna:

- 8 ounces lasagna sheets, cooked according to the instructions on the package
- 1 tablespoon minced garlic
- 1-pound firm tofu, crumbled
- 1 ½ packages (10 ounces each) frozen spinach, thawed, squeezed of excess moisture
- ¼ tsp ground pepper to taste
- 2 tablespoons chopped parsley
- 2 tablespoon chopped fresh basil
- ½ teaspoon Italian seasoning

Instructions:

1. Place a skillet over medium heat. Add oil. When the oil is heated, add onions and sauté until translucent. Stir in the garlic and cook for another 3-4 minutes.
2. Add rest of the ingredients for sauce and stir. Lower the heat and cover with a lid. Cook for about 45 minutes. Stir occasionally. Turn off the heat.
3. For lasagna: To the crumbled tofu, add garlic, salt, pepper and fresh herbs. Mash well.
4. To assemble: Take a square or rectangular baking dish of about 8 inches. Spread about ½ cup sauce on the bottom of the dish.
5. Place a layer of lasagna noodles. Spread 1/3 the tofu mixture over it.
6. Your next layer should be of spinach.
7. Spread 10-12 tablespoons of the sauce.
8. Repeat step 5 and 7 twice. Your topmost layer will be of sauce.
9. Cover the dish with foil.
10. Bake in a preheated oven at 400° F for 25-30 minutes.

Nutrition Facts Per Serving:
Calories 542, Total Fat 11.3g, Saturated Fat 1.8g, Cholesterol 40mg, Sodium 272mg, Total Carbohydrate 86.4g, Dietary Fiber 7.2g, Total Sugars 9.1g, Protein 29.5g, Vitamin D 0mcg, Calcium 384mg, Iron 6mg, Potassium 1460mg

Zucchini Gratin

Prep time 10 minutes / Cook time 20 minutes / Serves 3

Ingredients:

Gratin:
- 6 medium zucchinis, thinly sliced
- 1 cup water
- ¾ cup raw cashews
- 2 tbsp apple cider vinegar
- 2 tbsp nutritional yeast
- 1 tsp garlic powder
- ½ tsp onion powder
- ¼ tsp black pepper
- ½ tsp Salt

Toppings:
- 1 tbsp sesame seeds
- 1 tsp thyme

Instructions:
1. Preheat oven to 400F.
2. Blend all ingredients, except zucchini and the toppings, until smooth to form a batter.
3. In a bowl, coat the zucchini slices in the batter.
4. Arrange the zucchinis in a baking pan or cast-iron skillet. Pour remaining batter over the zucchinis.
5. Bake for 20 minutes in the oven.
6. Add toppings and serve.

Nutrition Facts Per Serving:
Calories 308, Total Fat 18.5g, Saturated Fat 3.6g, Cholesterol 0mg, Sodium 246mg, Total Carbohydrate 29.5g, Dietary Fiber 7.7g, Total Sugars 8.9g, Protein 13.8g, Vitamin D 0mcg, Calcium 121mg, Iron 6mg, Potassium 1422mg

Carrot Cashew Pate

Prep time 10 minutes / Cook time 0 minutes / Serves 4

Ingredients:
- 2 cups carrots, chopped into large pieces
- 1 cup cashews, soaked in water for an hour
- ¼ cup tahini
- ¼ cup lemon juice
- 1 tbsp peeled and grated ginger
- ½ cilantro, stems and leaves
- ½ tsp salt

Instructions:
1. Place carrots in a food processor and blend until there are no big chunks.
2. Drain cashews and add into the processor with tahini, lemon juice, ginger, cilantro, and salt.
3. Process until completely smooth. Add salt to taste.
4. Serve.

Nutrition Facts Per Serving:
Calories 318, Total Fat 24.2g, Saturated Fat 4.4g, Cholesterol 0mg, Sodium 357mg, Total Carbohydrate 21.3g, Dietary Fiber 4.2g, Total Sugars 4.9g, Protein 8.6g, Vitamin D 0mcg, Calcium 104mg, Iron 4mg, Potassium 495mg '

Taco Elbow Pasta

Prep time 10 minutes / Cook time 0 minutes / Serves 2

Ingredients:
- 1 ½ cups dry elbow pasta
- ½ can (from 15 ounces can) black beans, drained, rinsed
- 2 tomatoes, diced
- ½ Avocado slices to serve
- 1 ½ cups vegetable stock
- 1 bell pepper, diced
- 1 teaspoon taco seasoning or to taste
- 3 cups Water, as required

Instructions:
1. Add all the ingredients into a pot. Place the pot over medium heat. Add water only if required. Cook until pasta is al dente.
2. Divide into bowls. Place avocado slices on top if using and serve.

Nutrition Facts Per Serving:
Calories 806, Total Fat 13.3g, Saturated Fat 2.5g, Cholesterol 0mg, Sodium 289mg, Total Carbohydrate 144.1g, Dietary Fiber 29.7g, Total Sugars 11.3g, Protein 36.4g, Vitamin D 0mcg, Calcium 165mg, Iron 9mg, Potassium 2227mg

Cauliflower Steak with Sweet-pea Puree

Prep time 10 minutes / Cook time 30 minutes / Serves 2

Ingredients:

Cauliflower:
- 2 heads of cauliflower
- 1 tsp olive oil
- ¼ tsp Paprika
- 1 tsp Coriander
- ¼ tsp Black pepper

Sweet-pea puree:
- 1 10-ounce bag frozen green peas
- 1 small onion, chopped
- 2 tbsp fresh parsley
- ¼ cup unsweetened soy milk

Instructions:
1. Preheat oven to 425F.
2. Remove bottom core of cauliflower. Stand it on its base, starting in the middle, slice in half. Then slice steaks about ¾ inches thick.
3. Place steaks on baking pan.
4. Lightly coat the front and back of each steak with olive oil.
5. Sprinkle with coriander, paprika, and pepper.
6. Bake for 30 minutes, flipping once.
7. Meanwhile, steam the chopped onion and peas until soft.
8. Place these vegetables in a blender with milk and parsley and blend until smooth.

Nutrition Facts Per Serving:
Calories 234, Total Fat 3.8g, Saturated Fat 0.6g, Cholesterol 0mg, Sodium 106mg, Total Carbohydrate 40.3g, Dietary Fiber 15.1g, Total Sugars 17.2g, Protein 14.5g, Vitamin D 0mcg, Calcium 116mg, Iron 4mg, Potassium 1267mg

Creamy Cashew Alfredo

Prep time 8 minutes / Cook time 20 minutes / Serves 3

Ingredients:

For vegan Alfredo:
- ½ cup + 2 tablespoons raw cashews, soaked in hot water for 20 minutes, drained
- 2 tablespoons nutritional yeast
- Salt to taste
- ½ cup plain almond or rice milk or more if needed
- 1 ½ teaspoons arrowroot starch
- 1 clove garlic, crushed
- 1 tablespoon vegan Parmesan cheese

To assemble:
- 5 ounces fettuccini pasta, cooked
- Vegan Parmesan cheese, grated
- ½ cup Roasted tomatoes to serve

Instructions:
1. To make vegan Alfredo sauce: Add cashew, arrowroot, garlic, nutritional yeast, salt, nondairy milk and Parmesan into a blender and blend until smooth.
2. Taste and adjust garlic, nutritional yeast or vegan Parmesan and salt if required.
3. Pour into a saucepan. Place the saucepan over medium heat. Stir constantly until thick.
4. Add pasta and stir. Heat thoroughly.
5. Garnish with vegan Parmesan cheese and serve.
6. Serve with roasted tomatoes.

Nutritional values per:
Calories 439, Total Fat 28.1g, Saturated Fat 4.1g, Cholesterol 8mg, Sodium 968mg, Total Carbohydrate 39.3g, Dietary Fiber 4.9g, Total Sugars 3g, Protein 11.3g, Vitamin D 0mcg, Calcium 37mg, Iron 3mg, Potassium 326mg

Zucchini Pasta

Prep time 10 minutes / Cook time 3 minutes / Serves 2

Ingredients:
- 1-pound large zucchinis, trimmed
- 1 medium onion, chopped
- ½ pint cherry tomatoes, halved
- 2 tablespoons extra virgin olive oil
- 2 tbsp Zest of a lemon, grated
- ¼ cup basil leaves, finely sliced
- ¼ tsp pepper
- ¼ tsp Salt

- 2 cloves garlic, minced
- 1 tbsp lemon juice
- ½ cup grated vegan Parmesan cheese

Instructions:
1. Make noodles of the zucchini using a spiralizer or a julienne peeler.
2. Place a skillet. Add oil. When the oil is heated, add garlic and onion and sauté until translucent.
3. Add zucchini and tomatoes and mix well. Cook for 2-3 minutes.
4. Add Parmesan, red pepper and basil.
5. Stir and serve.

Nutrition Facts Per Serving:
Calories 288, Total Fat 19.8g, Saturated Fat 2.7g, Cholesterol 0mg, Sodium 442mg, Total Carbohydrate 25.6g, Dietary Fiber 7g, Total Sugars 12.5g , Protein 6.5g, Vitamin D 0mcg, Calcium 108mg, Iron 1mg, Potassium 922mg

Spicy Peanut Soba Noodles

Prep time 7 minutes / Cook time 17 minutes / Serves 3

Ingredients:
- 5 ounces uncooked soba noodles
- ½ tablespoon low sodium soy sauce
- 1 clove garlic, minced
- 4 teaspoons water
- 1 small head broccoli, cut into florets
- ½ cup carrot
- ¼ cup finely chopped scallions
- 3 tablespoons peanut butter
- 1 tablespoon honey
- 1 teaspoon crushed red pepper flakes
- 2 teaspoons vegetable oil
- 4 ounces button mushrooms, discard stems
- 3 tablespoons peanuts, dry roasted, unsalted

Instructions:
1. Cook soba noodles following the directions on the package.
2. Add peanut butter, honey, water, soy sauce, garlic and red pepper flakes. Whisk until well combined.
3. Place a skillet over medium heat. Add oil. When the oil is heated, add broccoli and sauté for a few minutes until crisp as well as tender.
4. Add mushrooms and sauté until the mushrooms are tender. Turn off the heat.
5. Add the sauce mixture and carrots and mix well.
6. Crush the peanuts by rolling with a rolling pin.
7. Divide the noodles into bowls. Pour sauce mixture over it. Sprinkle scallions and peanuts on top and serve.

Nutrition Facts Per Serving:
Calories 376, Total Fat 16.2g, Saturated Fat 3g, Cholesterol 0mg, Sodium 566mg, Total Carbohydrate 50.3g, Dietary Fiber 3g, Total Sugars 9.5g, Protein 15g, Vitamin D 136mcg, Calcium 41mg, Iron 5mg, Potassium 515mg

Barbeque Bean Tacos with Tropical Salsa

Prep time 9 minutes / Cook time 20 minutes / Serves 3

Ingredients:
- 2 15-ounce cans pinto beans
- 1 tablespoon maple syrup
- 2 tablespoons prepared Dijon mustard
- ¾ cup ketchup
- ½ teaspoon chili powder
- ½ teaspoon garlic powder
- ¾ teaspoon sea salt, divided
- 1 20-ounce can pineapple chunks, packed in juice
- ¼ cup cilantro, finely chopped
- ¼ cup red onion, minced
- 3 radishes, stemmed and thinly sliced
- 1 small green cabbage, cored and thinly sliced
- 1 lime, cut into wedges
- 4 corn tortillas

Instructions:
1. Drain and rinse the beans and pour into a heavy skillet.
2. Add the maple syrup, mustard, ketchup, chili powder, garlic powder and a half teaspoon of salt. Heat on low, stirring frequently, until the mixture heats through and thickens.

3. Meanwhile, drain and chop the pineapple chunks and put them in a bowl.
4. Add the cilantro, onion and the remaining salt and stir together.
5. Take a tortilla and place a fourth of the bean mixture on the side. Sprinkle with the radish and cabbage mixture and top with the pineapple mixture. Garnish the tops with more cilantro. Serve with lime wedges.

Nutrition Facts Per Serving:
Calories 1307, Total Fat 6.2g, Saturated Fat 1g, Cholesterol 0mg, Sodium 1498mg, Total Carbohydrate 253.8g, Dietary Fiber 55.9g, Total Sugars 51.1g, Protein 68.9g, Vitamin D 0mcg, Calcium 494mg, Iron 17mg, Potassium 4930mg

Burgundy Mushroom Sauce Over Polenta

Prep time 7 minutes / Cook time 15 minutes / Serves 4

Ingredients:
- 1 tablespoon olive oil
- 1 medium red onion, chopped
- 4 cloves garlic, minced
- 2 large carrots, peeled, cut in half and thinly sliced
- 24 ounces Cremini mushrooms, sliced
- 1 teaspoon dry mustard
- ½ teaspoon dried rosemary
- ½ teaspoon dried thyme
- ½ teaspoon sea salt
- ½ teaspoon ground black pepper
- 1½ cups red wine
- 1 15-ounce can diced tomatoes
- 2 tablespoon Worcestershire sauce
- 4 green onions, chopped
- 1 cup unsweetened non-dairy milk
- ¼ cup parsley, chopped

Instructions:
1. In a large pot over medium heat, heat the olive oil and the onion. Sauté for two to three minutes.
2. Add the garlic, carrots, dry mustard, rosemary, thyme, salt and pepper and sauté until the mushrooms turn golden and lose most of their liquid.
3. Deglaze with the wine; scrape the brown bits up from the bottom of the pan.
4. Add the tomatoes, Worcestershire sauce and green onions. Cook to reduce the liquid by half.
5. Make some polenta, rice, or quinoa and set it aside until ready to serve.
6. If you're using polenta, stir in enough of the non-dairy milk or vegetable broth until it becomes the consistency of mashed potatoes.
7. To serve, spoon the mushroom sauce over the polenta and sprinkle with the parsley.

Nutrition Facts Per Serving:
Calories 555, Total Fat 18.4g, Saturated Fat 13.2g, Cholesterol 0mg, Sodium 609mg, Total Carbohydrate 35.2g, Dietary Fiber 6.5g, Total Sugars 16g, Protein 8.2g, Vitamin D 0mcg, Calcium 134mg, Iron 4mg, Potassium 1482mg

Carrot Brown Rice Casserole with Spinach

Prep time 7 minutes / Cook time 55 minutes / Serves 4

Ingredients:
- 1 bunch fresh spinach leaves, chopped
- 2 tablespoons vegetable stock
- 3 cups shredded carrots
- 1 large onion, chopped
- 1 teaspoon sea salt
- ½ teaspoon dry thyme
- 1½ teaspoons garlic powder
- ¼ cup smooth peanut butter
- 3 cups water or vegetable stock
- 3 cups cooked brown rice
- 1 tablespoon soy sauce
- ¾ cup whole-grain crumbs

Instructions:
1. Coat the inside of a two-quart casserole with nonstick spray and preheat the oven to 350 degrees, Fahrenheit.
2. Spread the spinach on the bottom of the casserole dish.
3. Heat a large pot over medium high heat and add the two tablespoons of vegetable broth. This will keep everything from sticking to the pan.

4. Add the onions and carrots and sauté for five minutes.
5. Add the salt, thyme and garlic powder and stir in.
6. Add the peanut butter and water or vegetable stock and whisk until smooth.
7. Stir in the soy sauce along with the breadcrumbs and stir well.
8. Pour this on top of the spinach and cover with a lid or foil.

9. Bake for 45 minutes and take out of the oven. Let cool for 10 minutes, remove the cover and serve.

Nutrition Facts Per Serving:
Calories 727, Total Fat 12.4g, Saturated Fat 2.5g, Cholesterol 0mg, Sodium 859mg, Total Carbohydrate 136.8g, Dietary Fiber 11.2g, Total Sugars 8.9g, Protein 20.1g, Vitamin D 0mcg, Calcium 185mg, Iron 6mg, Potassium 1333mg

Cashew Topped Vegetable Stuffed Peppers

Prep time 10 minutes / Cook time 60 minutes / Serves 5

Ingredients:
- 1 tablespoon olive oil
- 2 cloves garlic, chopped
- 1 medium onion, chopped
- 8 ounces mushrooms, sliced
- 2 large Swiss chard leaves, coarsely chopped
- 15-ounce can kidney beans, rinsed and drained
- 8 sun-dried tomatoes, soaked
- 1 to 2 cups tomato sauce
- 1½ cups cooked brown rice or quinoa
- 3 large red peppers, cut into half lengthwise
- 1/3 cup raw cashews, finely chopped

Instructions:
1. Preheat the oven to 375 degrees, Fahrenheit.
2. Place the olive oil in a heated skillet and add the garlic, sautéing for two minutes.
3. Add the onions and mushrooms and sauté until the onion is soft.

4. Add the chard and beans and cook until the chard wilts.
5. Add the drained and chopped sun-dried tomatoes, tomato sauce and cooked rice or quinoa. Stir to combine everything.
6. Fill the pepper cups with the mixture and place in a baking dish that has been sprayed with nonstick spray. Cover with foil.
7. Bake for 40 minutes, remove from the oven and sprinkle cashews over the top. Bake for another 10 minutes.
8. Cool for 10 minutes before serving.

Nutrition Facts Per Serving:
Calories 1004, Total Fat 14.2g, Saturated Fat 2.5g, Cholesterol 0mg, Sodium 867mg, Total Carbohydrate 194.7g, Dietary Fiber 17.1g, Total Sugars 13.9g , Protein 27.6g, Vitamin D 163mcg, Calcium 168mg, Iron 9mg, Potassium 1744mg

Coconut Curry with Cauliflower and Tomato

Prep time 10 minutes / Cook time 30 minutes / Serves 6

Ingredients:
- 3 cups Cooked brown rice for serving
- 2 tablespoons olive oil
- 1 onion, chopped
- 1 pound sweet potato, unpeeled but chopped
- 1 head cauliflower, chopped
- 1 teaspoon kosher salt, divided
- 1 tablespoon garam masala
- 1 teaspoon cumin
- ¼ teaspoon cayenne pepper
- 2 tablespoons curry powder
- 1 23-ounce jar diced plum tomatoes
- 1 15-ounce can full-fat coconut milk

- 15-ounce can chickpeas, rinsed and drained
- 4 cups fresh spinach leaves
- 1 tbsp Cilantro for garnish

Instructions:
1. Heat the oil in a large pot over medium heat.
2. Sauté the onions for about three minutes, then add the sweet potato and sauté for another 3 minutes.
3. Add the cauliflower and a half teaspoon of the salt; sauté for five minutes.
4. Add the garam marsala, cumin, cayenne pepper and curry powder; stir to mix thoroughly.

5. Pour in the plum tomatoes, including their juice and the coconut milk; bring to a boil.
6. Reduce the heat and simmer, covered, for about 10 minutes. The cauliflower should be soft.
7. Add the chickpeas and spinach leaves, along with the rest of the salt; stir until the spinach wilts and the chickpeas are heated through.
8. Serve over brown rice and garnish with cilantro.

Nutrition Facts Per Serving:
Calories 1042, Total Fat 39.9g, Saturated Fat 29.2g, Cholesterol 0mg, Sodium 508mg, Total Carbohydrate 145.2g, Dietary Fiber 22g, Total Sugars 18.8g, Protein 28.1g, Vitamin D 0mcg, Calcium 170mg, Iron 11mg, Potassium 1769mg

Greek Style Stuffed Sweet Potatoes

Prep time 10 minutes / Cook time 30 minutes / Serves 4

Ingredients:
- 4 sweet potatoes
- ½ red onion, chopped
- 1 cucumber, peeled and chopped
- 2 large tomatoes, chopped
- 1 small jar Kalamata olives, chopped
- 3 tablespoons fresh mint, chopped
- 1 lime, juiced
- 1 clove garlic, processed into a paste
- 2 tablespoons lemon juice
- 1/3 cup Tahini sauce
- ¼ teaspoon salt
- 4 tablespoons lukewarm water
- 15-ounce can chickpeas, drained and rinsed

Instructions:
1. Preheat the oven to 375 degrees, Fahrenheit.
2. Cut the cleaned sweet potatoes in half lengthwise and place them, with cut side down, on a greased baking sheet. Bake for 20 to 30 minutes, until tender when poked with a fork. Remove from the oven to cool.
3. In a bowl, combine the onions, cucumber, tomatoes, olives, mint and lime juice. Mix well and set the bowl aside.
4. In another bowl, combine the garlic, lemon juice, Tahini sauce and salt. Start adding the water with two tablespoons and see if it becomes the right consistency. If it is thick and pasty, add more of the water up to six tablespoons. Set the mixture aside.
5. To assemble, place two potato halves on a plate right side up and mash with a fork lightly. Place the onion, cucumber tomato and olive mixture on top. Sprinkle with chickpeas and end up with the Tahini mixture on top and serve.

Nutrition Facts Per Serving:
Calories 703, Total Fat 16g, Saturated Fat 2g, Cholesterol 0mg, Sodium 579mg, Total Carbohydrate 119g, Dietary Fiber 28.6g, Total Sugars 16.7g, Protein 26.2g, Vitamin D 0mcg, Calcium 217mg, Iron 10mg, Potassium 2548mg

Imitation Crab Cakes With Tofu

Prep time 8 minutes / Cook time 20 minutes / Serves 4

Ingredients:
- 2 tablespoons ground flaxseed
- 4 tablespoons water
- 1 block tofu
- ½ cup red bell pepper, diced
- ¾ cup red onion, diced
- 1½ cups celery diced
- ¼ cup flat leaf parsley, chopped
- 1 tablespoons capers, drained
- ½ teaspoon Worcestershire sauce
- ¼ teaspoon hot sauce
- 1½ teaspoons Old Bay seasoning
- ¼ cup vegetable stock
- ¼ tsp salt
- ¼ tsp pepper
- 1 tablespoon lemon juice
- ½ tablespoon lemon zest
- ½ cup dry wheat bread crumbs
- 2 tablespoons Dijon mustard

Instructions:
1. Combine the flaxseed and water and let it soak until ready to use.
2. Cut the tofu block in half lengthwise, pressing each half between paper towels and wrapping in newspaper to make it as dry as

possible. Place something heavy on top and let it rest for 20 minutes.

3. Put the red bell pepper, the onion, celery, parsley, capers, Worcestershire sauce, hot sauce, Old Bay seasoning, vegetable stock, salt and pepper in a large pot over medium low heat. Cook for 15 minutes or until everything is soft. Cool to room temperature.
4. Place the tofu in a large bowl and mash it into small pieces
5. Add the lemon juice, lemon zest, breadcrumbs, mustard and the flaxseed, including the water. Mix well.
6. Add the vegetable mixture and mix well.

7. Cover the bowl and let it rest in the refrigerator for 30 minutes.
8. Preheat the oven to 375 degrees, Fahrenheit and cover a baking sheet with parchment paper.
9. Remove the mixture from the refrigerator and shape it into balls, place them on the parchment paper and press down to flatten.
10. Bake for five minutes on each side and serve.

Nutrition Facts Per Serving:
Calories 137, Total Fat 3.5g, Saturated Fat 0.6g, Cholesterol 0mg, Sodium 1442mg, Total Carbohydrate 20.3g, Dietary Fiber 5.3g, Total Sugars 5.1g, Protein 6.4g, Vitamin D 0mcg, Calcium 147mg, Iron 3mg, Potassium 551mg

Lentil and Mushroom Loaf (Fake Meatloaf)

Prep time 10 minutes / Cook time 60 minutes / Serves 8
Ingredients:
- 2 cloves garlic, finely chopped
- 1 small onion, chopped
- 3 cups mushrooms, finely chopped
- 1 cup green lentils, already cooked
- 1 cup red lentils, already cooked
- ½ cup old-fashioned rolled oats
- ¼ cup ground flaxseed
- 1 tablespoon Tamari or soy sauce
- 2 tablespoons dried thyme
- ½ teaspoon salt
- ¼ teaspoon pepper
- ½ cup water

Instructions:
1. Preheat the oven to 370 degrees, Fahrenheit.
2. Place the garlic, onion and mushrooms in a large mixing bowl.
3. Add the green and red lentils, oats, flaxseed, Tamari, thyme, salt and pepper; mix well with your hands. The mixture may be a little crumbly.

4. Add water, a little bit at a time and up to a half cup as needed until the mixture starts to stick together like a regular meatloaf. Add two tablespoons first, then add by two-tablespoon increments until the loaf gains the proper texture.
5. Place a strip of parchment paper on the bottom of the pan that extends up both sides and out of the pan on the small sides. This creates a sling that you can grasp to pull out the loaf after it's cooked.
6. Pack the loaf mixture into the pan and bake for 50 to 60 minutes.
7. Remove from oven and cool for 15 minutes. Lift the loaf out of the pan and set it on a cutting board to slice Serve while warm.

Nutrition Facts Per Serving:
Calories 136, Total Fat 1.8g, Saturated Fat 0.3g, Cholesterol 0mg, Sodium 279mg, Total Carbohydrate 21.4g, Dietary Fiber 9.6g, Total Sugars 1.5g, Protein 8.8g, Vitamin D 95mcg, Calcium 35mg, Iron 5mg, Potassium 387mg

Meatless Chick Nuggets

Prep time 10 minutes / Cook time 30 minutes / Serves 8
Ingredients:
- 1 15.5-ounce can chickpeas, rinsed and drained
- ½ teaspoon garlic powder
- 1 teaspoon granulated onion
- 1 tablespoon nutritional yeast
- 1 tablespoon whole-wheat bread crumbs
- ½ cup panko bread crumbs

Instructions:
1. Preheat the oven to 350 degrees, Fahrenheit and cover a rimmed baking pan with parchment paper.

80

2. Place the drained chickpeas in a food processor and pulse four to five times.
3. Add the garlic powder, granulated onion, nutritional yeast and the tablespoon of whole-wheat bread crumbs to the processor and process until you get a chunky, grainy mixture that sticks together.
4. Scoop out by teaspoonfuls and form balls.
5. Roll the balls in the panko crumbs and set on the baking sheet, flattening each ball so it looks more like a chicken nugget. Be sure to space them apart so they do not touch each other.
6. Bake for 20 minutes, remove from the oven and flip each nugget over with tongs. Return to the oven for 10 more minutes.
7. Cool for a few minutes and then serve with honey, barbecue sauce or Ranch dipping sauce.

Nutrition Facts Per Serving:
Calories 245, Total Fat 4.4g, Saturated Fat 0.4g, Cholesterol 0mg, Sodium 63mg, Total Carbohydrate 41.6g, Dietary Fiber 10.6g, Total Sugars 6.3g, Protein 12.5g, Vitamin D 0mcg, Calcium 71mg, Iron 4mg, Potassium 541mg

Portobello Bolognese With Zucchini Noodles

Prep time 6 minutes / Cook time 25 minutes / Serves 4

Ingredients:
- 3 tablespoons olive oil, divided
- ½ cup onion, minced
- 3 cloves of garlic, minced
- ½ cup carrot, peeled and minced
- ½ cup celery, minced
- 6 portobello mushroom caps, stems removed and finely chopped
- ½ teaspoon Kosher salt
- ½ teaspoon ground pepper
- 1 tablespoon tomato paste
- 1 28-ounce can crushed plum tomatoes
- ¼ teaspoon red pepper flakes, crushed
- ½ cup fresh basil leaves, finely chopped
- 2 teaspoons dried oregano
- 4 medium zucchini

Instructions:
1. Heat two tablespoons of the olive oil in a large skillet over medium high heat.
2. Add the onion, garlic, carrot and celery; sauté for about five minutes or until the onion turns translucent.
3. Add the mushrooms and sauté for another six to seven minutes, until the mushrooms shrink and lose their liquid. Stir constantly so they don't burn but turn a golden hue.
4. Stir in the tomato paste and cook, stirring frequently, for about two minutes.
5. Pour in the crushed tomatoes, red pepper flakes, basil and oregano. Reduce the heat to a simmer, cooking very low until the sauce thickens.
6. While the pot simmers, create the zucchini noodles and put them in cold water until they're all made. Drain the noodles and use tongs to place them in a skillet with a little water at the bottom. Toss and add some salt and pepper. They will only take a few minutes to soften and warm over medium heat.
7. Divide the noodles among four bowls and serve with the sauce on top; add a basil leaf on top as garnish.

Nutrition Facts Per Serving:
Calories 228, Total Fat 11.2g, Saturated Fat 1.6g, Cholesterol 0mg, Sodium 380mg, Total Carbohydrate 23.4g, Dietary Fiber 7.9g, Total Sugars 14.8g, Protein 8.1g, Vitamin D 0mcg, Calcium 104mg, Iron 5mg, Potassium 1000mg

Quesadilla With Black Beans and Sweet Potato

Prep time 10 minutes / Cook time 30 minutes / Serves 2

Ingredients:
- 1 medium-sized sweet potato, peeled and cut into cubes
- 3 teaspoons taco seasoning
- 4 whole-wheat tortillas
- ½ of a 15-ounce can of black beans, drained and rinsed

Instructions:
1. Bring a large pot of water to boil and drop in the sweet potato.

2. Boil for 10 to 20 minutes or until soft.
3. Drain the sweet potato and put in a bowl.
4. Add the taco seasoning and mash well.
5. To assemble the quesadilla, spread the sweet potato mixture on the tortilla.
6. Add the black beans and press them onto the potato mixture.
7. Cover with another tortilla.

8. Heat a nonstick skillet over medium high heat and lay the tortilla in it. Toast on both sides and serve immediately.

Nutrition Facts Per Serving:
Calories 520, Total Fat 3g, Saturated Fat 0.6g, Cholesterol 0mg, Sodium 80mg, Total Carbohydrate 99.8g, Dietary Fiber 21.1g, Total Sugars 6.5g, Protein 26.9g, Vitamin D 0mcg, Calcium 172mg, Iron 8mg, Potassium 1937mg

Quinoa-stuffed Acorn Squash

Prep time 10 minutes / Cook time 80 minutes / Serves 4

Ingredients:

- ½ cup quinoa, cooked per package instructions
- 2 acorn squash
- 1/8 cup water
- 1 large onion, chopped
- 1/8 teaspoon ground cloves
- 1/8 teaspoon ground cardamom
- ½ teaspoon ground ginger
- 1 teaspoon ground cinnamon
- ½ cup raisins
- 1/3 cup walnuts or pecans, chopped
- ½ teaspoon sea salt
- ¼ teaspoon ground black pepper

Instructions:

1. Preheat the oven to 350 degrees, Fahrenheit and pre-cook the quinoa. Set it aside until ready to use.
2. Poke the squash with a fork or knife to let the steam out (and to avoid a squash explosion). Place on a microwave safe dish and microwave on high for three to four minutes. This will soften the squash before you cut into it.
3. Let the squash cool for five minutes and then cut it in half. Carefully remove the seeds as they will still be hot. Place the halves, cut side down, on a parchment-lined baking sheet. Bake for 30 to 40 minutes, until the squash is soft.

4. While squash is cooking, pour the water into a skillet over medium high heat and sauté the onion.
5. Reduce the heat to low and add the cloves, cardamom, ginger and cinnamon, stirring to mix. Turn off the heat and set the mixture aside until the squash is finished baking.
6. Once the squash is soft inside, remove it from the oven, but do not turn off the heat. As soon as it can be handled, carefully scoop the squash meat from the shell without damaging the skin. Mash the squash meat.
7. Add the squash meat to the onion spice mix in the skillet and turn the heat back on to medium high, stirring to mix.
8. Add the raisins and nuts and stir while heating through. Season with salt and pepper.
9. Turn off the heat and pack the shells with the mixture in the pan. Put the squash shells back on the baking sheet, cover everything with foil and bake for another 20 minutes before serving.

Nutrition Facts Per Serving:
Calories 301, Total Fat 7.8g, Saturated Fat 0.6g, Cholesterol 0mg, Sodium 246mg, Total Carbohydrate 55.8g, Dietary Fiber 7.3g, Total Sugars 12.5g, Protein 8.3g, Vitamin D 0mcg, Calcium 113mg, Iron 3mg, Potassium 1121mg

Spicy Corn and Spinach Casserole

Prep time 12 minutes / Cook time 80 minutes / Serves 6

Ingredients:

- 1½ cups water
- ¾ cup unsweetened soy milk, divided
- 1¼ cups cornmeal
- 1 14-ounce block tofu, drained and rinsed
- 3 cloves garlic, minced
- 1 10-ounce package frozen corn, thawed, divided
- 2 4.5-ounce cans mild chilies, diced
- 1 10-ounce package frozen spinach, thawed
- 1 teaspoon baking powder
- ½ teaspoon cayenne pepper
- ½ teaspoon cumin
- ½ teaspoon salt
- ½ teaspoon pepper

Instructions:

1. Preheat the oven to 450 degrees, Fahrenheit.
2. Heat the water and a half cup of the soy milk in a medium saucepan, bringing it almost to a boil. Turn off the burner and slowly whisk in the cornmeal, letting It thicken. Scrape out into a bowl and set it aside until ready to use.
3. Wrap the tofu in a paper towel and press down to extract most of the liquid. This may require repeating several times, with fresh paper towels.
4. When the tofu is as dry as you can get it, place it in a food processor, along with the garlic, one cup of corn and the remaining soy milk. Process until smooth, then pour it into the bowl with the cornmeal, folding it in to combine thoroughly.
5. To the same bowl, add the rest of the corn, the chilies, spinach, baking powder, cayenne pepper, cumin, salt and pepper. The mixture will be thick but needs to be combined well. Use your muscles.
6. Pour the mixture into an oiled baking dish and bake for 60 to 70 minutes. The edges should be crispy and the middle should jiggle just a little bit.
7. Let the casserole stand for 20 minutes before serving.

Nutrition Facts Per Serving:
Calories 643, Total Fat 8.6g, Saturated Fat 1.4g, Cholesterol 0mg, Sodium 2210mg, Total Carbohydrate 120.9g, Dietary Fiber 17.8g, Total Sugars 20g, Protein 25.5g, Vitamin D 0mcg, Calcium 239mg, Iron 13mg, Potassium 1352mg

Summer Harvest Pizza

Prep time 20 minutes / Cook time 15 minutes / Serves 2

Ingredients:

- 1 Lavash flatbread, whole grain
- 4 Tbsp Feta spread, store-bought
- ½ cup cheddar cheese, shredded
- ½ cup corn kernels, cooked
- ½ cup beans, cooked
- ½ cup fire-roasted red peppers, chopped

Instructions:

1. Preheat oven to 350°F.
2. Cut Lavash into two halves. Bake crusts on a pan in the oven for 5 minutes.
3. Spread feta spread on both crusts. Top with remaining ingredients.
4. Bake for another 10 minutes.

Nutritional facts per serving:
Calories 270, Total Fat 17.8g, Saturated Fat 11.1g, Cholesterol 50mg, Sodium 435mg, Total Carbohydrate 16.6g, Dietary Fiber 2g, Total Sugars 2.8g, Protein 12.8g, Vitamin D 3mcg, Calcium 254mg, Iron 2mg, Potassium 189mg

Whole Wheat Pizza with Summer Produce

Prep time 15 minutes / Cook time 15 minutes / Serves 2

Ingredients:

- 1 pound whole wheat pizza dough
- 4 ounces goat cheese
- 2/3 cup blueberries
- 2 ears corn, husked
- 2 yellow squash, sliced
- 2 Tbsp olive oil

Instructions:

1. Preheat the oven to 450°F.

2. Roll the dough out to make a pizza crust.
3. Crumble the cheese on the crust. Spread remaining ingredients, then drizzle with olive oil.
4. Bake for about 15 minutes. Serve.

Nutritional facts per serving:
Calories 522, Total Fat 22.2g, Saturated Fat 8.2g, Cholesterol 30mg, Sodium 597mg, Total Carbohydrate 69.7g, Dietary Fiber 7.7g, Total Sugars 7.2g, Protein 20.5g, Vitamin D 0mcg, Calcium 269mg, Iron 3mg, Potassium 497mg

Spicy Chickpeas

Prep time 15 minutes / Cook time 20 minutes / Serves 8
Ingredients:
- 1 Tbsp extra-virgin olive oil
- 1 yellow onion, diced
- 1 tsp curry
- ¼ tsp allspice
- 1 can diced tomatoes
- 2 cans chickpeas, rinsed, drained
- ¼ tsp Salt
- ¼ tsp cayenne pepper

Instructions:
1. Simmer onions in 1 Tbsp oil for 4 minutes.
2. Add allspice and pepper, cook for 2 minutes.
3. Stir in tomatoes, and cook for another 2 minutes.
4. Add chickpeas, and simmer for 10 minutes.
5. Season with salt, and serve.

Nutritional facts per serving:
Calories 207, Total Fat 4.8g, Saturated Fat 0.6g, Cholesterol 0mg, Sodium 123mg, Total Carbohydrate 32.6g, Dietary Fiber 9.2g, Total Sugars 6.5g, Protein 10g, Vitamin D 0mcg, Calcium 60mg, Iron 3mg, Potassium 463mg

Beans & Greens Bowl

Prep time 2 minutes / Cook time 2 minutes / Serves 1
Ingredients:
- 1½ cups curly kale, washed, chopped
- ½ cup black beans, cooked
- ½ avocado
- 2 Tbsp feta cheese, crumbled

Instructions:
1. Mix the kale and black beans in a microwavable bowl and heat for about 1 ½ minutes.
2. Add the avocado and stir well. Top with feta.

Nutritional facts per serving:
Calories 830, Total Fat 29.6g, Saturated Fat 7.7g, Cholesterol 17mg, Sodium 410mg, Total Carbohydrate 113.7g, Dietary Fiber 39.5g, Total Sugars 14.6g, Protein 46.9g, Vitamin D 0mcg, Calcium 974mg, Iron 13mg, Potassium 4393mg

Faro with Pistachios & Herbs

Prep time 20 minutes / Cook time 45 minutes / Serves 10
Ingredients:
- 2 cups faro
- 4 cups water
- 1 tsp kosher salt, divided
- 2½ Tbsp extra-virgin olive oil
- 1 onion, chopped
- 2 cloves garlic, minced
- ½ tsp ground pepper, divided
- ½ cup parsley, chopped
- 4 oz salted shelled pistachios, toasted, chopped

Instructions:
1. Combine farro, water, and ¾ tsp salt, simmer for 40 minutes.
2. Cook onion and garlic in 2 Tbsp oil for 5 minutes.
3. Combine ½ tsp oil, ¼ tsp pepper, parsley, pistachios, and toss well.
4. Combine all. Season with salt and pepper.

Nutritional facts per serving:
Calories 277, Total Fat 20.6g, Saturated Fat 2.7g, Cholesterol 0mg, Sodium 298mg, Total Carbohydrate 19.3g, Dietary Fiber 4.3g, Total Sugars 1.3g, Protein 5.3g, Vitamin D 0mcg, Calcium 27mg, Iron 1mg, Potassium 37mg

84

Millet and Teff with Squash & Onions

Prep time 10 minutes / Cook time 20 minutes / Serves 6

Ingredients:

- 1 cup millet
- ½ cup teff grain
- 4½ cups of water
- 1 onion, sliced
- 1 butternut squash, chopped
- ¼ tsp Sea salt

Instructions:

1. Rinse millet, and put in a large pot.
2. Add remaining ingredients. Mix well.
3. Simmer 20 minutes until all the water is absorbed.
4. Serve hot.

Nutritional facts per serving:

Calories 218, Total Fat 1.7g, Saturated Fat 0.3g, Cholesterol 0mg, Sodium 111mg, Total Carbohydrate 45.2g, Dietary Fiber 6.6g, Total Sugars 2.3g, Protein 6.6g, Vitamin D 0mcg, Calcium 65mg, Iron 2mg, Potassium 346mg

Brown Rice Tabbouleh

Prep time 20 minutes / Cook time 0 minutes / Serves 6

Ingredients:

- 3 cups brown rice, cooked
- ¾ cup cucumber, chopped
- ¾ cup tomato, chopped
- ¼ cup mint leaves, chopped
- ¼ cup green onions, sliced
- ¼ cup olive oil
- ¼ cup lemon juice
- ¼ tsp Salt
- ¼ tsp pepper

Instructions:

1. Combine all ingredients in a large bowl.
2. Toss well and chill for 20 min.

Nutritional facts per serving:

Calories 428, Total Fat 11.1g, Saturated Fat 1.8g, Cholesterol 0mg, Sodium 106mg, Total Carbohydrate 74.6g, Dietary Fiber 4g, Total Sugars 1.1g, Protein 7.7g, Vitamin D 0mcg, Calcium 47mg, Iron 2mg, Potassium 370mg

Healthy Hoppin' John

Prep time 15 minutes / Cook time 1 hour / Serves 4

Ingredients:

- 1 Tbsp extra-virgin olive oil
- 1 onion, diced
- 2 garlic cloves, minced
- 1 cup of dried black-eyed peas
- 1 cup brown rice, uncooked
- 4 cups water
- ¼ tsp Salt
- ¼ tsp pepper

Instructions:

1. Cook the onions and garlic in oil for 3 minutes.
2. Combine the peas, salt, brown rice, and 4 cups of water and bring to a boil.
3. Add pepper. Simmer for 45 minutes.
4. Serve hot.

Nutritional facts per serving:

Calories 261, Total Fat 5.3g, Saturated Fat 0.8g, Cholesterol 0mg, Sodium 170mg, Total Carbohydrate 47.3g, Dietary Fiber 4.3g, Total Sugars 1.2g, Protein 6.9g, Vitamin D 0mcg, Calcium 43mg, Iron 2mg, Potassium 283mg

Black Beans & Brown Rice

Prep time 2 minutes / Cook time 45 minutes / Serves 4

Ingredients:

- 4 cups water
- 2 cups brown rice, uncooked
- 1 can no-salt black beans
- 3 cloves garlic, minced

Instructions:

1. Bring the water and rice to boil, simmer for 40 minutes.
2. In a pan, cook the black beans with their liquid and the garlic for 5 minutes.
3. Toss the rice and beans together, and serve.

Nutritional facts per serving:
Calories 429, Total Fat 3.3g, Saturated Fat 0.5g, Cholesterol 0mg, Sodium 19mg, Total Carbohydrate 87.3g, Dietary Fiber 8.5g, Total Sugars 0.8g, Protein 12.5g, Vitamin D 0mcg, Calcium 58mg, Iron 3mg, Potassium 467mg

Yucatan Bean & Pumpkin Seed Appetizer

Prep time 10 minutes / Cook time 3 minutes / Serves 8
Ingredients:
- ¼ cup pumpkin seeds
- 16 oz can white beans
- 1 tomato, chopped
- 1/3 cup onion, chopped
- 1/3 cup cilantro, chopped
- 1 lime, juiced
- ¼ tsp Salt
- ¼ tsp pepper

Instructions:

1. Toast the pumpkin seeds for 3 minutes to lightly brown. Let cool, and then chop in a food processor.
2. Mix in the remaining ingredients. Season with salt and pepper, and serve.

Nutritional facts per serving:
Calories 217, Total Fat 2.5g, Saturated Fat 0.5g, Cholesterol 0mg, Sodium 85mg, Total Carbohydrate 36.2g, Dietary Fiber 9.1g, Total Sugars 1.7g, Protein 14.5g, Vitamin D 0mcg, Calcium 141mg, Iron 7mg, Potassium 1089mg

Butter Bean Hummus

Prep time 5 minutes / Cook time 0 minutes / Serves 4
Ingredients:
- 1 can butter beans, drained, rinsed
- 2 garlic cloves, minced
- ½ lemon, juiced
- 1 Tbsp olive oil
- 4 sprigs of parsley, minced
- ¼ tsp Sea salt

Instructions:
1. Blend all ingredients in a food processor into a creamy mixture.

2. Serve as a dip for bread, crackers, or any types of vegetables.

Nutritional facts per serving:
Calories 84, Total Fat 3.9g, Saturated Fat 0.6g, Cholesterol 0mg, Sodium 121mg, Total Carbohydrate 10.2g, Dietary Fiber 2.2g, Total Sugars 2.1g, Protein 3.1g, Vitamin D 0mcg, Calcium 19mg, Iron 1mg, Potassium 226mg

Greek-style garbanzo beans

Prep time 8 hours 5 minutes / Cook time 10 hours / Serves 10
Ingredients:
- 12 ounces garbanzo beans
- 14 oz tomatoes with juice, chopped
- 2 stalks celery, diced
- 1 onion, diced
- 4 garlic cloves, minced
- ¼ tsp Salt

Instructions:
1. Soak beans in water for 8 hours.

2. Combine drained beans with the remaining ingredients. Stir, and pour water to cover.
3. Cook for 10 hours on low. Season with salt, and serve.

Nutritional facts per serving:
Calories 138, Total Fat 2.2g, Saturated Fat 0.2g, Cholesterol 0mg, Sodium 72mg, Total Carbohydrate 23.7g, Dietary Fiber 6.7g, Total Sugars 5.2g, Protein 7.1g, Vitamin D 0mcg, Calcium 46mg, Iron 2mg, Potassium 421mg

Brown Rice & Red Beans & Coconut Milk

Prep time 10 minutes / Cook time 1 hour / Serves 6

Ingredients:

- 2 cups brown rice, uncooked
- 4 cups water
- 1 Tbsp olive oil
- 1 onion, diced
- 3 cloves garlic, minced
- 2 cans red beans
- 1 can coconut milk

Instructions:

1. Bring brown rice in water to a boil, then simmer for 30 minutes.

2. Sauté onion in olive oil. Add garlic and cook until golden.
3. Mix the onions and garlic, beans, and coconut milk into rice. Simmer for 15 minutes.
4. Serve hot.

Nutritional facts per serving:

Calories 661, Total Fat 14.6g, Saturated Fat 9.3g, Cholesterol 0mg, Sodium 25mg, Total Carbohydrate 109.1g, Dietary Fiber 17.4g, Total Sugars 4.1g, Protein 26.7g, Vitamin D 0mcg, Calcium 115mg, Iron 8mg, Potassium 1560mg

Black-Eyed Peas with Herns

Prep time 10 minutes / Cook time 1 hour / Serves 8

Ingredients:

- 2 cans no-sodium black-eyed beans
- ½ cup extra-virgin olive oil
- 1 cup parsley, chopped
- 4 green onions, sliced
- 2 carrots, grated
- 2 Tbsp tomato paste
- 2 cups water
- ¼ tsp Salt
- ¼ tsp pepper

Instructions:

1. Drain the beans, reserve the liquid.

2. Sauté beans, parsley, onions, and carrots in oil for 3 minutes.
3. Add remaining ingredients, 2 cups reserved beans liquid, and water.
4. Cook for 30 minutes.
5. Season with salt, pepper and serve.

Nutritional facts per serving:

Calories 175, Total Fat 12.9g, Saturated Fat 1.8g, Cholesterol 0mg, Sodium 200mg, Total Carbohydrate 13.4g, Dietary Fiber 3.6g, Total Sugars 1.9g, Protein 3.7g, Vitamin D 0mcg, Calcium 51mg, Iron 2mg, Potassium 362mg

Smashing Sweet Potato Burger with Quinoa

Prep time 10 minutes / Cook time 1 hour 15 minutes / Serves 2

Ingredients:

- 1 12-ounce can, rinsed black beans
- 2 tablespoons, finely diced jalapeno
- 2 cups, mashed roasted sweet potatoes
- ½ cup, freshly diced purple onion
- 1/3 cup, roasted sunflower seeds
- 2 cups, cooked quinoa
- ¼ cup, oat flour
- 2 teaspoons, garlic powder
- 1 teaspoon, olive oil
- 1 tablespoon of ground cumin
- ¼ teaspoon of sea salt

Instructions:

1. Preheat the oven to 375o F. Spray some coconut oil on a baking sheet.

2. After cutting the sweet potatoes in half, arrange them on the baking sheet with a drizzle of olive oil.
3. Make perforations with a fork. Put them skin-side down on the tray, and bake them for about an hour.
4. Mix all of the other ingredients in a large bowl while the potatoes are roasting.
5. Allow the potatoes to cool for 10 minutes. Scoop out the flesh with a spoon. Mash the flesh with a spoon, and mix it with the rest of the ingredients.
6. Preheat the oven again to 375o F. Spray some coconut oil on the baking sheet.

7. In order to create burger patties, you need to scoop some of the sweet potato mixture and form a 1-inch patty with the mashed mix. You can moisten your hands to shape the patty properly. Put them in the oven, and bake them for 15 minutes.

8. Once the burgers are baked, heat some olive oil in a skillet.

9. Put the patties in the oil for 4-5 minutes, flipping half way through the cooking time.

You will know that the patties are ready when both sides are golden brown.

10. Once the patties are ready, top with your favorite salad and toppings, and enjoy your healthy burgers.

Nutritional Facts Per Serving:
Calories 989, Total Fat 14.6g, Saturated Fat 1.8g, Cholesterol 0mg, Sodium 368mg, Total Carbohydrate 172.6g, Dietary Fiber 30g, Total Sugars 11.1g, Protein 44.4g, Vitamin D 0mcg, Calcium 262mg, Iron 13mg, Potassium 2471mg

Famous Veg Caprese Bowl

Prep time 15 minutes / Cook time 35 minutes / Serves 4

Ingredients:
- 1 medium-sized zucchini
- 2 tablespoons, olive oil
- 1 cup, freshly chopped yellow onion
- 16 ounces, freshly sliced cremini mushrooms
- 1 tablespoon, finely chopped garlic
- 1 tablespoon, unsalted tomato paste
- 1 teaspoon, freshly ground black pepper
- 1 can, fire-roasted, diced, unsalted tomatoes, undrained
- 5 ounces, fresh baby spinach
- ¼ cup, fresh basil
- 1 teaspoon, freshly ground black pepper
- ¾ cup, part-skim mozzarella cheese
- ½ cup, part-skim ricotta cheese

Instructions:
1. Cut long strips of zucchini. In a colander, mix some salt with the zucchini. Allow it to stand for some time.

2. Over medium-high heat, warm some oil. Add the onion and garlic and cook until they are fragrant and tender. This will take about 3 minutes.

3. Add the mushrooms and stir. Cook the mushrooms until they are brown; this will take about 5 minutes.

4. Add the tomato paste and cook everything for 1 minute.

5. Add the pepper, tomatoes, and salt.

6. Decrease the heat to medium-low, and allow the veggies to simmer, stirring them until the ingredients have reduced. This will take about 6 minutes.

7. Add the spinach, cover the pot, and allow the spinach leaves to wilt. This will take another 3 minutes.

8. Remove the pot from the stove and add the zucchini strips.

9. In a small bowl, mix the mozzarella and ricotta cheese and microwave for about 30 seconds. Now top the mixture with the warmed cheese and some basil.

Nutritional Facts Per Serving:
Calories 209, Total Fat 10.8g, Saturated Fat 3.2g, Cholesterol 12mg, Sodium 130mg, Total Carbohydrate 17.3g, Dietary Fiber 4.4g, Total Sugars 7.7g, Protein 11.4g, Vitamin D 0mcg, Calcium 180mg, Iron 3mg, Potassium 982mg

Tempting Tempeh BLT

Prep time 15 minutes / Cook time 20 minutes / Serves 6

Ingredients:
- 1 tablespoon, pure maple syrup
- 1 ½ teaspoons, black pepper
- 1 ½ tablespoons, reduced sodium tamari
- 2 teaspoons, smoked paprika
- 1 package, tempeh cut into 16 slices
- 8 whole-wheat bread slices
- ½ cup, wild blackberry wood chips
- 5 teaspoons, canola mayonnaise
- 8 romaine lettuce leaves
- 1 heirloom tomato

Instructions:

1. Preheat the oven to 400o F. In a bowl, whisk together the maple syrup, tamari sauce, and smoked paprika. Add 1 teaspoon of pepper.
2. On a baking sheet place the tempeh and lather both sides with the prepared mixture.
3. Take a disposable aluminum foil pan and pierce 10 holes in the bottom.
4. Put the wood chips on top of the holes and allow the holed side to sit on a stopover burner. The temperature should be medium-high.
5. Heat until the wood chips begin to smoke. This will take about 1 minute. Remove from the heat.
6. Put a wire rack on the baking sheet and bake the tempeh at 400o F. You will know that the tempeh is ready when the slices are golden brown and slightly crispy. You should flip them once halfway through cooking.
7. Put the bread slices on the oven rack, and toast them for about 5 minutes.
8. Spread ¼ teaspoon of mayo on one side of the bread. Sprinkle some pepper on top. Now add the tomato slices, followed by lettuce, and then top it with tempeh. Finally, add the other toasted bread slice to form the BLT.

Nutritional Facts Per Serving:
Calories 142, Total Fat 4.5g, Saturated Fat 0.4g, Cholesterol 1mg, Sodium 462mg, Total Carbohydrate 20.4g, Dietary Fiber 3.2g, Total Sugars 5g, Protein 5.7g, Vitamin D 0mcg, Calcium 50mg, Iron 2mg, Potassium 181mg

Amazing Cavatappi with Pesto & Carrots

Prep time 10 minutes / Cook time 30 minutes / Serves 2

Ingredients:

- 10 ounces asparagus
- 1 lemon
- 8 ounces carrots
- 2 cloves garlic
- ¼ cup soy-free vegan parmesan
- 1 box Banza Cavatappi
- 4 ounces, baby arugula
- ½ cup almonds
- ¼ tsp Pepper
- 3 tablespoons, olive oil
- ¼ tsp Salt

Instructions:

1. Preheat the oven to 400o F.
2. Peel and slice the carrots, and trim the end of each asparagus. Chop the asparagus stalks into 1-inch pieces. Peel the garlic.
3. Put the carrots on a baking sheet, drizzle some olive oil over them, and sprinkle with salt and pepper. Roast the carrots until you can insert a fork through them. This will take about 10-12 minutes.
4. Put 1 cup of Cavatappi aside, and add the rest of the Cavatappi to the water. Bring to a boil, then reduce the heat and cook until al dente. The entire process will be done within 6-8 minutes. Remove ½ cup of pasta water, and drain the pasta.
5. In a food processor, add half of the lemon juice, garlic, carrots, and almonds along with ½ cup of arugula, water, salt, and 2 tablespoons of parmesan. Adjust salt to taste. Pulse the ingredients. Add some olive oil, and make a smooth puree.
6. Put the pot back on medium-high heat, and warm 2 tablespoons of olive oil. Add the chopped asparagus, and cook until they are crisp-tender. This will take about 2-3 minutes. Add the carrot pesto, Cavatappi, reserved water with remaining arugula, and the rest of the lemon juice. Stir everything so that the ingredients do not stick to the pot.
7. You will know that the dish is almost ready when the arugula wilts. Adjust the salt and pepper, and divide it into bowls. Sprinkle some more parmesan on the top, and enjoy this amazing pasta.

Nutritional Facts Per Serving:
Calories 570, Total Fat 34.1g, Saturated Fat 4g, Cholesterol 0mg, Sodium 583mg, Total Carbohydrate 51.2g, Dietary Fiber 11.6g, Total Sugars 12.2g, Protein 20.6g, Vitamin D 0mcg, Calcium 360mg, Iron 6mg, Potassium 1088mg

Vegan Mac n Cheese

Prep time 10 minutes / Cook time 20 minutes / Serves 6

Ingredients:

- 3 cups, vegetable broth
- 1.5 cups, rinsed quinoa
- 1 8.5-ounce jar, drained and sliced sun-dried tomatoes
- ¼ tsp Salt
- 1 tablespoon, minced garlic
- ¼ tsp Pepper
- 4 cups, deboned kale
- 2 tablespoons, EVOO
- Cheese sauce:
- 2 tablespoons, corn starch
- 2 cups, Blue Diamond Almond Breeze
- 2 cups, shredded mozzarella cheese

Instructions:

1. Boil the quinoa and vegetable broth in a medium-sized pot. Reduce the heat, cover the pot, and allow the quinoa to simmer for about 15 minutes or until it soaks up all of the liquid.
2. In the meantime, drain the tomatoes and slice them, but do not rinse them. After deboning the kale, chop it into bite-sized portions.
3. In a frying pan, add the EVOO, tomatoes, garlic, and kale and sauté for about 5 minutes. You will know that it is ready when the kale is wilted.
4. In a medium-sized pot, add 2 cups of almond milk and 2 tablespoons of corn starch, and bring to a boil. Reduce the heat to medium, and allow the ingredients to cook for 8 minutes. As the milk thickens, you can add the shredded cheese to form a smooth substance. Do not stop stirring.
5. In a large bowl, mix the quinoa, cheese sauce, and veggies. Dig into this one-of-a-kind mac n cheese!

Nutritional Facts Per Serving:

Calories 289, Total Fat 8.2g, Saturated Fat 1.8g, Cholesterol 5mg, Sodium 719mg, Total Carbohydrate 41.2g, Dietary Fiber 4.5g, Total Sugars 4.4g, Protein 13.2g, Vitamin D 0mcg, Calcium 198mg, Iron 3mg, Potassium 722mg

Thai-Style Eggplant

Prep time 10 minutes / Cook time 25 minutes / Serves 2

Ingredients:

- 1 eggplant
- ¾ cup jasmine rice
- 1 shallot
- 5 ounces coconut milk
- 3 cloves garlic
- 1 red bell pepper
- 1 jalapeno
- 1 tablespoon rice vinegar
- 2 scallions
- 2 tablespoons tamari
- ¼ tsp Salt
- 4 teaspoons turbinado sugar
- 3 tablespoons olive oil

Instructions:

1. Mix the jasmine rice with coconut milk and ½ cup of water with salt to cook the rice. Bring to a boil and then reduce the heat to cook the rice until the water is absorbed and the rice is fluffy. This will take about 15-20 minutes.
2. Chop the eggplant into 1-inch cubes. Mince the garlic and the shallot. Roughly chop the bell pepper. Chop the scallions into 2-inch pieces. Lastly, mince the jalapeno.
3. On medium-high heat, add 2 tablespoons of vegetable oil to a non-stick skillet. After the oil is warm, add the eggplant and cook until brown. The entire process will take about 4 minutes. You can transfer the eggplant to a plate.
4. Add 1 tablespoon of vegetable oil, and cook the garlic, shallot, and jalapeno. Stir occasionally. You will have fragrant aromatics in about 4 minutes.
5. Now, add the pepper, eggplant, scallions, tamari, turbinado sugar, and rice vinegar with ¼ cup of water.

6. Once the sauce starts to coat the eggplant (in about 1-2 minutes), adjust the seasoning.
7. Enjoy your jasmine rice with Thai-style eggplant curry!

Nutritional Facts Per Serving:
Calories 715, Total Fat 38.6g, Saturated Fat 18g, Cholesterol 0mg, Sodium 1318mg, Total Carbohydrate 86.6g, Dietary Fiber 14.3g, Total Sugars 19g, Protein 11.6g, Vitamin D 0mcg, Calcium 67mg, Iron 5mg, Potassium 960mg

Delicious Mediterranean Pinwheels

Prep time 5 minutes / Cook time 1 minute / Serves 16
Ingredients:
- 2 cups Tahini Sauce
- 1 clove garlic
- 3 tablespoons tahini paste
- ¼ tsp Salt
- 3 tablespoons lemon juice
- ½ cup water
- ¼ tsp Pepper
- 4 tablespoons white vinegar
- 4 Pinwheels
- 4 cups Olives
- 8 Gluten-free tortillas
- 8 Cherry tomatoes
- 4 Lettuce leaves
- 2 Artichokes

Instructions:
1. Combine all the ingredients for the tahini sauce in a small bowl.
2. Cut the artichokes, tomatoes, and olives.
3. On one tortilla, spread some tahini sauce. Add the veggies and, lastly, the salad.
4. Roll the tortillas tightly and cut them into pinwheels!

Nutritional Facts Per Serving:
Calories 240, Total Fat 14.4g, Saturated Fat 2g, Cholesterol 1mg, Sodium 656mg, Total Carbohydrate 22.8g, Dietary Fiber 4.8g, Total Sugars 2.6g, Protein 4.9g, Vitamin D 0mcg, Calcium 86mg, Iron 2mg, Potassium 250mg

Peanut and Ginger Tofu Wrap

Prep time 30 minutes / Cook time 10 minutes / Serves 4
Ingredients:
- 4 oz Crispy Tofu
- 2 tablespoons, avocado/peanut oil
- 1 piece 14-ounce extra-firm tofu
- 1 tbsp Peanut Ginger Spread
- 2 tablespoons, lime juice
- 1 tablespoon, water
- 6 tablespoons, creamy peanut butter
- 1 tablespoon, tamari
- 1 tablespoon, ginger juice
- 2 tablespoons, coconut sugar
- ¼ cup, cilantro leaves
- 4 large whole-grain tortillas
- ¼ cup, sliced green onions
- 1 freshly peeled and shredded carrot
- 2 Lime wedges
- 1 small red bell pepper, cored and cut into thin strips

Instructions:
1. Put a large skillet on medium-high heat. Heat some oil and add the tofu, cooking it for 5 minutes. The tofu will be crisp and brown on both sides. Shift the tofu to a paper-lined dish so that the excess oil is absorbed.
2. Whisk all the ingredients to make the peanut spread. If you want a less thick consistency, you can add a few drops of water to the mix.
3. Start assembling the tofu, pepper strips, carrot cilantro, and green onions on top of the peanut spread on the wraps. Add a dash of lime juice.
4. Your healthy wrap is ready to be eaten!

Nutritional Facts Per Serving:
Calories 890, Total Fat 41.7g, Saturated Fat 7.6g, Cholesterol 0mg, Sodium 1202mg, Total Carbohydrate 95g, Dietary Fiber 6g, Total Sugars 52.4g, Protein 40.1g, Vitamin D 0mcg, Calcium 201mg, Iron 6mg, Potassium 1002mg

Amazing Rotini with a Dash of Pesto

Prep time 10 minutes / Cook time 10 minutes / Serves 4

Ingredients:

- Pesto
- 1 tablespoon fresh lime juice
- 1 cup cilantro leaves
- 1 clove garlic
- ¼ tsp Salt
- 1 seeded and quartered jalapeno pepper
- ¼ cup extra virgin olive oil
- ¼ tsp Pepper
- ¼ cup, raw almonds
- ½ cup Pasta
- 1 cup halved grape tomatoes
- 2 ears husked corn
- 1 cup jalapeno cilantro pesto
- 8 ounces rotini

Instructions:

1. Mix all the ingredients for the pesto, except the salt and pepper, in a powerful blender. Once you have a smooth paste, add some salt. Keep it for later use.
2. Add water to a large pot and boil it. Once the water starts boiling, add the corn and cook for about 2 minutes. Using tongs, remove the corn and rinse it in cold water.
3. In the same pot, cook the rotini al dente. Follow the package instructions for cooking.
4. To remove the corn kernels, use a sharp knife or a corn zipper.
5. Remove ¼ cup of the cooked liquid from the pasta. Drain the rotini and put it back in the pot.
6. Stir in the pesto and see that the rotini is well-coated with the pesto sauce. If you need to thin the sauce a bit, add the liquid which you have taken out. Add the corn and tomatoes to the pasta.
7. Add some more salt and pepper if required. Adjust the seasoning as per your taste!

Nutritional Facts Per Serving:

Calories 579, Total Fat 26.1g, Saturated Fat 3.6g, Cholesterol 15mg, Sodium 832mg, Total Carbohydrate 75.2g, Dietary Fiber 6.9g, Total Sugars 9.5g, Protein 16g, Vitamin D 0mcg, Calcium 112mg, Iron 6mg, Potassium 423mg

Quick-Fix Veggie Wrap

Prep time 15 minutes / Cook time 15 minutes / Serves 8

Ingredients:

- 1 finely diced medium red onion
- ½ freshly diced large green bell pepper
- 4 freshly minced garlic cloves
- ½ freshly diced large red bell pepper
- 1 teaspoon, curry powder
- 4 cups, shredded butter lettuce
- 4 cups, chopped veggies: cauliflower, steamed potatoes, zucchini, broccoli, carrots, and green beans
- 3 tablespoons, vegan feta
- 8 flour tortillas
- ½ cup, hummus

Instructions:

1. In a large pan, sauté the curry powder, green and red bell peppers, onion, and garlic in little water for about 5 minutes.
2. To these sautéed ingredients, add the shredded lettuce and chopped veggies. Cover everything, reduce the heat, and steam for another 10 minutes.
3. On a non-stick skillet, warm the tortillas. You can also warm them in a microwave by wrapping them in a wet towel.
4. Spoon ½ cup of veggies in the middle of the tortilla and put 2 tablespoons of hummus on one side of the tortilla.
5. Fold the other side and then make a roll.
6. If you are hungry and need a quick fix, this healthy veggie wrap will never disappoint.

Nutritional Facts Per Serving:

Calories 130, Total Fat 2.3g, Saturated Fat 0.3g, Cholesterol 0mg, Sodium 258mg, Total Carbohydrate 21.2g, Dietary Fiber 4.6g, Total Sugars 3.6g, Protein 6.8g, Vitamin D 0mcg, Calcium 104mg, Iron 2mg, Potassium 177mg

Chickpea Lentil Stew in Moroccan Style

Prep time 10 minutes / Cook time 35 minutes / Serves 6

Ingredients:

- 1 cup diced yellow onion
- 1 tablespoon coconut oil
- ¾ teaspoon ground cumin
- ¼ teaspoon ground coriander
- 1/3 teaspoon, ground cinnamon
- 2 cups water
- ½ teaspoon red pepper flakes
- ½ teaspoon garlic cloves
- ½ teaspoon fine sea salt
- 2 cups vegetable broth
- 1 lemon
- 1 28-ounce can, crushed tomatoes
- 2 cups thinly sliced carrots
- 1 cup uncooked and dry French lentils
- ½ Full-fat coconut milk
- 1 15-ounce can cooked chickpeas

Instructions:

1. Heat some coconut oil in a large Dutch oven. Saute the onions in the oil for about 10 minutes. If the onions are a little charred, that is absolutely fine.
2. Add all the spices, like the cinnamon, cumin, and coriander, along with sea salt and red pepper flakes. Stir in the garlic and cook everything until it is fragrant, about 2 minutes.
3. Add the broth with tomatoes, lentils, and carrots. Bring everything to a boil and allow the ingredients to simmer for 25 minutes. As the stew cooks, it will thicken.
4. Add the chickpeas and simmer for another 10 minutes until both the lentils and the chickpeas become soft.
5. If you desire a thinner stew, add some more vegetable broth.
6. After removing the stew from the heat, squeeze some lemon juice into it. Adjust the salt as per taste.
7. Once you ladle the soup into bowls, garnish it with coconut cream and cilantro. Scoop the soft, fatty layer of the coconut cream and add it to the top. Serve it with lemon wedges and more coconut milk. Sprinkle fresh cilantro on top!

Nutritional Facts Per Serving:

Calories 493, Total Fat 8.4g, Saturated Fat 3.5g, Cholesterol 0mg, Sodium 713mg, Total Carbohydrate 79.9g, Dietary Fiber 28g, Total Sugars 18.8g, Protein 27.5g, Vitamin D 0mcg, Calcium 185mg, Iron 9mg, Potassium 1163mg

Alfredo Fusilli

Prep time 5 minutes / Cook time 15 minutes / Serves 4

Ingredients:

- 12 ounces fusilli

For Alfredo sauce:

- 2 teaspoons vegetable oil
- 6 large cloves, garlic
- 1 cup water, divided
- ½ teaspoon dried basil or oregano
- ½ teaspoon dried thyme
- 1 teaspoon white vinegar
- 4 tablespoons lemon juice
- 6 tablespoons nutritional yeast
- 1 teaspoon salt
- 1 cup chopped onions
- ½ cup raw pumpkin seeds
- 1 cup water
- ½ teaspoon red pepper flakes
- 1 teaspoon onion powder
- 1 teaspoon garlic powder
- Pepper powder to taste
- 2 tablespoons flour
- 4 teaspoons extra virgin olive oil
- 2 cups baby spinach
- 1 cup frozen peas, thawed
- 2 cups nondairy milk
- 2 tablespoons vegan Parmesan cheese

Instructions:

1. Place a skillet over medium heat. Add vegetable oil and heat. Add onions and garlic and sauté until the onions are pink.
2. Add pumpkin seeds and water and bring to a boil. Simmer for 10 minutes. Remove from heat and cool.

3. Transfer into a blender. Add nutritional yeast, milk, basil, thyme, lemon juice, vinegar, flour, salt, and olive oil and blend until smooth.
4. Pour the blended mixture back into the skillet. Place the skillet over medium heat. Add about ½ cup of water and stirring constantly, bring to a boil. Cook until the sauce thickens. This will take like 5 minutes. Taste and adjust the seasonings if necessary. Add more water if you find the sauce too thick.
5. Add pasta, spinach, and peas and toss well. Heat thoroughly.
6. Remove from heat. Cover and set aside for a couple of minutes.
7. Garnish with pepper flakes and vegan Parmesan cheese if using and serve.

Nutritional Facts Per Serving:
Calories 881, Total Fat 46.4g, Saturated Fat 28.5g, Cholesterol 0mg, Sodium 678mg, Total Carbohydrate 98g, Dietary Fiber 14.2g, Total Sugars 10.2g, Protein 29.5g, Vitamin D 0mcg, Calcium 130mg, Iron 13mg, Potassium 1083mg

Delicious Collard Wraps

Prep time 15 minutes / Cook time 0 minutes / Serves 4

Ingredients:
- 1 avocado
- 4 large collard leaves
- ½ lime
- 1 teaspoon extra virgin olive oil
- 1 red bell pepper
- 2 ounces alfalfa sprouts
- 1 avocado
- ½ teaspoon minced garlic
- 1 cup raw pecans
- ½ teaspoon grated ginger
- 1 tablespoon tamari

Instructions:
1. Wash the collard leaves thoroughly and cut off the white stem. Put them in warm water with a dash of lemon juice. Allow the leaves to soak for about 10 minutes. Dry the leaves with a paper towel and, with a sharp knife, cut off the central root.
2. Slice the pepper and avocado.
3. In a blender, combine the pecan, cumin, tamari, and olive oil. Pulse everything until you have a clumpy mix.
4. Spread a collard leaf and spoon the pecan mixture onto it. Top it with the red bell pepper and avocado slices. Add some lime juice. Lastly, add the alfalfa sprouts. Fold the bottom and top and then wrap on both sides.
    1. Slice the wrap in half and serve it to your guests!

Nutritional Facts Per Serving:
Calories 581, Total Fat 56.1g, Saturated Fat 7.8g, Cholesterol 0mg, Sodium 263mg, Total Carbohydrate 20.6g, Dietary Fiber 13.6g, Total Sugars 4.1g, Protein 9g, Vitamin D 0mcg, Calcium 84mg, Iron 2mg, Potassium 811mg

Spaghetti Puttanesca with Red Beans & Spinach

Prep time 10 minutes / Cook time 10 minutes / Serves 4

Ingredients:
- 7 ounces whole-wheat spaghetti
- 2 tablespoons rapeseed oil
- 4 cloves garlic, peeled, chopped
- 4 teaspoons apple cider vinegar
- 10 kalamata olives, pitted, halved
- 15 ounces kidney beans, drained, rinsed
- ½ cup chopped basil leaves
- ½ cup chopped parsley
- 2 large onions, finely chopped
- 2 red chilies, deseeded, sliced
- 7 ounces cherry tomatoes, halved
- 2 tablespoons capers
- 2 teaspoons smoked paprika
- 12 ounces spinach, shredded
- ¼ tsp Salt

Instructions:
1. Follow the directions on the package and cook the spaghetti. Retain the cooked liquid.
2. Place a large nonstick pan or a wok over medium -high heat. Add oil. When the oil is

heated, add onion and cook until golden brown.

3. Add chili, garlic and cherry tomatoes and mix well. Cook for 10 minutes until aromatic.
4. Add vinegar, olives, capers, paprika, salt and about a cup of cooked water. Mix well. Add beans and heat thoroughly.
5. Add spinach to the remaining cooked pasta liquid. Let it remain for a couple of minutes

in the water until it wilts. Drain and add into the skillet. Toss well. Turn off the heat.
6. Add herbs and toss well.
7. Serve immediately.

Nutritional Facts Per Serving:
Calories 572, Total Fat 10.4g, Saturated Fat 1g, Cholesterol 0mg, Sodium 463mg, Total Carbohydrate 93.6g, Dietary Fiber 23.8g, Total Sugars 7.8g, Protein 31.2g, Vitamin D 0mcg, Calcium 237mg, Iron 12mg, Potassium 2266mg

Garlicky Mushroom Penne

Prep time 5 minutes / Cook time 15 minutes / Serves 4

Ingredients:
- 15 ounces chickpeas with its liquid
- 2 large cloves garlic, peeled, minced
- 4 teaspoons tahini
- 8 ounces whole-wheat pasta
- 4 red onions, halved, sliced
- lemon Juice + extra to serve
- 2 teaspoons loose vegetable bouillon
- ½ teaspoon ground coriander
- 4 teaspoons rapeseed oil
- 14 ounces mushrooms, roughly chopped
- ½ cup chopped parsley
- ¼ tsp Salt

Instructions:
For hummus:
1. Add chickpeas, lemon juice, garlic, coriander, tahini and vegetable bouillon into a blender

and blend until slightly smooth. A few pieces of chickpeas should be visible in it.
2. Follow the directions on the package and cook the pasta.
3. Place a large nonstick pan or a wok over medium -high heat. Add oil. When the oil is heated, add onion and mushroom and cook for 15 minutes until tender.
4. Add pasta and toss well. Add hummus and toss lightly. Sprinkle some water if required.
5. Garnish with parsley and divide into plates. Drizzle some lemon juice on top and serve.

Nutritional Facts Per Serving:
Calories 762, Total Fat 15.5g, Saturated Fat 1.5g, Cholesterol 0mg, Sodium 201mg, Total Carbohydrate 123.8g, Dietary Fiber 24.7g, Total Sugars 18.1g, Protein 34.4g, Vitamin D 357mcg, Calcium 178mg, Iron 11mg, Potassium 1501mg

Penne alla Norma

Prep time 10 minutes / Cook time 5 minutes / Serves 6

Ingredients:
- 2 small eggplants
- 2 large cloves garlic, crushed
- 15 ounces plum tomato
- ¼ cup cheese, finely grated
- 4 teaspoons extra-virgin olive oil
- ¼ teaspoon red chili flakes
- 1 onion, chopped
- 10 ounces gluten free penne
- ½ cup torn fresh basil leaves
- ¼ tsp Salt
- ¼ tsp Pepper
- 2 tablespoons grated vegan cheese

Instructions:

1. Place eggplant cubes in a large bowl. Drizzle olive oil over it. Toss well.
2. Place a large nonstick pan over high heat. Add eggplant and cook until golden brown on all the sides. Transfer into a bowl.
3. Lower the heat and onions. Sprinkle a little water and sauté until translucent.
4. Stir in the chili and garlic and sauté for 5 minutes, until aromatic.
5. Add tomatoes, salt, pepper and 1 can water, fill water in the empty tomato can.
6. Mash the tomatoes slightly with a potato masher.

7. Add eggplants and stir. Cook until eggplants are tender.
8. Follow the directions on the package and cook pasta. Drain the pasta and retain a little of the cooked liquid.
9. Add pasta into the sauce and toss well. Add some retained liquid and cheese and toss well.

10. Serve in bowls. Garnish with basil and serve.

Nutritional Facts Per Serving:
Calories 168, Total Fat 5.7g, Saturated Fat 1.3g, Cholesterol 6mg, Sodium 365mg, Total Carbohydrate 26.2g, Dietary Fiber 8.3g, Total Sugars 8.1g, Protein 5.2g, Vitamin D 0mcg, Calcium 106mg, Iron 1mg, Potassium 456mg

Vegetable Lo Mein with Tofu

Prep time 5 minutes / Cook time 10 minutes / Serves 8

Ingredients:
- 16 ounces dried vegan lo Mein noodles

For sauce:
- 6 tablespoons soy sauce
- 4 tablespoons hoisin sauce
- 4 tablespoons organic brown sugar
- 2 teaspoons toasted sesame oil

For lo Mein:
- 6 tablespoons vegetable oil, divided
- 16 ounces white button mushrooms sliced
- 3 teaspoons freshly grated ginger
- 3 carrots, peeled, cut into matchsticks
- 14 ounces, extra firm tofu, drained
- 6 cloves garlic, peeled, minced
- 8 scallions, white parts finely chopped, green part sliced
- 3 cups fresh baby corn pieces

Instructions:
1. Cook the noodles following the directions on the package.
2. Add all the ingredients for sauce into a bowl and whisk well.
3. To make lo Mein: Place a large skillet over medium heat. Add 2 tablespoons oil and heat. Add tofu and sauté until brown all over.

4. Remove tofu with a slotted spoon and place on a plate lined with paper towels.
5. Again add 2 tablespoons oil into the skillet. Add mushrooms and cook until brown. Remove the mushrooms and place it along with tofu.
6. Add 2 tablespoons oil into the skillet again. When the oil is heated, white part of the scallion and sauté for 10 minutes. Add ginger and garlic and stir for a few seconds until aromatic.
7. Increase the heat to high heat. Add carrot and baby corn and sauté for a few minutes until the vegetables are crisp as well as tender.
8. Reduce the heat to medium heat. Pour the sauce mixture and heat for a couple of minutes.
9. Add noodles, tofu and mushrooms. Toss well. Heat thoroughly.
10. Turn off the heat.

Nutritional Facts Per Serving:
Calories 402, Total Fat 19.6g, Saturated Fat 3.3g, Cholesterol 0mg, Sodium 1178mg, Total Carbohydrate 49.5g, Dietary Fiber 5g, Total Sugars 13.4g, Protein 13.4g, Vitamin D 204mcg, Calcium 151mg, Iron 6mg, Potassium 584mg

Coconut Noodles

Prep time 5 minutes / Cook time 6 minutes / Serves 8

Ingredients:
- 16 ounces rice noodles
- 6 tablespoons tomato paste
- 13-ounce unsweetened coconut milk
- ½ cup shredded coconut
- 16 ounces bean sprouts
- 6 scallions thinly sliced
- ½ teaspoon chili powder
- 1 ½ tablespoons chili sauce

- 30 fresh large basil leaves, torn
- ¼ tsp Salt

Instructions:
1. Heat a large pan over medium flame. Add the coconut milk, chili powder, tomato paste, salt and chili sauce and mix it well.
2. Once it boils, lower the flame and let it simmer for about 2-3 minutes.

3. Add noodles and toss well. Cook for about 3 minutes
4. Divide into bowls. Divide the scallions, sprouts and basil among the bowls.
5. Garnish with shredded coconut if using and serve.

Nutritional Facts Per Serving:
Calories 217, Total Fat 13.2g, Saturated Fat 11.3g, Cholesterol 0mg, Sodium 182mg, Total Carbohydrate 23g, Dietary Fiber 2.9g, Total Sugars 3.6g, Protein 5g, Vitamin D 0mcg, Calcium 36mg, Iron 3mg, Potassium 413mg

Rainbow Veggie Noodle Stir-Fry

Prep time 5 minutes / Cook time 12 minutes / Serves 8

Ingredients:
- 15 ounces thick flat rice noodles
- 4 cloves garlic, peeled, sliced
- 2 red onions, thinly sliced
- 2 inches fresh ginger, peeled, cut into matchsticks
- 1 bunch fresh cilantro, chopped
- 2 red bell pepper, thinly sliced
- 1 large head broccoli, cut into florets,
- 12 ounces, firm tofu cubed
- 1 fresh red chili, thinly sliced
- 2 tablespoons vegetable oil
- 7 ounces fresh spinach, shredded
- 7 ounces snow peas
- 2 carrots, peeled into long ribbons
- 4 limes, juiced
- 7 ounces unsalted cashews, toasted until golden in color
- 2 teaspoons sesame oil
- 4 Lime wedges to serve

Instructions:
1. Follow the instructions on the package and cook the noodles.
2. Place a large nonstick pan or work over high heat. Add oil and heat. Add onion, ginger, garlic and cilantro stem and sauté until light golden brown in color.
3. Add broccoli, tofu, bell peppers and snow peas and stir-fry for 2 minutes.
4. Add spinach and cook for 10 minutes until it wilts. Stir in the noodles and carrot and toss well. Heat thoroughly.
5. Add lime juice, sesame oil to taste. Toss well.
6. Divide into plates. Garnish with chili, cashews and cilantro leaves.

Nutritional Facts Per Serving:
Calories 337, Total Fat 18.4g, Saturated Fat 3.6g, Cholesterol 0mg, Sodium 58mg, Total Carbohydrate 37.7g, Dietary Fiber 6g, Total Sugars 7g, Protein 10.9g, Vitamin D 0mcg, Calcium 171mg, Iron 4mg, Potassium 655mg

Stir fried Rice Noodles with Tofu and Vegetables

Prep time 5 minutes / Cook time 3 / Serves 8

Ingredients:
- 8 ounces rice noodles
- 14 ounces firm tofu
- 4 carrots, cut into thin strips
- 4 cups bean sprouts
- 8 scallions, thinly sliced
- 2 red bell peppers, deseeded, thinly sliced
- 6 tablespoons brown sugar
- 6 tablespoons soy sauce
- 4 tablespoons lime juice
- 1/3 cup roasted peanuts, roughly chopped
- ¾ cup fresh cilantro, chopped
- 2 tablespoons canola oil
- 1 ½ tablespoons fresh ginger, grated

Instructions:
1. Add brown sugar, soy sauce and lime juice to a bowl and whisk until sugar dissolves completely.
2. Place a large skillet or wok over medium high heat. Add oil. When oil is heated, add carrots, bell peppers and ginger and sauté for 3 minutes.
3. Add tofu and bean sprouts and sauté until the vegetables are crisp as well as tender. Turn off the heat.
4. Add half the sauce mixture and noodles into another skillet and toss well. Heat thoroughly.

5. Add cilantro and stir well. Transfer on a serving platter. Top with the vegetable mixture. Drizzle remaining sauce mixture on top.
6. Garnish with scallions, roasted peanuts and serve hot.

Nutritional Facts Per Serving:
Calories 293, Total Fat 9.4g, Saturated Fat 1.2g, Cholesterol 0mg, Sodium 768mg, Total Carbohydrate 44.1g, Dietary Fiber 3.2g, Total Sugars 10.7g, Protein 12.2g, Vitamin D 0mcg, Calcium 160mg, Iron 3mg, Potassium 551mg

Miso Shiitake Ramen

Prep time 10 minutes / Cook time 15 minutes / Serves 4

Ingredients:
- 6 cups vegetable stock
- 2 red chilies
- 4 tablespoons white miso paste
- 2 tablespoons vegetable oil
- 8 spring onions, thinly sliced
- 2 cloves garlic, smashed
- 14 ounces frozen vegan ramen
- 9 ounces shiitake mushrooms, sliced
- 4 heads Pak Choy, shredded
- 2 teaspoons sesame oil
- 1 teaspoon soy sauce
- 4-inch ginger, grated
- ¼ tsp Salt
- ¼ tsp Pepper

Instructions:
1. Add stock, sliced ginger, garlic and whole chili into a pot. Place the pot over high heat.
2. Let it boil for 10 minutes. Fish out the chili, ginger and garlic and throw it off.
3. Add miso and whisk until it dissolves completely. Lower the heat and let it simmer.
4. Cook the ramen following the directions on the package. Drain and place in cold water for a couple of minutes. Drain and set aside.
5. Place a skillet over medium heat. Add oil. When the oil is heated, add chopped chili, whites of the spring onion, grated ginger, mushrooms and Pak Choy and sauté for 3-4 minutes.
6. Stir in soy sauce and sesame oil and heat for 1 minute and then turn off the heat.
7. Place equal amount stir-fried vegetables among 4 bowls. Divide the simmering stock among the bowls. Garnish with greens of spring onion and serve.

Nutritional Facts Per Serving:
Calories 654, Total Fat 14.5g, Saturated Fat 2.2g, Cholesterol 0mg, Sodium 3896mg, Total Carbohydrate 106.5g, Dietary Fiber 20g, Total Sugars 20.4g , Protein 32.6g, Vitamin D 0mcg, Calcium 916mg, Iron 10mg, Potassium 2362mg

Chapter 7: Desserts & Snacks Recipes

Mango & Papaya After-Chop

Prep time 25 minutes / Cook time 0 minutes / Serves 1
Ingredients:
- ¼ of papaya, chopped
- 1 mango, chopped
- 1 Tbsp coconut milk
- ½ tsp maple syrup
- 1 Tbsp peanuts, chopped

Instructions:
1. Cut open the papaya. Scoop out the seeds, chop.
2. Peel the mango. Slice the fruit from the pit, chop.
3. Put the fruit in a bowl. Add remaining ingredients. Stir to coat.

Nutrition Facts Per Serving:
Calories 330, Total Fat 9.6g, Saturated Fat 4.2g, Cholesterol 0mg, Sodium 14mg, Total Carbohydrate 63.4g, Dietary Fiber 7.9g, Total Sugars 54.9g, Protein 5.8g, Vitamin D 0mcg, Calcium 66mg, Iron 1mg, Potassium 818mg

Sautéed Bosc Pears with Walnuts

Prep time 15 minutes / Cook time 16 minutes / Serves 6
Ingredients:
- 2 Tbsp salted butter
- ¼ tsp cinnamon
- ¼ tsp nutmeg, ground
- 6 Bosc pears, peeled, quartered
- 1 Tbsp lemon juice
- ½ cup walnuts, chopped, toasted

Instructions:
1. Melt butter in a skillet, add spices and cook for 30 seconds.
2. Add pears and cook for 15 minutes. Stir in lemon juice.
3. Serve topped with walnuts.

Nutrition Facts Per Serving:
Calories 221, Total Fat 10.3g, Saturated Fat 2.8g, Cholesterol 10mg, Sodium 31mg, Total Carbohydrate 33g, Dietary Fiber 7.3g, Total Sugars 20.6g, Protein 3.3g, Vitamin D 3mcg, Calcium 28mg, Iron 1mg, Potassium 302mg

Brown Rice Pudding

Prep time 5 minutes / Cook time 1 hour 30 minutes / Serves 6
Ingredients:
- 2 cups brown rice, cooked
- 3 cups light coconut milk
- 3 eggs
- 1 cup brown sugar
- 1 tsp vanilla
- ½ tsp salt
- ½ tsp cinnamon
- ¼ tsp nutmeg

Instructions:
1. Blend all ingredients well. Put mixture in a 2-quart casserole dish.
2. Bake at 300°F for 90 minutes.
3. Serve.

Nutrition Facts Per Serving:
Calories 632, Total Fat 32.5g, Saturated Fat 26.4g, Cholesterol 82mg, Sodium 252mg, Total Carbohydrate 79.1g, Dietary Fiber 4.9g, Total Sugars 27.8g, Protein 10.3g, Vitamin D 8mcg, Calcium 74mg, Iron 4mg, Potassium 549mg

Raw Energy Squares

Prep time 30 minutes / Cook time 0 minutes / Serves 6

Ingredients:

- 2 cups Medjool dates, chopped and pitted
- 2 cups cashews
- ½ cup almonds
- ¾ cup powder, cocoa
- Sea salt, to taste
- 2 Tbsp vanilla extract
- 3 Tbsp cold water

Instructions:

1. Blend first five ingredients in a food processor.
2. Add the vanilla and water, give a quick pulse.
3. Put the dough into a pan, making an even layer.
4. Cut into squares and serve.

Nutrition Facts Per Serving:
Calories 387, Total Fat 26.1g, Saturated Fat 4.5g, Cholesterol 0mg, Sodium 28mg, Total Carbohydrate 30.2g, Dietary Fiber 5g, Total Sugars 9.2g, Protein 11g, Vitamin D 0mcg, Calcium 43mg, Iron 5mg, Potassium 323mg

Date Porcupines

Prep time 20 minutes / Cook time 15 minutes / Serves 2

Ingredients:

- 2 eggs
- 1 Tbsp extra-virgin olive oil
- 1 tsp vanilla
- 1 cup Medjool dates, pitted, chopped
- 1 cup walnuts, chopped
- ¾ cup flour
- 1 cup coconut, shredded
- ½ tsp salt

Instructions:

1. Preheat oven to 350°F.
2. Beat the eggs, adding the oil and vanilla. Fold in the dates and walnuts. Add flour and salt to the mixture, mix well.
3. Form the mixture into small balls and roll in coconut. Bake for 15 minutes.
4. Serve cold.

Nutrition Facts Per Serving:
Calories 907, Total Fat 62.1g, Saturated Fat 16.4g, Cholesterol 164mg , Sodium 653mg, Total Carbohydrate 69.7g, Dietary Fiber 11.1g, Total Sugars 21.9g, Protein 27.8g, Vitamin D 15mcg, Calcium 70mg, Iron 11mg, Potassium 582mg

Raspberry Chia Pudding Shots

Prep time 1 hour / Cook time 15 minutes / Serves 2

Ingredients:

- ¼ cup chia seeds
- ½ cup raspberries
- ½ cup coconut milk
- ¼ cup almond milk
- 1 Tbsp cacao powder
- 1 Tbsp stevia

Instructions:

1. Combine all ingredients except raspberries in a jar.
2. Let sit for 2-3 minutes and transfer to shot glasses.
3. Refrigerate 1 hour, or overnight to serve as breakfast.
4. Serve with fresh raspberries.

Nutrition Facts Per Serving:
Calories 246, Total Fat 23.1g, Saturated Fat 19.4g, Cholesterol 0mg, Sodium 15mg, Total Carbohydrate 13.6g, Dietary Fiber 6.1g, Total Sugars 4.4g, Protein 3.6g, Vitamin D 0mcg, Calcium 48mg, Iron 2mg, Potassium 339mg

Banana Muffins

Prep time 15 minutes / Cook time 15 minutes / Serves 10

Ingredients:

- 3 bananas
- 2 eggs
- 2 cups whole wheat pastry flour
- 1/3 cup sugar
- 1 tsp salt
- 1 tsp baking soda
- ½ cup walnuts, chopped

Instructions:

1. Preheat oven to 350°F.
2. Grease and flour 10 cups of a muffin tin.
3. Mix bananas and eggs together. Add sifted dry ingredients.
4. Add nuts. Mix well.
5. Spoon into muffin tins. Bake for 20 minutes.

Nutrition Facts Per Serving:

Calories 199, Total Fat 4.9g, Saturated Fat 0.6g, Cholesterol 33mg, Sodium 372mg, Total Carbohydrate 34.5g, Dietary Fiber 2g, Total Sugars 11.2g, Protein 5.6g, Vitamin D 3mcg, Calcium 14mg, Iron 2mg, Potassium 198mg

Avocado-based Chocolate Mousse

Prep time 7 minutes / Cook time 0 minutes / Serves 3

Ingredients:

- 4 ripe avocados
- 1 cup agave syrup, divided
- 1 cup cacao, divided
- ¼ teaspoon salt
- ¼ teaspoon vanilla extract

Instructions:

1. Prepare the avocados and place the meat in a food processor. Process until smooth.
2. Add half the agave syrup, half the cacao, the salt and the vanilla; process until smooth.
3. Taste to see if it needs more agave syrup or cacao and add anything that's lacking.
4. Refrigerate for at least two hours, or overnight, before serving.

Nutrition Facts Per Serving:

Calories 950, Total Fat 57.6g, Saturated Fat 14.3g, Cholesterol 0mg, Sodium 285mg, Total Carbohydrate 124.8g, Dietary Fiber 26g, Total Sugars 1.4g, Protein 10.4g, Vitamin D 0mcg, Calcium 83mg, Iron 5mg, Potassium 1367mg

Banana Creamy Pie

Prep time 10 minutes / Cook time 0 minutes / Serves 4

Ingredients:

- 2 large pitted dates
- 1 pre-made pie crust, cooled
- 2 very ripe bananas, peeled and sliced, plus one a little less ripe for garnish
- 1 tablespoon coconut sugar
- 1 cup coconut milk
- ½ teaspoon vanilla
- ¼ salt

Instructions:

1. Soak the dates for about an hour, then drain and dry them.
2. Place the dates and banana slices in a food processor and pulse to break them up.
3. Add the coconut sugar, coconut milk, vanilla and salt and process until smooth and creamy.
4. Pour the filling into a cooled pie crust. It must be cool, or it will make the crust soggy.
5. Cover with plastic wrap and place the pie in the freezer for at least two hours.
6. Remove from the freezer and let it thaw a bit. Slice the remaining banana and place it on top. Serve while still partially frozen.

Nutrition Facts Per Serving:

Calories 511, Total Fat 29.4g, Saturated Fat 15.9g, Cholesterol 0mg, Sodium 363mg, Total Carbohydrate 61.9g, Dietary Fiber 4.1g, Total Sugars 37.8g, Protein 4.6g, Vitamin D 0mcg, Calcium 27mg, Iron 3mg, Potassium 450mg

Banana Mango Ice Cream

Prep time 30 minutes / Cook time 0 minutes / Serves 2

Ingredients:
- 1 banana, peeled and sliced
- 2 ripe mangos with the skin removed and the flesh cubed
- 3 tablespoons almond or cashew milk, chilled

Instructions:
1. Lay out the banana and mango slices on a baking sheet lined with parchment paper and place them in the freezer.
2. Once they are frozen solid, remove the fruit and place it in the food processor.
3. Add the cold milk and process until smooth, about three to four minutes.
4. Taste and add sweetener as needed.
5. Serve immediately.

Nutrition Facts Per Serving:
Calories 306, Total Fat 6.8g, Saturated Fat 5.1g, Cholesterol 0mg, Sodium 7mg, Total Carbohydrate 65.1g, Dietary Fiber 7.4g, Total Sugars 53.9g, Protein 3.9g, Vitamin D 0mcg, Calcium 44mg, Iron 1mg, Potassium 835mg

Strawberry Mango Shave Ice

Prep time 5 hours 30 minutes / Cook time 0 minutes / Serves 4

Ingredients:
- ½ cup superfine sugar, divided
- 1-cup strawberries, diced
- 2 diced mangos
- 2 cups mango juice
- ½ cup coconut, toasted

Instructions:
1. Add 1 cup water and ¾ cup sugar to a pot and boil over medium heat.
2. Once boiled, remove from heat and add 2 more cups of water.
3. Freeze this mixture stirring after every 45 minutes.
4. Take a blender and add all remaining ingredients and blend until smooth.
5. Strain the mixture into a container with a pour spout.
6. For serving, divide the ice into glasses and pour juice and mixture over them.
7. Serve and enjoy.

Nutritional facts per serving:
Calories 306, Total Fat 4.1g, Saturated Fat 3.1g, Cholesterol 0mg, Sodium 29mg, Total Carbohydrate 70g, Dietary Fiber 4.3g, Total Sugars 65.8g, Protein 2g, Vitamin D 0mcg, Calcium 24mg, Iron 2mg, Potassium 373mg

Chocolate Avocado Mousse

Prep time 10 minutes / Cook time 10 minutes / Serves 6

Ingredients:
- 1¼ cups almond milk, unsweetened
- 1 lb. dairy-free dark chocolate, coarsely chopped
- 4 small ripe avocados, pitted, peeled, and chopped
- ¼ cup agave syrup
- 1 tbsp orange zest, finely grated
- 2 tbsp puffed quinoa
- 2 tsp Maldon sea salt
- 2 tsp Aleppo pepper flakes
- 1 tbsp extra virgin olive oil

Instructions:
1. Heat almond milk in a saucepan. After 5 to 10 minutes, add in chopped chocolate.
2. Take all remaining ingredients and blend them until smooth.
3. Mix both and let cool for a while.
4. Refrigerate for about 2 hours before serving.

Nutrition Facts Per Serving:
Calories 1007, Total Fat 77.3g, Saturated Fat 44.8g, Cholesterol 17mg, Sodium 718mg, Total Carbohydrate 76.1g, Dietary Fiber 14.3g, Total Sugars 43.3g, Protein 11.4g, Vitamin D 0mcg, Calcium 183mg, Iron 5mg, Potassium 1251mg

Fudge

Prep time 10 minutes / Cook time 5 minutes / Serves 2

Ingredients:

- 1 cup vegan chocolate chips
- ½ cup soy milk

Instructions:

1. Line an 8-inch portion skillet with wax paper. Set aside. Clear some space in your refrigerator for this dish as you will need it later.
2. Melt chocolate chips in a double boiler or add chocolate and almond spread to a medium, microwave-safe bowl. Melt it in the microwave in 20-second increments until chocolate melts. In between each 20-second burst, stir the chocolate until it is smooth.
3. Empty the melted chocolate mixture into the lined skillet. Tap the sides of the skillet to make sure the mixture spreads into an even layer. Alternatively, use a spoon to make swirls on top.
4. Move skillet to the refrigerator until it is firm. Remove the skillet from the refrigerator and cut fudge into 18 squares.

Nutrition Facts Per Serving:
Calories 193, Total Fat 9.1g, Saturated Fat 4.1g, Cholesterol 0mg, Sodium 51mg, Total Carbohydrate 23.9g, Dietary Fiber 2.4g, Total Sugars 20.4g, Protein 4g, Vitamin D 0mcg, Calcium 15mg, Iron 3mg, Potassium 72mg

Chocolate Chip Cookies

Prep time 20 minutes / Cook time 0 minutes / Serves 8

Ingredients:

- 1½ cups roasted, salted cashews
- 8 oz pitted Medjool dates
- 3 tbsp coconut oil
- 2 tsp vanilla extract
- 2 cups old-fashioned oats
- 1 cup semi-sweet or dark chocolate chips

Instructions:

1. Line a baking sheet with parchment paper.
2. In the bowl of a food processor, add the cashews, dates, coconut oil, vanilla, and oats.
3. Pulse until combined, and all lumps are broken up.
4. On the off chance that the batter appears to be dry, add 1 more tbsp of coconut oil and a sprinkle of water. Mix in the chocolate chips.
5. Divide the mixture into 18 to 20 tbsp-size balls and place them on the prepared baking sheet. Using the palm of your hand, delicately press down each ball into flat circles. Move the sheet to the refrigerator for 10 to 15 minutes or until cookies are firm.
6. Serve and enjoy.

Nutrition Facts Per Serving:
Calories 815, Total Fat 54.2g, Saturated Fat 15.8g, Cholesterol 0mg, Sodium 17mg, Total Carbohydrate 76g, Dietary Fiber 7.2g, Total Sugars 31g, Protein 18.8g, Vitamin D 0mcg, Calcium 64mg, Iron 7mg, Potassium 794mg

Oatmeal & Peanut Butter Bar

Prep Time 4 minutes / Cook Time 6 minutes / Serves 2

Ingredients

- 1½ cups date, pit removed
- ½ cup peanut butter
- ½ cup old-fashioned rolled oats

Instructions:

1. Grease and line an 8" x 8" baking tin with parchment and pop to one side.
2. Grab your food processor, add the dates and whizz until chopped.
3. Add the peanut butter and the oats and pulse.
4. Scoop into the baking tin then pop into the fridge or freezer until set and serve.

Nutrition value per serving:
Calories 1837, Total Fat 35.7g, Saturated Fat 7.2g, Cholesterol 0mg, Sodium 307mg, Total Carbohydrate 393.8g, Dietary Fiber 45.1g, Total Sugars 316.4g, Protein 30.8g, Vitamin D 0mcg, Calcium 204mg, Iron 12mg, Potassium 3704mg

Chocolate Chip Banana Pancake

Prep Time 5 minutes / Cook Time 10 minutes / Serves 6

Ingredients

- 1 large ripe banana, mashed
- 2 tablespoons coconut sugar
- 3 tablespoons coconut oil, melted
- 1 cup coconut milk
- 1 ½ cups whole wheat flour
- 1 teaspoon baking soda
- ½ cup vegan chocolate chips
- Olive oil, for frying

Instructions:

1. Grab a large bowl and add the banana, sugar, oil and milk. Stir well.
2. Add the flour and baking soda and stir again until combined.
3. Add the chocolate chips and fold through then pop to one side.
4. Place a skillet over a medium heat and add a drop of oil.
5. Pour ¼ of the batter into the pan and move the pan to cover.
6. Cook for 3 minutes then flip and cook on the other side.
7. Repeat with the remaining pancakes then serve and enjoy.

Nutritional facts per serving:

Calories 346, Total Fat 20.4g, Saturated Fat 15.4g, Cholesterol 0mg, Sodium 221mg, Total Carbohydrate 38.6g, Dietary Fiber 2.6g, Total Sugars 11.2g,
Protein 4.7g, Vitamin D 0mcg, Calcium 12mg, Iron 3mg, Potassium 220mg

Avocado and 'Sausage' Sandwich

Prep Time 5 minutes / Cook Time 10 minutes / Serves 1

Ingredients

- 1 vegan sausage patty
- 1 cup kale, chopped
- 2 teaspoons extra virgin olive oil
- 1 tablespoon pepitas
- Salt and pepper, to taste

For the spicy mayo

- 1 tablespoon vegan mayo
- 1/8 teaspoon chipotle powder
- 1 teaspoon jalapeno chopped
- 1 English muffin, toasted
- ¼ avocado, sliced

Instructions:

1. Place a sauté pan over a high heat and add a drop of oil.
2. Add the vegan patty and cook for 2 minutes.
3. Flip the patty then add the kale and pepitas.
4. Season well then cook for another few minutes until the patty is cooked.
5. Find a small bowl and add the mayo, chipotle powder and the jalapeno. Stir well to combine.
6. Place the muffin onto a flat surface, spread with the spicy may then top with the patty.
7. Add the sliced avocado then serve and enjoy.

Nutritional facts per serving:

Calories 540Total Fat 32.9g, Saturated Fat 5.7g, Cholesterol 8mg, Sodium 743mg, Total Carbohydrate 46.7g, Dietary Fiber 7.4g, Total Sugars 4.2g, Protein 18.3g, Vitamin D 0mcg, Calcium 193mg, Iron 5mg, Potassium 762mg

Black Bean Burritos

Prep Time 6 minutes / Cook Time 24 minutes / Serves 2

Ingredients

For the rice

- ¾ cup white rice
- 1 ½ cups water
- ¼ tsp salt
- ½ lime, juiced
- ¼ cup chopped fresh cilantro

For the potato and onion mixture

- 3 medium red potatoes, cut into bite-sized pieces
- ½ red onion, sliced into rings
- 1 tbsp. olive oil
- Salt & pepper, to taste

For the beans

- 1 cup cooked black beans

- ¼ teaspoon each ground cumin garlic powder, and chili powder
- Salt & pepper, to taste

For the slaw...
- ¼ avocado
- 2 tbsps. lime juice
- 1 cup thinly sliced purple cabbage
- 1 thinly sliced jalapeno
- ¼ tsp. salt
- ¼ tsp. black pepper

To serve
- 2 large vegan flour tortillas
- ½ sliced avocado
- Hot sauce optional
- ¼ cup salsa

Instructions:
1. Place the rice, water and salt in a pan and bring to the boil.
2. Cover and cook on low until fluffy then remove from the heat and pop to one side.
3. Place a skillet over a medium heat, add 1-2 tablespoons olive oil and add the potatoes and onion.

4. Season well then leave to cook for 10 minutes, stirring often.
5. Remove from the heat and pop to one side.
6. Take a small pan then add the beans, cumin, garlic and chili. Stir well.
7. Pop over a medium heat and bring to simmer. Reduce the heat to remain warm.
8. Take a small bowl and add the lime juice and avocado. Mash together.
9. Add the cabbage and jalapeno and stir well. Season then pop to one side.
10. Add the cilantro and lime juice to the cooked rice then toss with a fork.
11. Gently warm the tortillas in a microwave for 10-20 seconds then add the fillings.
12. Roll up, serve and enjoy.

Nutritional facts per serving:
Calories 1174, Total Fat 29.8g, Saturated Fat 5.8g, Cholesterol 0mg, Sodium 607mg, Total Carbohydrate 199g, Dietary Fiber 32.3g, Total Sugars 10.7g, Protein 37g, Vitamin D 0mcg, Calcium 251mg, Iron 12mg, Potassium 3803mg

Coconut Yogurt Chia Pudding

Prep time 5 minutes / Cook time 0 minutes / Serves 1
Ingredients:
- ½ cup vanilla coconut yogurt
- 2 tbsp chia seeds
- 3 tbsp almond milk

Instructions:
1. Mix all ingredients in a bowl until well combined.
2. Place in the freezer for an hour or overnight.

3. When thickened, top with your favorite garnishes and serve.

Nutrition Facts Per Serving:
Calories 466, Total Fat 29.6g, Saturated Fat 12.6g, Cholesterol 7mg, Sodium 102mg, Total Carbohydrate 35g, Dietary Fiber 20.5g, Total Sugars 10.1g, Protein 17.4g, Vitamin D 0mcg, Calcium 589mg, Iron 5mg, Potassium 635mg

Peanut Butter Ice Cream

Prep time 20 minutes / Cook time 8 hours / Serves 3
Ingredients:
- 1 cup dark chocolate chips
- 3 cans coconut cream, divided
- ¼ cup peanut butter
- ½ cup granulated sugar
- 2 tsp vanilla extract
- ¼ tsp salt
- ¼ cup graham cracker crumbs

Instructions:

1. Reserve ½ cup of the coconut cream and add the rest to the blender along with peanut butter, sugar, vanilla extract, and salt.
2. Blend until smooth and freeze the mixture for 2 hours.
3. Heat the remaining ½ cup of the coconut cream in a small pot over low heat until it starts to boil.
4. Remove the pot from the heat and add the chocolate chips to the coconut cream.

5. Let this sit for 5 minutes then stir the mixture to combine the chocolate and the cream. The chocolate chips should be completely softened by this point.
6. Let the mixture cool to room temperature.
7. Meanwhile, take out the frozen mixture and mix with the coconut cream chocolate mixture and graham cracker crumbs in a bowl.

8. Let cool for 8 hours in the refrigerator.
9. Scoop out and serve chilled.

Nutrition Facts Per Serving:
Calories 1029, Total Fat 79.4g, Saturated Fat 59.7g, Cholesterol 0mg, Sodium 391mg, Total Carbohydrate 83.7g, Dietary Fiber 7g, Total Sugars 66.4g, Protein 14g, Vitamin D 0mcg, Calcium 40mg, Iron 7mg, Potassium 775mg

Cashew Cream Cheese

Prep time 10 minutes / Cook time 0 minutes / Serves 6

Ingredients:
- 1 cup raw cashews, soaked overnight
- 2-3 tbsp water
- ¼ cup lemon juice
- ½ tsp apple cider vinegar
- 2 tbsp nutritional yeast
- Salt, to taste

Instructions:
1. Wash soaked cashews in a colander then transfer them to a blender or food processor and blend them with 2 to 3 tbsp of water until smooth.

2. Add in the rest of the ingredients and mix until combined.
3. If you'd like a vegetable cream "cheese," add chopped herbs, chives, peppers, carrots, and onions to the mixture.

Nutritional facts per serving:
Calories 145, Total Fat 10.8g, Saturated Fat 2.2g, Cholesterol 0mg, Sodium 35mg, Total Carbohydrate 9.2g, Dietary Fiber 1.6g, Total Sugars 1.4g, Protein 5.1g, Vitamin D 0mcg, Calcium 14mg, Iron 2mg, Potassium 222mg

Cinnamon Apples

Prep time 20 minutes / Cook time 60 minutes / Serves 2

Ingredients:
- 2 apples
- 1 tsp cinnamon

Instructions:
1. Pre-heat stove to 220 degrees F.
2. Core the apples or cut them into rounds with a sharp blade or mandolin slicer.
3. Place them in a bowl and sprinkle them with cinnamon. Use your hands to make sure the apples are coated completely.
4. Arrange the apple cuts in a single layer on a silicone tray or a baking sheet lined with parchment paper.

5. Bake for 1 hour then flip the apples.
6. Bake for 1 more hour. Then, turn the oven off and leave the sheet in the stove until cooled.
7. Serve when desired or store in a sealed container for up to a week.

Nutrition Facts Per Serving:
Calories 119, Total Fat 0.4g, Saturated Fat 0g, Cholesterol 0mg, Sodium 2mg, Total Carbohydrate 31.7g, Dietary Fiber 6g, Total Sugars 23.2g , Protein 0.7g, Vitamin D 0mcg, Calcium 13mg, Iron 1mg, Potassium 244mg

Roasted Chickpeas

Prep time 10 minutes / Cook time 25 minutes / Serves 4

Ingredients:
- 1 can chickpeas, rinsed and drained
- 2 tsp freshly squeezed lemon juice
- 2 tsp tamari
- ½ tsp fresh rosemary, chopped
- 1/8 tsp sea salt

- 1/8 tsp pure maple syrup or agave nectar

Instructions:
1. Preheat stove to 400°F. Line a baking sheet with parchment paper.

2. Toss all ingredients together and spread the chickpeas out on the baking sheet.
3. Roast for around 25 minutes, stirring the chickpeas every 5 minutes or so. Note, until the tamari and lemon juice dry up, the chickpeas will seem delicate, not crunchy.
4. Serve warm or at room temperature.

Nutrition Facts Per Serving:
Calories 185, Total Fat 3.1g, Saturated Fat 0.3g, Cholesterol 0mg, Sodium 239mg, Total Carbohydrate 30.8g, Dietary Fiber 8.8g, Total Sugars 5.6g, Protein 10g, Vitamin D 0mcg, Calcium 55mg, Iron 3mg, Potassium 449mg

Baked Sesame Fries

Prep time 10 minutes / Cook time 20 minutes / Serves 4
Ingredients:
- 3 tbsp sesame seeds
- 2 lb. Yukon gold potatoes, not peeled and wedged
- 1 tbsp avocado, grapeseed, or sunflower oil
- 1½ tbsp potato starch
- 1½ tbsp nutritional yeast, optional
- Black pepper and salt

Instructions:
1. Preheat stove to 420°F.
2. Line a parchment paper on a metal baking sheet.
3. Toss potatoes with all of the ingredients until covered. Drizzle a little more oil if seeds don't stick.
4. Spread potatoes onto the prepared sheet in an even layer and bake for about 20 minutes, flipping midway through, until potatoes are crispy.
5. Serve immediately with desired toppings.

Nutrition Facts Per Serving:
Calories 705, Total Fat 7.7g, Saturated Fat 0.9g, Cholesterol 0mg, Sodium 70mg, Total Carbohydrate 148.2g, Dietary Fiber 6.8g, Total Sugars 0.6g, Protein 9.3g, Vitamin D 0mcg, Calcium 88mg, Iron 5mg, Potassium 724mg

Chocolate Peanut Butter Energy Bites

Prep time 15 minutes / Cook time 10 minutes / Serves 8
Ingredients
- 1 ½ cup old fashioned rolled oats, divided
- ½ cup natural creamy peanut butter
- 3 tablespoons chia seeds
- 1/8 teaspoon sea salt
- ¼ cup flax seeds
- ¼ cup unsweetened cocoa powder, raw or regular
- 1/3 cup honey or maple syrup
- 1 teaspoon vanilla extract

Instructions:
1. Line a baking sheet or storage container with parchment paper and pop to one side.
2. Grab your bender and add ½ cup oats and all the flax seeds.
3. Whizz until they form a powder then transfer to a large bowl.
4. Add the remaining oats, cocoa powder, salt and chia seeds. Stir well.
5. Find a small bowl and add the honey, peanut butter and vanilla extract.
6. Stir well to combine then add to the dry ingredients.
7. Use your hands to form into small balls.
8. Pop onto the baking sheet or storage container then pop into the fridge.
9. Serve and enjoy.

Nutritional facts per serving:
Calories 274, Total Fat 13.8g, Saturated Fat 2.6g, Cholesterol 0mg, Sodium 137mg, Total Carbohydrate 32.2g, Dietary Fiber 7.9g, Total Sugars 13.4g, Protein 9g, Vitamin D 0mcg, Calcium 80mg, Iron 4mg, Potassium 307mg

Banana Chocolate Nice Cream

Prep time 10 minutes / Cook time 0 minutes / Serves 2

Ingredients

- 2 large ripe bananas cut into small pieces, freeze for at least 12 hours
- ½ cup unsweetened almond milk
- ¼ cup chopped walnuts
- Cacao nibs or vegan chocolate chips

Instructions:

1. Grab your blender and add the almond milk and bananas and whizz until smooth.
2. Add more milk as required.
3. Sprinkle with the walnuts then serve and enjoy.

Nutritional facts per serving:

Calories 268, Total Fat 12.6g, Saturated Fat 1.8g, Cholesterol 0mg, Sodium 52mg, Total Carbohydrate 38.1g, Dietary Fiber 5.4g, Total Sugars 21.3g, Protein 6g, Vitamin D 0mcg, Calcium 91mg, Iron 2mg, Potassium 616mg

Avocado Fudge Brownie

Prep time 45 minutes / Cook time 30 minutes / Serves 12

Ingredients

- 3 large overly ripe bananas
- 1 medium avocado, ripe but not brown
- 1 cup crunchy natural peanut butter
- 1 teaspoon vanilla
- ½ cup cacao powder
- ¼ cup almond flour
- ½ cup millet
- ¼ cup cacao nibs
- ½ cup walnut pieces

Instructions:

1. Preheat your oven to 350°F and line an 8 x 8" baking pan with parchment paper.
2. Grab a large bowl and add the banana and avocado. Mash well with a fork.
3. Add the peanut butter and vanilla and stir well until smooth.
4. Add the cacao, almond meal, millet, cacao nibs and walnuts. Stir well until combined.
5. Pour into the baking pan then pop into the oven for 30 minutes until set in the middle.
6. Remove from the oven and leave to cool for several hours.
7. Serve and enjoy.

Nutritional facts per serving:

Calories 269, Total Fat 12.3g, Saturated Fat 2.3g, Cholesterol 0mg, Sodium 312mg, Total Carbohydrate 37.6g, Dietary Fiber 8.2g, Total Sugars 22.9g, Protein 6.4g, Vitamin D 0mcg, Calcium 52mg, Iron 3mg, Potassium 528mg

No-Bake Chocolate-Covered Cookie Dough Bars

Prep time 10 minutes / Cook time 10 minutes / Serves 10

Ingredients

- 1 cup almond flour
- 2 tablespoons coconut flour
- ¼ teaspoon salt
- 1/3 cup pure maple syrup
- 1/3 cup almond butter
- ½ teaspoon vanilla extract
- 3/4 cup vegan chocolate chips

For the chocolate topping…

- 1 cup vegan chocolate chips
- 2 tablespoons almond butter

Instructions:

1. Line a 9 x 9" baking pan with parchment paper and pop to one side.
2. Grab a large bowl and add all the ingredients except the chocolate chips.
3. Stir well then add the chocolate chips.
4. Transfer to your baking tin then press down.
5. Pop into the fridge and leave until firm.
6. Meanwhile, find a small pan and add the chocolate chips and almond butter.
7. Melt together, stirring often for 10 minutes
8. Pour over the cookie dough then leave to set.
9. Serve and enjoy.

Nutritional facts per serving:

Calories 111, Total Fat 4.8g, Saturated Fat 1.6g, Cholesterol 0mg, Sodium 67mg, Total Carbohydrate 15.8g, Dietary Fiber 1.7g, Total Sugars 12.7g, Protein 1.7g, Vitamin D 0mcg, Calcium 13mg, Iron 1mg, Potassium 28mg

Caramel Apple Parfait

Prep time 15 minutes / Cook time 0 minutes / Serves 4

Ingredients

- 2 cups almond milk
- ¼ cup chia seeds
- 1 teaspoon ground cinnamon
- ¼ cup coconut oil, melted
- ¼ cup pure maple syrup
- 2 tablespoons almond butter
- ½ cup apples, peeled and diced
- ½ cup granola

Instructions:

1. Find a small bowl and add the almond milk, chia seeds and cinnamon.
2. Stir well then cover and pop into the fridge for an hour.
3. Take another small bowl and add the coconut oil, maple syrup and almond butter.
4. Whisk until smooth.
5. Grab four bowls and add the coconut mixture to each.
6. Top with a layer of granola, chopped apples and then a drizzle of the caramel.
7. Serve and enjoy.

Nutritional facts per serving:

Calories 579, Total Fat 56.4g, Saturated Fat 39g, Cholesterol 0mg, Sodium 29mg, Total Carbohydrate 44.9g, Dietary Fiber 9.6g, Total Sugars 25.1g, Protein 10.3g, Vitamin D 0mcg, Calcium 109mg, Iron 6mg, Potassium 642mg

Carrot Spice Oatmeal Cookies

Prep time 20 minutes / Cook time 10 minutes / Serves 12

Ingredients

- 1 cup oats
- ¾ cup wheat flour
- 1 ½ teaspoon baking powder
- 1 teaspoon ground cinnamon
- ½ teaspoon ground cloves
- 2 tablespoons melted coconut oil
- ½ cup coconut milk
- ½ cup applesauce
- 1 teaspoon almond extract
- 1 cup granulated coconut sugar
- 1 cup carrots, finely grated

Instructions:

1. Heat the oven to 325°F and line a baking sheet with parchment paper. Pop to one side.
2. Add the oats, flour, cinnamon baking powder, and clove in a medium bowl
3. Stir well then pop to one side.
4. Take a large mixing bowl and add the oil, coconut milk, applesauce, almond extract and coconut sugar.
5. Stir well then slowly add the mixture of flour
6. Add the carrot and fold through.
7. Drop onto the baking sheet then pop into the oven for 8-10 minutes.
8. Cool slightly then serve and enjoy.

Nutritional facts per serving:

Calories 168, Total Fat 5.2g, Saturated Fat 4.3g, Cholesterol 0mg, Sodium 10mg, Total Carbohydrate 29.7g, Dietary Fiber 1.6g, Total Sugars 17.9g, Protein 2.1g, Vitamin D 0mcg, Calcium 39mg, Iron 1mg, Potassium 162mg

Coconut Peppermint Fudge

Prep time 30 minutes / Cook time 2 minutes / Serves 20

Ingredients

- 2 ½ cups vegan chocolate chips
- 1/3 cup canned coconut milk
- ¼ cup sugar
- 1 tablespoon coconut oil
- Sea salt, to taste
- 1 teaspoon pure peppermint extract
- ¼ cup Vanilla extract, to taste
- ½ cup diced walnuts

Instructions:

1. Grease a 1-quart casserole dish and pop to one side.
2. Find a heavy saucepan and add the chocolate chips, coconut milk, sugar, coconut oil and salt. Stir well to combine.
3. Pop over a low heat for 2 minutes and allow the chocolate to melt.

4. Remove from the heat and add the peppermint, stirring well to combine.
5. Add the walnuts then leave to cool to room temperature.
6. Pour the fudge into the dish then cover and leave to set.
7. Cut into 30 squares then serve and enjoy.

Nutritional facts per serving:
Calories 91, Total Fat 5.5g, Saturated Fat 2.6g, Cholesterol 0mg, Sodium 29mg, Total Carbohydrate 8.4g, Dietary Fiber 0.8g, Total Sugars 7.5g, Protein 1.3g, Vitamin D 0mcg, Calcium 3mg, Iron 1mg, Potassium 31mg

Chocolate Banana Nut Bread

Prep time 1 hour 15 minutes / Cook time 1 hour / Serves 8

Ingredients
- 4 overly ripe bananas
- 1 cup sugar
- ¼ cup water
- 1 teaspoon vanilla
- 1 ¾ cup whole wheat flour
- ¼ cup cocoa powder
- ½ teaspoon baking soda
- 1 teaspoon cinnamon
- 1 teaspoon baking powder
- ¼ cup vegan chocolate chips
- ¼ cup chopped walnuts

Instructions:
1. Preheat your oven to 350°F and grease a loaf pan.
2. Find a large bowl and add the bananas. Mash well using a fork.
3. Add the sugar and vanilla, stirring well to combine.
4. Add the water and stir through.
5. Take another bowl and add the flour, cocoa powder, baking soda, cinnamon and baking powder. Stir well.
6. Add the dry ingredients to the wet and mix well.
7. Add the chocolate chips and nuts, stir well then pour into the loaf pan.
8. Bake for 1 hour until cooked through.
9. Leave to cool completely before cutting.
10. Serve and enjoy.

Nutritional facts per serving:
Calories 289, Total Fat 3.6g, Saturated Fat 0.7g, Cholesterol 0mg, Sodium 83mg, Total Carbohydrate 63.1g, Dietary Fiber 3.6g, Total Sugars 33.6g, Protein 5g, Vitamin D 0mcg, Calcium 43mg, Iron 2mg, Potassium 394mg

Raw Vegan Lemon Cranberry Cheesecake

Prep time 10 minutes / Serves 22

Ingredients
For the crust...
- 2 cups raw almonds
- 2 cups chopped pitted dates
- ½ cup raw cacao powder

For the filling...
- 3 cups raw cashews (soaked for 2 hours)
- 1 ½ cup fresh cranberries
- 1 cup coconut oil
- 3/4 cup raw agave
- ½ cup fresh lemon juice
- ½ cup filtered water
- 1 tablespoon lemon zest
- 1 teaspoon vanilla extract
- ½ tsp sea salt

Instructions:
1. Grab your food processor and add the almonds, dates and cacao powder. Whizz until combined.
2. Use your hands to roll this mixture into a bal.
3. Grease a 9" springform cake tin with oil then press the crust into the bottom.
4. Wipe out the blender, add the filling ingredients and whizz until smooth.
5. Pour the filling into the tin.
6. Cover with foil and then pop into the freezer for 5-10 hours until set.

Nutritional facts per serving:
Calories 349, Total Fat 24.1g, Saturated Fat 11.8g, Cholesterol 0mg, Sodium 48mg, Total Carbohydrate 31.9g, Dietary Fiber 4.3g, Total Sugars 20.7g, Protein 6.2g, Vitamin D 0mcg, Calcium 40mg, Iron 3mg, Potassium 296mg

Coconut Mango Ice Cream

Prep time 10 minutes / Cook time 0 minutes / Serves 6

Ingredients

- 1 cup canned coconut milk
- 3 cups diced mango, frozen
- 1 tablespoon honey
- 1/3 cup raspberries
- 3 tablespoons maple syrup, optional
- 1 teaspoon chia

Instructions:

1. Grab your blender and add the coconut milk, mango and maple syrup.
2. Scoop into serving dishes then enjoy.

Nutritional facts per serving:
Calories 186, Total Fat 10.2g, Saturated Fat 8.5g, Cholesterol 0mg, Sodium 8mg, Total Carbohydrate 25.4g, Dietary Fiber 3g, Total Sugars 21.7g, Protein 1.9g, Vitamin D 0mcg, Calcium 30mg, Iron 1mg, Potassium 276mg

Skinny Strawberry Banana Bread

Prep time 30 minutes / Cook time 10 minutes / Serves 24

Ingredients

- 1 cup mashed over-ripe bananas
- 2/3 cup coconut milk
- 3 tablespoons maple syrup
- 2 ½ tablespoons chia seeds
- 2 tablespoons coconut oil, melted
- 1 tablespoon vanilla
- 1 ¼ cup all-purpose flour
- 2 ½ teaspoons baking powder
- 1 tablespoon cinnamon
- 1 cup finely chopped fresh strawberries

Instructions:

1. Preheat the oven to 350°F then grease a 24-count mini load tin.
2. Take a large bowl and add the bananas, coconut milk, maple syrup, chia, coconut oil and vanilla.
3. Stir well together then leave to stand for five minutes.
4. Take another bowl and add the flour, baking powder and cinnamon. Stir together then add to the wet ingredients.
5. Add the strawberries and fold through.
6. Divide between the muffin tins and bake for 10 minutes until cooked through.
7. Remove from the oven then drizzle with coconut cream and chia seeds.
8. Serve and enjoy.

Nutritional facts per serving:
Calories 80, Total Fat 3.7g, Saturated Fat 2.5g, Cholesterol 0mg, Sodium 3mg, Total Carbohydrate 10.7g, Dietary Fiber 1.8g, Total Sugars 2.9g, Protein 1.4g, Vitamin D 0mcg, Calcium 49mg, Iron 1mg, Potassium 128mg

Chocolate, Quinoa & Zucchini Muffins

Prep time 10 minutes / Cook time 20 minutes / Serves 8

Ingredients:

- ½ cup dry quinoa
- 2 tbsp. coconut oil
- 1½ cups almond flour
- ½ cup walnuts, chopped
- 2 large bananas
- ½ cup applesauce
- ¼ cup maple syrup
- ½ cup zucchini, shredded
- 1 cup vegan protein powder, vanilla or chocolate flavor
- ½ cup vegan dark chocolate chips
- 4 tbsp. almond milk
- 2 tsp. baking powder
- ½ tsp. cinnamon
- ½ tsp. vanilla extract
- ½ tsp. nutmeg
- ¼ tsp salt
- ½ cup water

Instructions:

1. Preheat the oven to 400°F
2. Line an 8-cup muffin pan with baking cups, spray with coconut oil, and set aside.

3. In a large bowl, mix together the flour, cooked quinoa, nutmeg, walnuts, cinnamon, salt, and baking powder.
4. Take a second bowl and mash the bananas with a fork, and then combine the mashed bananas with the applesauce.
5. Stir in the vanilla, maple syrup, protein powder, and almond milk until all the ingredients are distributed evenly; if necessary, add the optional water.
6. Combine the separate mixtures into one large bowl. Stir until the batter is smooth and lumps have dissolved.
7. Finally, carefully fold in the shredded zucchini and chocolate chips.
8. Fill each of the muffin cups halfway.
9. Bake in the oven until the muffins are fluffy all the way through, for about 20 minutes.
10. Remove from the oven and cool for at least 15 minutes before serving or storing and enjoy!

Nutritional facts per serving:
Calories 394, Total Fat 24.4g, Saturated Fat 8.1g, Cholesterol 0mg, Sodium 104mg, Total Carbohydrate 39.9g, Dietary Fiber 4.8g, Total Sugars 13g, Protein 11.7g, Vitamin D 0mcg, Calcium 118mg, Iron 3mg, Potassium 420mg

Oil-Free Chocolate Muffins

Prep time 40 minutes / Cook time 1 hour / Serves 12
Ingredients
- 15 oz. can black beans
- ¾ cup cacao powder
- ½ heaping cup coconut sugar
- 1 small banana
- ¼ cup unsweetened applesauce
- 6 tablespoons water
- 2 heaping tablespoons ground flax seed
- 1 ½ teaspoon baking powder
- 1 teaspoon arrowroot powder
- 1 teaspoon vanilla extract
- ¼ teaspoon salt

Instructions:

1. Preheat the oven to 350°F then grease a 12-serve muffin tin.
2. Grab your blender and add all the ingredients. Whizz until smooth.
3. Pour into the muffin tin then bake for 30 minutes until set.
4. Leave to cook for 30 minutes.
5. Serve and enjoy.

Nutritional facts per serving:
Calories 64, Total Fat 1.5g, Saturated Fat 0.7g, Cholesterol 0mg, Sodium 183mg, Total Carbohydrate 12.3g, Dietary Fiber 3.8g, Total Sugars 2g, Protein 3.2g, Vitamin D 0mcg, Calcium 50mg, Iron 2mg, Potassium 239mg

Gluten-Free Energy Crackers

Prep time 10 minutes / Cook time 55 minutes / Serves 6
Ingredients:
- ¼ cup flax seeds
- ¼ cup chia seeds
- ¾ cup water
- 1 tbsp. garlic, minced
- ½ tbsp. dried onion flakes
- ½ cup pumpkin seeds, chopped
- ¼ cup peanuts, crushed
- ¼ cup cashews, crushed
- ¼ cup sesame seeds
- ¼ tsp. paprika powder
- ¼ tsp Salt
- ¼ tsp pepper

Instructions:

1. Preheat the oven to 350°F
2. Take a large bowl and combine the water, garlic, onion flakes, and paprika. Whisk until everything is combined thoroughly.
3. To the same bowl, add the flax seeds, chia seeds, pumpkin seeds, peanuts, cashews, and sesame seeds.
4. Stir everything well, while adding pinches of salt and pepper to taste, until it is thoroughly combined.
5. Line a baking sheet with parchment paper and spread out the mixture in a thin and even layer across the parchment paper.
6. Bake for 20-25 minutes.

7. Remove the pan from the oven and flip over the flat chunk so that the other side can crisp.
8. Cut the chunk into squares or triangles, depending on preference and put the pan back into the oven and bake until the bars have turned golden brown, around 30 minutes.

9. Allow the crackers to cool before serving or storing. Enjoy!

Nutritional Facts per serving:
Calories 198, Total Fat 15.7g, Saturated Fat 2.6g, Cholesterol 0mg, Sodium 104mg, Total Carbohydrate 9g, Dietary Fiber 3.6g, Total Sugars 0.9g, Protein 7.5g, Vitamin D 0mcg, Calcium 85mg, Iron 5mg, Potassium 253mg

Raw Lemon Pie Bars

Prep time 10 minutes / Cook time 0 minutes / Serves 6

Ingredients:
- ¼ cup chia seeds
- ¼ cup pecan pieces
- ⅓ cup raw cashews
- ⅓ cup sunflower seeds
- 2 cups of pitted dates
- ½ cup vegan protein powder
- 2 tbsp. organic lemon juice
- ¼ tsp. salt

Instructions:
1. Soak the chia seeds according to the method and drain the excess water.
2. Place the pecans, cashews, chia seeds, and sunflower seeds in a food processor and pulse on low until it is a crumbly mixture.
3. Add the dates, lemon or lime juice, and salt to the processor. Continue pulsing while

adding protein powder until the mixture is a bit chunky but doughy.
4. Transfer the dough to a baking sheet lined with parchment paper and press it out with your fingers or rolling pin until it forms a ½-inch thick square.
5. Place the sheet pan into the freezer until the chunk is solid, or for about 1 hour.
6. Slice the chunk into 8 equally-sized bars. Store, or enjoy right away.

Nutritional facts per serving:
Calories 247, Total Fat 6g, Saturated Fat 1g, Cholesterol 5mg, Sodium 105mg, Total Carbohydrate 48.5g, Dietary Fiber 5.7g, Total Sugars 38.3g, Protein 5.3g, Vitamin D 0mcg, Calcium 45mg, Iron 1mg, Potassium 477mg

Matcha Energy Balls

Prep time 15 minutes / Cook time 0 minutes / Serves 4

Ingredients:
- 1 cup raw cashews
- ½ cup pistachios
- ½ cup pitted dates, packed
- ½ cup vanilla vegan protein powder
- ¼ cup finely shredded coconut
- ¼ cup crushed hazelnuts
- 1 tbsp. matcha powder
- 1 tbsp. maple syrup

Instructions:
1. Add all the ingredients—except the hazelnuts—to a food processor and blend on low until everything is finely crushed and combined, around 45 seconds.

2. Use a tablespoon to scoop out rounded heaps of the mixture, and then use your hands to roll them into balls.
3. Pour the crushed hazelnuts out into a bowl and roll the matcha balls in the hazelnuts until they are evenly coated on all sides.
4. Refrigerate for about 30 minutes until the balls are solid, and store or serve right away!

Nutritional facts per serving:
Calories 375, Total Fat 24.2g, Saturated Fat 5.3g, Cholesterol 8mg, Sodium 54mg, Total Carbohydrate 35.2g, Dietary Fiber 4.7g, Total Sugars 19.9g, Protein 11.2g, Vitamin D 0mcg, Calcium 55mg, Iron 4mg, Potassium 506mg

Sunflower Protein Bars

Prep time 15 minutes / Cook time 30 seconds / Serves 6

Ingredients:
- 1 cup old fashioned oats
- 1 cup puffy rice cereal
- 1 cup vegan protein powder
- ½ cup maple syrup
- ½ cup sunflower butter
- 2 tsp. pure vanilla extract
- 1 tsp. cinnamon
- ¼ tsp. nutmeg
- ¼ tsp. salt

Instructions:
1. In a large bowl, mix together the oats, rice cereal, protein powder, cinnamon, nutmeg, and salt; set aside.
2. Take a smaller bowl, add the sunflower butter, maple syrup, and heat in the microwave for 30 seconds.
3. Remove the melted sunflower butter mixture from the microwave and mix the heated ingredients into the large bowl with the dry ingredients.
4. Stir everything thoroughly, add the vanilla extract, and use a whisk to mix everything together until all the lumps have dissolved to create a smooth mixture.
5. Spread the mixture into a shallow dish lined with parchment paper, and then pack it down firmly with a spoon to make sure no air bubbles remain.
6. Transfer the dish to the freezer and let it sit for at least 20 minutes.
7. Take the dish out and cut the chunk into 6 equal-sized bars; store or enjoy right away!

Nutritional facts per serving:
Calories 446, Total Fat 17.7g, Saturated Fat 10.3g, Cholesterol 51mg, Sodium 219mg, Total Carbohydrate 61.3g, Dietary Fiber 3.2g, Total Sugars 16.8g, Protein 9.4g, Vitamin D 11mcg, Calcium 66mg, Iron 3mg, Potassium 241mg

High Protein Cake Batter Smoothie

Prep time 10 minutes / Cook time 0 minutes / Serves 2

Ingredients:
- 1 large banana, frozen
- 1 cup almond milk
- ¼ cup quick oats
- 4 tbsp. vegan protein powder
- 1 tbsp. cashew butter
- 1 tsp. cinnamon
- 1 tsp. pure vanilla extract
- ¼ tsp. nutmeg

Instructions:
1. Mix the oats and almond milk in a small bowl or jar.
2. Place the bowl in the fridge until the oats have softened, for about 1 hour.
3. Add the oats and milk mixture along with the remaining ingredients to a blender.
4. Blend on high speed until it is smooth and all lumps have disappeared.
5. Serve in tall glasses with an extra sprinkle of cinnamon on top, or store to enjoy later.

Nutritional facts per serving:
Calories 676, Total Fat 39.1g, Saturated Fat 31.1g, Cholesterol 144mg, Sodium 171mg, Total Carbohydrate 37.8g, Dietary Fiber 6.1g, Total Sugars 14.7g, Protein 49.3g, Vitamin D 4mcg, Calcium 242mg, Iron 4mg, Potassium 957mg

Almond Vanilla Popcorn

Prep time 5 minutes / Cook time 10 minutes / Serves 4

Ingredients:
- ½ cup popcorn kernels
- 2 Medjool dates
- 2 tablespoons coconut oil
- 2 tablespoons slivered almonds
- 2 teaspoons vanilla
- 1 tablespoon water

Instructions:

1. Preheat the oven to 325 degrees, Fahrenheit and prepare casserole dishes or baking sheets with parchment paper.
2. Pop the popcorn and place in a large bowl.
3. Combine the dates, coconut, almonds, vanilla and water in a food processor and process until smooth, scraping down the sides a few times.
4. Pour the sauce into the popcorn and mix to be sure it is all well coated.
5. Spread the popcorn out on the parchment paper, it will be wet, so you'll need baking sheets with shallow sides.
6. Place the popcorn in the oven and bake for 8 to 10 minutes, stirring with a wooden spoon every two minutes. The popcorn is ready when it is dry.
7. Cool and store in an airtight container.

Nutritional facts per serving:
Calories 97, Total Fat 8.4g, Saturated Fat 6g, Cholesterol 0mg, Sodium 0mg , Total Carbohydrate 4.8g, Dietary Fiber 0.9g, Total Sugars 3g, Protein 0.9g, Vitamin D 0mcg, Calcium 10mg, Iron 0mg, Potassium 55mg

Carrot Hotdogs with Red Cabbage

Prep time 10 minutes / Cook time 1 hour 3 minutes / Serves 4

Ingredients:
- 4 carrots
- ¼ cup tamari sauce
- 1 tablespoon maple syrup
- ¼ cup water
- 1 tablespoon liquid smoke
- 1 teaspoon garlic powder
- 1 tablespoon paprika
- 2 tablespoons nutritional yeast
- 3 tablespoons olive oil
- 1 small onion, sliced
- 2 apples, peeled, cored and cut into slices
- 2 more tablespoons maple syrup
- 1 small head red cabbage
- 2 tablespoons apple cider vinegar
- Salt and pepper to taste
- 1 more cup water
- 1 more tablespoon olive oil
- 4 whole-grain hot dog buns
- Ketchup and mustard

Instructions:
1. Boil the carrots for 12 to 14 minutes or until tender, in enough salt water to cover them. Drain and set the carrots aside to cool.
2. Combine the tamari, a tablespoon of maple syrup, the water, liquid smoke, garlic powder, paprika and nutritional yeast in a shallow dish. Add the carrots after they are cool, cover them and place them in the refrigerator for 24 hours to marinate.
3. Make the red cabbage slaw by heating the three tablespoons of olive oil in a Dutch oven and adding the onion. Sauté until translucent.
4. Add the apple slices and the remaining two tablespoons of maple syrup, then sauté for four to five minutes until the apples are tender
5. Cut the cabbage into strips and combine them with the apple cider vinegar in another pot on the stove. Stir, cover and simmer for about 10 minutes.
6. Add the salt and pepper to taste with the water. Stir and simmer for 30 minutes. Drain out any leftover liquid.
7. Place the final tablespoon of olive oil in a skillet over medium heat and fry the carrots on all sides, cooking them for two to three minutes on each side.
8. Slice the buns, add a little cabbage slaw and a carrot and serve with ketchup and mustard.

Nutritional facts per serving:
Calories 473, Total Fat 23.8g, Saturated Fat 3.6g, Cholesterol 0mg, Sodium 1323mg, Total Carbohydrate 59.9g, Dietary Fiber 8.2g, Total Sugars 26.5g, Protein 10.2g, Vitamin D 0mcg, Calcium 118mg, Iron 4mg,Potassium 665mg

Broccoli Slaw Stir-fry with Tofu

Prep time 5 minutes / Cook time 6 minutes / Serves 6

Ingredients:

For tofu:
- 28 ounces extra firm tofu
- 4 cloves garlic, sliced
- ½ cup rice wine
- 2 tablespoons soy sauce

For the stir-fry:
- 1 large onion, sliced
- 1 red bell pepper, sliced
- 12-ounce, broccoli slaw
- ¼ cup water
- 4 cloves garlic, sliced
- 2 teaspoons minced ginger
- ¼ teaspoon red chili flakes
- 1 teaspoon sesame oil
- 2 tablespoons soy sauce
- Salt to taste

Instructions:

1. Add tofu, garlic, rice wine and soya sauce into a large zip lock plastic bag. Seal the bag and turn the bag around a few times to coat well. Set aside for an hour

2. Place a large nonstick skillet over medium high heat. Remove tofu from the bag and add to the skillet. Pour the remaining marinade into a large bowl.

3. Cook tofu until brown. Remove and place in the bowl of marinade. Cover and keep warm.

4. Add onions into the same skillet and sauté for a couple of minutes. Add rest of the ingredients except water and sesame oil and sauté for 2-3 minutes.

5. Add water, cover and cook for 2-3 minutes until the broccoli slaw is tender and crisp.

6. Add the tofu and marinade. Mix well and heat thoroughly. Serve immediately.

Nutritional facts per serving:

Calories 39, Total Fat 6.8g, Saturated Fat 1.4g, Cholesterol 47mg, Sodium 850mg, Total Carbohydrate 18g, Dietary Fiber 2.3g, Total Sugars 8.4g, Protein 29.3g, Vitamin D 0mcg, Calcium 290mg, Iron 3mg, Potassium 483mg

Eggplant and Sesame Stir-Fry

Prep time 5 minutes / Cook time 10 minutes / Serves 4

Ingredients:
- 2 tablespoons sesame oil
- 4 spring onions, sliced
- 2 red chilies, deseeded, sliced
- 2 tablespoons soy sauce
- 2 tablespoons mirin
- 2 teaspoons sesame seeds
- 6 cloves garlic, crushed
- 4 inches pieces ginger, shredded
- 8 baby eggplant, cut into wedges
- 2 tablespoons rice wine vinegar
- 2 teaspoons cornstarch
- Salt to taste
- Hot steamed rice to serve

Instructions:

1. Place a wok over medium-high heat. Add oil. When the oil is heated, add garlic and sauté for about a minute until aromatic.

2. Stir in the spring onions, chili and ginger and sauté for a couple of minutes.

3. Stir in the eggplant and sprinkle some water. Lower the heat and cook until soft.

4. Raise the heat to high heat. Add soy sauce, vinegar and mirin and cook until slightly thick.

5. Mix together cornstarch with 1-2 tablespoons of water and add into the wok, stirring constantly.

6. Cook for 10 minutes until thick.

7. Serve over hot steamed rice. Sprinkle sesame seeds and a few chili slices. Also garnish with some spring onions and serve.

Nutritional facts per serving:

Calories 557, Total Fat 10g, Saturated Fat 1.2g, Cholesterol 0mg, Sodium 583mg, Total Carbohydrate 111.1g, Dietary Fiber 40.3g, Total Sugars 35.6g, Protein 15.6g, Vitamin D 0mcg, Calcium 149mg, Iron 5mg, Potassium 2676mg

Vegetable Teriyaki Stir-fry

Prep time 4 minutes / Cook time 15 minutes / Serves 3

Ingredients:

For stir-fry:

- 1 tablespoon olive oil
- 2 cloves garlic, minced
- 1 small onion, diced
- ½ tablespoon minced ginger
- ½ cup sliced bell pepper
- ¾ cup sugar snap peas
- 6 tablespoons roasted salted cashews
- 1 green onion, sliced
- 1 heaping cup shredded carrot
- 1 medium head broccoli, cut into florets
- 1 cup cooked brown rice or quinoa
- ½ cup edamame
- Salt to taste
- Pepper to taste

For sauce:

- ½ can pineapple chunks in pineapple juice, with its liquid
- 1 tablespoon honey or sugar or stevia
- ½ tablespoon chia seeds
- 2 tablespoons soy sauce
- ½ tablespoon seasoned rice vinegar

- 1 teaspoon Sriracha sauce

Instructions:

To make sauce:

1. Add all the ingredients for sauce into a blender and blend until smooth.
2. To make stir-fry: Place a large skillet or wok over medium heat. Add oil. When the oil is heated, add onion and cook until translucent.
3. Sir in the ginger and garlic and cook for 5 minutes.
4. Add all the vegetables except edamame and cook until tender.
5. Stir in rice, edamame and cashews and heat thoroughly for 10 minutes
6. Add sauce and mix well. Add salt and pepper to taste.
7. Sprinkle spring onions and cashews on top and serve.

Nutritional facts per serving:

Calories 546, Total Fat 19g, Saturated Fat 3.1g, Cholesterol 0mg, Sodium 675mg, Total Carbohydrate 81.8g, Dietary Fiber 9.3g, Total Sugars 14g, Protein 16.8g, Vitamin D 0mcg, Calcium 192mg, Iron 5mg, Potassium 906mg

Chickpea Burgers

Prep time 5 minutes / Cook time 6 minutes / Serves 8

Ingredients:

- 1 15-ounce can chickpeas, rinsed and drained well
- ½ cup green onions, finely chopped
- ⅓ cup fresh dill, finely chopped
- 2 tablespoons dry whole-wheat breadcrumbs
- 2 tablespoons lemon juice
- ½ teaspoon salt
- ¼ teaspoon pepper
- ¼ teaspoon ground cumin
- 2 tablespoons tahini
- ¼ cup vegetable oil

Instructions:

1. Pour have the chickpeas in a bowl and mash with a potato masher.
2. Add the green onions, dill, bread crumbs and lemon juice and mix well.

3. Place the rest of the chickpeas in a food processor and add the salt, pepper, cumin and tahini. Process until smooth.
4. Add to the mashed chickpeas in the bowl and mix well, using your hands. Shape them into six to eight patties.
5. Heat up a 12-inch skillet over medium heat and pour in the vegetable oil. Let it heat up, then add the patties and cook them until crispy and dark golden on both sides, for about six minutes. Only flip them once.
6. Drain on paper towels and serve alone or in buns with condiments.

Nutritional facts per serving:

Calories 291, Total Fat 12.3g, Saturated Fat 2g, Cholesterol 0mg, Sodium 183mg, Total Carbohydrate 36g, Dietary Fiber 10.2g, Total Sugars 6g, Protein 11.7g, Vitamin D 0mcg, Calcium 116mg, Iron 5mg, Potassium 574mg

Chickpea Crust Pizza with Veggie Topping

Prep time 10 minutes / Cook time 52 minutes / Serves 2

Ingredients:

- 1 cup chickpea flour
- 1 cup unsweetened soy milk
- 1 tablespoon apple cider vinegar
- 1 tablespoon tahini
- ¼ teaspoon baking powder
- ¼ teaspoon sea salt
- ⅛ teaspoon ground pepper
- 1 zucchini, diced
- 1 red bell pepper, seeds removed and diced
- ½ cup cauliflower florets, chopped
- 1 cup marinara sauce
- ¼ teaspoon crushed red pepper flakes

Instructions:

1. Pour the chickpea flour, soy milk, apple cider vinegar, tahini, baking powder, salt and pepper into a blender and blend into a smooth batter.
2. Coat a skillet with nonstick spray and cook the batter over medium heat for 20 minutes. Keep the heat down so it doesn't burn. Use a wide spatula to flip the crust over and cook for another 10 minutes. Transfer to a cooling rack. Cool completely before topping.
3. Preheat the oven to 350 degrees, Fahrenheit and line a baking sheet with parchment paper. Make the topping.
4. Spray another skillet with butter flavored nonstick spray and sauté the zucchini, bell pepper and cauliflower for five to seven minutes until tender crisp. Add a little water if they start to burn or stick.
5. Top the crust with marinara sauce and spread the topping over it.
6. Bake for 10 to 15 minutes or until the marinara starts to bubble.

Nutritional facts per serving:
Calories 627, Total Fat 16g, Saturated Fat 2.4g, Cholesterol 3mg, Sodium 861mg, Total Carbohydrate 96.8g, Dietary Fiber 24.7g, Total Sugars 32g, Protein 29.1g, Vitamin D 0mcg, Calcium 248mg, Iron 9mg, Potassium 1964mg

Dark Chocolate Hazelnut Popcorn

Prep time 7 minutes / Cook time 0 minutes / Serves 5

Ingredients:

- 3 tablespoons coconut oil, divided
- ¼ cup unpopped popcorn kernels
- 2 tablespoons cocoa powder
- ½ cup unsweetened coconut flakes
- ½ cup chopped hazelnuts
- 2 tablespoons maple syrup
- ¼ teaspoon kosher salt

Instructions:

1. Place two tablespoons of the coconut oil in a large pot with a lid.
2. Add the popcorn kernels, heat, shake and allow them to pop.
3. Once all the corn has popped, remove the pan from the heat and stir in the cocoa powder, coconut, hazelnuts, maple syrup and salt.
4. Mix well so that all the popcorn is coated; spread the kernels out on a baking sheet until they are dry.
5. Store at room temperature in an airtight container.

Nutritional facts per serving:
Calories 203, Total Fat 16.1g, Saturated Fat 9.9g, Cholesterol 0mg, Sodium 119mg, Total Carbohydrate 16.8g, Dietary Fiber 3.7g, Total Sugars 5.6g, Protein 2.9g, Vitamin D 0mcg, Calcium 17mg, Iron 2mg, Potassium 150mg

Greek Pizza

Prep time 7 minutes / Cook time 20 minutes / Serves 1

Ingredients:

- ½ to 1 cup hummus
- 1 handful sliced Kalamata olives
- ½ red pepper, seeded and sliced
- ½ small red onion, diced
- 8 to 10 fresh basil leaves

Instructions:

1. Preheat the oven to 375 degrees, Fahrenheit.
2. Spread hummus on the crust to about a half inch from the edge.
3. Sprinkle on the olives, red pepper and onion evenly over the surface of the pizza.
4. Place the basil leaves evenly on the pizza.
5. Put in the oven and cook for about 20 minutes (this is without a precooked crust). Check after 15 minutes and the pizza is done when the crust turns a light golden brown and the vegetables are cooked through.

Nutritional facts per serving:
Calories 246, Total Fat 12.7g, Saturated Fat 1.9g, Cholesterol 0mg, Sodium 515mg, Total Carbohydrate 26g, Dietary Fiber 9.3g, Total Sugars 4.5g, Protein 11g, Vitamin D 0mcg, Calcium 72mg, Iron 4mg, Potassium 460mg

Mexican Pizza

Prep time 5 minutes / Cook time 20 minutes / Serves 4
Ingredients:
- ½ to 1 cup refried beans
- ½ package mild taco seasoning
- ½ cup salsa
- ½ small yellow onion, diced
- 1 handful sliced black olives
- 1 tomato, stemmed and thinly sliced
- 1 handful fresh spinach leaves
- ¼ cup fresh cilantro, chopped

Instructions:
1. Preheat the oven to 375 degrees, Fahrenheit.
2. In a small bowl, mix the cold refried beans with the taco seasoning and spread over the pizza crust to within a half inch of the edge.
3. Spread the salsa on top
4. Sprinkle the onion and olives over the surface of the pizza.
5. Place the thin slices of tomato over the surface of the pizza and top with spinach leaves and cilantro.
6. Cook for 15 to 20 minutes or until crust is crispy and the vegetables are soft. The refried beans and salsa should be bubbly hot too.

Nutritional facts per serving:
Calories 93, Total Fat 3.2g, Saturated Fat 1.6g, Cholesterol 10mg, Sodium 403mg, Total Carbohydrate 11.9g, Dietary Fiber 2.7g, Total Sugars 1.9g, Protein 5.2g, Vitamin D 0mcg, Calcium 55mg, Iron 1mg, Potassium 309mg

Cinnamon Roll Popcorn

Prep time 10 minutes / Cook time 0 minutes / Serves 3
Ingredients:
- 2 teaspoons vegetable oil
- ⅓ cup popcorn kernels
- 2 tablespoons coconut palm sugar
- ½ teaspoon ground cinnamon
- 2 tablespoons vegan butter
- 1 tablespoon maple syrup

Instructions:
1. Use the vegetable oil in a large pan with a lid to make the popcorn according to package instructions.
2. Once the popcorn is popped, place the coconut palm sugar, cinnamon, butter and maple syrup in a saucepan over medium high heat. Stir constantly until everything melts and is well combined.
3. Place the popcorn in a large bowl and drizzle the sauce over the top. Toss with two large spoons to combine and let it cool before serving.
4. Store it at room temperature in an airtight container.

Nutritional facts per serving:
Calories 195, Total Fat 11.6g, Saturated Fat 5.5g, Cholesterol 20mg, Sodium 185mg, Total Carbohydrate 24.6g, Dietary Fiber 3.8g, Total Sugars 6.5g, Protein 2.5g, Vitamin D 5mcg, Calcium 11mg, Iron 1mg, Potassium 127mg

Pumpkin Flavored Popcorn

Prep time 5 minutes / Cook time 10 minutes / Serves 10

Ingredients:

- 10 cups popped popcorn
- 2 tablespoons maple syrup
- 2 tablespoons coconut oil, melted
- 1 tablespoon pumpkin puree
- ¼ teaspoon cinnamon
- ½ teaspoon salt

Instructions:

1. Make the popcorn and place it in a large bowl, reserving two cups of the popcorn to be placed in a four-cup measuring cup.
2. Preheat the oven to 325 degrees, Fahrenheit.
3. In a small saucepan, combine the maple syrup, coconut oil, puree, cinnamon and salt and put over medium heat. Stir constantly while it cooks, for about two minutes.
4. Put all the popcorn except the reserved two cups into a large roasting pan lined with aluminum foil.
5. Pour the sauce over the popcorn in the roasting pan and stir until it is all coated.
6. Place in the oven for eight minutes, stirring every two or three minutes.
7. Remove from oven and let it cool; the popcorn will harden.
8. Pour the two cups of plain popcorn on top and stir to break up the hardened popcorn and incorporate all together.
9. Store at room temperature in an airtight container.

Nutritional facts per serving:

Calories 66, Total Fat 3.1g, Saturated Fat 2.4g, Cholesterol 0mg, Sodium 117mg, Total Carbohydrate 9.1g, Dietary Fiber 1.2g, Total Sugars 2.5g, Protein 1.1g, Vitamin D 0mcg, Calcium 4mg, Iron 0mg, Potassium 38mg

Quinoa Tacos

Prep time 10 minutes / Cook time 1 hour / Serves 6

Ingredients:

- 1 cup quinoa
- ¾ cup water
- 1 cup vegetable broth
- 1 tablespoon nutritional yeast
- ½ cup salsa
- ½ teaspoon garlic powder
- 2 teaspoons chili powder
- 2 teaspoon cumin
- ½ teaspoon sea salt
- ½ teaspoon ground pepper
- 1 tablespoon olive oil

Instructions:

1. Rinse the quinoa and drain.
2. Heat a saucepan over medium heat and toast the quinoa for about four minutes stirring constantly.
3. Add the water and vegetable broth and bring to a boil.
4. Reduce to a simmer, cover and cook for 15 to 20 minutes or until the liquid is all absorbed. Fluff with a fork, put the lid back on and set to cool 10 minutes.
5. Preheat the oven to 375 degrees, Fahrenheit and cover a shallow sided baking sheet with aluminum foil.
6. Place the cooled quinoa in a mixing bowl and add the nutritional yeast, salsa, garlic powder, chili powder, cumin, salt, pepper and oil and stir to combine.
7. Spread on prepared baking sheet and bake 20 minutes, stir around in the pan and bake another 15 or 20 minutes or until it starts to smell good and becomes light brown.
8. Serve in taco shells or on tostadas.

Nutritional facts per serving:

Calories 149, Total Fat 4.7g, Saturated Fat 0.7g, Cholesterol 0mg, Sodium 427mg, Total Carbohydrate 21.5g, Dietary Fiber 3.2g, Total Sugars 0.9g, Protein 6.2g, Vitamin D 0mcg, Calcium 33mg, Iron 2mg, Potassium 333mg

Sweet Potato Burgers with Maple Flavor

Prep time 5 minutes / Cook time 25 minutes / Serves 4

Ingredients:

- 1 large sweet potato, peeled, cubed and steamed until tender
- ¾ cup water
- ¼ cup dry millet
- 2 dates, pitted
- 1 cup baby portobello mushrooms, quartered
- 2 teaspoons cilantro
- 1 chipotle pepper
- 1 teaspoon cumin
- ½ teaspoon kosher salt
- 1 lime, juiced
- 1 tablespoon maple syrup
- ¼ cup Old fashioned rolled oats
- 1 tablespoon pumpkin seeds
- Canola oil

Instructions:

1. Attach the "S" blade in the food processor and add in the sweet potato cubes.
2. In a saucepan, place the water and bring it to a boil. Add the millet, cover the pot and simmer for 15 minutes or until all the liquid is absorbed. Let the millet cool.
3. Place the dates, mushrooms, cilantro, chipotle pepper, cumin and salt in the food processor and process until everything is well diced and still chunky.
4. Preheat the oven to 350 degrees, Fahrenheit and cover a shallow-edged baking sheet with foil.
5. Place the sweet potato mixture in a large bowl and add the millet.
6. Add the lime juice, maple syrup, oats and seeds and mix with your hands. Divide into four portions and form patties.
7. In a skillet, heat up about a tablespoon of canola oil and place one patty in and fry until both sides brown. Place on the prepared baking sheets. Do the same with the other three patties adding more canola oil if necessary.
8. Place the baking sheet in the oven for 10 minutes.
9. Serve the patties on a bun with lettuce and condiments.

Nutritional facts per serving:

Calories 190, Total Fat 5.7g, Saturated Fat 0.6g, Cholesterol 0mg, Sodium 313mg, Total Carbohydrate 32.4g, Dietary Fiber 4.4g, Total Sugars 9.8g, Protein 4.6g, Vitamin D 63mcg, Calcium 25mg, Iron 4mg, Potassium 433mg

Sweet Potato Macaroni and Cheese

Prep time 8 minutes / Cook time 40 minutes / Serves 6

Ingredients:

- 1 14-ounce package whole grain macaroni
- 1 large (12 ounces) sweet potato, peeled and chopped
- 1 cup onion, chopped
- ½ teaspoon dried rosemary, crushed
- ½ teaspoon grated nutmeg
- 2 cloves garlic, minced
- ¼ teaspoon sea salt
- ¼ teaspoon ground pepper

Instructions:

1. Preheat the oven to 425 degrees, Fahrenheit and coat the inside of a two-quart casserole with nonstick spray.
2. Cook the macaroni per package instructions, drain it and dump it into a large bowl.
3. In a medium saucepan over medium heat cook the sweet potato in enough salted water to cover it. Boil for 15 to 20 minutes or until the potato is tender. Drain off the water.
4. In a blender process the drained sweet potato and onion until chunky.
5. Add the milk and process until smooth and creamy, scraping down the sides as necessary.
6. Add the rosemary, nutmeg, garlic, salt and pepper and process until smooth.
7. Pour the sauce over the cooked macaroni and stir well. Pour into the prepared casserole and bake for 15 to 20 minutes or until brown and bubbly.

Nutritional facts per serving:

Calories 307, Total Fat 1.2g, Saturated Fat 0.2g, Cholesterol 0mg, Sodium 103mg, Total Carbohydrate 63.5g, Dietary Fiber 4.5g, Total Sugars 6.3g, Protein 10.1g, Vitamin D 0mcg, Calcium 24mg, Iron 4mg, Potassium 452mg

Tofu Hot Dogs

Prep time 10 minutes / Cook time 1 hour / Serves 8

Ingredients:

- 8 ounces firm tofu, drained and dried with paper towels
- 3 tablespoons olive oil
- ¼ cup water
- 2 tablespoons tamari sauce
- 1 teaspoon onion powder
- 1 teaspoon garlic powder
- 1 teaspoon coriander
- 1 teaspoon dry mustard
- 1 tablespoon paprika, smoked
- ½ teaspoon ground cardamom
- ¼ teaspoon allspice
- 1 cup vital wheat gluten
- 1 teaspoon granulated
- 1 teaspoon salt
- ½ teaspoon ground pepper
- ⅔ cup oat flour
- 1 teaspoon cornstarch
- Whole wheat buns and condiments

Instructions:

1. Preheat the oven to 350 degrees, Fahrenheit.
2. Crumble the tofu into a food processor and add the olive oil, water and tamari. Blend until smooth.
3. Add the onion powder, garlic powder, coriander, dry mustard, paprika, cardamom, allspice, wheat gluten, sweetener, salt, pepper, oat flour and cornstarch; process until smooth.
4. Remove the ball of dough from the food processor and knead it with your hands for about two minutes. Divide it into eight equal portions.
5. Shape each portion like a hot dog and wrap it in a piece of aluminum foil, twisting the ends. Place them seam side down in a baking dish.
6. Pour about a half inch of water into the bottom of the dish and bake for 1 hour.
7. Let it cool a little and carefully unwrap each tofu dog. (Watch out for steam!)
8. Place on a plate and cover with plastic wrap, storing it in refrigerator overnight.
9. Simmer in hot water, fry in a skillet, or cook on the grill and serve on buns with condiments.

Nutritional facts per serving:
Calories 138, Total Fat 7.5g, Saturated Fat 1.2g, Cholesterol 0mg, Sodium 573mg, Total Carbohydrate 11.5g, Dietary Fiber 1.7g, Total Sugars 1.4g, Protein 7.5g, Vitamin D 0mcg, Calcium 77mg, Iron 1mg, Potassium 117mg

Vegan Caramel Popcorn

Prep time 5 minutes / Cook time 1 hour / Serves 8

Ingredients:

- 8 cups popped popcorn
- ½ cup vegan butter
- ⅔ cups brown sugar
- 2 tablespoons agave nectar
- ¼ teaspoon baking soda
- 1 pinch salt
- 1 teaspoon vanilla

Instructions:

1. Preheat the oven to 250 degrees, Fahrenheit and line a baking sheet with parchment paper.
2. Spread the popped popcorn on the baking sheet and set it aside.
3. In a saucepan, over medium heat, melt the butter.
4. Add the brown sugar and whisk constantly until it starts to bubble.
5. Add the agave nectar, baking soda, salt and vanilla and stir. Because of the baking soda it will foam quite a bit; just keep stirring until the foam goes down.
6. Once the foaming stops, pour it onto the popcorn and use a spatula to turn the popcorn while drizzling in a stream. Make sure all the corn is coated and pat smooth with the spatula.
7. Bake for one hour, stirring it up every 15 minutes. You're done when the popcorn is crispy.

Nutritional facts per serving:
Calories 180, Total Fat 11.9g, Saturated Fat 7.3g, Cholesterol 31mg, Sodium 143mg, Total Carbohydrate 18.2g, Dietary Fiber 1.2g, Total Sugars 11.9g, Protein 1.2g, Vitamin D 8mcg, Calcium 14mg, Iron 0mg, Potassium 47mg

Zucchini Nuggets

Prep time 5 minutes / Cook time 40 minutes / Serves 8

Ingredients:

- 6 to 7 small potatoes, peeled
- 2 medium zucchinis, grate
- ½ teaspoon sweet paprika
- ¼ teaspoon salt
- ¼ teaspoon ground pepper
- Olive oil

Instructions:

1. Cook the potatoes in boiling water until they are tender when poked with a fork. Drain and let them cool so they can be handled.
2. Preheat the oven to 425 degrees, Fahrenheit and line two baking sheets with parchment paper. It is hard to get them all on one baking sheet, but the second may only be half full.
3. Grate the zucchini and squeeze out the liquid by wrapping it in a clean kitchen towel and twisting and squeezing. Place in a medium bowl.
4. Grate the cooked potatoes and place them in the bowl with the zucchini.
5. Add the paprika, salt and pepper, adjusting to your taste and mix with your hands.
6. Scoop out 1½ to two tablespoons of the mixture at a time and shape them into nuggets or tot shapes. Brush each one with olive oil on all sides. Place on baking sheets.
7. Bake for 35 to 40 minutes or until they are crisp.

Nutritional facts per serving:

Calories 111, Total Fat 2g, Saturated Fat 0.3g, Cholesterol 0mg, Sodium 86mg, Total Carbohydrate 21.8g, Dietary Fiber 3.7g, Total Sugars 2.3g, Protein 2.8g, Vitamin D 0mcg, Calcium 19mg, Iron 1mg, Potassium 651mg

Hummus without Oil

Prep time 5 minutes / Cook time 0 minutes / Serves 6

Ingredients

- 2 tablespoons, lemon juice
- 1 15-ounce can, chickpeas
- 2 tablespoons, tahini
- 1-2 freshly chopped/minced garlic cloves
- Red pepper hummus
- 2 tablespoons, almond milk pepper

Instructions:

1. Rinse the chickpeas and put them in a high-speed blender with garlic. Blend them until they break into fine pieces.
2. Add the other ingredients and blend everything until you have a smooth paste. Add some water if you want a less thick consistency.
3. Your homemade hummus dip is ready to be served with eatables!

Nutritional facts per serving:

Calories 480, Total Fat 26.4g, Saturated Fat 17.9g, Cholesterol 0mg, Sodium 47mg, Total Carbohydrate 49.3g, Dietary Fiber 14.8g, Total Sugars 10.6g, Protein 16.7g, Vitamin D 0mcg, Calcium 111mg, Iron 6mg, Potassium 878mg

Tempting Quinoa Tabbouleh

Prep time 10 minutes / Cook time 10 minutes / Serves 6

Ingredients

- 1 cup, well-rinsed quinoa
- 1 finely minced garlic clove
- ½ teaspoon, kosher salt
- ½ cup, extra virgin olive oil
- 2 tablespoons, fresh lemon juice
- Freshly ground black pepper
- 2 Persian cucumbers
- 2 thinly sliced scallions
- 1-pint, halved cherry tomatoes
- ½ cup, chopped fresh mint
- 2/3 cup, chopped parsley

Instructions:

1. Put a medium saucepan on high heat and boil the quinoa mixed with salt in 1 ¼ cups of water. Decrease the heat to medium-low, cover the pot, and simmer everything until

the quinoa is tender. The entire process will take 10 minutes. Remove the quinoa from heat and allow it to stand for 5 minutes. Fluff it with a fork.

2. In a small bowl, whisk the garlic with the lemon juice. Add the olive oil gradually. Mix the salt and pepper to taste.

3. On a baking sheet, spread the quinoa and allow it to cool. Shift it to a large bowl and mix ¼ of the dressing.

4. Add the tomatoes, scallions, herbs, and cucumber. Give them a good toss and season everything with pepper and salt. Add the remaining dressing.

Nutritional facts per serving:
Calories 26, Total Fat 0.3g, Saturated Fat 0.2g, Cholesterol 0mg, Sodium 7mg, Total Carbohydrate 5.7g, Dietary Fiber 1g, Total Sugars 3g, Protein 1.2g, Vitamin D 11mcg, Calcium 24mg, Iron 1mg, Potassium 241mg

Quick Peanut Butter Bars

Prep time 10 minutes / Cook time 0 minutes / Serves 1

Ingredients:
- 20 soft-pitted Medjool dates
- 1 cup, raw almonds
- 1 ¼ cup, crushed pretzels
- 1/3 cup, natural peanut butter

Instructions:
1. Put the almonds in a food processor and mix them until they are broken.
2. Add the peanut butter and the dates. Blend them until you have a thick dough
3. Crush the pretzels and put them in the processor. Pulse enough to mix them with the rest of the ingredients. You can also give them a good stir with a spoon.

4. Take a small, square pan and line it with parchment paper. Press the dough onto the pan, flattening it with your hands or a spoon.

5. Put it in the freezer for about 2 hours or in the fridge for about 4 hours.

6. Once it is fully set, cut it into bars. Store them and enjoy them when you are hungry. Just remember to store them in a sealed container.

Nutritional facts per serving:
Calories 1807, Total Fat 93.4g, Saturated Fat 13.2g, Cholesterol 0mg, Sodium 1417mg, Total Carbohydrate 221.2g, Dietary Fiber 32.5g, Total Sugars 119.3g, Protein 53.4g, Vitamin D 0mcg, Calcium 337mg, Iron 17mg, Potassium 2445mg

Healthy Cauliflower Popcorn

Prep time 10 minutes / Cook time 12 hours / Serves 2

Ingredients:
- 2 heads, cauliflower
- Spicy Sauce
- ½ cup, filtered water
- ½ teaspoon, turmeric
- 1 cup, dates
- 2-3 tablespoons, nutritional yeast
- ¼ cup, sun-dried tomatoes
- 2 tablespoons, raw tahini
- 1-2 teaspoons, cayenne pepper
- 2 teaspoons, onion powder
- 1 tablespoon, apple cider vinegar
- 2 teaspoons, garlic powder

Instructions:
1. Chop the cauliflower into small pieces so that you can have crunchy popcorn.

2. Put all the ingredients for the spicy sauce in a blender and create a mixture with a smooth consistency.

3. Coat the cauliflower florets in the sauce. See that each piece is properly covered.

4. Put the spicy florets in a dehydrator tray.

5. Add some salt and your favorite herb if you want.

6. Dehydrate the cauliflower for 12 hours at 115°F. Keep dehydrating until it is crunchy.

7. Enjoy the cauliflower popcorn, which is a healthier alternative!

Nutritional facts per serving:
Calories 184, Total Fat 8.7g, Saturated Fat 1.2g, Cholesterol 0mg, Sodium 129mg, Total Carbohydrate 21.4g, Dietary Fiber 9.6g, Total Sugars 7.8g, Protein 10.6g, Vitamin D 16mcg, Calcium 128mg, Iron 4mg, Potassium 1026mg

Hummus Made with Sweet Potato

Prep time 15 minutes / Cook time 55 minutes / Serves 4

Ingredients:

- 2 cups, cooked chickpeas
- 2 medium sweet potatoes
- 3 tablespoons, tahini
- 3 tablespoons, olive oil
- 3 freshly peeled garlic gloves
- Freshly squeezed lemon juice
- Ground sea salt
- ¼ teaspoon, cumin
- Zest from half a lemon
- ½ teaspoon, smoked paprika
- 1 ½ teaspoons, cayenne pepper

Instructions:

1. Preheat the oven to 400°F. Put the sweet potatoes on the middle rack of the oven and bake them for about 45 minutes. You can also bake the potatoes in a baking dish. You will know that they are ready when they become soft and squishy.
2. Allow the sweet potatoes to cool down. Blend all the other ingredients in a food processor.
3. After the sweet potatoes have sufficiently cooled down, use a knife to peel off the skin.
4. Add the sweet potatoes to a blender and blend well with the rest of the ingredients.
5. Once you have a potato mash, sprinkle some sesame seeds and cayenne pepper and serve it!

Nutritional facts per serving:
Calories 621, Total Fat 22.9g, Saturated Fat 3.1g, Cholesterol 0mg, Sodium 164mg, Total Carbohydrate 86.6g, Dietary Fiber 22.1g, Total Sugars 12g, Protein 22.8g, Vitamin D 0mcg, Calcium 175mg, Iron 8mg, Potassium 1584mg

Avocado-Spinach Panini

Prep time 6 minutes / Cook time 5 minutes / Serves 2

Ingredients:

- 1 avocado, peeled, pitted, thinly sliced
- 1 tablespoon diced red onion
- 4 ounces ciabatta rolls, split
- ½ ounce smoked sun-dried tomatoes, julienned
- 1 cup lightly packed baby spinach

Instructions:

1. Divide equally the vegetables and sundried tomatoes and place on the bottom half of the ciabatta rolls.
2. Cover with the top halves of the rolls.
3. Grease the Panini maker with some cooking spray and preheat it. Place the sandwich in the Panini maker and grill to the desired doneness, about 4-5 minutes.
4. Remove from the Panini maker and place on your cutting board. Cut into the desired shape and serve.
5. Repeat step 3 and make the other sandwich.

Nutritional facts per serving:
Calories 329, Total Fat 22g, Saturated Fat 4.1g, Cholesterol 0mg, Sodium 18mg, Total Carbohydrate 28.6g, Dietary Fiber 8.4g, Total Sugars 1g, Protein 6.4g, Vitamin D 0mcg, Calcium 29mg, Iron 1mg, Potassium 595mg

Veggie Sandwich

Prep time 10 minutes / Cook time 0 minutes / Serves 2

Ingredients:

- 4 slices whole grain bread
- 4 leaves Romaine lettuce
- 2 tablespoons shredded carrots
- ½ large apple, cored, thinly sliced
- ½ large avocado, peeled, pitted, sliced
- ½ teaspoon extra-virgin olive oil
- Pepper to taste
- Salt to taste
- 4 tablespoons hummus
- ½ cup micro greens
- 8-12 red onion slices
- ½ cup thinly sliced red bell pepper
- 8-12 cucumber slices
- 4 teaspoons pumpkin seeds

Instructions:

1. Spread a tablespoon of hummus on each bread slices.
2. Take 2 slices of bread and layer with equal quantity of lettuce. Layer with the remaining vegetables.
3. Scatter pumpkin seeds on top. Drizzle ¼ teaspoon oil if using. Season with salt and pepper.
4. Cover with the remaining bread slices.
5. Cut into the desired shape if desired and serve.

Nutritional facts per serving:
Calories 502, Total Fat 18.5g, Saturated Fat 3.7g, Cholesterol 0mg, Sodium 343mg, Total Carbohydrate 83.2g, Dietary Fiber 14.7g, Total Sugars 36.2g, Protein 15g, Vitamin D 0mcg, Calcium 256mg, Iron 7mg, Potassium 2419mg

French Dip Sandwiches

Prep time 5 minutes / Cook time 5 minutes / Serves 4

Ingredients:

- 4 tablespoons olive oil, divided
- 4 cloves garlic, minced
- 2 cups vegetable broth
- 2 tablespoons vegan Worcestershire sauce
- ½ teaspoon liquid smoke
- 2 medium onions,
- 40 ounces Portobello mushroom caps
- 2 tablespoons soy sauce
- 1 teaspoon dried thyme
- Freshly ground pepper to taste

To serve:

- Horseradish mustard
- 4 sandwich rolls 6 inches

Instructions:

1. Place a large skillet over medium-low heat. Add 2 tablespoons oil.
2. When the oil is heated, add the onions and stir until the onions are well coated with the oil.
3. Cook until the onions turn golden brown. Stir occasionally.
4. Add garlic and sauté for 5 minutes, until aromatic.
5. Remove the onions with a slotted spoon and place over layers of paper towels.
6. Add remaining oil into the skillet. Increase the heat to medium heat.
7. Add mushrooms. Do not stir for a while. Cook until the underside is light brown. Flip sides and cook the other side.
8. Add the caramelized onions into the skillet. Pour broth and stir. Add soy sauce, Worcestershire sauce, pepper, thyme and liquid smoke and mix until well combined.
9. Simmer for a few minutes until the liquid in the skillet reduces to half its original quantity.

To serve:

1. Spread horseradish in the inside of the rolls. Remove the mushrooms with a slotted spoon and place over the rolls. Pour the liquid remaining in the pan into a bowl, which is to be served as dipping sauce.
2. Serve the sandwiches with dipping sauce. The mushrooms will give you the meaty taste and I bet you will never miss your meat in this sandwich.

Nutritional facts per serving:
Calories 256, Total Fat 15.6g, Saturated Fat 2.3g, Cholesterol 0mg, Sodium 935mg, Total Carbohydrate 23.5g, Dietary Fiber 5.8g, Total Sugars 9.5g, Protein 11g, Vitamin D 0mcg, Calcium 56mg, Iron 3mg, Potassium 1593mg

Vegan "BLT" Sandwich

Prep time 10 minutes / Cook time 0 minutes / Serves 2

Ingredients:

- 4 slices sandwich bread
- 4 tablespoons vegan mayonnaise
- 1 tomato, thinly sliced
- 10-12 slices eggplant bacon
- ½ medium onion, thinly sliced
- 4 lettuce leaves

Instructions:

1. If you like toasted bread, go ahead and toast it.
2. Heat the eggplant bacon in a pan on both the sides.

3. Spread mayonnaise on one side of the bread slices.
4. Place 2 of the bread slices on a serving platter. Layer with eggplant bacon, tomato, onion and lettuce. Cover with the remaining bread slices.
5. Cut into the desired shape and serve.

Nutritional facts per serving:
Calories 800, Total Fat 13.2g, Saturated Fat 0g, Cholesterol 0mg, Sodium 569mg, Total Carbohydrate 168.7g, Dietary Fiber 82.9g, Total Sugars 74.8g, Protein 27.1g, Vitamin D 0mcg, Calcium 416mg, Iron 6mg, Potassium 5372mg

BBQ Tofu Sandwiches

Prep time 5 minutes / Cook time 10 minutes / Serves 2
Ingredients:
- 8 ounces extra-firm tofu, drained
- 2 ounces canned, chopped green chilies, drained
- ½ tablespoon tamari or soy sauce
- ¼ teaspoon smoked paprika
- ¼ teaspoon onion powder
- 2 sandwich rolls split, toasted
- ½ tablespoon olive oil
- ½ cup vegan BBQ sauce
- 1 teaspoon prepared mustard
- ¼ teaspoon liquid smoke
- Salt to taste
- Pepper to taste

Instructions:
1. Place tofu on a plate lined with paper towels. Place something heavy on it like a heavy bottomed pan. Let it remain like this for 20-30 minutes. Cut into slices.
2. Place a large skillet over medium heat. Add oil and heat. Add tofu slices and cook for 10 minutes until the underside is brown and crisp. Flip sides and cook the other side until brown and crisp.
3. Remove with a slotted spoon and place on a plate lined with paper towels.
4. When tofu is cool enough to handle, cut into thick slices.
5. Add tofu into the skillet. Add rest of the ingredients except sandwich rolls and stir.
6. Place the saucepan over medium-low heat and cook until most of the liquid has been absorbed by the tofu.
7. Taste and adjust the seasoning if required.
8. Divide into 2 portions and place on the bottom half of the rolls.
9. Place the desired toppings and serve.

Nutritional facts per serving:
Calories 427, Total Fat 12.4g, Saturated Fat 2.2g, Cholesterol 0mg, Sodium 1274mg, Total Carbohydrate 66.9g, Dietary Fiber 10.8g, Total Sugars 31.6g, Protein 17.3g, Vitamin D 0mcg, Calcium 319mg, Iron 5mg, Potassium 898mg

Jackfruit "Philly Cheesesteak" Sandwich

Prep time 10 minutes / Cook time 20 minutes / Serves 2
Ingredients:
- 1 tablespoon extra-virgin olive oil, divided
- 20 ounces jackfruit in brine, drained, rinsed well
- ¼ teaspoon onion powder
- ¼ teaspoon celery seeds
- Pepper to taste
- Salt
- Cayenne pepper
- 2 tablespoons vegetable broth
- ½ tablespoon balsamic vinegar
- 2 tablespoons vegan mayonnaise
- 1 small onion, sliced
- ¼ teaspoon garlic powder
- ¼ teaspoon paprika
- ½ tablespoon chickpea flour
- 1 tablespoon vegan Worcestershire sauce
- 2 whole-wheat rolls, split
- ½ cup vegan cheddar cheese

Instructions:
1. Place a skillet over medium heat. Add ½ tablespoon oil and heat. Add onion and sauté until translucent.
2. Lower the heat and cook until golden brown. Stir occasionally. Remove onto a plate.

3. Dry the jackfruit by placing over a kitchen towel. Cut into triangular pieces and add into a bowl.
4. Add spices and salt and mix until well coated.
5. Place a skillet over medium-high heat. Add jackfruit and cook for about 5 minutes. Stir occasionally.
6. Add remaining oil into the skillet and mix well. Stir in the browned onions.
7. Add chickpea flour and mix until well coated.
8. Stir in broth, vinegar and Worcestershire sauce.
9. Reduce the heat to medium heat and cover the pan with a lid. Cook until jackfruit is tender. Stir occasionally.
10. Turn off the heat. When cool enough to handle, shred the jackfruit with a pair of forks and place on a lined baking sheet, in a single layer.
11. Bake in a preheated oven at 350° F for 15 minutes.
12. Spread 1-tablespoon mayonnaise on the bottom part of the rolls. Dust with garlic powder. Divide the jackfruit and place on the bottom part of the rolls. Sprinkle cheese on top.
13. Set the oven to broiler mode and preheat the oven. Broil for a couple of minutes.
14. Cover with the top half of the rolls and serve immediately.

Nutritional facts per serving:
Calories 684, Total Fat 24.8g, Saturated Fat 8g, Cholesterol 30mg, Sodium 456mg, Total Carbohydrate 105.5g, Dietary Fiber 10.2g, Total Sugars 4.5g, Protein 18.7g, Vitamin D 3mcg, Calcium 341mg, Iron 5mg, Potassium 1180mg

Meatless Mexican Sloppy Joes

Prep time 10 minutes / Cook time 14 minutes / Serves 3

Ingredients:
- ¼ red onion, diced
- 2 tablespoons water, divided
- ½ jalapeño pepper, discard seeds and membranes, diced
- ¾ cup cooked or canned pinto beans, rinsed, drained
- ¾ cup cooked or canned black beans, rinsed, drained
- ½ cup corn kernels, fresh or frozen
- 3 burger buns, split
- 1 clove garlic, minced
- ½ red bell pepper, diced
- A handful fresh cilantro, chopped
- Guacamole, to serve

For Mexican BBQ sauce:
- 10 tablespoons salsa
- 2 tablespoons coconut sugar
- 1 teaspoon ground cumin
- ½ teaspoon dried oregano
- Juice of a lime
- ½ tablespoon chili powder
- 1 teaspoon smoked paprika
- Salt to taste
- Pepper to taste

Instructions:
To make Mexican BBQ sauce:

1. Add all the ingredients for sauce into a bowl and whisk well. Set aside for a while for the flavors to blend in.
2. Place a skillet over medium-high heat. Add a tablespoon of water and onion and cook until soft.
3. Stir in the garlic and sauté for a few seconds until aromatic.
4. Stir in the bell pepper and jalapeño. Also add a tablespoon of water and cook for 2-3 minutes.
5. Add sauce and mix well. Lower the heat and cook for 5-6 minutes.
6. Stir in the corn and beans. Cook for 4-5 minutes. Taste and add more salt and pepper if desired.
7. Stir in the cilantro and turn off the heat.
8. Place the bun halves on a serving platter, with the cut side facing up. Divide the bean mixture among the buns.
9. Spoon some guacamole and jalapeño slices and serve.

Nutritional facts per serving:
Calories 575, Total Fat 6.8g, Saturated Fat 1.2g, Cholesterol 0mg, Sodium 662mg, Total Carbohydrate 106g, Dietary Fiber 20.1g, Total Sugars 17.6g, Protein 27.9g, Vitamin D 0mcg, Calcium 218mg, Iron 8mg, Potassium 1807mg

Hearty Lentil and Brown Rice Burger

Prep time 10 minutes / Cook time 2 hours 30 minutes / Serves 5

Ingredients:

- 1 cup dried green lentils, rinsed
- 2 medium yellow onions, chopped
- 8 cloves garlic, minced
- 2 teaspoons ground sage
- 3 cups water
- 1 cup brown rice
- 2 carrots, grated
- 6 teaspoons ground cumin
- 2 teaspoons sea salt
- 2 cups vegetable broth

Instructions:

1. Add lentils, onion, cumin, salt, brown rice, carrot, sage, water, broth and garlic into a saucepan.
2. Place the saucepan over medium heat. When the mixture begins to boil, lower the heat and simmer until tender. It may take like 2 hours to cook. Transfer into a colander and drain off the extra liquid from the lentils. Let it sit for 3-4 minutes.
3. Transfer into the food processor bowl and process until quite smooth.
4. Divide the mixture into 12 equal portions and shape into patties. Spray some cooking spray over the patties.
5. Bake in a preheated oven at 350° F for about 25-30 minutes or until brown.
6. Serve over whole-wheat buns with toppings of your choice.

Nutritional facts per serving:

Calories 334, Total Fat 2.6g, Saturated Fat 0.5g, Cholesterol 0mg, Sodium 1086mg, Total Carbohydrate 61.7g, Dietary Fiber 15g, Total Sugars 4.2g, Protein 16.2g, Vitamin D 0mcg, Calcium 97mg, Iron 6mg, Potassium 762mg

Vegan Pizza

Prep time 8 minutes / Cook time 20 minutes / Serves 4

Ingredients:

For pizza:

- 1 garlic herb pizza crust
- 2/3 cup chopped onion
- 1 cup chopped red bell pepper
- 1 cup chopped green bell pepper
- 1 cup chopped orange bell pepper
- 2 cups chopped mushrooms
- ½ teaspoon salt or to taste
- 1 teaspoon dried oregano
- 1 teaspoon dried basil
- 1 teaspoon garlic powder
- 2 tablespoons olive oil

For tomato sauce:

- 15 ounces tomato sauce
- Salt to taste
- 1 teaspoon dried oregano
- 1 teaspoon dried basil
- 1 teaspoon garlic powder
- 1 teaspoon granulated sugar

For toppings:

- Red pepper flakes
- Dried oregano
- 1 cup shredded vegan Parmesan cheese

Instructions:

1. Place rack in the center of the oven. Place a round sheet of parchment paper in a round baking sheet.
2. Place a large skillet over medium heat. Add oil. When the oil is heated, add onion and all the peppers and sauté for a couple of minutes.
3. Stir in the salt, garlic powder and all the dried herbs. Cook until the vegetables are slightly brown.
4. Add mushrooms and cook for 2-3 minutes. Turn off the heat.
5. To make sauce: Add all the ingredients for sauce into a bowl and whisk well. If the consistency is thick, add a little water to dilute. Taste and adjust the seasonings if required.
6. Dust your countertop with a little flour. Place the dough on the countertop and roll the dough into a circle.
7. Place the dough in the prepared baking sheet.
8. Spread tomato sauce (less or more or all of it, depending on your preference) over the pizza crust.

9. Scatter the sautéed vegetables over the pizza. Sprinkle half the vegan Parmesan cheese on top.
10. Carefully slide the parchment paper with crust (not the baking sheet) on the rack in the oven.
11. Bake in a preheated oven at 425° F for about 17 to 20 minutes or to the desired doneness.
12. Sprinkle oregano, chili flakes and remaining Parmesan on top.
13. Cut into 4 equal wedges and serve.

Nutritional facts per serving:
Calories 205, Total Fat 9.7g, Saturated Fat 2.2g, Cholesterol 5mg, Sodium 1036mg, Total Carbohydrate 26.4g, Dietary Fiber 4.3g, Total Sugars 13g, Protein 7.6g, Vitamin D 126mcg, Calcium 98mg, Iron 3mg, Potassium 699mg

Tortilla Vegetable Pizza

Prep time 5 minutes / Cook time 15 minutes / Serves 2

Ingredients:
- 2 low fat tortillas
- 4 heaping tablespoons nutritional yeast
- Olive oil cooking spray
- Arrabbiata sauce
- ½ red onion, sliced
- 1 cup sliced mixed bell peppers
- ½ courgette, diced
- A handful fresh basil, finely chopped
- 2 cloves garlic, minced

For quick Arrabbiata sauce:
- ½ cup canned tomatoes or passata
- 2 clove garlic, peeled
- 1 teaspoon dried chili flakes
- 4-5 fresh basil leaves
- Salt to taste

Instructions:
To make Arrabbiata sauce:
1. Add all the ingredients for Arrabbiata sauce into a blender and blend until smooth.
2. Place rack in the center of the oven. Place a round sheet of parchment paper in a round baking sheet.
3. Place a large skillet over medium heat. Spray some cooking oil. When the pan is heated, add onion, garlic, courgette and all the peppers and sauté for 3 minutes.
4. Stir in the basil. Cook until the vegetables are slightly brown and tender. Sprinkle some water while cooking if the vegetables are getting burnt. Turn off the heat.
5. Place a tortilla in the prepared pan. Spread some Arrabbiata or tomato sauce over it. Sprinkle half the nutritional yeast.
6. Spread half the vegetables over the tortilla. Slide tortilla onto the rack. Carefully pull off the parchment paper so that the tortilla is directly on the rack.
7. Repeat steps 5-6 and place the other tortilla.
8. Bake in a preheated oven at 375° F for about 10 to 12 minutes or until crisp.
9. Sprinkle basil on top and serve hot.

Nutritional facts per serving:
Calories 138, Total Fat 1.9g, Saturated Fat 0.3g, Cholesterol 0mg, Sodium 47mg, Total Carbohydrate 25.3g, Dietary Fiber 6.5g, Total Sugars 4.3g, Protein 8.7g, Vitamin D 0mcg, Calcium 66mg, Iron 3mg, Potassium 666mg

Pizza Burrito

Prep time 10 minutes / Cook time 20 minutes / Serves 2

Ingredients:
For pizza sauce:
- 3 tablespoons tomato sauce
- ½ teaspoon maple syrup

For burrito pizza:
- 2 tortillas
- ½ cup sliced mushrooms
- ½ cup fresh packed spinach
- 2 tablespoons vegan sausage crumbles
- 3 tablespoons vegan cream sauce
- 1 tablespoon fresh basil

Instructions:
To make pizza sauce:
- Add pizza sauce and maple syrup into a small bowl and stir.

130

To assemble:
1. Warm the tortillas following the instructions on the package.
2. Place tortillas on your countertop. Spread half the sauce on each tortilla.
3. Scatter half the spinach on each. Drizzle half the cream sauce on each and spread it.
4. Scatter half the sausage crumbles or chopped chickpeas on each followed by half the mushrooms.
5. Fold like a burrito. Place on a baking sheet lined with parchment paper, with the seam side facing down.
6. Bake in a preheated oven at 350° F for about 18-20 minutes or until crisp.

Nutritional facts per serving:
Calories 80, Total Fat 1.8g, Saturated Fat 0.7g, Cholesterol 3mg, Sodium 144mg, Total Carbohydrate 14.5g, Dietary Fiber 2.2g, Total Sugars 2.9g, Protein 2.6g, Vitamin D 63mcg, Calcium 38mg, Iron 1mg, Potassium 232mg

Black Eyed Peas and Tofu Pizza

Prep time 10 minutes / Cook time 30 minutes / Serves 8

Ingredients:

For black eyed peas:
- 1 ½ cups dried black eyed peas
- 1 medium onion, chopped
- 2 bay leaves
- 4 teaspoons olive oil
- 1 green bell pepper, deseeded, chopped
- 1 Serrano chili pepper
- 1 cup tomato sauce
- Salt to taste

For tofu thyme ricotta layer:
- 16 ounces firm tofu, crumbled
- 2 teaspoons Italian seasoning
- 2 teaspoons garlic powder
- 2 tablespoons dried thyme
- Salt to taste
- 2 tablespoons extra- virgin olive oil
- 4 teaspoons apple cider vinegar

For pizza:
- 2 pizza crusts
- 4 cups marinara sauce
- 2 cups fresh mushrooms, sliced
- Green bell pepper sliced
- 1 cup shredded nondairy cheese

Instructions:

To make black-eyed peas:
1. Place a large skillet over medium heat. Add oil. When oil is heated, add onions, bay leaf, bell pepper and Serrano chili and sauté until onions are golden brown.
2. Add tomato sauce and salt and sauté for a minute.
3. Add drained black-eyed peas. Stir-fry for a minute and add water to fully cover the black-eyed peas.
4. Lower heat, cover and cook until black-eyed peas are tender and nearly dry. Taste and adjust the seasoning if necessary.
5. To make tofu thyme ricotta layer: Add all the ingredients for tofu thyme ricotta layer and mix well. Taste and adjust the seasonings if necessary.
6. Takes 2 round baking dishes of about 8 inches each. Roll each portion of dough. Until it is a round of about 9 inches each. Place the dough in the baking dish. Press it onto the bottom as well as the sides of the baking dish. Spray water on the dough.
7. Bake in a preheated oven at 400° F for about 8-10 minutes.
8. Divide and spread the black-eyed peas over the crusts. Divide and spread tofu ricotta over the black-eyed pea's layer.
9. Sprinkle mushrooms and bell peppers over. Spread marinara sauce or tomato sauce over the vegetables. Sprinkle nondairy cheese on top, if using.
10. Bake for about 20 minutes.
11. Remove from oven. Slice each pizza into 4 wedges and serve.

Nutritional facts per serving:
Calories 398, Total Fat 17.4g, Saturated Fat 5.4g, Cholesterol 18mg, Sodium 904mg, Total Carbohydrate 50.3g, Dietary Fiber 13.2g, Total Sugars 17.2g, Protein 20g, Vitamin D 65mcg, Calcium 283mg, Iron 6mg, Potassium 743mg

Sriracha BBQ Tofu Pizza

Prep time 5 minutes / Cook time 0 minutes / Serves 4

Ingredients:

For no rise spelt crust:
- ¾ cup warm water
- 4 teaspoons active yeast
- 2 tablespoons cornstarch
- 4 teaspoons extra- virgin olive oil
- 1 ½ cups spelt flour
- 2 teaspoons maple syrup
- 2/3 teaspoon salt

For BBQ tofu:
- 4 tablespoons BBQ sauce
- 2 cloves garlic, sliced
- 5-6 teaspoons Sriracha sauce
- 2 cups cubed firm tofu

For toppings:
- 1 onion, halved, sliced
- 1 red bell pepper, sliced
- Marinara sauce
- 1 cup almond milk pepper Jack cheese, shredded
- 2 tablespoons cilantro, chopped

Instructions:

For BBQ tofu:
1. Place the tofu over kitchen towels for a while. Keep something heavy over it for about 30 minutes to drain off excess moisture.
2. Add tofu, BBQ sauce, Sriracha sauce, garlic to a bowl and toss well. Let it marinate for a while.
3. Meanwhile, make spelt crust as follows: Mix together in a large bowl, water, yeast, and maple syrup and keep it aside for 5-7 minutes or until it becomes frothy.
4. Mix together in another bowl, spelt flour, corn flour and salt.
5. Add this dry mixture into the frothy mixture. Add oil and knead until you get smooth dough.
6. Divide and roll the dough into 2 ovals of about 12 inches size. Place on a baking sheet. Leave it at a warm place for about 10 minutes.
7. Spread marinara sauce over the rolled dough. Place onions and peppers over it. Season with salt and pepper.
8. Place the tofu pieces over it. Pour the remaining marinade over it. Sprinkle cheese all over it.
9. Bake in a preheated oven at 450° F for about 12-13 minutes. Remove from oven.
10. Garnish with cilantro and serve.

Nutritional facts per serving:
Calories 573, Total Fat 26.7g, Saturated Fat 15g, Cholesterol 1mg, Sodium 869mg, Total Carbohydrate 68.2g, Dietary Fiber 7.4g, Total Sugars 17.2g, Protein 19.9g, Vitamin D 0mcg, Calcium 304mg, Iron 7mg, Potassium 817mg

Apple Glazed Vegetable & Edamame Stir-Fry

Prep time 5 minutes / Cook time 10 minutes / Serves 8

Ingredients:
- 2 cups cubed squash
- 2 cups cubed sweet potato
- 2 cups cubed carrots
- 1 large bell pepper, deseeded, cut into squares
- 1 large onion, cut into 1-inch square pieces, separate the layers
- 1 cup water
- 1 cup applesauce
- 2 teaspoons ground ginger
- 6 tablespoons rice wine vinegar
- 4 tablespoons soy sauce or hoisin sauce
- 1 cup cooked edamame beans
- 1 teaspoon Old Bay seasoning
- ½ cup brown or white sugar
- Salt to taste
- Pepper to taste
- ½ teaspoon red pepper flakes
- 1 teaspoon minced garlic
- Cooking spray

Instructions:
1. Place a large nonstick pan or wok over high heat. Spray some cooking spray over it.
2. Add onion and garlic sauté for a couple of minutes. Add rest of the vegetables except edamame and cover with a lid. Cook until tender.

3. Add rest of the ingredients except edamame into a bowl and stir. Pour into the pan and mix until well coated.
4. Lower the heat to medium-low and cook for 10 minutes until tender.
5. Add edamame and mix well. Heat thoroughly and serve.

Nutritional facts per serving:
Calories 152, Total Fat 0.4g, Saturated Fat 0g, Cholesterol 0mg, Sodium 594mg, Total Carbohydrate 35g, Dietary Fiber 4.3g, Total Sugars 22.6g , Protein 2.8g, Vitamin D 0mcg, Calcium 31mg, Iron 2mg, Potassium 535mg

Satay Sweet Potato Curry

Prep time 6 minutes / Cook time 10 minutes / Serves 8
Ingredients:
- 2 tablespoons coconut oil
- 4 cloves garlic, grated
- 6 tablespoons Thai red curry paste
- 2 pounds sweet potato, peeled, cubed
- 14 ounces spinach
- 2 onions, chopped
- 3 tablespoons minced ginger
- 2 tablespoons smooth peanut butter
- 14 ounces coconut milk
- Juice, 2 limes
- Roasted peanuts
- Salt to taste
- 2 cups water
- Cooked rice to serve

Instructions:
1. Place a large saucepan over medium heat. Add oil. When the oil is heated, add onions and sauté until onions turn translucent.
2. Stir in garlic and ginger and sauté for a few seconds until aromatic.
3. Add Thai curry paste, sweet potatoes and peanut butter and mix well.
4. Add coconut milk and water and stir.
5. When it begins to boil, lower the heat and cook until sweet potato is fork tender. Do not cover while cooking.
6. Add spinach and salt cook for 10 minutes until sweet potatoes are very soft.
7. Turn off the heat. Add lime juice and stir.
8. Serve over cooked rice. Garnish with peanuts and serve.

Nutritional facts per serving:
Calories 453, Total Fat 23.1g, Saturated Fat 15.3g, Cholesterol 0mg, Sodium 698mg, Total Carbohydrate 55.5g, Dietary Fiber 7.9g, Total Sugars 11.2g, Protein 9.1g, Vitamin D 0mcg, Calcium 88mg, Iron 9mg, Potassium 1106mg

Chickpea Curry

Prep time 5 minutes / Cook time 5 minutes / Serves 4
Ingredients:
- 2 tablespoons canola oil
- Salt to taste
- 1 ½ teaspoons ground ginger
- 1 ½ teaspoons garam masala
- 2/3 cup full fat coconut milk
- 4 cups canned or cooked chickpeas, drained, rinsed
- 2 ½ cups tomato puree
- A handful fresh cilantro, chopped, to garnish

Instructions:
1. Place a large pot over medium-high heat. Add oil. When the oil is heated, add chickpeas, salt and the spices and mix well. Stir frequently.
2. Lower the heat to low heat. Stir in the tomato puree and coconut milk.
3. Simmer thoroughly heated. Taste and adjust the seasonings and coconut milk if required.
4. Garnish with cilantro.
5. Serve over with hot steamed rice or naan bread or any other flat bread of your choice.

Nutritional facts per serving:
Calories 944, Total Fat 29g, Saturated Fat 10.3g, Cholesterol 0mg, Sodium 139mg, Total Carbohydrate 138.1g, Dietary Fiber 38.8g, Total Sugars 30.3g, Protein 42.2g, Vitamin D 0mcg, Calcium 246mg, Iron 16mg, Potassium 2555mg

Chickpea and Squash Coconut Curry

Prep time 3 minutes / Cook time 4 minutes / Serves 8

Ingredients:

- 2 onions, chopped
- 2 inches ginger, peeled, chopped
- 2 cloves garlic, peeled
- 2 red chilies, sliced
- 1 teaspoon turmeric powder
- 2 teaspoons ground cumin
- 2 teaspoons ground coriander
- 2 teaspoons garam masala
- 28 ounces butternut squash, peeled, diced
- 14 ounces, half fat coconut milk
- ounces baby spinach
- 1 tablespoon oil
- 2 cups vegetable stock or water
- Juice, lime
- Lime wedges to serve
- Salt to taste

Instructions:

1. Add onion, chili, garlic and ginger into a blender. Add a tablespoon of water and blend until smooth.
2. Place a large skillet over medium heat. Add oil. When the oil is heated, add the ground paste and sauté for a few minutes until aromatic.
3. Add salt and all the spices and cook for a few seconds until aromatic.
4. Add squash and chickpeas and mix well.
5. Stir in the coconut milk and stock. When it begins to boil, lower the heat and cook until squash is soft.
6. Add spinach and cook for 3-4 minutes. Add lime juice and stir.
7. Serve over rice. Serve with lime wedges.

Nutritional facts per serving:

Calories 149, Total Fat 2.5g, Saturated Fat 0.4g, Cholesterol 41mg, Sodium 68mg, Total Carbohydrate 16.5g, Dietary Fiber 3.3g, Total Sugars 3.8g, Protein 16.7g, Vitamin D 0mcg, Calcium 74mg, Iron 2mg, Potassium 591mg

Cinnamon Apple Chips with Dip

Prep time 10 minutes / Cook time 3 hours / Serves 4

Ingredients:

- 1 cup raw cashews
- 2 apples, thinly sliced
- 1 lemon
- 1½ cups water, divided
- Cinnamon
- Another medium cored apple quartered
- 1 tablespoon honey
- 1 teaspoon cinnamon
- ¼ teaspoon sea salt

Instructions:

1. Place the cashews in a bowl of warm water, deep enough to cover them and let them soak overnight.
2. Preheat the oven to 200 degrees, Fahrenheit. Line two baking sheets with parchment paper.
3. Juice the lemon into a large glass bowl and add two cups of the water. Place the sliced apples in the water as you cut them and when done, swish them around and drain.
4. Spread the apple slices across the baking sheet in a single layer and sprinkle with a little cinnamon. Bake for 90 minutes.
5. Remove the slices from the oven and flip each of them over. Put them back in the oven and bake for another 90 minutes, or until they are crisp. Remember, they will get crisper as they cool.
6. While the apple slices are cooking, drain the cashews and put them in a blender, along with the quartered apple, the honey, a teaspoon of cinnamon and a half cup of the remaining water. Process until thick and creamy. I like to refrigerate my dip for about an hour to chill, before serve alongside the room temperature apple slices.

Nutritional facts per serving:

Calories 312, Total Fat 16.3g, Saturated Fat 3.2g, Cholesterol 0mg, Sodium 135mg, Total Carbohydrate 42.7g, Dietary Fiber 7.3g, Total Sugars 23.9g, Protein 6g, Vitamin D 0mcg, Calcium 64mg, Iron 3mg, Potassium 413mg

Eggplant Mushroom and Potato Curry

Prep time 5 minutes / Cook time 10 minutes / Serves 8

Ingredients:
- 2 tablespoons oil
- 2 pounds button mushrooms
- 2 large potatoes, peeled, chopped into chunks
- 2 eggplants, chopped into chunks
- 2 onions, chopped
- 1 ¼ cups vegetable stock
- 4 tablespoons curry paste
- 2 cans light coconut milk
- 2 tablespoons cilantro
- Salt to taste

Instructions:
1. Place a large saucepan over medium heat. Add oil. When oil is heated, add onions and potatoes. Sauté for a couple of minutes. Cover and cook for about 5 minutes.
2. Add eggplants and mushrooms. Stir well. Cook for about 5 minutes.
3. Add curry paste, stock and coconut milk.
4. When it begins to boil, lower the heat and simmer until the potatoes are cooked. Garnish with cilantro and serve with hot rice or naan bread.

Nutritional facts per serving:
Calories 353, Total Fat 22.8g, Saturated Fat 13.1g, Cholesterol 0mg, Sodium 52mg, Total Carbohydrate 34.5g, Dietary Fiber 10.2g, Total Sugars 10.4g, Protein 8.6g, Vitamin D 408mcg, Calcium 37mg, Iron 5mg, Potassium 1249mg

Black Bean Dip

Prep time 5 minutes / Cook time 0 minutes / Serves 10

Ingredients:
- 2 15-ounce cans black beans, rinsed and drained
- 1 jalapeno pepper, seeded and minced
- ½ red bell pepper, seeded and diced
- ½ yellow bell pepper, seeded and diced
- ½ small red onion, diced
- 1 cup fresh cilantro, finely chopped
- 1 lime Zest
- 1 lime, Juice
- 1 10-ounce can Rotel, drained
- ½ teaspoon Kosher salt
- ¼ teaspoon ground black pepper

Instructions:
1. In a large bowl, combine the garlic, green onions, beans, jalapeno, red and yellow bell pepper, onion, cilantro and mix together well.
2. Add the lime zest and juice, Rotel, salt and pepper and mix. Adjust seasoning to your own taste.
3. Refrigerate for at one hour, minimum, before serving, so the flavors have time to blend. Serve with wheat tortilla slices that have been crisped in the oven or with wheat or sesame crackers.

Nutritional facts per serving:
Calories 298, Total Fat 1.3g, Saturated Fat 0.3g, Cholesterol 0mg, Sodium 122mg, Total Carbohydrate 55.2g, Dietary Fiber 13.5g, Total Sugars 2.7g, Protein 18.6g, Vitamin D 0mcg, Calcium 110mg, Iron 4mg, Potassium 1308mg

Crunchy Asparagus Spears

Prep time 5 minutes / Cook time 25 minutes / Serves 4

Ingredients:
- 1 bunch asparagus spears
- ¼ cup nutritional yeast
- 2 tablespoons hemp seeds
- 1 teaspoon garlic powder
- ¼ teaspoon paprika
- ⅛ teaspoon ground pepper
- ¼ cup whole-wheat breadcrumbs
- Juice, ½ lemon

Instructions:
1. Preheat the oven to 350 degrees, Fahrenheit. Line a baking sheet with parchment paper.
2. Wash the asparagus, snapping off the white part at the bottom. Save it for making vegetable stock.

3. Mix together the nutritional yeast, hemp seed, garlic powder, paprika, pepper and breadcrumbs.
4. Place asparagus spears on the baking sheets giving them a little room in between and sprinkle with the mixture in the bowl.
5. Bake for up to 25 minutes, until crispy.

6. Serve with lemon juice if desired.

Nutritional facts per serving:
Calories 91, Total Fat 2.7g, Saturated Fat 0.3g, Cholesterol 0mg, Sodium 56mg, Total Carbohydrate 11.8g,Dietary Fiber 3.6g, Total Sugars 1g, Protein 7.1g, Vitamin D 0mcg, Calcium 28mg, Iron 3mg, Potassium 327mg

Cucumber Bites with Chive and Sunflower Seeds

Prep time 10 minutes / Cook time 0 minutes / Serves 4
Ingredients:
- 1 cup raw sunflower seed
- ½ teaspoon salt
- ½ cup chopped fresh chives
- 1 clove garlic, chopped
- 2 tablespoons red onion, minced
- 2 tablespoons lemon juice
- ½ cup water
- 4 large cucumbers

Instructions:
1. Place the sunflower seeds and salt in the food processor and process to a fine powder. It will take only about 10 seconds.
2. Add the chives, garlic, onion, lemon juice and water and process until creamy, scraping

down the sides frequently. The mixture should be very creamy; if not, add a little more water.
3. Cut the cucumbers into 1½-inch coin-like pieces.
4. Spread a spoonful of the sunflower mixture on top and set on a platter. Sprinkle more chopped chives on top and refrigerate until ready to serve.

Nutritional facts per serving:
Calories 82, Total Fat 6.1g, Saturated Fat 0.6g, Cholesterol 0mg, Sodium 296mg, Total Carbohydrate 5.3g, Dietary Fiber 1.6g, Total Sugars 1.7g, Protein 3.1g, Vitamin D 0mcg, Calcium 27mg, Iron 1mg, Potassium 189mg

Garlicky Kale Chips

Prep time 10 minutes / Cook time 1 hour / Serves 5
Ingredients:
- 4 cloves garlic
- 1 cup olive oil
- 8 to 10 cups fresh kale, chopped
- 1 tablespoon, garlic-flavored olive oil
- ½ teaspoon garlic salt
- ½ teaspoon pepper
- 1 pinch red pepper flakes

Instructions:
1. Peel and crush the garlic clove and place it in a small jar with a lid. Pour the olive oil over the top, cover tightly and shake. This will keep in the refrigerator for several days. When you're ready to use it, strain out the garlic and retain the oil.

2. Preheat the oven to 175 degrees, Fahrenheit.
3. Spread out the kale on a baking sheet and drizzle with the olive oil. Sprinkle with garlic salt, pepper and red pepper flakes.
4. Bake for an hour, remove from the oven and let the chips cool.
5. Store in an airtight container if you don't plan to eat them right away.

Nutritional facts per serving:
Calories 749, Total Fat 80.7g, Saturated Fat 11.5g, Cholesterol 0mg, Sodium 47mg, Total Carbohydrate 12.4g, Dietary Fiber 1.8g, Total Sugars 0.1g, Protein 3.4g, Vitamin D 0mcg, Calcium 150mg, Iron 2mg, Potassium 543mg

Hummus-stuffed Baby Potatoes

Prep time 5 minutes / Cook time 20 minutes / Serves 4
Ingredients:
- 12 small red potatoes, walnut-sized
- Hummus
- 2 green onions, thinly sliced

- ¼ teaspoon paprika, for garnish

Instructions:

1. Place two to three inches of water in a saucepan, set a steamer inside and bring the water to a boil.
2. Place the whole potatoes in the steamer basket and steam for about 20 minutes or until soft. Keep the pan from boiling dry by adding additional hot water as needed.
3. Dump the potatoes into a colander and run cold water over them until they can be handled.
4. Cut each potato open and scoop out most of the pulp, leaving the skin and a thin layer of potato intact.
5. Mix the hummus with most of the green onions (keep enough for garnish) and spoon a little into the area where the potato has been scooped out.
6. Sprinkle each filled potato half with paprika and serve.

Nutritional facts per serving:
Calories 366, Total Fat 1.1g, Saturated Fat 0.2g, Cholesterol 0mg, Sodium 45mg, Total Carbohydrate 82.2g, Dietary Fiber 9.1g, Total Sugars 5.3g, Protein 10.1g, Vitamin D 0mcg, Calcium 58mg, Iron 4mg, Potassium 2352mg

Homemade Trail Mix

Prep time 10 minutes / Cook time 0 minutes / Serves 5
Ingredients:
- ½ cup uncooked old-fashioned oatmeal
- ½ cup chopped dates
- 2 cups whole grain cereal
- ¼ cup raisins
- ¼ cup almonds
- ¼ cup walnuts

Instructions:
1. Mix all the ingredients in a large bowl.
2. Place in an airtight container until ready to use.

Nutritional facts per serving:
Calories 245, Total Fat 7.1g, Saturated Fat 0.6g, Cholesterol 0mg, Sodium 94mg, Total Carbohydrate 44.7g, Dietary Fiber 6.7g, Total Sugars 24.3g, Protein 6.2g, Vitamin D 0mcg, Calcium 39mg, Iron 5mg, Potassium 400mg

Nut Butter Maple Dip

Prep time 10 minutes / Cook time 0 minutes / Serves 6
Ingredients:
- ½ tablespoon ground flaxseed
- 1 teaspoon ground cinnamon
- ½ tablespoon maple syrup
- 2 tablespoons cashew milk
- ¾ cups crunchy, unsweetened peanut butter

Instructions:
1. In a bowl, combine the flaxseed, cinnamon, maple syrup, cashew milk and peanut butter.
2. Use a fork to mix everything in. I stir it like I'm scrambling eggs. The mixture should be creamy. If it's too runny, add a little more peanut butter; if it's too thick, add a little more cashew milk.
3. Refrigerate for about an hour, covered and serve.

Nutritional facts per serving:
Calories 200, Total Fat 16.5g, Saturated Fat 3.5g, Cholesterol 0mg, Sodium 151mg, Total Carbohydrate 8.2g, Dietary Fiber 2.3g, Total Sugars 4.3g, Protein 8.4g, Vitamin D 0mcg, Calcium 12mg, Iron 3mg, Potassium 222mg

Pumpkin Orange Spice Hummus

Prep time 10 minutes / Cook time 0 minutes / Serves 4
Ingredients:
- 1 cup canned, unsweetened pumpkin puree
- 1 16-ounce can garbanzo beans, rinsed and drained
- 1 tablespoon apple cider vinegar
- 1 tablespoon maple syrup
- ¼ cup tahini
- 1 tablespoon fresh orange juice
- ½ teaspoon orange zest and additional zest for garnish
- ⅛ teaspoon ground cinnamon

- ⅛ teaspoon ground ginger
- ⅛ teaspoon ground nutmeg
- ¼ teaspoon salt

Instructions:
1. Pour the pumpkin puree and garbanzo beans into a food processor and pulse to break up.
2. Add the vinegar, syrup, tahini, orange juice and orange zest pulse a few times.
3. Add the cinnamon, ginger, nutmeg and salt and process until smooth and creamy.
4. Serve in a bowl sprinkled with more orange zest with wheat crackers alongside.

Nutritional facts per serving:
Calories 583, Total Fat 15.8g, Saturated Fat 2.4g, Cholesterol 3mg, Sodium 267mg, Total Carbohydrate 85.4g, Dietary Fiber 22g, Total Sugars 23.4g, Protein 29.5g, Vitamin D 51mcg, Calcium 383mg, Iron 9mg, Potassium 1315mg

Quick English Muffin Mexican Pizzas

Prep time 5 minutes / Cook time 15 minutes / Serves 4

Ingredients:
- 2 whole-wheat English muffins separated
- ⅓ cup tomato salsa
- ¼ cup refried beans
- 1 small jalapeno, seeded and sliced
- ¼ cup onion, sliced
- 2 tablespoons diced plum or cherry tomato
- ⅓ cup vegan cheese shreds

Instructions:
1. Preheat the oven to 400 degrees, Fahrenheit and cover a baking sheet with foil. The foil makes the crust crispier.
2. Separate the English muffin and spread on some salsa and refried beans.
3. Place some of the jalapenos and onions on top and sprinkle the cheese over all.
4. Place on the baking sheet and bake for 10 to 15 minutes or until brown. You can turn on the broiler for a minute or two to melt the cheese.

Nutritional facts per serving:
Calories 134, Total Fat 3.9g, Saturated Fat 2.3g, Cholesterol 11mg, Sodium 357mg, Total Carbohydrate 18.5g, Dietary Fiber 2.8g, Total Sugars 3.1g, Protein 6.2g, Vitamin D 1mcg, Calcium 131mg, Iron 2mg, Potassium 251mg

Quinoa Trail Mix Cups

Prep time 10 minutes / Cook time 12 minutes / Serves 6

Ingredients:
- 2 tablespoons ground flaxseed
- ⅓ cup unsweetened soy milk
- 1 cup old-fashioned rolled oats
- 1 cup cooked and cooled quinoa
- ¼ cup brown sugar
- 1 teaspoon ground cinnamon
- ¼ teaspoon salt
- ¼ cup pumpkin or sunflower seeds
- ¼ cup shredded coconut
- ½ cup almonds
- ½ cup raisins or dried cherries/cranberries

Instructions:
1. Whisk the flaxseed and milk together in a small bowl and set aside for 10 minutes so the seed can absorb the milk.
2. Preheat the oven to 350 degrees, Fahrenheit and coat a muffin tin with coconut oil.
3. In a large bowl, mix the oats, quinoa, brown sugar, cinnamon, salt, pumpkin seeds, coconut, almonds and raisins.
4. Stir in the flaxseed and milk mixture and combine thoroughly.
5. Place two heaping teaspoons of the trail mix mixture in each muffin cup. When done, wet your fingers and press down on each muffin cup to compact the trail mix.
6. Bake for 12 minutes.
7. Cool completely before removing and each little cup will fall out. Store in an airtight container.

Nutritional facts per serving:
Calories 297, Total Fat 8.7g, Saturated Fat 1.8g, Cholesterol 0mg, Sodium 111mg, Total Carbohydrate 47.8g, Dietary Fiber 6.3g, Total Sugars 14.6g, Protein 9g, Vitamin D 0mcg, Calcium 63mg, Iron 4mg, Potassium 435mg

Chapter 8: Soups, Stews and Chili Recipes

Sniffle Soup

Prep time 5 minutes / Cook time 33 minutes / Serves 6

Ingredients:

- 1½ tbsp plus 4 cups water, divided
- 1½ cups onion, diced
- 1 cup carrot, diced
- 1 cup celery, diced
- 3 large cloves garlic, minced
- 1 tsp paprika
- 1 tsp mild curry powder
- ½ tsp sea salt
- ¼ tsp dried thyme
- ¼ tsp ground black pepper
- 2 cups dried red lentils
- 3 cups vegetable stock
- 1½ tbsp apple cider vinegar

Instructions:

1. Heat a large pot over medium heat.
2. Add all ingredients to the pot and stir occasionally.
3. Cook for 8 minutes.
4. Increase heat and bring it to a boil.
5. Once it is boiled, let it simmer for 25 minutes.
6. Serve and enjoy.

Nutrition Facts Per Serving:

Calories 293, Total Fat 1g, Saturated Fat 0.1g, Cholesterol 0mg, Sodium 222mg, Total Carbohydrate 53.2g, Dietary Fiber 23.1g, Total Sugars 7.4g, Protein 18.5g, Vitamin D 0mcg, Calcium 90mg, Iron 6mg, Potassium 912mg

French Lentil Soup with Paprika

Prep time 10 minutes / Cook time 43 minutes / Serves 5

Ingredients:

- 1 cup water
- 1½ cups onion, diced
- 1 cup carrot, cut into disks
- 4 cloves garlic, minced
- 1½ tsp dried thyme
- 1¼ tbsp smoked paprika
- 1 tsp Dijon mustard
- ¾ tsp sea salt
- ¼ tsp ground black pepper
- 2 cups French lentils, rinsed
- 2 cups vegan vegetable stock
- 5 cups water
- ¼ cup tomato paste
- 1 bay leaf

Instructions:

1. Heat a large pot over medium heat.
2. Add all ingredients in it to the pot and cook for 8 minutes, stirring occasionally.
3. Increase heat and bring it to a boil.
4. Once it is boiled, let it simmer for 35 minutes.
5. Remove bay leaf.
6. Serve and enjoy.

Nutrition Facts Per Serving:

Calories 370, Total Fat 2.6g, Saturated Fat 1.1g, Cholesterol 0mg, Sodium 629mg, Total Carbohydrate 68.5g, Dietary Fiber 29.6g, Total Sugars 10.8g, Protein 23g, Vitamin D 0mcg, Calcium 141mg, Iron 10mg, Potassium 1244mg

Squash Soup

Prep time 10 minutes / Cook time 1 hour 5 minutes / Serves 4

Ingredients:

- 3 lb. butternut squash, whole and unpeeled
- 1 large or 2 small onions, whole and unpeeled
- 2 cups water plus more to thin
- ½ cup raw cashews, presoaked and drained
- 1 tbsp lemon juice, freshly squeezed
- 1 tsp fresh rosemary

- 1 tsp sea salt
- ¼ tsp cinnamon
- 1/8 tsp allspice
- 1 medium-large clove garlic, minced

Instructions:
1. Preheat oven to 450 F.
2. Take a baking dish and line it with parchment paper.
3. Place onion and squash on the baking dish and bake for an hour.
4. Take a blender and add water, cashews, lemon juice, rosemary, sea salt, cinnamon, allspice, and garlic.
5. Puree until smooth.
6. Chop baked onions and squash and transfer to the blender with the skin and seeds removed.
7. Blend until smooth.
8. Transfer the soup to a pot and heat over low heat for 3 to 5 minutes and serve.

Nutrition Facts Per Serving:
Calories 270, Total Fat 8.4g, Saturated Fat 1.7g, Cholesterol 0mg, Sodium 491mg, Total Carbohydrate 49.5g, Dietary Fiber 8.4g, Total Sugars 10g, Protein 6.5g, Vitamin D 0mcg, Calcium 190mg, Iron 4mg, Potassium 1362mg

Chickpea Lentil Soup

Prep time 10 minutes / Cook time 31 minutes / Serves 6

Ingredients:
- 3 cups Water
- 2 cups onion, diced
- ¾ tsp sea salt
- ¼ tsp ground black pepper
- 1 tsp mustard seeds
- 1 tsp cumin seeds
- 1½ tsp paprika
- ½ tsp dried oregano
- ½ tsp dried thyme
- 1 cup dried red lentils
- 3½ cups chickpeas, cooked
- 2 cups tomatoes, chopped
- 3 cups vegetable stock
- 2 cups water
- 2 dried bay leaves
- ¼ cup fresh lemon juice

Instructions:
1. Heat a large pot over medium heat.
2. Add all ingredients to it and cook for 6 minutes, stirring occasionally.
3. Increase heat and bring it to a boil.
4. Once it is boiled, let it simmer for 25 minutes.
5. Remove bay leaf.
6. Serve and enjoy.

Nutrition Facts Per Serving:
Calories 765, Total Fat 11.3g, Saturated Fat 1.3g, Cholesterol 0mg, Sodium 316mg, Total Carbohydrate 129.4g, Dietary Fiber 41.9g, Total Sugars 22.5g, Protein 42.3g, Vitamin D 0mcg, Calcium 239mg, Iron 15mg, Potassium 2043mg

Beans and Lentils Soup

Prep time 10 minutes / Cook time 48 minutes / Serves 4

Ingredients:
- 2 tbsp water
- 1½ cups onion, diced
- 3 cups potatoes, cut in chunks
- ½ cup celery, diced
- 1 cup carrots, diced
- 4 cloves garlic, minced
- 1½ tsp dried rosemary leaves
- 1 tsp dried thyme leaves
- 1½ tsp ground mustard
- 1 tsp sea salt
- ¼ tsp ground black pepper
- 1 cup green lentils, rinsed
- 2 cups vegetable stock
- 5 cups water
- 1 tbsp red miso
- 1½ tbsp blackstrap molasses
- 2 dried bay leaves
- 15-oz white beans

Instructions:
1. Heat a large pot over medium heat.
2. Add all ingredients to it and cook for 8 minutes, stirring occasionally.
3. Increase heat and bring it to a boil.
4. Once it is boiled, let it cook for 40 minutes.

140

5. Remove bay leaf.
6. Serve and enjoy.
Nutrition Facts Per Serving:
Calories 810, Total Fat 3.8g, Saturated Fat 0.6g, Cholesterol 0mg, Sodium 762mg, Total Carbohydrate 156.3g, Dietary Fiber 40.5g, Total Sugars 29.3g, Protein 43.6g, Vitamin D 0mcg, Calcium 481mg, Iron 19mg, Potassium 3663mg

Barley Lentil Stew

Prep time 5 minutes / Cook time 50 minutes / Serves 3
Ingredients:
- ½ onion, chopped
- 2 stalks celery, chopped
- 1 carrot, diced
- 1 tablespoon olive oil
- 3 cups vegetable stock
- 2 small red potatoes, skin on, chopped
- ¼ cup dry, uncooked barley
- ¾ cup cooked lentils

Instructions:
1. Place a large pot over medium high heat and add the oil. Once it is heated, add the vegetables and sauté for three to four minutes, until slightly softened.
2. Add the vegetable stock and the potatoes and bring the pot to a boil.
3. Reduce the heat to a simmer and add the barley and lentils.
4. Simmer gently for 45 minutes, adding water if needed until the barley is plump and soft.
5. Serve hot.

Nutrition Facts Per Serving:
Calories 367, Total Fat 5.8g, Saturated Fat 0.9g, Cholesterol 0mg, Sodium 85mg, Total Carbohydrate 63.1g, Dietary Fiber 20.8g, Total Sugars 4.9g, Protein 17.3g, Vitamin D 0mcg, Calcium 59mg, Iron 5mg, Potassium 1165mg

Chickpea Noodle Soup

Prep time 8 minutes / Cook time 5 minutes / Serves 3
Ingredients:
- 1 tablespoon olive
- 1 clove garlic, minced
- 1 onion, diced
- 6 stalks celery, diced
- 4 carrots, peeled and diced
- 4 cups vegetable stock
- 4 cups water
- 2 heaping tablespoons white miso paste
- 4 ounces whole-wheat pasta
- 15-ounce can chickpeas, rinsed and drained
- ¼ tsp salt
- ¼ tsp pepper
- 2 handfuls baby spinach

Instructions:
1. Place the oil in a large pot over medium high heat.
2. Sauté the garlic for one to two minutes, then add the onion and sauté for another couple minutes, until softened.
3. Add the celery and carrot and sauté for another two to three minutes.
4. Add the vegetable stock and water and bring the pot to a boil.
5. Pour in the pasta; as soon as it is cooked al dente, add the miso paste and chickpeas and turn down the heat to a simmer.
6. Season with salt and pepper to taste, simmering until everything is heated through.
7. If you are freezing your soup, stop here and let the soup cool before putting into freezer containers. However, if you plan to serve the soup immediately, toss in the spinach, turn off the heat and let the pot set there just long enough to wilt the spinach.
8. Serve the soup hot.

Nutrition Facts Per Serving:
Calories 743, Total Fat 10.8g, Saturated Fat 0.9g, Cholesterol 11mg, Sodium 731mg, Total Carbohydrate 130.5g, Dietary Fiber 29.7g, Total Sugars 23.4g, Protein 37.7g, Vitamin D 0mcg, Calcium 212mg, Iron 9mg, Potassium 1968mg

Creamy Carrot and White Bean Soup

Prep time 6 minutes / Cook time 35 minutes / Serves 5

Ingredients:

- 2 pounds carrots, peeled and chopped
- 2 tablespoons maple syrup
- 14-ounce can coconut milk
- 1½ cups vegetable stock
- 1 14-ounce can white beans
- ¼ tsp turmeric
- ¼ tsp curry powder
- ¼ tsp salt
- ¼ tsp pepper

Instructions:

1. Preheat the oven to 350 degrees, Fahrenheit and line a rimmed baking sheet with parchment paper.
2. Place the chopped carrots in a bowl and pour in the maple syrup. Toss and make sure each carrot piece is coated with the syrup.
3. Spread the carrots on the baking sheet, making sure they don't overlap. Bake for 35 minutes.
4. Remove the carrots from the oven and cool for at least 15 minutes.
5. Scrape the carrots into a blender or food processor; add the coconut milk and vegetable stock and blend until smooth.
6. Add the beans, turmeric, curry, salt and pepper; blend until smooth and creamy.
7. Pour back into the pot and heat through before serving.

Nutrition Facts Per Serving:

Calories, 550, Total Fat 19.7g, Saturated Fat 17g, Cholesterol 0mg, Sodium 322mg, Total Carbohydrate 76.7g, Dietary Fiber 18.9g, Total Sugars 18.8g, Protein 22.3g, Vitamin D 0mcg, Calcium 269mg, Iron 10mg, Potassium 2236mg

Creamy Leek and Potato Soup

Prep time 5 minutes / Cook time 20 minutes / Serves 3

Ingredients:

- 3 large leeks, cleaned and chopped in pieces
- 1 tablespoon vegan butter
- 1½ tablespoons olive oil
- 1 pinch sea salt
- 1 small onion, diced
- 3 medium potatoes, peeled and chopped
- 3 cloves garlic, minced
- ½ teaspoon dried rosemary
- 1½ teaspoons dried thyme
- ½ teaspoon ground coriander
- 5 cups vegetable stock
- 1 teaspoon more sea salt
- ¼ teaspoon pepper
- 2 bay leaves
- 1 cup coconut milk
- 1 green onion, chopped

Instructions:

1. Prepare the leeks and drain them well
2. Put the butter and oil in a large pot over medium heat and add a pinch of salt.
3. When the butter is melted, add the leeks and onion and sauté for five to six minutes, until soft.
4. Add the potatoes, garlic, rosemary, thyme and coriander and sauté for about three minutes.
5. Pour in the vegetable broth, salt, pepper and bay leaves and bring to a boil.
6. Immediately turn the heat down to a simmer and let it cook for 15 minutes.
7. Remove the bay leaves and pour in the coconut milk. Taste and season with salt and pepper.
8. Use an immersion blender (or process in batches in a blender) and blend until smooth and creamy.
9. Pour back into the pot if it was removed; heat through until hot.
10. Ladle into bowls and top with chopped green onion and a little more pepper.

Nutrition Facts Per Serving:

Calories 694, Total Fat 48.4g, Saturated Fat 21.9g, Cholesterol 0mg, Sodium 298mg, Total Carbohydrate 64.5g, Dietary Fiber 11.5g, Total Sugars 11.9g, Protein 8.9g, Vitamin D 0mcg, Calcium 154mg, Iron 8mg, Potassium 1323mg

Green Cream of Broccoli Soup

Prep time 10 minutes / Cook time 25 minutes / Serves 4

Ingredients:

- 6 cups fresh broccoli florets
- 1 teaspoon olive
- 1 clove garlic, chopped
- 1 teaspoon tamari sauce
- 2 cups cold coconut milk
- 1 teaspoon dry Italian seasoning
- ¼ teaspoon sea salt
- ¼ teaspoon ground pepper
- 1 dash of cayenne pepper

Instructions:

1. Cut up the broccoli into florets and place in a steamer basket over a pan of boiling water. Steam the florets for seven to eight minutes, until they are tender crisp.
2. Place oil in a large soup pot over medium heat and let it heat up. Add the garlic and sauté for about two minutes.
3. Add the tamari sauce and coconut milk, stir and add the steamed broccoli.
4. Add the Italian seasoning, salt and the black and cayenne pepper; turn off the heat while you use an immersion blender to process the mixture until it's smooth and creamy.
5. If the soup is too thick for your liking, add more coconut milk, two tablespoons at a time, until you get to the proper consistency.
6. Turn the burner back on over medium heat and simmer for 10 to 15 minutes.

Nutrition Facts Per Serving:

Calories 330, Total Fat 29.5g, Saturated Fat 25.4g, Cholesterol 1mg, Sodium 258mg, Total Carbohydrate 16.4g, Dietary Fiber 6.3g, Total Sugars 6.5g, Protein 6.8g, Vitamin D 0mcg, Calcium 86mg, Iron 3mg, Potassium 754mg

Chilled Sweet Corn Soup

Prep time 10 minutes / Cook time 0 minutes / Serves 8

Ingredients:

- 12 fresh ears corn, shucked
- 1 teaspoon ground cinnamon
- 1 ½ cups sliced watermelon
- ½ cup fresh basil leaves
- 2 cups plain almond milk
- 8 tablespoons maple syrup
- ½ pint blackberries

Instructions:

1. Remove the corn from the cobs. Add corn, cinnamon and milk into a blender and blend until smooth.
2. Pass the mixture thorough a nut milk bag and strain the milk into a bowl. Throw off the solids.
3. Add maple syrup and stir.
4. Divide into bowls. Divide the watermelon and blackberries into the bowls. Garnish with basil and refrigerate until use.

Nutrition Facts Per Serving:

Calories 278, Total Fat 3.8g, Saturated Fat 0.5g, Cholesterol 0mg, Sodium 74mg, Total Carbohydrate 61.3g, Dietary Fiber 7.8g, Total Sugars 22g, Protein 8.2g, Vitamin D 0mcg, Calcium 31mg, Iron 7mg, Potassium 745mg

Pea and Mint Soup

Prep time 10 minutes / Cook time 0 minutes / Serves 8

Ingredients:

- 2 tablespoons extra-virgin olive oil
- 2 medium onions, finely chopped
- 10 cups shelled fresh peas
- 8 cups vegetable stock
- 2 ounces vegan butter
- 2 cloves garlic, peeled, minced
- 2 cups mint leaves
- ¼ tsp Salt
- ¼ tsp Pepper
- Vegan Parmesan cheese

Instructions:

1. Place a soup pot over medium heat. Add oil and butter. When it heats, add onion and sauté until translucent.

2. Stir in the garlic and cook for about 2-3 minutes.
3. Add 8 cups peas, mint and 6 cups stock. Cover and cook until soft.
4. Turn off the heat and transfer into a blender. Blend until smooth.
5. Pour into the pot. Add rest of the stock and peas. Add salt and pepper to taste.
6. Place pot over medium heat. Cook until peas are soft.
7. Add cheese if using. Simmer until cheese melts.
8. Add a few drops of olive oil and stir.
9. Cool completely.
10. Ladle into bowls and serve.

Nutrition Facts Per Serving:
Calories 257, Total Fat 9.1g, Saturated Fat 1.7g, Cholesterol 0mg, Sodium 184mg, Total Carbohydrate 27.1g, Dietary Fiber 9.6g, Total Sugars 8.8g, Protein 14.1g, Vitamin D 0mcg, Calcium 58mg, Iron 3mg, Potassium 148mg

Greek Meatball Soup

Prep time 10 minutes / Cook time 30 minutes / Serves 4

Ingredients:
- ¾ cup dry brown lentils, rinsed
- ½ small onion, chopped
- 2 ½ cups vegetable broth
- Juice of a large lemon
- 2 tablespoons breadcrumbs
- ¼ tsp Salt
- ¼ tsp Pepper
- 7 tablespoons long grain brown rice
- ¼ cup flour
- ½ tablespoon cornstarch mixed
- 2 tablespoons parsley, chopped
- 1 tablespoon olive oil
- 1 tablespoon ground flaxseeds
- 2 cups water

Instructions:
1. Add 2 cups broth and lentils into a saucepan and place over medium-high heat.
2. When it begins to boil, reduce the heat and simmer until lentils are cooked. Strain lentils and retain cooked water.
3. Place another small saucepan with 6 tablespoons rice and remaining broth and cook until rice is soft. Add half the rice into a blender.
4. Add the retained liquid back to the saucepan. Also add water and place over medium heat.
5. Meanwhile, add lentils into the blender and pulse until coarsely mashed.
6. Transfer into a bowl. Add remaining cooked rice, parsley, oil, breadcrumbs and flaxseeds and mix until well combined.
7. Divide the mixture 12 equal portions and shape into balls.
8. Add remaining tablespoon of uncooked rice to the simmering broth and lower the lentil balls into it.
9. Reduce heat and simmer for about 30 minutes.
10. Add cornstarch mixture to the simmering broth and stir gently. Add lemon juice, salt and pepper.
11. Ladle into soup bowls.

Nutrition Facts Per Serving:
Calories 309, Total Fat 6.1g, Saturated Fat 0.9g, Cholesterol 0mg, Sodium 657mg, Total Carbohydrate 48.5g, Dietary Fiber 13g, Total Sugars 3.3g, Protein 15.4g, Vitamin D 0mcg, Calcium 53mg, Iron 5mg, Potassium 583mg

Tomato and Basil Soup

Prep time 10 minutes / Cook time 20 minutes / Serves 8

Ingredients:
- 4 pounds tomatoes, quartered
- 4 cups vegetable broth
- 4 tablespoons balsamic vinegar
- Freshly ground pepper to taste
- 2 bunches fresh basil, chopped
- 4 cloves garlic, peeled
- ¼ tsp Salt to taste

Instructions:
1. Add all the ingredients into a blender and blend until the preferred consistency.

144

2. Strain if desired and pour into a large saucepan. Place over low heat. Let it cook for 20 minutes.
3. Cool completely and serve in bowls.
Nutrition Facts Per Serving:

Calories 64, Total Fat 1.1g, Saturated Fat 0.3g, Cholesterol 0mg, Sodium 467mg, Total Carbohydrate 9.9g, Dietary Fiber 2.8g, Total Sugars 6.4g, Protein 4.5g, Vitamin D 0mcg, Calcium 32mg, Iron 1mg, Potassium 654mg

Mushroom Barley Soup

Prep time 5 minutes / Cook time 4 minutes / Serves 6
Ingredients:
- 2 cups sliced fresh mushrooms
- 2 tablespoons vegan butter
- 2/3 cup medium pearl barley
- 2 medium carrots, sliced
- ¼ tsp Salt to taste
- ¼ tsp Pepper to taste
- 4 cloves garlic, minced
- 4 cans vegetable broth
- 2 tablespoons soy sauce
- 1 teaspoon dill weed

Instructions:
1. Place a soup pot over medium heat. Add vegan butter. When it melts, add mushroom and garlic and sauté for about 3-4 minutes.
2. Add barley, broth and soy sauce.
3. When it begins to boil, lower the heat and cover the pot partially. Simmer until tender.
4. If the barley is not cooked and there is not sufficient broth, add more broth and cook until barley is tender.
5. Add carrot, dill, salt and pepper. Cover and cook until carrots are tender.

Nutrition Facts Per Serving:
Calories 328, Total Fat 8.3g, Saturated Fat 2.3g, Cholesterol 0mg, Sodium 1706mg, Total Carbohydrate 50.5g, Dietary Fiber 5g, Total Sugars 37.9g, Protein 14.8g, Vitamin D 84mcg, Calcium 55mg, Iron 2mg, Potassium 624mg

Miso Soup

Prep time 10 minutes / Cook time 8 minutes / Serves 4
Ingredients:
- 4 cups water
- 1 cup chopped green onion
- 2 sheets dried nori, chopped
- 1 cup chopped green chard
- ½ cup cubed tofu
- 7 tablespoons white miso paste
- ¼ tsp Salt

Instructions:
1. Add water into a saucepan. Place saucepan over high heat. When it begins to boil, add nori and cover with lid. Cook for 2-3 minutes.
2. Add green onion, green chard and tofu and cook for about 5 minutes. Turn off the heat.
3. Whisk together in a bowl, miso and hot water.
4. Pour into the hot soup. Stir and taste the soup. Add more salt or miso if desired.
5. Cool slightly.
6. Ladle into soup bowls and serve

Nutrition Facts Per Serving:
Calories 455, Total Fat 0.7g, Saturated Fat 0.1g, Cholesterol 0mg, Sodium 1143mg, Total Carbohydrate 18.7g, Dietary Fiber 1.1g, Total Sugars 0.6g, Protein 7g, Vitamin D 0mcg, Calcium 61mg, Iron 1mg, Potassium 71mg

Wonder Soup

Prep time 4 minutes / Cook time 5 minutes / Serves 6
Ingredients:
- 3 onions, chopped
- 2 medium tomatoes, chopped
- 1 medium bunch celery, trimmed, chopped
- 1 large green bell pepper, deseeded, chopped
- 1 medium cabbage, chopped into bite size pieces
- 1 medium carrot, chopped
- 1 cup sliced mushrooms
- 1 cup Fresh herbs
- 1 tsp Italian Seasoning
- ¼ tsp Salt
- 3 cups water

Instructions:
1. Place a soup pot over medium heat.
2. Add all the ingredients and stir. Bring to a boil.
3. Lower the heat and simmer for 5 minutes until the vegetables are tender.
4. Ladle into soup bowls and serve.

Nutrition Facts Per Serving:
Calories 98, Total Fat 0.8g, Saturated Fat 0.1g, Cholesterol 1mg, Sodium 148mg, Total Carbohydrate 22.1g, Dietary Fiber 8.5g, Total Sugars 10.2g, Protein 4.4g, Vitamin D 42mcg, Calcium 207mg, Iron 4mg, Potassium 753mg

Tortilla Soup

Prep time 5 minutes / Cook time 20 minutes / Serves 3
Ingredients:
- ½ cup salsa
- ½ teaspoon chili powder
- ½ can chickpeas, drained, rinsed
- 1 small onion, chopped
- 2 cups vegetable stock
- ½ teaspoon ground cumin
- ¼ tsp Salt
- ½ can corn, drained, rinsed
- 2 cloves garlic, minced
- 2 tbsp juice
- ½ Avocado, sliced
- Tortilla chips
- 2 tbsp Chopped cilantro

Instructions:
1. Add all the ingredients into a soup pot. Place the pot over medium heat.
2. Cover and simmer for 20-30 minutes.
3. Add lime juice and stir.
4. Ladle into soup bowls and serve with suggested toppings.

Nutrition Facts Per Serving:
Calories 427, Total Fat 11.6g, Saturated Fat 2.1g, Cholesterol 0mg, Sodium 538mg, Total Carbohydrate 74.9g, Dietary Fiber 16g, Total Sugars 15.7g, Protein 15.9g, Vitamin D 0mcg, Calcium 72mg, Iron 9mg, Potassium 1270mg

Creamy Curried Cauliflower Soup

Prep time 10 minutes / Cook time 10 minutes / Serves 3
Ingredients:
- 2 tablespoons extra-virgin olive oil
- 1 medium head cauliflower trimmed, chopped into florets
- 1 small white onion, thinly sliced
- 1 large clove garlic, peeled, minced
- 2 ¼ cups vegetable broth or water
- 1/3 cup fresh coconut milk
- ¾ teaspoon ground cumin
- ¼ teaspoon ground coriander
- ¼ teaspoon turmeric powder
- ½ teaspoon curry powder
- ¼ tsp Salt
- ¼ tsp ground pepper
- 2 tablespoons chopped, roasted cashew nuts
- 2 tablespoons chopped fresh Italian parsley
- ½ teaspoon red chili flakes to garnish

Instructions:
1. Place a soup pot over medium heat. Add oil. When oil is heated, add onions and a large pinch of salt and sauté for 10 minutes until soft. Add garlic and sauté until aromatic.
2. Stir in the cauliflower, broth, coriander, curry powder, cumin, turmeric and salt. Mix well.
3. When it begins to boil, lower the heat and cover with a lid. Simmer until tender. Turn off the heat and cool for a while.
4. Transfer into a blender and blend until smooth. Pour the soup back into the pot.
5. Place the pot back over medium heat. Add coconut milk, and pepper and stir. Taste and adjust the seasoning if necessary.
6. Ladle into soup bowls. Sprinkle parsley, and cashew nuts top
7. Drizzle some olive oil on top and serve immediately.

Nutrition Facts Per Serving:
Calories 240, Total Fat 18.8g, Saturated Fat 7.6g, Cholesterol 0mg, Sodium 288mg, Total Carbohydrate 16.5g, Dietary Fiber 6.4g, Total Sugars 6.8g, Protein 5.8g, Vitamin D 0mcg, Calcium 71mg, Iron 2mg, Potassium 755mg

Lemongrass Lime Mushroom Soup

Prep time 6 minutes / Cook time 21 minutes / Serves 6

Ingredients:

- 1 tablespoon olive oil
- 1 tablespoon sesame oil
- 2 cloves garlic, minced
- ½ red onion, finely chopped
- 1 celery stalk, finely chopped
- 1 tablespoon fresh ginger, peeled and chopped
- 1 cup shitake mushrooms, thinly sliced
- 2 14-ounce cans coconut milk
- 1½ cups vegetable stock
- 1 small red chili pepper, seeded and minced
- 1 stalk fresh lemongrass, whole and pounded
- 1 tablespoons of lemongrass, minced
- ¼ tsp Sea salt
- ¼ tsp ground pepper
- 1 handful fresh basil leaves
- 1 lime, juiced
- ½ cup red bell pepper, julienned

Instructions:

1. Place a soup pot over medium high heat and add the olive oil and sesame oil.
2. Sauté the garlic for one or two minutes, then add the onion, celery, ginger and mushrooms. Sauté for six minutes.
3. Add the coconut milk, vegetable broth, chili pepper, lemongrass stalk and minced lemongrass.
4. Season with salt and pepper.
5. Bring to a simmer and let it cook for around 15 minutes; you want everything to be piping hot.
6. Stir in the basil leaves and turn the heat off.
7. Squeeze in the lime juice, stir the pot and serve with a fresh basil leaf on top of each bowlful.

Nutrition Facts Per Serving:

Calories 377, Total Fat 36.4g, Saturated Fat 28.7g, Cholesterol 0mg, Sodium 205mg, Total Carbohydrate 14.7g, Dietary Fiber 4.5g, Total Sugars 6.9g, Protein 4.3g, Vitamin D 0mcg, Calcium 35mg, Iron 3mg, Potassium 449mg

Creamy Cauliflower Soup

Prep time 10 minutes / Cook time 0 minutes / Serves 8

Ingredients:

- 4 tablespoons extra-virgin olive oil
- 1 onion, chopped
- 4 cups vegetable broth
- 1 teaspoon salt or to taste
- ½ cup nutritional yeast
- 8 cloves garlic, chopped
- 2 heads cauliflower, cut into florets
- 1 teaspoon pepper or to taste
- 2 cups plant-based milk, unsweetened

Instructions:

1. Place a soup pot over medium-high heat. Add oil and heat. Add onions and garlic and sauté until onions are nearly caramelized.
2. Add rest of the ingredients except nutritional yeast and stir. When it begins to boil, lower the heat and cook until cauliflower is super soft.
3. Turn off the heat. Cool for a while. Transfer into a blender and blend until smooth.
4. Pour the soup back into the pot. Add nutritional yeast and stir. Heat thoroughly. Taste and adjust the seasonings if necessary.

Nutrition Facts Per Serving:

Calories 172, Total Fat 9.6g, Saturated Fat 2g, Cholesterol 5mg, Sodium 728mg, Total Carbohydrate 13.9g, Dietary Fiber 4.6g, Total Sugars 5.3g, Protein 10.7g, Vitamin D 0mcg, Calcium 109mg, Iron 3mg, Potassium 612mg,

Healthy Lentil Soup

Prep time 10 minutes / Cook time 5 minutes / Serves 8

Ingredients:

- 2 teaspoons vegetable oil
- 2 carrots, sliced
- 2 onions, chopped
- 2 cups brown dry lentils, rinsed, soaked
- 4 bay leaves
- 2 tablespoons lemon juice

- 8 cups vegetable broth
- ½ teaspoon dried thyme
- Salt to taste
- Pepper to taste

Instructions:

1. Place a soup pot over medium heat. Add oil and heat. Add onions and carrots and sauté until onions are translucent.
2. Add rest of the ingredients except lemon juice and stir.

3. When it begins to boil, lower the heat and cover with a lid. Simmer for 5 minutes until the lentils are soft. Discard the bay leaves.
4. Add lemon juice just before serving and stir.
5. Ladle into soup bowls and serve.

Nutrition Facts Per Serving:
Calories 237, Total Fat 3.1g, Saturated Fat 0.7g, Cholesterol 0mg, Sodium 798mg, Total Carbohydrate 34.2g, Dietary Fiber 15.7g, Total Sugars 3.7g, Protein 17.7g, Vitamin D 0mcg, Calcium 52mg, Iron 4mg, Potassium 761mg

Lemon Coconut Lentil Soup

Prep time 10 minutes / Cook time 10 minutes / Serves 12

Ingredients:

- 4 tablespoons coconut oil
- 6 cloves garlic, peeled, minced
- 4 carrots, peeled, chopped
- 1 yellow onion, minced
- 4 stalks celery, chopped
- 3 teaspoons ground cumin
- 3 teaspoons smoked paprika
- 1 teaspoon ground coriander
- Crushed red pepper flakes
- ½ cup tomato paste
- 8 cups water
- 8 cups vegetable broth
- 4 cups red lentils
- 4 tablespoons lemon juice
- Salt to taste
- Pepper to taste
- 2/3 cup full-fat coconut milk
- A handful fresh cilantro, chopped, to garnish

Instructions:

1. Place a soup pot over medium heat. Add oil and heat. Add onions and carrots and sauté until onions are translucent.
2. Add garlic and cook for a few seconds until aromatic. Add carrot, celery and spices and cook for 10 minutes.
3. Add lentils, water, tomato paste and broth and stir.
4. When it begins to boil, lower the heat and cover with a lid. Simmer until the lentils are soft.
5. Add lemon juice, coconut milk and cilantro just before serving and stir.
6. Ladle into soup bowls. Garnish with red pepper flakes and serve.

Nutrition Facts Per Serving:
Calories 351, Total Fat 9.6g, Saturated Fat 7.2g, Cholesterol 0mg, Sodium 563mg, Total Carbohydrate 46.1g, Dietary Fiber 21.4g, Total Sugars 5.2g, Protein 21.2g, Vitamin D 0mcg, Calcium 73mg, Iron 6mg, Potassium 1027mg

Macaroni and Vegetable Soup

Prep time 4 minutes / Cook time 5 minutes / Serves 8

Ingredients:

- 5 small zucchinis, chopped into cubes
- ¾ cup frozen green beans
- 3 large carrots, peeled, chopped
- 4 cloves garlic, minced
- ½ cup frozen pearl onions
- 2 stalks celery, chopped into thick slices
- 3 cans, 14.5 ounces each vegetable broth
- 1 ½ cans (15 ounces each) kidney beans, drained

- 1 ½ cans (28 ounces each) peeled, crushed tomatoes
- 2 bay leaves
- 1 teaspoon dried basil
- 1 ½ tablespoons dried parsley
- ¾ cup macaroni
- 1 ½ vegetable bouillon cubes
- Salt to taste
- Pepper to taste

Instructions:

1. Place a soup pot over medium heat. Add broth, tomatoes, carrots, beans, celery, onions, garlic, parsley, basil, bay leaf along with vegetable bouillon cubes and stir.
2. When it begins to boil, add rest of the ingredients and bring to a boil again.
3. Lower heat and simmer for 5 minutes until macaroni is al dente.
4. Remove from heat and discard bay leaves.
5. Ladle into soup bowls and serve.

Nutrition Facts Per Serving:
Calories 204, Total Fat 1.3g, Saturated Fat 0.3g, Cholesterol 0mg, Total Carbohydrate 37.5g, Dietary Fiber 7.9g, Total Sugars 6.5g, Protein 12.3g, Vitamin D 0mcg, Calcium 68mg, Iron 3mg, Potassium 919mg,

Italian Potato, Bean, and Kale Soup

Prep time 5 minutes / Cook time 8 minutes / Serves 3

Ingredients:

- 1 cup onions, chopped
- 4 cups vegetable broth
- ½ pound small potatoes, chopped into bite sized pieces
- 5 -6 cups kale leaves, chopped, discard hard stems and ribs
- 3 cloves garlic, minced
- 1 can (15 ounces) pinto beans or borlotti beans, drained or
- ½ teaspoon dried basil
- ½ teaspoon dried oregano
- ¼ teaspoon dried rosemary, crushed
- ¼ teaspoons red pepper flakes
- ¼ teaspoon fennel seeds
- ¼ cup nondairy milk
- 1 tablespoon nutritional yeast
- Salt to taste
- 1-2 tablespoons water

Instructions:

1. Place a soup pot over medium heat. Add onions and a tablespoon of water and sauté until onions turn soft. Add garlic and sauté for a minute or so until aromatic.
2. Add spices and stir for a few seconds until aromatic. Add beans, broth and potatoes and bring to a boil.
3. Lower the heat and cover with a lid. Cook until the potatoes are tender.
4. Add kale, cover, and cook for 5-8 minutes until kale turn bright green in color and tender as well.
5. Remove about half the soup and blend in a blender until smooth. Pour the soup back to the pot.
6. Heat thoroughly. Taste and adjust the seasonings and herbs if necessary.
7. Add milk and nutritional yeast. Mix well. Heat thoroughly.
8. Ladle into soup bowls and serve.

Nutrition Facts Per Serving:
Calories 426, Total Fat 3.5g, Saturated Fat 1g, Cholesterol 2mg, Sodium 1104mg, Total Carbohydrate 72.5g, Dietary Fiber 15.4g, Total Sugars 5.8g, Protein 27.7g, Vitamin D 0mcg, Calcium 291mg, Iron 7mg, Potassium 2199mg

White Bean and Roasted Butternut Squash Soup

Prep time 10 minutes / Cook time 1 hour 30 minutes / Serves 8

Ingredients:

- 2 butternut squashes, halved lengthwise, deseeded
- 2 onions, diced
- 2 cans (15 ounces each) white beans, rinsed, drained
- 2 cups unsweetened almond milk
- ¼ teaspoon ground nutmeg
- 2 teaspoons olive oil
- 4 cloves garlic, minced
- 5 cups vegetable broth
- Salt to taste
- Pepper to taste
- 2 teaspoons chopped fresh sage

Instructions:

1. Place a sheet of foil on a large baking sheet. Spray some cooking spray over it.

2. Place the squash on it, with the skin side facing up.
3. Bake in a preheated oven at 375° F for 60-90minutes or until fork tender.
4. Remove from the oven and set aside to cool. When cool enough to handle, peel the skin and break into smaller pieces.
5. Place a soup pot over medium heat. Add oil and heat. Add onion and garlic and cook until soft. Turn off the heat.
6. Transfer into a blender. Also add beans and half the broth and blend. Transfer into the soup pot.
7. Add butternut squash into the blender along with remaining broth and blend until smooth.
8. Transfer into the soup pot. Place the soup pot over medium- low heat. Add almond milk and stir. Season with salt, pepper, nutmeg and sage and stir frequently. Cook for about 15 minutes.
9. Ladle into soup bowls and serve.

Nutrition Facts Per Serving:
Calories 226, Total Fat 3.4g, Saturated Fat 0.6g, Cholesterol 0mg, Sodium 551mg, Total Carbohydrate 34.7g, Dietary Fiber 8.6g, Total Sugars 2.7g, Protein 15.5g, Vitamin D 0mcg, Calcium 214mg, Iron 6mg, Potassium 1131mg

Cream of Mushroom Soup

Prep time 4 minutes / Cook time 5 minutes / Serves 12

Ingredients:
- 4 tbsps. Olive oil
- 2 shallots
- ½ cup, cherry cooking wine
- Salt
- 1 tsp dried thyme
- ½ cup, cashews
- 1-pound cremini mushrooms, chopped
- 2 cloves garlic, peeled, chopped
- 6 cups vegetable broth
- Pepper
- Fresh thyme leaves

Instructions:
1. Place a soup pot over medium heat. Add oil and heat. Add shallot, garlic and mushrooms and cook until mushrooms are tender.
2. Add wine and let it boil until it is half its original quantity.
3. Meanwhile, make the cashew cream as follow: Drain the soaked water but retain it. Add cashews and a little of the soaked water into a blender and blend until smooth and thick. Transfer into a bowl. Add more water if required. The consistency should be like yogurt. Use 6 tablespoons of the mixture and save the rest for use in some other recipe.
4. Add broth, salt, pepper and thyme into the simmering wine in the soup pot.
5. Cook for 5 minutes. Stir in the cashew cream.
6. Whisk well. Blend with an immersion blender until the cashew cream is well combined if you like it chunky. If you like it smooth, then transfer the soup into a blender in batches and blend until smooth.
7. Ladle into soup bowls. Garnish with fresh thyme leaves and serve.

Nutrition Facts Per Serving:
Calories 72, Total Fat 5.4g, Saturated Fat 0.9g, Cholesterol 0mg, Sodium 396mg, Total Carbohydrate 2.6g, Dietary Fiber 0.3g, Total Sugars 1g, Protein 3.5g, Vitamin D 3mcg, Calcium 15mg, Iron 1mg, Potassium 283mg

Simple Pumpkin Soup

Prep time 5 minutes / Cook time 56 minutes / Serves 8

Ingredients:
- 4 sugar pumpkins, halved, deseeded, discard strings
- 6 cloves garlic, minced
- 2 cups light coconut milk
- Salt to taste
- Pepper to taste
- ½ teaspoon ground cinnamon
- ½ teaspoon ground nutmeg
- 4 shallots, diced
- 4 cups vegetable broth
- 4 tablespoons maple syrup
- Oil, to brush

- For garlic kale sesame topping
- 2 cups roughly chopped kale, discard hard stems and ribs
- 4 tablespoons raw sesame seeds
- 2 large cloves garlic, minced
- 1/8 teaspoon salt or to taste
- 2 tablespoons olive oil

Instructions:

1. Line a baking sheet with parchment paper.
2. Brush the cut side of the pumpkin with oil and place on the baking sheet, with the cut side facing down.
3. Bake in a preheated oven at 350° F for about 40-50 minutes or until tender.
4. Remove the baking sheet from the oven. When cool enough to handle, discard the skin and add pumpkin into a bowl.
5. Place a soup pot over medium heat. Add oil. When the oil is heated, add shallots and garlic and sauté until translucent.
6. Add rest of the ingredients including pumpkin and stir.
7. When it begins to boil, lower the heat and simmer for 5-6 minutes.
8. Turn off the heat. Blend with an immersion blender until smooth.
9. Place the pot back over heat. Heat thoroughly.
10. Taste and add more seasonings if necessary.
11. Meanwhile, make the kale sesame topping as follows: Place a small skillet over medium heat. Add sesame seeds and toast until light golden brown. Remove from heat.
12. Add kale and salt and stir. Cover with a lid. Cook until kale wilts.
13. Add sesame seeds and mix well.
14. Ladle soup into soup bowls. Top with kale sesame topping and serve.

Nutrition Facts Per Serving:

Calories 313, Total Fat 22.9g, Saturated Fat 14.1g, Cholesterol 0mg, Sodium 410mg, Total Carbohydrate 25.3g, Dietary Fiber 5.8g, Total Sugars 12.4g, Protein 6.8g, Vitamin D 0mcg, Calcium 129mg, Iron 4mg, Potassium 668mg

Grilled Gazpacho

Prep time 5 minutes / Cook time 0 minutes / Serves 3

Ingredients:

- 1 pound ripe plum tomatoes
- 2 small cucumbers, peeled, seeded, chopped
- 1 small red bell pepper
- 2 cloves garlic
- 2 tablespoons red wine vinegar
- 1/8 teaspoon hot Spanish paprika
- ½ tablespoon fresh parsley, minced
- A large pinch cayenne pepper
- 1 tablespoon extra-virgin olive oil
- Salt to taste
- Freshly ground black pepper to taste
- 2 slices bread, crust removed, chopped

Instructions:

1. Grill the tomatoes and bell pepper in a preheated grill at medium high. Grill until the skin of the tomatoes and bell pepper is charred slightly. Remove from the grill and set aside to cool.
2. When cool enough to handle, chop the tomatoes. Chop the bell pepper.
3. Blend together the tomatoes, half the bell pepper, half the cucumber, bread, garlic, vinegar, parsley, salt, pepper and cayenne pepper.
4. Blend until smooth. Pour the olive oil and blend again.
5. Pour into clear Spanish tumblers. Chill until use.
6. Add the remaining cucumber and bell pepper. Mix well and serve.

Nutrition Facts Per Serving:

Calories 116, Total Fat 5.4g, Saturated Fat 0.8g, Cholesterol 0mg, Sodium 114mg, Total Carbohydrate 16.2g, Dietary Fiber 2.8g, Total Sugars 9g, Protein 3.1g, Vitamin D 0mcg, Calcium 44mg, Iron 1mg, Potassium 473mg

Three Bean Chili with Spring Pesto

Prep time 10 minutes / Cook time 0 minutes / Serves 8

Ingredients:

- 15 ounces chickpeas, rinsed, drained
- 15 ounces kidney beans, rinsed, drained
- 16 ounces cannellini beans, rinsed, drained
- 2 cans (15.5 ounces each) diced tomatoes with its liquid
- 1 large yellow onion, chopped
- 2 cloves garlic, peeled, minced
- 4 carrots, chopped
- ½ cup fresh flat leaf parsley, chopped
- 6 tablespoons pine nuts
- 10 tablespoons extra- virgin olive oil, divided
- 4 cups water
- Salt to taste
- Pepper to taste
- Crusty bread

Instructions:

1. Place a soup pot over medium-high heat. Add 2 tablespoons oil and heat. Add onions and carrots and sauté until onions are translucent.
2. Add tomatoes, water, salt, pepper and all the variety of beans. Heat thoroughly.
3. In a small bowl, mix together garlic, 2 tablespoons oil, salt, pepper, pine nuts and parsley. This is your spring pesto.
4. Serve in bowls. Divide the spring pesto among the bowls and serve with crusty bread if desired.

Nutrition Facts Per Serving:

Calories 805, Total Fat 27.5g, Saturated Fat 3.6g, Cholesterol 1mg, Sodium 106mg, Total Carbohydrate 108.4g, Dietary Fiber 33.3g, Total Sugars 11.2g , Protein 37.8g,Vitamin D 0mcg, Calcium 209mg, Iron 12mg,Potassium 2227mg

Mushroom Chili

Prep time 7 minutes / Cook time 20 minutes / Serves 12

Ingredients:

- 2 pounds whole baby Bella mushrooms, minced
- 1 bell pepper, finely chopped
- 2 medium onions, chopped
- 4 jalapeño peppers, minced
- 2 tablespoons olive oil
- 3 teaspoons salt or to taste
- 2 tablespoons chili powder
- 5 tablespoons ground cumin
- 2 tablespoons raw sugar
- 4 cans (15 ounces each) tomato sauce
- 6 cans (15 ounces each) dark kidney beans, rinsed, drained
- 2 cans (14.5 ounces each) fire-roasted diced tomatoes, with its juice
- 1 bunch fresh cilantro, finely chopped

Instructions:

1. Place a soup pot over medium-high heat. Add oil and heat. Add onions, garlic, mushroom, jalapeño and bell pepper. Cook until mushrooms are tender.
2. Add rest of the ingredients except cilantro and stir.
3. When it begins to boil, lower the heat and simmer for about 20 minutes.
4. Ladle into bowls. Sprinkle a generous amount of cilantro on top and serve.

Nutrition Facts Per Serving:

Calories 402, Total Fat 4.6g, Saturated Fat 0.6g, Cholesterol 0mg, Sodium 1166mg, Total Carbohydrate 70.5g, Dietary Fiber 17.6g, Total Sugars 10.7g , Protein 25.3g, Vitamin D 272mcg, Calcium 123mg, Iron 11mg, Potassium 1927mg

Tofu Chili

Prep time 5 minutes / Cook time 30 minutes / Serves 4

Ingredients:

- 1 ½ tablespoons vegetable oil
- 1 small onion, chopped
- 2 cloves garlic, minced
- ½ package firm or extra firm tofu, crumbled
- ½ green bell pepper, diced
- ½ cup sliced mushrooms
- 1 ½ tablespoons chili powder
- ¼ teaspoon ground cumin

- 1/8 teaspoon cayenne pepper
- Salt to taste
- Pepper to taste
- 14 ounces tomato sauce
- 28 ounces kidney beans, drained, rinsed
- 28 ounces whole or diced tomatoes with its liquid
- ½ tablespoon sugar

Instructions:
1. Place a soup pot over medium-high heat. Add oil and heat. Add the vegetables, spices, salt and sauté for a few minutes until slightly tender.
2. Add rest of the ingredients and stir.
3. Lower the heat and simmer for about 30 minutes. Stir occasionally.
4. Ladle into bowls and serve.

Nutrition Facts Per Serving:
Calories 815, Total Fat 9.1g, Saturated Fat 1.6g, Cholesterol 0mg, Sodium 597mg, Total Carbohydrate 141.7g, Dietary Fiber 35.9g, Total Sugars 17.1g, Protein 50.1g, Vitamin D 32mcg, Calcium 246mg, Iron 16mg, Potassium 3664mg

Sweet Potato & Black Bean Chili

Prep time 5 minutes / Cook time 7 minutes / Serves 8

Ingredients:
- 4 tablespoons extra-virgin olive oil
- 2 large onions, diced
- 4 tablespoons chili powder
- 1 teaspoon ground chipotle chili
- 5 cups water
- 2 cans (14 ounces each) diced tomatoes
- 4 cans (15 ounces each) black beans, rinsed
- 2 medium-large sweet potatoes, peeled, cubed
- 8 cloves garlic, minced
- 8 teaspoons ground cumin
- Salt to taste
- 1 cup fresh cilantro, chopped
- 8 teaspoons lime juice

Instructions:
1. Place a soup pot over medium high heat. Add oil and heat. Add onions and sweet potatoes and cook until the onions are translucent.
2. Add garlic and sauté for a few seconds until fragrant. Add spices and salt and stir. Sauté for a few seconds until fragrant.
3. Add water and stir.
4. When it begins to boil, lower the heat and cover with a lid. Simmer until the sweet potatoes are tender.
5. Add lime juice, beans and tomatoes and stir. Raise the heat to high heat and bring to the boil.
6. Lower heat and simmer for 5-7 minutes.
7. Turn off the heat and add cilantro and stir.
8. Ladle into bowls and serve.

Nutrition Facts Per Serving:
Calories 490, Total Fat 9.7g, Saturated Fat 1.5g, Cholesterol 0mg, Sodium 82mg, Total Carbohydrate 83.2g, Dietary Fiber 19.2g, Total Sugars 5.6g, Protein 23.4g, Vitamin D 0mcg, Calcium 184mg, Iron 7mg, Potassium 2040mg

Indian Vegetable Stew

Prep time 5 minutes / Cook time 10 minutes / Serves 3

Ingredients:
- ½ tablespoon extra-virgin olive oil
- 2 cloves garlic, minced
- 2 large onions, chopped
- ½ pound baby carrots, rinsed, trimmed
- ½ cup fresh cilantro, chopped
- ½ pound new potatoes, scrubbed, rinsed, quartered
- 19 ounces chickpeas, rinsed, drained
- 14 ounces crushed fire roasted tomatoes
- ½ teaspoon cumin seeds
- ½ teaspoon ground cumin
- ½ teaspoon ground coriander
- 1/8 teaspoon ground cardamom
- 1/8 teaspoon cayenne pepper
- 1 cup water
- Salt to taste

Instructions:
1. Place a soup pot over medium heat. Add oil and heat. Add cumin seeds and onions and sauté until light brown. Add garlic and sauté until fragrant.

2. Add all the spices. Sauté for a couple of minutes until fragrant.
3. Add potatoes, water and salt.
4. When it begins to boil, lower the heat and cover with a lid. Cook for about 10 minutes. Add chickpeas, tomatoes and carrots and mix it all well. Partially cover the pot and cook until the vegetables are tender. Add more water if required.

5. Add cilantro and stir.
6. Ladle into bowls and serve.

Nutrition Facts Per Serving:
Calories 823, Total Fat 13.9g, Saturated Fat 1.5g, Cholesterol 0mg, Sodium 173mg, Total Carbohydrate 142.7g, Dietary Fiber 39.2g, Total Sugars 31.5g , Protein 39g, Vitamin D 0mcg, Calcium 271mg, Iron 13mg, Potassium 2555mg

Okra Stew

Prep time 10 minutes / Cook time 10 minutes / Serves 8

Ingredients:
- 3 pounds fresh okra, trimmed cut into about 1 ½ inch long pieces
- 2 medium onions, chopped
- 2 tablespoons minced garlic
- 1 teaspoon ground cumin
- Freshly ground pepper to taste
- Salt to taste
- 2 tablespoons extra-virgin olive oil
- 2 teaspoon paprika
- 2 cans (26 ounces each) chopped tomatoes, with its liquid

Instructions:
1. Place a heavy pot or pan over medium-high heat. Add oil and heat. Stir in the onions and salt and sauté until translucent.
2. Stir in the garlic and cook for a few seconds until aromatic.

3. Add spices and cook for a few seconds until aromatic.
4. Next add in the okra and stir-fry for 10 minutes.
5. Add tomatoes and stir.
6. Reduce the heat to medium-low and cover with a lid. Cook until okra is tender. Stir once in a while. Add salt and cook for a few more minutes.
7. Add pepper to taste.
8. Ladle into bowls and serve.

Nutrition Facts Per Serving:
Calories 119, Total Fat 4g, Saturated Fat 0.6g, Cholesterol 0mg, Sodium 34mg, Total Carbohydrate 17.2g, Dietary Fiber 6.6g, Total Sugars 4.4g, Protein 4g, Vitamin D 0mcg, Calcium 155mg, Iron 2mg, Potassium 628mg

Vegetarian Chili with Quinoa

Prep time 5 minutes / Cook time 30 minutes / Serves 12

Ingredients:
- 2 large onions, chopped
- 2 red bell peppers, deseeded, chopped
- 28 ounces fire roasted diced tomatoes
- 8 ounces tomato sauce
- 2 tablespoons chili powder
- 2 tablespoons smoked paprika
- 2 tablespoons ground cumin
- 2 teaspoons ground coriander
- ½ teaspoon black pepper
- 1 teaspoon salt or to taste
- 1 teaspoon chili flakes or to taste
- 4 cups cooked quinoa
- 2 cloves garlic, minced
- 15 ounces chili beans
- 7 cups water

- 2 poblano peppers, deseeded, sliced
- 2 green onions, sliced to serve

Instructions:
1. Add all the ingredients into a soup pot. Place the pot over medium heat.
2. Cover and simmer for 20-30 minutes.
3. Taste and adjust the seasonings if necessary.
4. Ladle into soup bowls. Garnish with green onions and serve.

Nutrition Facts Per Serving:
Calories 300, Total Fat 6.1g, Saturated Fat 1.3g, Cholesterol 6mg, Sodium 650mg, Total Carbohydrate 51.4g, Dietary Fiber 8.3g, Total Sugars 6g, Protein 12g, Vitamin D 0mcg, Calcium 87mg, Iron 6mg, Potassium 817mg

Prep time 5 minutes / Cook time 15 minutes / Serves 3

Ingredients:

- ½ tablespoon vegetable oil
- 1 medium clove garlic, minced
- 1 medium red bell pepper, diced
- 1 medium onion, chopped
- 1 medium sweet potato (about 2/3 pound), peeled, cubed
- ½ can (from a 14.5 ounces can) diced tomatoes
- 1 can (16 ounces black beans) drained, rinsed
- 2 tablespoons chopped fresh cilantro
- ½ small hot green chili pepper
- ½ ripe mango, peeled, pitted, diced
- Salt to taste

Instructions:

1. Place a soup pot over medium high heat. Add oil and heat. Add onions and cook until the onions are translucent.

2. Add garlic and sauté until onions turn golden brown. Add bell pepper and sweet potato and stir. Add spices and salt and stir. Sauté for a few seconds until fragrant.
3. Add tomatoes and stir.
4. When it begins to boil, lower heat and cover with a lid. Simmer for 15 minutes until the sweet potato is tender.
5. Add in the beans and stir.
6. Ladle into bowls. Garnish with cilantro and mangoes and serve.

Nutrition Facts Per Serving:
Calories 343, Total Fat 3.7g, Saturated Fat 0.8g, Cholesterol 0mg, Sodium 72mg, Total Carbohydrate 64.6g, Dietary Fiber 13.7g, Total Sugars 15.9g, Protein 16.4g, Vitamin D 0mcg, Calcium 104mg, Iron 5mg, Potassium 1443mg

Prep time 7 minutes / Cook time 25 minutes / Serves 8

Ingredients:

- 14.5 ounces diced tomatoes with juice
- 16 ounces cannellini beans
- 6 cloves garlic, sliced
- 6 tablespoons olive oil
- ½ cup white wine
- ¼ cup water
- 1 teaspoon dried thyme
- 3 teaspoons ground sage
- 2 bay leaves
- Salt to taste
- Pepper to taste

Instructions:

1. Place a soup pot over medium-high heat. Add oil. When oil is heated, add garlic and sauté until light brown.

2. Add wine, tomatoes, water, salt, pepper, sage, thyme and bay leaf. When it starts boiling, lower the heat and simmer for about 20-25 minutes.
3. Add beans and mix well. Simmer until thick. Discard the bay leaves.
4. Ladle into bowls and serve.

Nutrition Facts Per Serving:
Calories 305Total Fat 11.1g, Saturated Fat 1.6g, Cholesterol 0mg, Sodium 37mg, Total Carbohydrate 37.5g, Dietary Fiber 15g, Total Sugars 2.8g, Protein 14g, Vitamin D 0mcg, Calcium 100mg, Iron 5mg, Potassium 947mg

Prep time 5 minutes / Cook time 15 minutes / Serves 8

Ingredients:

- 15 ounces pinto beans, drained, rinsed
- 19 ounces enchilada sauce
- 2 cubes vegetarian bouillon
- ½ teaspoon chili powder
- 1 teaspoon garlic powder
- ½ teaspoon ground cumin
- 16 ounces diced tomatoes
- 2 cups frozen corn, thawed
- 1 cup diced tofu
- 3 cups water
- 6 inches tortillas cut into strips
- 2 tablespoons chopped fresh cilantro
- Salt to taste
- Pepper to taste

Instructions:
1. Add enchilada sauce, and water to a large pot. Stir well. Add bouillon cubes. When the cube dissolves, place the pot over medium heat.
2. Add beans, enchilada sauce, tomatoes, corn, cumin, chili powder, garlic powder tortillas, salt, pepper and cilantro and bring to a boil.
3. Add tofu, and tortilla. Stir well and heat thoroughly for 15 minutes.
4. Ladle into bowls. Garnish with cilantro and serve.

Nutrition Facts Per Serving:
Calories 468, Total Fat 5.5g, Saturated Fat 1.3g, Cholesterol 0mg, Sodium 420mg, Total Carbohydrate 95.8g, Dietary Fiber 29.3g, Total Sugars 5.1g, Protein 24.6g, Vitamin D 0mcg, Calcium 444mg, Iron 24mg, Potassium 1927mg

Broccoli Cheese Soup

Prep time 10 minutes / Cook time 40 minutes / Serves 6

Ingredients
- 2 tablespoons coconut
- 1 large yellow onion, thinly sliced
- 3-4 cloves garlic
- 16 oz. fresh or frozen broccoli, chopped and divided
- 1 large russet potato, chopped
- 3 cups vegetable broth
- 2 cups unsweetened soymilk
- 8 oz. vegan cheddar cheese
- 3 tablespoons nutritional yeast
- Salt and pepper, to taste

To serve...
- Pan-fried onions
- Fresh broccoli florets

Instructions:
1. Pop a large pan over a medium heat and add the oil.
2. Throw in the onions and garlic and cook for 5 minutes until cost.
3. Add the potato and broccoli and cook for another 5 minutes.
4. Add the broth and milk, stir well and simmer.
5. Cook for 30 minutes until the veggies are tender.
6. Remove from the heat and add the vegan cheese and nutritional yeast.
7. Use an immersion blender to whizz to perfection then season well.
8. Serve with the optional toppings. Enjoy.

Nutrition Facts Per Serving:
Calories 315, Total Fat 15.8g, Saturated Fat 8.9g, Cholesterol 40mg, Sodium 674mg, Total Carbohydrate 24.8g, Dietary Fiber 6.4g, Total Sugars 4.6g, Protein 20.5g, Vitamin D 5mcg, Calcium 437mg, Iron 3mg, Potassium 947

Roasted Cauliflower Soup

Prep time 5 minutes / Cook time 45 minutes / Serves 5

Ingredients
- 1 large head cauliflower, de-stemmed and florets broken up
- 1 1/2 tablespoons olive oil
- Salt and pepper, to taste
- 5 cloves garlic, smashed with skins still on
- 1/2 large onion, chopped
- 2-3 sprigs thyme, stems removed
- 4 1/2 cups vegetable broth

Instructions:
1. Preheat your oven to 450°F and line a baking sheet with baking paper.
2. Grab a bowl and add the cauliflower, 1 tablespoon oil, ½ teaspoon of pepper and salt to taste.
3. Stir well then transfer to the baking sheet.
4. Pop into the oven and roast for 15 minutes.
5. Place a pan over a medium heat, add ½ tablespoon oil and cook the onions for 5 minutes until soft.
6. Throw in the cooked cauliflower, the garlic, thyme and broth.
7. Stir well then bring to a boil.
8. Reduce the heat and simmer for 15 minutes then remove from the heat.
9. Use an immersion blender to whizz as required then serve and enjoy.

Nutrition Facts Per Serving:
Calories 87, Total Fat 5.5g, Saturated Fat 1g, Cholesterol 0mg, Sodium 694mg, Total Carbohydrate 4.5g, Dietary Fiber 1g, Total Sugars 1.8g, Protein 5.2g, Vitamin D 0mcg, Calcium 30mg, Iron 1mg, Potassium 284mg

Spicy Mexican Chili

Prep time 5 minutes / Cook time 10 minutes / Serves 4

Ingredients:

- ¼ cup chopped onion
- 1 tablespoon minced garlic
- 2 tablespoons salsa from jar
- ½ tablespoon hot Mexican chili powder
- ½ teaspoon ground coriander
- ½ tablespoon ground cumin
- ½ red bell pepper, deseeded, chopped
- 3 ounces tomato paste
- 1 tablespoon cilantro base
- 15 ounces black beans, drained, rinsed
- 1 small sweet potato, grated
- ½ cup uncooked quinoa
- 1 tablespoon chopped fresh cilantro
- ½ tablespoon Sriracha sauce
- 2 cups vegetable broth
- 15 ounces fire roasted tomatoes
- Salt to taste
- Cooking spray

Instructions:

1. Place a soup pot over medium heat. Spray some cooking spray.
2. Add onion, garlic and bell pepper and sauté until onion is light brown.
3. Stir in the cilantro base, salsa, tomato paste, cumin, coriander and stir-fry for a couple of minutes.
4. Add broth, beans, tomatoes and sweet potatoes and let it simmer for 10 minutes.
5. Stir in the quinoa and lower the heat. Cover and cook until quinoa is cooked and the chili is thick.
6. Stir in lime juice, cilantro and Sriracha sauce.
7. Ladle into bowls and serve.

Nutrition Facts Per Serving:
Calories 532, Total Fat 4.4g, Saturated Fat 0.8g, Cholesterol 0mg, Sodium 504mg, Total Carbohydrate 95.9g, Dietary Fiber 21.2g, Total Sugars 10.4g, Protein 31.3g, Vitamin D 0mcg, Calcium 183mg, Iron 9mg, Potassium 2441mg

Moroccan Chickpea Stew

Prep time 5 minutes / Cook time 3 minutes / Serves 8

Ingredients:

- ½ cup vegetable stock
- 1 cup canned or cooked chickpeas, drained, rinsed
- 2 teaspoons honey
- 1 canned pumpkin or butternut squash puree
- A large handful fresh spinach leaves, torn
- ¼ teaspoon ground coriander
- ¼ teaspoon ground cumin
- ¼ teaspoon ground cinnamon
- Pepper to taste
- Salt to taste

To serve:

- Toasted country bread

Instructions:

1. Add stock pumpkin, spinach, chickpeas, salt and spices into a microwave safe bowl and stir.
2. Cover with a lid.
3. Microwave on High for 2-3 minutes.
4. Serve with toasted country bread.

Nutrition Facts Per Serving:
Calories 119, Total Fat 1.8g, Saturated Fat 0.2g, Cholesterol 0mg, Sodium 51mg, Total Carbohydrate 21.3g, Dietary Fiber 5.5g, Total Sugars 5.4g, Protein 5.6g, Vitamin D 0mcg, Calcium 39mg, Iron 2mg, Potassium 291mg

Black Bean and Sweet Potato Chili

Prep time 5 minutes / Cook time 10 minutes / Serves 8

Ingredients:

- 3 ½ tablespoons extra-virgin olive oil
- 2 large onions, chopped
- 2 medium sweet potatoes, peeled, diced
- 8 cloves garlic, minced
- 15ounces black beans, drained, rinsed
- 4 tablespoons chili powder
- 1 teaspoon ground chipotle pepper
- 5 cups water
- 8 teaspoons ground cumin
- Salt to taste
- 14 ounces diced tomatoes
- Juice of 2 limes

Instructions:

1. Place a heavy bottomed saucepan or a soup pot over medium high heat. Add oil. When the oil is heated, add sweet potato and onion and sauté until the onion is translucent.

2. Add garlic and sauté for a few seconds until fragrant. Add chipotle pepper, chili powder, salt and cumin and mix well.
3. Add tomatoes, water and black beans and stir.
4. When it begins to boil, lower the heat and cover with a lid. Simmer for 10 minutes until sweet potatoes are cooked and the chili is thick in consistency.
5. Add lime juice and salt. Mix well. Remove from heat.
6. Ladle into bowls. Garnish with cilantro and serve with toppings of your choice.

Nutrition Facts Per Serving:
Calories 329, Total Fat 8.2g, Saturated Fat 1.2g, Cholesterol 0mg, Sodium 76mg, Total Carbohydrate 54.1g, Dietary Fiber 12.9g, Total Sugars 4.7g, Protein 14g, Vitamin D 0mcg, Calcium 129mg, Iron 5mg, Potassium 1401mg

Tri-colored Chili

Prep time 8 minutes / Cook time 20 minutes / Serves 4
Ingredients:
- 3 tablespoons hulled barley
- Water, as required
- 1 ½ cups chopped onions
- 1 green bell pepper, deseeded, chopped
- 2 cloves garlic, minced
- 1 cup corn, fresh or frozen
- ¾ cup cooked or canned red kidney beans, drained
- ¾ cup cooked or canned black beans, drained
- 1 teaspoon chili powder
- 1 teaspoon ground cumin
- 1 ½ teaspoons Tabasco sauce or to taste
- Salt to taste
- Baked tortilla chips to serve
- Lime wedges to serve
- Cooking spray

Instructions:
1. Cook barley following the instructions on the package.
2. Place a soup pot over medium heat. Spray with cooking spray. Add onions and sauté until translucent.
3. Add garlic, chili powder, cumin, bell pepper and Tabasco sauce and sauté until slightly tender.
4. Add rest of the ingredients and stir.
5. When it begins to boil, lower the heat and cover with a lid. Simmer for about 20 minutes.
6. Taste and adjust the seasoning and Tabasco sauce if necessary.
7. Ladle into soup bowls. Serve with tortilla chips and lemon wedges.

Nutrition Facts Per Serving:
Calories 356, Total Fat 2.3g, Saturated Fat 0.4g, Cholesterol 0mg, Sodium 78mg, Total Carbohydrate 69.3g, Dietary Fiber 15.8g, Total Sugars 6.6g, Protein 19.5g, Vitamin D 0mcg, Calcium 111mg, Iron 6mg, Potassium 1329mg

Quick Mexican Stew with Kale and Chipotle

Prep time 5 minutes / Cook time 30 minutes / Serves 4
Ingredients:
- 2-3 cups water
- 15 ounces black beans
- 15 ounces pinto beans
- ½ small can tomato paste
- 1 medium red bell pepper, chopped into bite size pieces
- 1 clove garlic, minced or ½ teaspoon garlic powder
- 2 red potatoes, chopped into bite size pieces
- 4 ounces baby carrots, chopped into bite size pieces
- ½ small onion, chopped
- 1 ½ cups baby kale
- ½ teaspoon ground cumin
- A large pinch oregano
- Cayenne pepper to taste
- ¼ teaspoon ground coriander
- Himalayan pink salt to taste
- Chipotle pepper to taste
- ½ tablespoon coconut oil

Optional toppings:
- Salsa
- Kale chips
- Spicy potato chips etc.

Instructions:
1. Place a soup pot over medium heat. Add oil. When the oil is heated, add onion and garlic and sauté until translucent.
2. Add rest of the ingredients.
3. Cover and simmer for 20-30 minutes or until vegetables are tender.
4. Taste and adjust the seasonings if necessary.

158

5. Ladle into soup bowls and serve with optional toppings if desired.

Nutrition Facts Per Serving:
Calories 933, Total Fat 7.8g, Saturated Fat 3g, Cholesterol 0mg, Sodium 548mg, Total Carbohydrate 170g, Dietary Fiber 38.7g, Total Sugars 13.4g, Protein 51.6g, Vitamin D 0mcg, Calcium 349mg, Iron 14mg, Potassium 4342mg

Spicy Vegetable Stew

Prep time 5 minutes / Cook time 10 minutes / Serves 3
Ingredients:
- 1 small onion, chopped
- 1 small red bell pepper, chopped
- 1 small green bell pepper, chopped
- 3 small cloves garlic, minced
- A handful spinach chopped
- 1 small head cauliflower, cut into florets
- ½ tablespoon pure maple syrup
- ½ tablespoon curry powder
- 7 ounces canned diced roasted tomatoes
- ½ cup fresh cilantro, chopped
- 14 ounces chickpeas, rinsed, drained
- ½ tablespoon olive oil
- ½ teaspoon cumin seeds
- ½ tablespoon minced fresh ginger
- 1 cup water or vegetable broth
- ½ cup light coconut milk
- Cayenne pepper to taste
- Salt to taste

Instructions:
1. Place a soup pot over medium heat. Add oil and heat, toss in cumin seeds. When seeds crackle, add onions and bell peppers, sauté until tender. Add garlic and ginger and sauté. Stir in spices, sauté for 2 minutes until fragrant.
2. Add remaining ingredients and bring to boil, lower heat and simmer for 10 minutes, covered.
3. Add cilantro, mix well and serve.
4. Ladle into bowls and serve.

Nutrition Facts Per Serving:
Calories 685, Total Fat 20.6g, Saturated Fat 9.7g, Cholesterol 0mg, Sodium 91mg, Total Carbohydrate 102.8g, Dietary Fiber 29.2g, Total Sugars 26.5g, Protein 30.5g, Vitamin D 0mcg, Calcium 208mg, Iron 11mg, Potassium 1959mg

Irish "Lamb" Stew

Prep time 5 minutes / Cook time 20 minutes / Serves 4
Ingredients:
- ½ cup Textured vegetable protein (TVP) chunks or soy chunks
- Salt and pepper to taste
- 3 cloves garlic, minced
- 2 stalks celery, chopped
- 2 potatoes, peeled, chopped into chunks
- 1 ½ - 2 ½ cups vegetable stock
- ½ tablespoon minced, fresh rosemary
- 2 tablespoons all-purpose flour
- 1 medium onion, chopped
- 1 cup button mushrooms, halved
- 1 medium carrot, cut into thin, round slices
- ¼ bottle beer or ¼ cup wine
- ½ tablespoon minced, fresh thyme
- 1 tablespoon vegetable oil

Instructions:
1. Add TVP into a bowl of hot water and soak for 30-40 minutes. Drain and set aside for 5-7 minutes.
2. Add flour, salt and pepper into a bowl and stir. Roll the TVP chunks in the flour mixture, shaking off the extra flour.
3. Place a Dutch oven over medium heat. Heat the oil. Stir in TVP and cook until brown. Remove and place on layers of paper towels.
4. Add ½ teaspoon oil into the oven and heat. Add garlic, seasonings and onion, sauté until onions are pink. Add vegetables and herbs and mix well. Add the remaining flour mixture and sauté for 1-2 minutes.
5. Stir in the TVP, beer and stock. Stir constantly until it begins to boil.
6. Lower the heat and cover with a lid. Cook until tender. Stir occasionally.
7. Add more water or stock if you like to dilute the stew, Season with salt and pepper.
8. Ladles it into bowls and serve.

Nutrition Facts Per Serving:
Calories 169, Total Fat 3.8g, Saturated Fat 0.8g, Cholesterol 0mg, Sodium 60mg, Total Carbohydrate 27.3g, Dietary Fiber 4.7g, Total Sugars 3.9g, Protein 6.5g, Vitamin D 63mcg, Calcium 48mg, Iron 2mg, Potassium 683mg

Chapter 9: Salads Recipes

Prep time: 10 minutes / Cook time: 3 minutes / Serves: 4

Ingredients:

Salad:
- 4 cups baby spinach, rinsed, drained
- ½ cup pickled red cabbage

Dressing:
- 1-inch piece ginger, finely chopped
- 1 tsp. chili garlic paste
- 1 tbsp. soy sauce
- ½ tbsp. rice vinegar
- 1 tbsp. sesame oil
- 3 tbsp. avocado oil

Toppings:
- ½ cup raw cashews, unsalted
- ¼ cup fresh cilantro, chopped

Instructions:
1. Put the spinach and red cabbage in a large bowl. Toss to combine and set the salad aside.
2. Toast the cashews in a frying pan over medium-high heat, stirring occasionally until the cashews are golden brown. This should take about 3 minutes. Turn off the heat and set the frying pan aside.
3. Mix all the dressing ingredients in medium-sized bowl and use a spoon to mix them into a smooth dressing.
4. Pour the dressing over the spinach salad and top with the toasted cashews.
5. Toss the salad to combine all ingredients and transfer the large bowl to the fridge. Allow the salad to chill for up to one hour – doing so will guarantee a better flavor. Alternatively, the salad can be served right away, topped with the optional cilantro.

Nutritional facts per serving:
Calories 160, Total Fat 12.9g, Saturated Fat 2.4g, Cholesterol 0mg, Sodium 265mg, Total Carbohydrate 9.1g, Dietary Fiber 2.1g, Total Sugars 1.4g, Protein 4.1g, Vitamin D 0mcg, Calcium 45mg, Iron 2mg, Potassium 344mg

Prep Time: 10 minutes / Cook Time: 0 minutes / Serves: 2

Ingredients:

Dressing:
- 1 tbsp. olive oil
- ¼ cup chopped basil
- 1 tsp. lemon juice
- ¼ tsp Salt
- 1 medium avocado, halved, diced
- ¼ cup water

Salad:
- ¼ cup dry chickpeas
- ¼ cup dry red kidney beans
- 4 cups raw kale, shredded
- 2 cups Brussel sprouts, shredded
- 2 radishes, thinly sliced
- 1 tbsp. walnuts, chopped
- 1 tsp. flax seeds
- Salt and pepper to taste

Instructions:
1. Prepare the chickpeas and kidney beans according to the method.
2. Soak the flax seeds according the method, and then drain excess water.
3. Prepare the dressing by adding the olive oil, basil, lemon juice, salt, and half of the avocado to a food processor or blender, and pulse on low speed.
4. Keep adding small amounts of water until the dressing is creamy and smooth.
5. Transfer the dressing to a small bowl and set it aside.
6. Combine the kale, Brussel sprouts, cooked chickpeas, kidney beans, radishes, walnuts, and remaining avocado in a large bowl and mix thoroughly.
7. Store the mixture, or, serve with the dressing and flax seeds, and enjoy!

Nutritional facts per serving:
Calories 266, Total Fat 26.6g, Saturated Fat 5.1g, Cholesterol 0mg, Sodium 298mg, Total Carbohydrate 8.8g, Dietary Fiber 6.8g, Total Sugars 0.6g, Protein 2g, Vitamin D 0mcg, Calcium 19mg, Iron 1mg, Potassium 500mg

Cucumber Edamame Salad

Prep time: 5 minutes / Cook time: 8 minutes / Serves: 2

Ingredients:

- 3 tbsp. avocado oil
- 1 cup cucumber, sliced into thin rounds
- ½ cup fresh sugar snap peas, sliced or whole
- ½ cup fresh edamame
- ¼ cup radish, sliced
- 1 large Hass avocado, peeled, pitted, sliced
- 1 nori sheet, crumbled
- 2 tsp. roasted sesame seeds
- 1 tsp. salt

Instructions:

1. Bring a medium-sized pot filled half way with water to a boil over medium-high heat.
2. Add the sugar snaps and cook them for about 2 minutes.
3. Take the pot off the heat, drain the excess water, transfer the sugar snaps to a medium-sized bowl and set aside for now.
4. Fill the pot with water again, add the teaspoon of salt and bring to a boil over medium-high heat.
5. Add the edamame to the pot and let them cook for about 6 minutes.
6. Take the pot off the heat, drain the excess water, transfer the soybeans to the bowl with sugar snaps and let them cool down for about 5 minutes.
7. Combine all ingredients, except the nori crumbs and roasted sesame seeds, in a medium-sized bowl.
8. Carefully stir, using a spoon, until all ingredients are evenly coated in oil.
9. Top the salad with the nori crumbs and roasted sesame seeds.
10. Transfer the bowl to the fridge and allow the salad to cool for at least 30 minutes.
11. Serve chilled and enjoy!

Nutritional facts per serving:
Calories 182, Total Fat 10.9g, Saturated Fat 1.3g, Cholesterol 0mg, Sodium 1182mg, Total Carbohydrate 14.2g, Dietary Fiber 5.4g, Total Sugars 1.9g, Protein 10.7g, Vitamin D 0mcg, Calcium 181mg, Iron 4mg, Potassium 619mg

Spinach and Mashed Tofu Salad

Prep time: 20 minutes / Serves: 4

Ingredients:

- 2 8-oz. blocks firm tofu, drained
- 4 cups baby spinach leaves
- 4 tbsp. cashew butter
- 1½ tbsp. soy sauce
- 1tbsp ginger, chopped
- 1 tsp. red miso paste
- 2 tbsp. sesame seeds
- 1 tsp. organic orange zest
- 1 tsp. nori flakes
- 2 tbsp. water

Instructions:

1. Use paper towels to absorb any excess water left in the tofu before crumbling both blocks into small pieces.
2. In a large bowl, combine the mashed tofu with the spinach leaves.
3. Mix the remaining ingredients in another small bowl and, if desired, add the optional water for a more smooth dressing.
4. Pour this dressing over the mashed tofu and spinach leaves.
5. Transfer the bowl to the fridge and allow the salad to chill for up to one hour. Doing so will guarantee a better flavor. Or, the salad can be served right away. Enjoy!

Nutritional facts per serving:
Calories 623, Total Fat 30.5g, Saturated Fat 5.8g, Cholesterol 0mg, Sodium 2810mg, Total Carbohydrate 48g, Dietary Fiber 5.9g, Total Sugars 3g, Protein 48.4g, Vitamin D 0mcg, Calcium 797mg, Iron 22mg, Potassium 2007mg

Roasted Almond Protein Salad

Prep Time: 30 minutes / Cook Time: 0 minutes / Serves: 4

Ingredients:
- ½ cup dry quinoa
- ½ cup dry navy beans
- ½ cup dry chickpeas
- ½ cup raw whole almonds
- 1 tsp. extra virgin olive oil
- ½ tsp. salt
- ½ tsp. paprika
- ½ tsp. cayenne
- Dash of chili powder
- 4 cups spinach, fresh or frozen
- ¼ cup purple onion, chopped

Instructions:
1. Prepare the quinoa according to the recipe. Store in the fridge for now.
2. Prepare the beans according to the method. Store in the fridge for now.
3. Toss the almonds, olive oil, salt, and spices in a large bowl, and stir until the ingredients are evenly coated.
4. Put a skillet over medium-high heat, and transfer the almond mixture to the heated skillet.
5. Roast while stirring until the almonds are browned, around 5 minutes. You may hear the ingredients pop and crackle in the pan as they warm up. Stir frequently to prevent burning.
6. Turn off the heat and toss the cooked and chilled quinoa and beans, onions, and spinach or mixed greens in the skillet. Stir well before transferring the roasted almond salad to a bowl.
7. Enjoy the salad with a dressing of choice, or, store for later!

Nutritional facts per serving:
Calories 347, Total Fat 10.5g, Saturated Fat 1g, Cholesterol 0mg, Sodium 324mg, Total Carbohydrate 49.2g, Dietary Fiber 14.7g, Total Sugars 4.7g, Protein 17.2g, Vitamin D 0mcg, Calcium 139mg, Iron 5mg, Potassium 924mg

Colorful Veggie Salad

Prep time 8 minutes / Serves 3

Ingredients:
- ½ head purple cabbage, shredded
- 1 medium carrot, cut into matchsticks
- ½ small head romaine lettuce, shredded
- For the tahini dressing:
- ¼ cup raw tahini
- 1 tablespoon olive oil
- ½ teaspoon salt
- ¼ cup fresh lemon juice

Instructions:
1. Add all the ingredients for dressing into a blender. Blend until smooth.
2. Add all the salad ingredients in a serving bowl. Toss well.
3. Add dressing and toss well. Serve immediately.

Nutritional facts per serving:
Calories 203, Total Fat 15.7g, Saturated Fat 2.4g, Cholesterol 0mg, Sodium 451mg, Total Carbohydrate 13.9g, Dietary Fiber 5.5g, Total Sugars 5.4g, Protein 5.3g, Vitamin D 0mcg, Calcium 141mg, Iron 3mg, Potassium 388mg

Lentil, Lemon & Mushroom Salad

Prep Time: 10 minutes / Cook Time: 0 minutes / Serves: 2

Ingredients:
- ½ cup dry lentils of choice
- 2 cups vegetable broth
- 3 cups mushrooms, thickly sliced
- 1 cup sweet or purple onion, chopped
- 4 tsp. extra virgin olive oil
- 2 tbsp. garlic powder
- ¼ tsp. chili flakes
- 1 tbsp. lemon juice
- 2 tbsp. cilantro, chopped
- ½ cup arugula

162

- ¼ tsp Salt
- ¼ tsp pepper

Instructions:

1. Sprout the lentils according the method. (Don't cook them).
2. Place the vegetable stock in a deep saucepan and bring it to a boil.
3. Add the lentils to the boiling broth, cover the pan, and cook for about 5 minutes over low heat until the lentils are a bit tender.
4. Remove the pan from heat and drain the excess water.
5. Put a frying pan over high heat and add 2 tablespoons of olive oil.
6. Add the onions, garlic, and chili flakes, and cook until the onions are almost translucent, around 5 to 10 minutes while stirring.
7. Add the mushrooms to the frying pan and mix in thoroughly. Continue cooking until the onions are completely translucent and the mushrooms have softened; remove the pan from the heat.
8. Mix the lentils, onions, mushrooms, and garlic in a large bowl.
9. Add the lemon juice and the remaining olive oil. Toss or stir to combine everything thoroughly.
10. Serve the mushroom/onion mixture over some arugala in bowl, adding salt and pepper to taste, or, store and enjoy later!

Nutritional facts per serving:

Calories 365, Total Fat 11.7g, Saturated Fat 1.9g, Cholesterol 0mg, Sodium 1071mg, Total Carbohydrate 45.2g, Dietary Fiber 18g, Total Sugars 8.2g, Protein 22.8g, Vitamin D 378mcg, Calcium 67mg, Iron 8mg, Potassium 1212mg

Sweet Potato & Black Bean Protein Salad

Prep Time: 15 minutes / Cook Time: 0 minutes / Serves: 2

Ingredients:

- 1 cup dry black beans
- 4 cups of spinach
- 1 medium sweet potato
- 1 cup purple onion, chopped
- 2 tbsp. olive oil
- 2 tbsp. lime juice
- 1 tbsp. minced garlic
- ½ tbsp. chili powder
- ¼ tsp. cayenne
- ¼ cup parsley
- ¼ tsp Salt
- ¼ tsp pepper

Instructions:

1. Prepare the black beans according to the method.
2. Preheat the oven to 400°F.
3. Cut the sweet potato into ¼-inch cubes and put these in a medium-sized bowl. Add the onions, 1 tablespoon of olive oil, and salt to taste.
4. Toss the ingredients until the sweet potatoes and onions are completely coated.
5. Transfer the ingredients to a baking sheet lined with parchment paper and spread them out in a single layer.
6. Put the baking sheet in the oven and roast until the sweet potatoes are starting to turn brown and crispy, around 40 minutes.
7. Meanwhile, combine the remaining olive oil, lime juice, garlic, chili powder, and cayenne thoroughly in a large bowl, until no lumps remain.
8. Remove the sweet potatoes and onions from the oven and transfer them to the large bowl.
9. Add the cooked black beans, parsley, and a pinch of salt.
10. Toss everything until well combined.
11. Then mix in the spinach, and serve in desired portions with additional salt and pepper.
12. Store or enjoy!

Nutritional facts per serving:

Calories 558, Total Fat 16.2g, Saturated Fat 2.5g, Cholesterol 0mg, Sodium 390mg, Total Carbohydrate 84g, Dietary Fiber 20.4g, Total Sugars 8.9g, Protein 25.3g, Vitamin D 0mcg, Calcium 220mg, Iron 10mg, Potassium 2243mg

Lentil Radish Salad

Prep Time: 15 minutes / Cook Time: 0 minutes / Serves: 3

Ingredients:

Dressing:
- 1 tbsp. extra virgin olive oil
- 1 tbsp. lemon juice
- 1 tbsp. maple syrup
- 1 tbsp. water
- ½ tbsp. sesame oil
- 1 tbsp. miso paste, yellow or white
- ¼ tsp. salt
- ¼ tsp Pepper

Salad:
- ½ cup dry chickpeas
- ¼ cup dry green or brown lentils
- 1 14-oz. pack of silken tofu
- 5 cups mixed greens, fresh or frozen
- 2 radishes, thinly sliced
- ½ cup cherry tomatoes, halved
- ¼ cup roasted sesame seeds

Instructions:
1. Prepare the chickpeas according to the method.
2. Prepare the lentils according to the method.
3. Put all the ingredients for the dressing in a blender or food processor. Mix on low until smooth, while adding water until it reaches the desired consistency.
4. Add salt, pepper (to taste), and optionally more water to the dressing; set aside.
5. Cut the tofu into bite-sized cubes.
6. Combine the mixed greens, tofu, lentils, chickpeas, radishes, and tomatoes in a large bowl.
7. Add the dressing and mix everything until it is coated evenly.
8. Top with the optional roasted sesame seeds, if desired.
9. Refrigerate before serving and enjoy, or, store for later!

Nutritional facts per serving:
Calories 621, Total Fat 19.6g, Saturated Fat 2.8g, Cholesterol 0mg, Sodium 996mg, Total Carbohydrate 82.7g, Dietary Fiber 26.1g, Total Sugars 20.7g, Protein 31.3g, Vitamin D 0mcg, Calcium 289mg, Iron 9mg, Potassium 1370mg

Colorful Protein Power Salad

Prep Time: 20 minutes / Cook Time: 0 minutes / Serves: 2

Ingredients:
- ½ cup dry quinoa
- 2 cups dry navy beans
- 1 green onion, chopped
- 2 tsp. garlic, minced
- 3 cups green or purple cabbage, chopped
- 4 cups kale, fresh or frozen, chopped
- 1 cup shredded carrot, chopped
- 2 tbsp. extra virgin olive oil
- 1 tsp. lemon juice
- ¼ tsp Salt
- ¼ tsp pepper

Instructions:
1. Prepare the quinoa according to the recipe.
2. Prepare the beans according to the method.
3. Heat up 1 tablespoon of the olive oil in a frying pan over medium heat.
4. Add the chopped green onion, garlic, and cabbage, and sauté for 2-3 minutes.
5. Add the kale, the remaining 1 tablespoon of olive oil, and salt. Lower the heat and cover until the greens have wilted, around 5 minutes. Remove the pan from the stove and set aside.
6. Take a large bowl and mix the remaining ingredients with the kale and cabbage mixture once it has cooled down. Add more salt and pepper to taste.
7. Mix until everything is distributed evenly.
8. Serve topped with a dressing, or, store for later!

Nutritional facts per serving:
Calories 1100, Total Fat 19.9g, Saturated Fat 2.7g, Cholesterol 0mg, Sodium 420mg, Total Carbohydrate 180.8g, Dietary Fiber 60.1g, Total Sugars 14.4g , Protein 58.6g, Vitamin D 0mcg, Calcium 578mg, Iron 16mg, Potassium 3755mg

Southwest Style Salad

Prep Time: 10 minutes / Cook Time: 0 minutes / Serves: 3

Ingredients:

- ½ cup dry black beans
- ½ cup dry chickpeas
- 1/3 cup purple onion, diced
- 1 red bell pepper, pitted, sliced
- 4 cups mixed greens, fresh or frozen, chopped
- 1 cup cherry tomatoes, halved or quartered
- 1 medium avocado, peeled, pitted, and cubed
- 1 cup sweet kernel corn, canned, drained
- ½ tsp. chili powder
- ¼ tsp. cumin
- ¼ tsp Salt
- ¼ tsp pepper
- 2 tsp. olive oil
- 1 tbsp. vinegar

Instructions:

1. Prepare the black beans and chickpeas according to the method.
2. Put all of the ingredients into a large bowl.
3. Toss the mix of veggies and spices until combined thoroughly.
4. Store, or serve chilled with some olive oil and vinegar on top!

Nutritional facts per serving:

Calories 635, Total Fat 19.9g, Saturated Fat 3.6g, Cholesterol 0mg, Sodium 302mg, Total Carbohydrate 95.4g, Dietary Fiber 28.1g, Total Sugars 18.8g, Protein 24.3g, Vitamin D 0mcg, Calcium 160mg, Iron 7mg, Potassium 1759mg

Shaved Brussel Sprout Salad

Prep Time: 25 minutes / Cook Time: 0 minutes / Serves: 4

Ingredients:

Dressing:

- 1 tbsp. brown mustard
- 1 tbsp. maple syrup
- 2 tbsp. apple cider vinegar
- 2 tbsp. extra virgin olive oil
- ½ tbsp. garlic minced

Salad:

- ½ cup dry red kidney beans
- ¼ cup dry chickpeas
- 2 cups Brussel sprouts
- 1 cup purple onion
- 1 small sour apple
- ½ cup slivered almonds, crushed
- ½ cup walnuts, crushed
- ½ cup cranberries, dried
- ¼ tsp Salt
- ¼ tsp pepper

Instructions:

1. Prepare the beans according to the method.
2. Combine all dressing ingredients in a bowl and stir well until combined.
3. Refrigerate the dressing for up to one hour before serving.
4. Using a grater, mandolin, or knife to thinly slice each Brussel sprout. Repeat this with the apple and onion.
5. Take a large bowl to mix the chickpeas, beans, sprouts, apples, onions, cranberries, and nuts.
6. Drizzle the cold dressing over the salad to coat.
7. Serve with salt and pepper to taste, or, store for later!

Nutritional facts per serving:

Calories 432, Total Fat 23.5g, Saturated Fat 2.2g, Cholesterol 0mg, Sodium 197mg, Total Carbohydrate 45.3g, Dietary Fiber 12.4g, Total Sugars 14g, Protein 15.9g, Vitamin D 0mcg, Calcium 104mg, Iron 4mg, Potassium 908mg

Edamame & Ginger Citrus Salad

Prep Time: 15 minutes / Cook Time: 0 minutes / Serves: 3

Ingredients:

Dressing:

- ¼ cup orange juice
- 1 tsp. lime juice
- ½ tbsp. maple syrup
- ½ tsp. ginger, finely minced
- ½ tbsp. sesame oil

Salad:

- ½ cup dry green lentils

- 2 cups carrots, shredded
- 4 cups kale, fresh or frozen, chopped
- 1 cup edamame, shelled
- 1 tablespoon roasted sesame seeds
- 2 tsp. mint, chopped
- Salt and pepper to taste
- 1 small avocado, peeled, pitted, diced

Instructions:
1. Prepare the lentils according to the method.
2. Combine the orange and lime juices, maple syrup, and ginger in a small bowl. Mix with a whisk while slowly adding the sesame oil.

3. Add the cooked lentils, carrots, kale, edamame, sesame seeds, and mint to a large bowl.
4. Add the dressing and stir well until all the ingredients are coated evenly.
5. Store or serve topped with avocado and an additional sprinkle of mint.

Nutritional facts per serving:
Calories 507, Total Fat 23.1g, Saturated Fat 4g, Cholesterol 0mg, Sodium 303mg, Total Carbohydrate 56.8g, Dietary Fiber 21.6g, Total Sugars 8.4g, Protein 24.6g, Vitamin D 0mcg, Calcium 374mg, Iron 8mg, Potassium 1911mg

Taco Tempeh Salad

Prep Time: 25 minutes / Cook Time: 0 minutes / Serves: 3

Ingredients:
- 1 cup dry black beans
- 1 8-oz. package tempeh
- 1 tbsp. lime or lemon juice
- 2 tbsp. extra virgin olive oil
- 1 tsp. maple syrup
- ½ tsp. chili powder
- ¼ tsp. cumin
- ¼ tsp. paprika
- 1 large bunch of kale, fresh or frozen, chopped
- 1 large avocado, peeled, pitted, diced
- ½ cup salsa
- ¼ tsp Salt
- ¼ tsp pepper

Instructions:
1. Prepare the beans according to the method.
2. Cut the tempeh into ¼-inch cubes, place in a bowl, and then add the lime or lemon juice, 1

tablespoon of olive oil, maple syrup, chili powder, cumin, and paprika.
3. Stir well and let the tempeh marinate in the fridge for at least 1 hour, up to 12 hours.
4. Heat the remaining 1 tablespoon of olive oil in a frying pan over medium heat.
5. Add the marinated tempeh mixture and cook until brown and crispy on both sides, around 10 minutes.
6. Put the chopped kale in a bowl with the cooked beans and prepared tempeh.
7. Store, or serve the salad immediately, topped with salsa, avocado, and salt and pepper to taste.

Nutritional facts per serving:
Calories 627, Total Fat 31.7g, Saturated Fat 6.1g, Cholesterol 0mg, Sodium 493mg, Total Carbohydrate 62.7g, Dietary Fiber 16g, Total Sugars 4.5g, Protein 31.4g, Vitamin D 0mcg, Calcium 249mg, Iron 7mg, Potassium 1972mg

Lebanese Potato Salad

Prep time 5 minutes / Cook time 10 minutes / Serves 4

Ingredients:
- 1-pound Russet potatoes
- 1 ½ tablespoons extra virgin olive oil
- 2 scallions, thinly sliced
- Freshly ground pepper to taste
- 2 tablespoons lemon juice
- ¼ teaspoon salt or to taste
- 2 tablespoons fresh mint leaves, chopped

Instructions:

1. Place a saucepan half filled with water over medium heat. Add salt and potatoes and cook for 10 minutes until tender. Drain the potatoes and place in a bowl of cold water. When cool enough to handle, peel and cube the potatoes. Place in a bowl.

To make dressing:

2. Add oil, lemon juice, salt and pepper in a bowl and whisk well. Drizzle dressing over the potatoes. Toss well.
3. Add scallions and mint and toss well.
4. Divide into 4 plates and serve.

Nutritional facts per serving:
Calories 129, Total Fat 5.5g, Saturated Fat 0.9g, Cholesterol 0mg, Sodium 158mg, Total Carbohydrate 18.8g, Dietary Fiber 3.2g, Total Sugars 1.6g, Protein 2.2g, Vitamin D 0mcg, Calcium 22mg, Iron 1mg, Potassium 505mg

Chickpea and Spinach Salad

Prep time 5 minutes / Cook time 0 minutes / Serves 4
Ingredients:
- 2 cans (14.5 ounces each) chickpeas, drained, rinsed
- 7 ounces vegan feta cheese, crumbled or chopped
- 1 tablespoon lemon juice
- 1/3 -½ cup olive oil
- ½ teaspoon salt or to taste
- 4-6 cups spinach, torn
- ½ cup raisins
- 2 tablespoons honey
- 1-2 teaspoons ground cumin
- 1 teaspoon chili flakes

Instructions:
1. Add cheese, chickpeas and spinach into a large bowl.
2. To make dressing: Add rest of the ingredients into another bowl and mix well.
3. Pour dressing over the salad. Toss well and serve.

Nutritional facts per serving:
Calories 822, Total Fat 42.5g, Saturated Fat 11.7g, Cholesterol 44mg, Sodium 910mg, Total Carbohydrate 89.6g, Dietary Fiber 19.7g, Total Sugars 32.7g, Protein 29g, Vitamin D 0mcg, Calcium 417mg, Iron 9mg, Potassium 1347mg

Tempeh "Chicken" Salad

Prep time 10 minutes / Cook time 0 minutes / Serves 2
Ingredients:
- 4 tablespoons light mayonnaise
- 2 scallions, sliced
- Pepper to taste
- 4 cups mixed salad greens
- 4 teaspoons white miso
- 2 tablespoons chopped fresh dill
- 1 ½ cups crumbled tempeh
- 1 cup sliced grape tomatoes

Instructions:
To make dressing:
1. Add mayonnaise, scallions, miso, dill and pepper into a bowl and whisk well.

2. Add tempeh and fold gently.
To serve:
3. Divide the greens into 4 plates. Divide the tempeh among the plates. Top with tomatoes and serve.

Nutritional facts per serving:
Calories 452, Total Fat 24.5g, Saturated Fat 4.4g, Cholesterol 8mg, Sodium 733mg, Total Carbohydrate 37.2g, Dietary Fiber 2.6g, Total Sugars 5.3g, Protein 29.9g, Vitamin D 0mcg, Calcium 261mg, Iron 8mg, Potassium 1377mg

Spinach & Dill Pasta Salad

Prep time 5 minutes / Cook time 0 minutes / Serves 4
Ingredients:
For salad:
- 3 cups cooked whole-wheat fusilli
- 2 cups cherry tomatoes, halved
- ½ cup vegan cheese, shredded
- 4 cups spinach, chopped

- 2 cups edamame, thawed
- 1 large red onion, finely chopped
For dressing:
- 2 tablespoons white wine vinegar
- ½ teaspoon dried dill

- 2 tablespoons extra-virgin olive oil
- Salt to taste
- Pepper to taste

Instructions:

To make dressing:

1. Add all the ingredients for dressing into a bowl and whisk well. Set aside for a while for the flavors to set in.

To make salad:

2. Add all the ingredients of the salad in a bowl. Toss well.
3. Drizzle dressing on top. Toss well.
4. Divide into 4 plates and serve.

Nutritional facts per serving:

Calories 684, Total Fat 33.6g, Saturated Fat 4.6g, Cholesterol 4mg, Sodium 632mg, Total Carbohydrate 69.5g, Dietary Fiber 12g, Total Sugars 6.4g, Protein 31.7g, Vitamin D 0mcg, Calcium 368mg, Iron 8mg, Potassium 1241mg

Italian Veggie Salad

Prep time 10 minutes / Cook time 0 minutes / Serves 8

Ingredients:

For salad:

- 1 cup fresh baby carrots, quartered lengthwise
- 1 celery rib, sliced
- 3 large mushrooms, thinly sliced
- 1 cup cauliflower florets, bite sized, blanched
- 1 cup broccoli florets, blanched
- 1 cup thinly sliced radish
- 4-5 ounces hearts of romaine salad mix to serve

For dressing:

- ½ package Italian salad dressing mix
- 3 tablespoons white vinegar
- 3 tablespoons water
- 3 tablespoons olive oil
- 3-4 pepperoncino, chopped

Instructions:

To make salad:

1. Add all the ingredients of the salad except hearts of romaine to a bowl and toss.

To make dressing:

2. Add all the ingredients of the dressing in a small bowl. Whisk well.
3. Pour dressing over salad and toss well. Refrigerate for a couple of hours.
4. Place romaine in a large bowl. Place the chilled salad over it and serve.

Nutritional facts per serving:

Calories 84, Total Fat 6.7g, Saturated Fat 1.2g, Cholesterol 3mg, Sodium 212mg, Total Carbohydrate 5g, Dietary Fiber 1.4g, Total Sugars 1.6g, Protein 2g, Vitamin D 31mcg, Calcium 27mg, Iron 1mg, Potassium 193mg

Best Broccoli Salad

Prep time 15 minutes / Serves 8

Ingredients:

- 8 cups diced broccoli
- ¼ cup sunflower seeds
- 3 tablespoons Apple cider vinegar
- ½ cup dried cranberries
- 1/3 cup cubed onion
- 1 cup mayonnaise
- ½ cup bacon bits
- 2 tablespoons sugar
- ½ teaspoon salt and ground black pepper

Instructions:

1. In a bowl mix vinegar, salt, pepper, mayonnaise, and sugar. Mix it well. In another bowl mix all the remaining ingredients and pour the prepared mayonnaise dressing and mix it well. before serving to refrigerate it for at least an hour.

Nutritional facts per serving:

Calories 177, Total Fat 11.4g, Saturated Fat 1.7g, Cholesterol 9mg, Sodium 299mg, Total Carbohydrate 17.1g, Dietary Fiber 2.8g, Total Sugars 6.7g, Protein 3.6g, Vitamin D 0mcg, Calcium 50mg, Iron 1mg, Potassium 323mg

Spicy Sweet Potato Salad

Prep time 10 minutes / Serves 2

Ingredients:
- 2 large sweet potatoes, peeled, chopped into chunks
- Salt to taste
- Freshly ground pepper to taste
- 1 small red bell pepper, cored, seeded, quartered
- ¼ cup scallions, sliced
- ¼ cup extra-virgin olive oil, divided
- 2 tablespoons red wine vinegar
- 1 teaspoon ground cumin
- ½ teaspoon orange zest, grated
- ¼ cup fresh mint leaves
- 1 fresh jalapeño pepper, minced
- 2 tablespoons raisins

Instructions:
1. Place sweet potatoes on a baking sheet. Trickle a tablespoon of oil over it. Toss well. Season with salt and pepper.
2. Roast in a preheated oven at 400° F for about 30minutes or until fork tender.
3. Remove from the oven and set aside to cool. Add sweet potatoes into a bowl. Also add scallion, mint, chilies and raisins and toss well.
4. To make dressing: Add 3 tablespoons oil, vinegar, bell pepper, cumin, salt, pepper and orange zest into a blender and blend until smooth.
5. Add about ¾ of the dressing. Toss well. Taste and add the remaining dressing if necessary.
6. Serve immediately.

Nutritional facts per serving:
Calories 458, Total Fat 26g, Saturated Fat 3.7g, Cholesterol 0mg, Sodium 315mg, Total Carbohydrate 56.7g, Dietary Fiber 8.8g, Total Sugars 9.7g, Protein 4.1g, Vitamin D 0mcg, Calcium 80mg, Iron 4mg, Potassium 1540mg

Smashed Avocado Chickpea Salad

Prep time 15 minutes / Serves 8

Ingredients:
- 2 ripe avocadoes, peeled, pitted, chopped
- Juice of a lemon
- 1 cucumber, peeled, diced
- 2 large carrots, peeled, chopped
- 4 tablespoons fresh dill
- 4 stalks celery, chopped
- 16 cherry tomatoes, halved
- ½ cup tahini
- 2 cans (15 ounce each) chickpeas, rinsed, drained
- 6 tablespoons salted sunflower seeds
- Sea salt to taste
- Pepper to taste
- 4 English muffins, halved, toasted

Instructions:
1. Add chickpeas avocado, tahini, and lemon juice into a large bowl. Mash coarsely with a potato masher.
2. Add cucumber, celery, carrot, salt, pepper, dill and sunflower seeds. Mix well.
3. Place the English muffins on a serving platter, with the cut side facing up. Place some chickpea mixture over one half of the muffin. Layer with 4 slices of tomatoes on each and serve.

Nutritional facts per serving:
Calories 548, Total Fat 25.2g, Saturated Fat 4.1g, Cholesterol 0mg, Sodium 248mg, Total Carbohydrate 67.8g, Dietary Fiber 19.7g, Total Sugars 15.3g, Protein 20.4g, Vitamin D 0mcg, Calcium 245mg, Iron 8mg, Potassium 1625mg

Coronation Chickpea and Apple Salad

Prep time 20 minutes / Serves 2

Ingredients:
- 2 spring onions, chopped
- 1 green apple, cored, diced
- ½ can (from 14.5 ounces can) chickpeas, rinsed, drained
- 1 little gems lettuce, leaves separated
- 1 stalk celery, cut into slices diagonally
- 1 tablespoon golden sultanas
- A handful fresh cilantro, chopped

For dressing:
- 1 teaspoon curry paste
- 1 ½ tablespoons almond juice
- 1 tablespoon mango chutney
- Lime juice
- Salt to taste
- Pepper to taste

Instructions:
To make salad:
1. Add all the ingredients of the salad except lettuce and a little of the cilantro to a bowl and toss.

To make dressing:
1. Add all the ingredients of the dressing in a small bowl. Whisk well.
2. Pour dressing over salad and toss well.
3. Place lettuce in a large bowl. Place the salad over it. Garnish with remaining cilantro and serve.

Nutritional facts per serving:
Calories 885, Total Fat 17.1g, Saturated Fat 3.7g, Cholesterol 0mg, Sodium 371mg, Total Carbohydrate 149.9g, Dietary Fiber 40.5g, Total Sugars 39.4g, Protein 41.3g, Vitamin D 0mcg, Calcium 254mg, Iron 14mg, Potassium 2172mg

Plant-Power Chopped Salad

Prep time 10 minutes / Cook time 0 minutes / Serves 3

Ingredients:
- 1 large head of Romaine lettuce, washed and chopped
- 2 cups baby arugula, chopped
- 1 medium zucchini, ends cut off and cut into slices
- 1 14-ounce can artichoke hearts, drained, dried and chopped
- 1 14-ounce can chickpeas, rinsed, drained and dried
- 2 medium carrots, peeled, quartered lengthwise and thinly sliced
- ¾ cup tomatoes, diced
- salt and pepper as desired
- 4 tablespoons shelled sunflower seeds

Instructions:
1. Place the chopped lettuce in a large salad bowl; add the arugula and toss to mix.
2. Add the zucchini, artichoke hearts, chickpeas, carrots and tomatoes; toss to combine.
3. Add salt and pepper to your liking and sprinkle the top with sunflower seeds.
4. Serve with creamy ranch dressing

Nutritional values per serving:
Calories 799, Total Fat 27.2g, Saturated Fat 2.9g, Cholesterol 0mg, Sodium 198mg, Total Carbohydrate 109.9g, Dietary Fiber 36.8g, Total Sugars 21.6g, Protein 39.8g, Vitamin D 0mcg, Calcium 301mg, Iron 14mg, Potassium 2132mg

Rainbow Orzo Salad

Prep time 10 minutes / Cook time 20 minutes / Serves 1

Ingredients:
- 1 chopped onion
- 1-ounce grated feta cheese
- 2 sliced bell peppers
- 1 tablespoon olive oil
- 6 sliced tomatoes
- 2 tablespoons chopped basil
- 1-ounce orzo pasta

Instructions:
1. Preheat the oven at 350F temperature. Prepare a baking sheet and place the onion and bell peppers and drizzle half olive oil.
2. Bake it for around 15 minutes. Add tomatoes on it and bake for additional 5 minutes. Meanwhile cook the orzo according to the given instructions on the pack and cool it.
3. Now toss it with the baked vegetables and top it with cheese, basil and remaining oil and serve it.

Nutritional facts per serving:
Calories 531, Total Fat 22.9g, Saturated Fat 6.5g, Cholesterol 46mg, Sodium 370mg, Total Carbohydrate 73.8g, Dietary Fiber 14.5g, Total Sugars 37.3g, Protein 17.5g, Vitamin D 0mcg, Calcium 273mg, Iron 5mg, Potassium 2442mg

Broccoli Pasta Salad

Prep time 15 minutes / Cook time 0 minutes / Serves 12

Ingredients:

- 1-pound cooked pasta
- 2 diced broccoli florets
- 1 chopped onion
- 1 cup grated cheese
- 12 ounce cooked and finely chopped bacon
- ¾ teaspoon salt
- ¾ teaspoon ground black pepper
- 1 cup mayonnaise

Instructions:

1. Take a bowl and mix all the ingredients until all of them combined well.

2. Cover it with the plastic wrap and place it in the refrigerator for at least 30 minutes and serve it. You can keep it in the refrigerator for 3 days.

Nutritional facts per serving:

Calories 386, Total Fat 22.4g, Saturated Fat 7g, Cholesterol 74mg, Sodium 1015mg, Total Carbohydrate 27.9g, Dietary Fiber 0.6g, Total Sugars 2g, Protein 17.8g, Vitamin D 1mcg, Calcium 89mg, Iron 2mg, Potassium 302mg

Cherry Tomato Couscous Salad

Prep time 05 minutes / Cook time 15 minutes / Serves 5

Ingredients:

- 1 cup couscous
- ½ cup small fresh basil leaves
- 2 tablespoons minced shallots
- 8-ounce sliced cherry tomatoes
- 1 tablespoon olive oil
- 3 tablespoons vinegar
- ¾ teaspoon ground black pepper
- ½ teaspoon salt

Instructions:

1. In a saucepan add water and salt and bring it to boil. Now toast couscous in a small pan and cook it over medium flame.

2. Cook it for around 7 minutes and move it in a circular motion. Add it immediately in the salty boiling water and cook for additional 6 minutes and drain and rinse it.

3. Now take a bowl and mix all the remaining ingredients and cooked couscous. Mix them well and serve them after 15 minutes.

Nutritional facts per serving:

Calories 168Total Fat 3.1g, Saturated Fat 0.5g, Cholesterol 0mg, Sodium 123mg, Total Carbohydrate 29.6g, Dietary Fiber 2.4g, Total Sugars 1.2g, Protein 5g, Vitamin D 0mcg, Calcium 21mg, Iron 1mg, Potassium 196mg

Spicy Watermelon Tomato Salad

Prep time 20 minutes / Serves 8

Ingredients:

- 1 diced yellow tomato
- 2 cups diced seeded watermelon
- ¼ cup vinegar
- 1 cubed red tomato
- 2 teaspoons honey
- ¼ cup olive oil
- 2 tablespoons chili-garlic sauce
- 1 tablespoon chopped lemon basil
- ½ teaspoon salt
- ½ teaspoon black pepper

Instructions:

1. Drain some moisture from watermelon and red and yellow tomatoes by spreading it over the paper towel. Now put all the ingredients including the drained ingredients.

2. Mix all the ingredients well and serve it.

Nutritional facts per serving:

Calories 84, Total Fat 6.4g, Saturated Fat 0.9g, Cholesterol 0mg, Sodium 250mg, Total Carbohydrate 7.3g, Dietary Fiber 0.5g, Total Sugars 5.3g, Protein 0.6g, Vitamin D 0mcg, Calcium 8mg, Iron 0mg, Potassium 137mg

Eggplant & Roasted Tomato Farro Salad

Prep time 1 hour / Cook time 1 hour 30 minutes / Serves 3

Ingredients:

- 4 small eggplants
- 1 ½ cups chopped cherry tomatoes
- ¾ cup uncooked faro
- 1 tablespoon olive oil
- 1 minced garlic clove
- ½ cup rinsed and drained chickpeas
- 1 tablespoon basil
- 1 tablespoon arugula
- ½ teaspoon salt and ground black pepper
- 1 tablespoon vinegar
- ½ cup toasted pine nuts

Instructions:

1. Preheat the oven at 300F temperature and prepare a baking sheet.
2. Place cherry tomatoes on the baking liner and drizzle olive oil, salt, and black pepper on it and bake it for 30 to 35 minutes.
3. Cook the faro in the salted water for 30 to 40 minutes. Slice the eggplant and salt it and leave it for 30 minutes. After that rinse it with water and dry it kitchen towel. Now peeled and sliced the eggplants.
4. Now place these slices on the baking liner and season it with salt, pepper and olive oil. Bake it for 15 to 20 minutes in the preheated oven at the 450F temperature.
5. Flip the sides of eggplant and bake it for additional 15 to 20 minutes. Bake the pine nuts for 5 minutes and sauté the garlic.
6. Now mix all the ingredients in a bowl and serve it.

Nutritional facts per serving:

Calories 322, Total Fat 22.8g, Saturated Fat 2.1g, Cholesterol 0mg, Sodium 162mg, Total Carbohydrate 27g, Dietary Fiber 8.1g, Total Sugars 6.5g, Protein 7.6g, Vitamin D 0mcg, Calcium 45mg, Iron 2mg, Potassium 682mg

Sweet Pepper Panzanella

Prep time 10 minutes / Cook time 20 minutes / Serves 4

Ingredients:

- 2 lb. red or orange bell peppers
- ½ thinly sliced onion
- 2 minced garlic cloves
- 8 tablespoons olive oil
- 2 tablespoons vinegar
- 2 minced garlic cloves
- 2 tablespoons fresh oregano
- ½ teaspoon salt and ground black pepper
- ¼ teaspoon crushed red pepper flakes
- 4 ounces fresh mozzarella
- ½ crushed loaf bread
- ¼ cup fresh mint leaves

Instructions:

1. Preheat the boiler and toss the bell peppers with olive oil, salt, and black pepper. Cook it for around 10 to 12 minutes.
2. In a large bowl add peppers, onion, garlic, vinegar, red pepper flakes. Olive oil and mix it well. Now bake the bread and season it with remaining oil, salt, and pepper.
3. Bake it for around 8 to 10 minutes in the preheated oven at the 400F temperature. Now mix all the baked and raw materials and mix them well.

Nutritional facts per serving:

Calories 367, Total Fat 33.6g, Saturated Fat 7.1g, Cholesterol 15mg, Sodium 196mg, Total Carbohydrate 11g, Dietary Fiber 2.6g, Total Sugars 3.9g, Protein 9.6g, Vitamin D 0mcg, Calcium 84mg, Iron 2mg, Potassium 214mg

Summer Corn Salad

Prep time 5 minutes / Cook time 0 minutes / Serves 8

Ingredients:

- 4 ears corn
- 2 diced red bell peppers
- 1 cubed onion
- 2 tablespoons olive oil
- 1 tablespoon lemon juice
- ½ cup chopped fresh cilantro

- ½ teaspoon salt and ground black pepper

Instructions:

1. Shave the corns off from the cob. Take a bowl and mix all the ingredients until all the ingredients combined well and it is ready to serve.

Nutritional facts per serving:
Calories 112, Total Fat 4.5g, Saturated Fat 0.7g, Cholesterol 0mg, Sodium 14mg, Total Carbohydrate 18.2g, Dietary Fiber 2.9g, Total Sugars 4.6g, Protein 3g, Vitamin D 0mcg, Calcium 7mg, Iron 2mg, Potassium 293mg

Best Tomato and Avocado Salad

Prep time 5 minutes / Cook time 0 minutes / Serves 4

Ingredients:

- 2 cups sliced tomatoes
- ¼ sliced onion
- 1 tablespoon lemon juice
- 2 cubed avocados
- ¼ cup chopped parsley
- ½ teaspoon red pepper flakes
- 2 tablespoons olive oil
- ½ teaspoon salt and ground black pepper

Instructions:

1. Add tomatoes, cilantro, and avocado in a salad bowl. Now add remaining ingredients in it and mix it well.
2. Now it is ready to serve. It is up to you. Whether you serve it immediately or serve it after refrigerating it.

Nutritional facts per serving:
Calories 235, Total Fat 21.9g, Saturated Fat 4.2g, Cholesterol 0mg, Sodium 12mg, Total Carbohydrate 11.1g, Dietary Fiber 6.5g, Total Sugars 3.2g, Protein 2.5g, Vitamin D 0mcg, Calcium 26mg, Iron 1mg, Potassium 619mg

Purple Potato and Green Bean Salad

Prep time 15 minutes / Cook time 20 minutes / Serves 8

Ingredients:

- 2 pounds diced potatoes
- ½ cup chopped celery
- 2 cups fresh green beans
- 1 tablespoon salt
- ¾ cup mayonnaise
- ½ cup chopped onion
- 2 tablespoons lime juice
- 2 teaspoons chopped the dill
- ¾ cup mayonnaise
- 2 tablespoons sour cream
- ½ teaspoon ground black pepper

Instructions:

1. Put the potatoes in the saucepan and cover it with salty water. Cook it for around 15 minutes. Boil the beans for around 5 to 7 minutes.
2. In a bowl add all the ingredients and merge them well and it is ready to serve.

Nutritional facts per serving:
Calories 187, Total Fat 8.2g, Saturated Fat 1.5g, Cholesterol 7mg, Sodium 1045mg, Total Carbohydrate 27.2g, Dietary Fiber 4g, Total Sugars 3.7g, Protein 2.9g, Vitamin D 0mcg, Calcium 38mg, Iron 1mg, Potassium 575mg

Broccoli, Edamame & Cabbage Millet Salad

Prep time 10 minutes / Serves 3

Ingredients:

- 3 tablespoons extra-virgin olive oil
- 1 tablespoon minced shallot
- Pepper to taste
- Salt to taste
- 1 cup cooked, shelled edamame
- ¾ cup chopped red cabbage
- 3 tablespoons white wine vinegar
- 1 ½ cups cooked millet
- ¾ cup chopped broccoli florets
- 2 tablespoons chopped, dried apricots

Instructions:

1. Add all the ingredients into a bowl and toss well.
2. Set aside for a while for the flavors to blend in.
3. Toss well and serve.

Nutritional facts per serving:
Calories 644, Total Fat 24.2g, Saturated Fat 3.4g, Cholesterol 0mg, Sodium 41mg, Total Carbohydrate 86.2g, Dietary Fiber 13.3g, Total Sugars 1.6g, Protein 23.1g, Vitamin D 0mcg, Calcium 197mg, Iron 6mg, Potassium 865mg

Mediterranean Salad

Prep time 10 minutes / Cook time 0 minutes / Serves 3
Ingredients:
For dressing:
- 2 tablespoons extra virgin olive oil
- ½ teaspoon garlic powder
- Juice of ½ lemon
- Salt to taste
- Pepper to taste

For salad:
- 1 ½ Persian cucumbers, chopped
- ½ green bell pepper, deseeded, chopped
- ½ red bell pepper, deseeded, chopped
- 2 tomatoes, chopped

Instructions:
1. Add all the ingredients for dressing into a bowl and whisk well.
2. Add rest of the ingredients and toss well.
3. Refrigerate for 15-20 minutes. Toss again and serve.

Nutritional facts per serving:
Calories 131, Total Fat 9.8g, Saturated Fat 1.4g, Cholesterol 0mg, Sodium 58mg, Total Carbohydrate 12.3g, Dietary Fiber 2.6g, Total Sugars 6.3g, Protein 2.2g, Vitamin D 0mcg, Calcium 40mg, Iron 1mg, Potassium 485mg

Quinoa Salad

Prep time 10 minutes / Cook time 10 minutes / Serves 4
Ingredients:
For quinoa:
- ¾ cup quinoa, rinsed
- 1 clove garlic, peeled, minced
- 1 cup + 2 tablespoons water
- Salt to taste

For the salad:
- 1 large tomato, finely chopped
- 1 medium cucumber, peeled, deseeded, diced
- ¼ cup thinly sliced scallions
- ½ cup corn, cooked
- ¾ cup canned or cooked chickpeas
- 2 tablespoons minced fresh mint
- 1/3 cup minced parsley
- 1 small jalapeño pepper, deseeded, thinly sliced
- 1 small ripe avocado, peeled, pitted, chopped

For the dressing:
- 2 tablespoons vegetable broth
- 2 tablespoons fresh lime juice
- ¼ teaspoon chipotle chili pepper
- Freshly ground pepper to taste
- Salt to taste

- 1 small clove garlic, peeled, minced

Instructions:
1. Add all the ingredients of quinoa into a saucepan.
2. Place the saucepan over medium heat. When it begins to boil, lower the heat and cover with a lid. Cook until dry for like 10 minutes
3. Uncover and fluff with a fork. Cool completely.

To make dressing:
1. Add all the ingredients for dressing into a bowl and whisk well.
2. Mix together all the vegetables of the salad in a large bowl.
3. Add quinoa and mix well. Pour the dressing over it and toss well.
4. Chill for a few hours.
5. Scatter avocado on top and serve.

Nutritional facts per serving:
Calories 418, Total Fat 14.7g, Saturated Fat 2.6g, Cholesterol 0mg, Sodium 103mg, Total Carbohydrate 61.3g, Dietary Fiber 14.5g, Total Sugars 8.2g, Protein 15.2g, Vitamin D 0mcg, Calcium 111mg, Iron 6mg, Potassium 1126mg

Japanese Cucumber Salad

Prep time 10 minutes / Cook time 0 minutes / Serves 2

Ingredients:

- 1 medium cucumber
- ½ teaspoon raw sugar
- 1 tablespoon sesame seeds, toasted
- 2 tablespoons rice vinegar
- Salt to taste

Instructions:

1. Peel cucumbers along the length alternately, leaving a gap between 2 peelings. (You should peel once along the length and leave the peel on once and repeat this on the entire cucumber)
2. Thinly slice the cucumbers and place in a bowl.
3. Place the cucumber slices in between layers of paper towels to remove excess moisture and press lightly.
4. Add sugar, salt and vinegar into a bowl. Mix until sugar dissolves completely.
5. Pour over the cucumbers. Toss well.
6. Sprinkle sesame seeds on top and serve.

Nutritional facts per serving:

Calories 62, Total Fat 2.4g, Saturated Fat 0.4g, Cholesterol 0mg, Sodium 81mg, Total Carbohydrate 7.5g, Dietary Fiber 1.3g, Total Sugars 3.5g, Protein 1.8g, Vitamin D 0mcg, Calcium 68mg, Iron 1mg, Potassium 242mg

Chickpea Shawarma Salad

Prep time 10 minutes / Cook time 30 minutes / Serves 4

Ingredients:

For chickpeas:

- 2 cans (15 ounces each) chickpeas, rinsed, drained, dried
- 3 teaspoons ground cumin
- ½ teaspoons turmeric powder
- 1 teaspoon ground cinnamon
- 1 ½ teaspoons smoked paprika
- 1 teaspoon sea salt
- ½ teaspoon ground ginger
- A large pinch cardamom powder
- A large pinch ground coriander
- A large pinch pepper powder

For salad:

- 10 ounces spring mix lettuce
- ½ cup red onion, thinly sliced
- 40 pita chips, slightly crushed
- 20 cherry tomatoes, chopped
- 1 ½ cups fresh parsley, chopped

For dressing:

- 1 cup hummus
- 2 teaspoons dried dill
- Warm water, as required
- 6 cloves garlic, finely minced
- 4 tablespoons lemon juice

Instructions:

1. Add all the ingredients of chickpeas into a bowl. Toss well. Mash half the chickpeas lightly using a fork. Taste and adjust the seasonings if necessary.
2. Transfer on to a baking sheet. Spread it in a single layer.
3. Roast in a preheated oven at 425 F° for 20-30 minutes or until crisp and golden brown. Set aside to cool.
4. Set aside the pita chips and add rest of the ingredients of salad into a bowl. Toss well.

To make dressing:

1. Add all the ingredients for dressing into a bowl. Whisk well. Add a little warm water and whisk until well combined.

To serve:

1. Add pita chips and baked chickpeas into the bowl of salad and toss well.
2. Pour half the dressing and toss again.
3. Divide the salad among 4 serving plates. Drizzle remaining dressing on top and serve.
4. You can make your own pita chips or use store bought ones.

Nutritional facts per serving:

Calories 2351, Total Fat 88.5g, Saturated Fat 6.3g, Cholesterol 0mg, Sodium 4958mg, Total Carbohydrate 334g, Dietary Fiber 39.7g, Total Sugars 30.7g, Protein 71g, Vitamin D 0mcg, Calcium 749mg, Iron 22mg, Potassium 1931mg

Soy Bean and Fennel Salad

Prep time 8 minutes / Cook time 0 minutes / Serves 2

Ingredients:

- 2 cups cooked soy beans
- 6 cherry tomatoes, quartered
- ¾ cup sliced fennel bulb
- 2 tablespoons minced onion
- 1 clove garlic, peeled, pressed
- 2 tablespoons chopped fresh parsley
- 1 ½ tablespoons chopped walnuts
- 1 ½ fresh lemon juice
- Extra- virgin olive oil, to taste
- Salt to taste
- Pepper to taste

Instructions:

1. After mincing the onion and pressing the garlic, let it sit for 5 minutes.
2. Add all the ingredients and add into a large bowl and toss well. Set aside for at least an hour.
3. Serve.

Nutritional facts per serving:

Calories 1018, Total Fat 48.7g, Saturated Fat 7g, Cholesterol 0mg, Sodium 126mg, Total Carbohydrate 75.9g, Dietary Fiber 23.7g, Total Sugars 24.6g, Protein 73.5g, Vitamin D 0mcg, Calcium 585mg, Iron 31mg, Potassium 4469mg

Guacamole Chopped Salad

Prep time 10 minutes / Cook time 0 minutes / Serves 2

Ingredients:

- 1 tablespoon corn oil
- 1 small clove garlic, grated
- Ground pepper to taste
- Salt to taste
- 1 tablespoon lime juice
- 2 cups romaine lettuce, chopped
- 1 ripe avocado, peeled, pitted, diced
- 2 tablespoons slivered red onion
- ½ cup quartered grape tomatoes
- ½ tablespoon chopped pickled jalapeño pepper

Instructions:

1. Add oil, garlic, pepper, salt and lime juice into a bowl and whisk well.
2. Add lettuce, avocado, onion, tomatoes and pickled jalapeño pepper and mix well.
3. Divide into 2 plates and serve.

Nutritional facts per serving:

Calories 293, Total Fat 26.6g, Saturated Fat 5g, Cholesterol 0mg, Sodium 59mg, Total Carbohydrate 15.4g, Dietary Fiber 8g, Total Sugars 3.1g, Protein 2.9g, Vitamin D 0mcg, Calcium 26mg, Iron 2mg, Potassium 722mg

Chapter 10: Smoothies Recipes

Chilled Cantaloupe Smoothie

Prep time 10 minutes / Serves 2

Ingredients:

- 1½ cups cantaloupe, diced
- 2 Tbsp frozen orange juice concentrate
- ¼ cup white wine
- 2 ice cubes
- 1 Tbsp lemon juice
- ½ cup Mint leaves, for garnish

Instructions:

1. Blend all ingredients to create a smooth mixture.
2. Top with mint leaves, and serve.

Nutritional facts per serving:

Calories 349, Total Fat 13.1g, Saturated Fat 11.3g, Cholesterol 0mg, Sodium 104mg, Total Carbohydrate 50.5g, Dietary Fiber 5.5g, Total Sugars 46.4g, Protein 6.5g, Vitamin D 0mcg, Calcium 117mg, Iron 5mg, Potassium 1320mg

High Protein Peanut Butter Smoothie

Prep time 3 minutes / Serves 2

Ingredients

- 2 cups kale
- 1 banana
- 2 tbsp. hemp seeds
- 1 tbsp. peanut butter
- 2/3 cup water
- 2 cups ice
- 1 cup almond or cashew milk
- 2 tbsp. cacao powder
- 1 scoop Vega vanilla protein powder

Instructions:

1. Pop the kale and banana in a blender, then add the hemp seeds and peanut butter.
2. Add the milk, water and ice and blend until ingredients are combined.
3. Add the protein powder.
4. Pour into glasses and serve.

Nutritional facts per serving:

Calories 687, Total Fat 50.4g, Saturated Fat 38g, Cholesterol 0mg, Sodium 176mg, Total Carbohydrate 46.5g, Dietary Fiber 9.9g, Total Sugars 23.7g, Protein 20.4g, Vitamin D 0mcg, Calcium 150mg, Iron 8mg, Potassium 979mg

Pineapple and Kale Smoothie

Prep time 3 minutes / Serves 2

Ingredients

- 1 cup Greek yogurt
- 1½ cups cubed pineapple
- 3 cups baby kale
- 1 cucumber
- 2 tbsp, hemp seeds

Instructions:

1. Pop everything in a blender and blitz
2. Pour into glasses and serve.

Nutritional facts per serving:

Calories 509, Total Fat 8.9g, Saturated Fat 3.3g, Cholesterol 10mg, Sodium 127mg, Total Carbohydrate 87.1g, Dietary Fiber 10.3g, Total Sugars 55.3g, Protein 30.6g, Vitamin D 0mcg, Calcium 438mg, Iron 5mg, Potassium 1068mg

Vanilla and Almond Smoothie

Prep time 3 minutes / Serves 1

Ingredients

- 2 scoops vegan vanilla protein powder
- ½ cup almonds
- 1 cup water

Instructions:

1. Pop everything in a blender and blitz
2. Pour into glasses and serve.

Nutritional facts per serving:
Calories 415, Total Fat 33.8g, Saturated Fat 1.8g, Cholesterol 0mg, Sodium 108mg, Total Carbohydrate 18.2g, Dietary Fiber 7.9g, Total Sugars 2g, Protein 42.1g, Vitamin D 0mcg, Calcium 255mg, Iron 9mg, Potassium 351mg

Berry Blast Smoothie

Prep time 3 minutes / Serves 2

Ingredients

- 1 cup raspberries
- 1 cup frozen blueberries
- 1 cup frozen blackberries
- 1 cup almond milk
- ¼ cup Soy Yogurt

Instructions:

1. Pop everything in a blender and blitz
2. Pour into glasses and serve.

Nutritional facts per serving:
Calories 404, Total Fat 30.4g, Saturated Fat 25.5g, Cholesterol 0mg, Sodium 22mg, Total Carbohydrate 34.5g, Dietary Fiber 12.5g, Total Sugars 19.6g, Protein 6.3g, Vitamin D 0mcg, Calcium 112mg, Iron 4mg, Potassium 581mg

Choc-Banana Smoothie

Prep time 3 minutes / Serves 2

Ingredients

- 1 banana
- 2 tbsp. hemp seeds
- 2/3 cup water
- 2 cups ice
- 1 cup almond or cashew milk
- 2 scoop Vegan chocolate protein powder
- 2 tbsp. cacao powder

Instructions:

1. Pop everything in a blender and blitz
2. Pour into glasses and serve.

Nutritional facts per serving:
Calories 676, Total Fat 52.3g, Saturated Fat 38.1g, Cholesterol 0mg, Sodium 46mg, Total Carbohydrate 41.6g, Dietary Fiber 8.7g, Total Sugars 25.2g, Protein 22.4g, Vitamin D 0mcg, Calcium 80mg, Iron 6mg, Potassium 528mg

Greens and Berry Smoothie

Prep time 3 minutes / Serves 2

Ingredients

- 1 cup frozen berries
- 1 cup kale or spinach
- ¾ cup milk almond, oat or coconut milk
- ½ tbsp chia seeds

Instructions:

1. Pop everything in a blender and blitz
2. Pour into glasses and serve.

Nutritional facts per serving:
Calories 298, Saturated Fat 19.3g, Cholesterol 0mg, Sodium 29mg, Total Carbohydrate 20g, Dietary Fiber 7.4g, Total Sugars 8g, Protein 4.7g, Vitamin D 0mcg, Calcium 114mg, Iron 3mg, Potassium 520mg

The 'Green Machine' Smoothie

Prep time 3 minutes / Serves 2

Ingredients

- 1 cup spinach
- ½ cup broccoli
- 2 Sticks of Celery
- 4 tbsp desiccated coconut
- 1 banana
- 1 scoop vegan unflavored protein powder
- 1 cup almond milk
- 1 cup water

Instructions:
1. Pop everything in a blender and blitz
2. Pour into glasses and serve.

Nutritional facts per serving:
Calories 780, Total Fat 66.5g, Saturated Fat 57.9g, Cholesterol 0mg, Sodium 224mg, Total Carbohydrate 38.8g, Dietary Fiber 15g, Total Sugars 18.4g, Protein 19.6g, Vitamin D 0mcg, Calcium 82mg, Iron 5mg, Potassium 1108mg

Sweet Coffee and Cacao Smoothie

Prep time 3 minutes / Serves 2

Ingredients

- 2 tsp Coffee
- ½ a Banana
- 1 cup Almond Milk
- 1 tsp Cashew Butter
- 2 tsp Cacao Powder
- 1 tsp maple Syrup
- 1 scoop vegan protein powder
- ½ cup Chocolate

Instructions:
1. Pop everything in a blender and blitz
2. Pour into glasses and serve.

Nutritional facts per serving:
Calories 614, Total Fat 43.2g, Saturated Fat 34.6g, Cholesterol 10mg, Sodium 146mg, Total Carbohydrate 44.7g, Dietary Fiber 5.4g, Total Sugars 31.2g, Protein 17.6g, Vitamin D 0mcg, Calcium 104mg, Iron 4mg, Potassium 614mg

Amazing Blueberry Smoothie

Prep time 5 minutes / Serves 2

Ingredients:

- ½ avocado
- 1 cup frozen blueberries
- 1 cup raw spinach
- ¼ tsp sea salt
- 1 cup soy
- 1 frozen banana

Instructions:
1. Blend everything in a powerful blender until you have a smooth, creamy shake.
2. Enjoy your healthy shake and start your morning on a fresh note!

Nutritional facts per serving:
Calories 269, Total Fat 12.3g, Saturated Fat 2.3g, Cholesterol 0mg, Sodium 312mg, Total Carbohydrate 37.6g, Dietary Fiber 8.2g, Total Sugars 22.9g, Protein 6.4g, Vitamin D 0mcg, Calcium 52mg, Iron 3mg, Potassium 528mg

Go-Green Smoothie

Prep time 5 minutes / Serves 1

Ingredients:

- 2 tablespoons, natural cashew butter
- 1 ripe banana
- 2/3 cup, unsweetened coconut
- ½ cup kale

Instructions:
1. Put everything inside a powerful blender.
2. Blend until you have a smooth, creamy shake.
3. Enjoy your special green smoothie.

Nutritional facts per serving:
Calories 500, Total Fat 33.2g, Saturated Fat 18.9g, Cholesterol 0mg, Sodium 161mg, Total Carbohydrate 48.6g, Dietary Fiber 10.4g, Total Sugars 19.8g, Protein 9.1g, Vitamin D 0mcg, Calcium 72mg, Iron 9mg, Potassium 777mg

Creamy Chocolate Shake

Prep time 10 minutes / Serves 2

Ingredients:
- 2 frozen ripe bananas, chopped
- 1/3 cup frozen strawberries
- 2 tbsp cocoa powder
- 2 tbsp salted almond butter
- 2 cups unsweetened vanilla almond milk
- 1 dash Stevia or agave nectar
- 1/3 cup ice

Instructions:

1. Add all ingredients in a blender and blend until smooth.
2. Take out and serve.

Nutritional facts per serving:

Calories 272, Total Fat 14.3g, Saturated Fat 1.5g, Cholesterol 0mg, Sodium 315mg, Total Carbohydrate 37g, Dietary Fiber 7.3g, Total Sugars 16.8g, Protein 6.2g, Vitamin D 2mcg, Calcium 735mg, Iron 2mg, Potassium 732mg

Hidden Kale Smoothie

Prep time 5 minutes / Serves 2

Ingredients:
- 1 medium ripe banana, peeled and sliced
- ½ cup frozen mixed berries
- 1 tbsp hulled hemp seeds
- 2 cups frozen or fresh kale
- 2/3 cup 100% pomegranate juice
- 2¼ cups filtered water

Instructions:

1. Add all ingredients in a blender and blend until smooth.
2. Take out and serve.

Nutritional facts per serving:

Calories 164, Total Fat 2g, Saturated Fat 0.2g, Cholesterol 0mg, Sodium 51mg, Total Carbohydrate 34.2g, Dietary Fiber 3.9g, Total Sugars 17.7g, Protein 4.1g, Vitamin D 0mcg, Calcium 124mg, Iron 2mg, Potassium 776mg

Orange Smoothie

Prep time 5 minutes / Serves 2

Ingredients:
- 1 cup orange slices
- 1 cup mango chunks
- 1 cup strawberries, chopped
- 1 cup coconut water
- Pinch freshly grated ginger
- 1-2 cups crushed ice

Instructions:

1. Place everything in a blender, blend, and serve.

Nutritional facts per serving:

Calories 269, Total Fat 12.3g, Saturated Fat 2.3g, Cholesterol 0mg, Sodium 312mg, Total Carbohydrate 37.6g, Dietary Fiber 8.2g, Total Sugars 22.9g, Protein 6.4g, Vitamin D 0mcg, Calcium 52mg, Iron 3mg, Potassium 528m

Raspberry Lime Smoothie

Prep time 5 minutes / Serves 2

Ingredients:
- 1 cup water
- 1 cup fresh or frozen raspberries
- 1 large frozen banana
- 2 tbsp fresh juice, lime
- 1 tsp oil, coconut
- 1 tsp agave

Instructions:

1. In a blender put all ingredients and blend until smooth.
2. Take out and serve

Nutritional facts per serving:

Calories 227, Total Fat 4g, Saturated Fat 1.3g, Cholesterol 0mg, Sodium 7mg, Total Carbohydrate 47.8g, Dietary Fiber 6g, Total Sugars 40.7g, Protein 0.9g, Vitamin D 0mcg, Calcium 22mg, Iron 1mg, Potassium 144mg

Blueberry Protein Shake

Prep time 5 minutes / Serves 1

Ingredients:
- ½ cup cottage cheese
- 3 tbsp vanilla protein powder
- ½ cup frozen blueberries
- ½ tsp maple extract
- ¼ tsp vanilla extract
- 2 tsp flaxseed meal
- Sweetener, choice
- 10-15 ice cubes
- ¼ cup water

Instructions:
1. Add all ingredients in a blender and blend until smooth.
2. Take out and serve.

Nutritional facts per serving:
Calories 559, Total Fat 4.2g, Saturated Fat 1.9g, Cholesterol 14mg, Sodium 659mg, Total Carbohydrate 31.1g, Dietary Fiber 4.5g, Total Sugars 20.7g, Protein 98g, Vitamin D 0mcg, Calcium 518mg, Iron 3mg, Potassium 676mg

Peppermint Monster Smoothie

Prep time 5 minutes / Serves 1

Ingredients:
- 1 large frozen banana, peeled
- 1½ cups non-dairy milk
- A handful of fresh mint leaves, stems removed
- 1-2 handfuls spinach

Instructions:
1. Add all ingredients in a blender and blend until smooth.
2. Take out and serve

Nutritional facts per serving:
Calories 799, Total Fat 28.1g, Saturated Fat 16.7g, Cholesterol 110mg , Sodium 645mg, Total Carbohydrate 98.4g, Dietary Fiber 4.5g, Total Sugars 77.2g, Protein 46.2g, Vitamin D 7mcg, Calcium 1634mg, Iron 2mg, Potassium 1366mg

Banana Green Smoothie

Prep time 5 minutes / Serves 1

Ingredients:
- 1 cup coconut water
- ¾ cup plant-based milk
- ¼ tsp vanilla extract
- 1 heaping cup loosely packed spinach
- 2-3 cups frozen bananas, sliced

Instructions:
1. Blend everything until smooth and serve.

Nutritional facts per serving:
Calories 364, Total Fat 4.8g, Saturated Fat 2.6g, Cholesterol 15mg, Sodium 111mg, Total Carbohydrate 78g, Dietary Fiber 8g, Total Sugars 45.1g, Protein 9.6g, Vitamin D 1mcg, Calcium 257mg, Iron 1mg, Potassium 1241mg

Cinnamon Coffee Shake

Prep time 5 minutes / Serves 2

Ingredients:

- 1 cup cooled coffee, regular or decaf
- ¼ cup almond or non-dairy milk
- A few pinches cinnamon
- 2 tbsp hemp seeds
- Splash vanilla extract
- 2 frozen bananas, sliced into coins
- Handful of ice

Instructions:

1. Chill some coffee in a sealed container for a couple of hours (or overnight) before making this smoothie, or be ready to use more ice.
2. Add the non-dairy milk, cinnamon, vanilla, and hemp seeds to a blender and blend until smooth. Add the coffee and cut bananas and keep blending until smooth.
3. Add the ice and keep blending on high until there are no lumps remaining. Taste for sweetness and add your preferred plant-based sugar or sugar alternative.
4. Transfer to a glass and serve.

Nutritional facts per serving:
Calories 197, Total Fat 6.4g, Saturated Fat 0.6g, Cholesterol 0mg, Sodium 5mg, Total Carbohydrate 31.3g, Dietary Fiber 5.2g, Total Sugars 15.8g, Protein 4g, Vitamin D 0mcg, Calcium 53mg, Iron 1mg, Potassium 582mg

Pumpkin Smoothie

Prep time 5 minutes / Serves 2

Ingredients:

- 1 cup unsweetened non-dairy milk
- 2 medium bananas, peeled and cut into quarters and frozen
- 2 medjool dates, pitted
- 1 cup pumpkin puree, canned or fresh
- 2 cups ice cubes
- ¼ tsp cinnamon
- 2 tbsp ground flaxseeds
- 1 tsp pumpkin spice

Instructions:

1. Blend all ingredients in a blender and serve.

Nutritional facts per serving:
Calories 272, Total Fat 5.6g, Saturated Fat 2.2g, Cholesterol 10mg, Sodium 75mg, Total Carbohydrate 51.9g, Dietary Fiber 9.5g, Total Sugars 29.4g, Protein 8.2g, Vitamin D 1mcg, Calcium 204mg, Iron 4mg, Potassium 865mg

Turmeric Smoothie

Prep time 5 minutes / Serves 2

Ingredients:

- 2 cups non-dairy milk like coconut, almond
- 2 medium bananas, frozen
- 1 cup mango, frozen
- 1 tsp turmeric, ground grated, peeled
- 1 tsp fresh ginger, grated, peeled
- 1 tbsp chia seeds
- ¼ tsp vanilla extract
- ¼ tsp cinnamon, ground
- 1 pinch pepper, ground

Instructions:

1. Blend all ingredients in a blender and serve

Nutritional facts per serving:
Calories 785, Total Fat 62.4g, Saturated Fat 51.5g, Cholesterol 0mg, Sodium 41mg, Total Carbohydrate 60.2g, Dietary Fiber 15g, Total Sugars 33.9g, Protein 10g, Vitamin D 0mcg, Calcium 149mg, Iron 6mg, Potassium 1292mg

Veggie Smoothie

Prep time 10 minutes / Serves 1

Ingredients:

- 1 stalk celery
- 1 carrot peeled and roughly chopped
- ½ cup broccoli sprouts
- 1 cup kale, chopped
- ½ cup curly parsley
- ½ tomato roughly chopped
- ½ avocado
- 1 banana
- ½ green apple
- ½ cup non-dairy milk
- 1 tbsp chia seeds
- 1 tbsp flaxseeds

Instructions:

1. Place all ingredients in a blender.
2. Blend until smooth. Serve immediately.

Nutritional facts per serving:

Calories 696, Total Fat 34.1g, Saturated Fat 7g, Cholesterol 10mg, Sodium 190mg, Total Carbohydrate 90.5g, Dietary Fiber 29.5g, Total Sugars 37.2g, Protein 18.5g, Vitamin D 1mcg, Calcium 527mg, Iron 9mg, Potassium 2223mg

Very Berry Smoothie

Prep time 5 minutes / Serves 2

Ingredients:

- 2 cups, plant-based Milk
- 2 cups, Frozen or fresh berries
- ½ cup Frozen ripe bananas
- 2 teaspoons, Flax Seeds
- ¼ tsp, Vanilla
- ¼ tsp, Cinnamon

Instructions:

1. Mix together milk, flax seeds, and fruit. Blend in a high-power blender.
2. Add cinnamon and vanilla. Blend until smooth.
3. Serve and enjoy!

Nutritional facts per serving:

Calories 269, Total Fat 12.3g, Saturated Fat 2.3g, Cholesterol 0mg, Sodium 312mg, Total Carbohydrate 37.6g, Dietary Fiber 8.2g, Total Sugars 22.9g, Protein 6.4g, Vitamin D 0mcg, Calcium 52mg, Iron 3mg, Potassium 528mg

Conclusion

Thank you for getting to end of this plant-based book. What you need to know is that it is not easy at the start but in the long run you will get used to it.

Plant-based diet are numerous benefits for you. If you adhere to this diet, you will get all these benefits for yourself.

All the best in your plant-based diet journey.

CPSIA information can be obtained
at www.ICGtesting.com
Printed in the USA
LVHW060256191020
669130LV00010B/344

9 781952 832741